Electronic Warfare

PERGAMON POLICY STUDIES ON SECURITY AFFAIRS

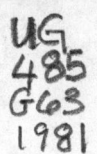

Electronic Warfare
Element of Strategy and Multiplier of Combat Power

Don E. Gordon

Pergamon Press
NEW YORK • OXFORD • TORONTO • SYDNEY • PARIS • FRANKFURT

Pergamon Press Offices:

U.S.A.	Pergamon Press Inc., Maxwell House, Fairview Park, Elmsford, New York 10523, U.S.A.
U.K.	Pergamon Press Ltd., Headington Hill Hall, Oxford OX3 OBW, England
CANADA	Pergamon Press Canada Ltd., Suite 104, 150 Consumers Road, Willowdale, Ontario M2J 1P9, Canada
AUSTRALIA	Pergamon Press (Aust.) Pty. Ltd., P.O. Box 544, Potts Point, NSW 2011, Australia
FRANCE	Pergamon Press SARL, 24 rue des Ecoles, 75240 Paris, Cedex 05, France
FEDERAL REPUBLIC OF GERMANY	Pergamon Press GmbH, Hammerweg 6 6242 Kronberg/Taunus, Federal Republic of Germany

Copyright © 1981 Pergamon Press Inc.

The views of the author do not purport to reflect the positions of the Department of the Army or the Department of Defense.

All Rights reserved. No part of this publication may be reproduced, stored in a retrieval system or transmitted in any form or by any means: electronic, electrostatic, magnetic tape, mechanical, photocopying, recording or otherwise, without permission in writing from the publishers.

Printed in the United States of America

CONTENTS

Foreword   vii

Chapter

I   Introduction   1

     Changing the Definition of Electronic Warfare   6
     A New Definition of Electronic Warfare   8
     Background   9

II   The Strategy   14

     The German Strategy   19
     Strategic Tasks   22

III   Cryptology   27

     An Electronic Warfare Weapon   27
     British Cryptology   27
     The Battle of Jutland   28
     Between Wars   31
     Two Vital Decisions   33
     Polish Cryptology   34
     Enigma   35
     French Cryptology   38
     The Polish Gift   38
     How Enigma Worked   38
     German Cryptology   47
     United States Cryptology   52

IV   Microwave Radar   54

     An Electronic Warfare Weapon   54
     How Radar Works   54
     The Development of Radar   56
     A Comparison of Technological Policies   59
     A Policy to Protect the Electronic Warfare
        Capability   65
     The Dynamic Electronic Warfare Duo   67

V	The German Surface Fleet	73
	The First Target	73
	Invasion of Norway	75
	The Second Target—Bismarck	80
	Radio Direction Finding	86
	Intelligence Must Be Disseminated	88
	The Loss of Bismarck, a Decisive Strategic Factor	94
VI	A Unique Trilogy: Tirpitz, Convoy PQ 17 and Raiders	98
	Tirpitz, The Third Target	98
	Convoy PQ 17	100
	Intelligence Work Was Good	104
	Anatomy of a Disaster	108
	Merchant Raiders, The Fourth Target	110
VII	U-Boats	114
	The U-Boat, A Strategic Weapon, The Fifth Target	114
	A Description of the Weapon	116
	The Battle	125
	German Vulnerability	133
	Cryptologic Revelations	135
VIII	Can the United States Win the Next War?	138
	Is the U.S. Navy Prepared to Fight An Electronic Battle of the Atlantic?	140
	Comparison of Two World Wars—WW II and WW III	143
	The Threat	143
	The Strategy	144
	Capabilities	144
	Is The U.S. Army Prepared to Fight the Electronic Battle?	146
	An Electronic Warfare Policy Recommendation	155

Notes	157
Bibliography	172
Index	177

FOREWORD

General W. E. DePuy, USA Ret

Although much of Colonel Gordon's book deals with the decisive influence of Electronic Warfare on the Battle of the Atlantic, he uses that fascinating discussion to make a larger point. He points to the fact that Electronic Warfare, reserved to the highest authorities in World War II in the form of critical signals intercept and decryption, is now expanding into every aspect of military operations and tactics down to the smallest unit and weapons level.

Since the cloak of secrecy has been at least partially removed by the genre of books and articles following the ULTRA revelations we have all seen the enormous impact of allied intelligence exploits on some of the most celebrated battles of the last great war. We now know how much the already great advantages of Montgomery over Rommel in terms of strength and resources were multiplied by Montgomery's knowledge, through ULTRA, of the desperate situation within Panzer Army Africa. This exploitation of the electronic spectrum we regard as strategic in nature. The Battle of the Atlantic brought Electronic Warfare down into the operational arena as German submarine wolf packs were detected, located, avoided or attacked. So too did the advent of radar intrude decisively into the operational aspects of the Battle of Britain. Air Forces have tended to lead the way in the development and exploitation of Electronic Warfare as they were thrown early into the life and death battle with the radars of the air defense systems.

The electronic battles over North Vietnam brought an explosion in countermeasure technology. Electronic Warfare is now firmly lodged in the midst of the tactical battlefield. The question becomes that of exploiting the full range of potentialities or conceding that advantage to the opposing force.

It would be nice to think that we could overwhelm our opponents with countermeasures while protecting our own Command Control and Communications as well as our electronically dependent weapons systems. The facts are that our chief opponent, the Soviet Union, is producing and deploying Electronic Warfare equipment at least equal to ours in quality and in greatly superior numbers just as he has done in tanks, artillery, helicopters and air defense weapons.

Our only hope for success on the battlefield is to prevail through the concentration of combat power and superior tactical performance at the critical times and places even though elsewhere and otherwise we are badly outnumbered and outgunned. The complete integration of Electronic Warfare into the combined arms teams of the battlefield is a prerequisite to victory.

But the Army is not yet comfortable with Electronic Warfare. The senior leaders have little first hand experience and thus little confidence or skill in its use and tend to leave it—unintegrated—in the hands of specialists. The specialists, in turn, are faced with a tradition and structure of secrecy and compartmentation hangover in part from the days of ULTRA.

Colonel Gordon is a leader of the new breed who *are* comfortable in the world of EW—have operated there successfully—who see the opportunities and necessities. Colonel Gordon proposed that we must control the electromagnetic spectrum for tactical and operational purposes. He suggests that our emphasis must move from the traditionally narrower focus on intelligence exploitation to the broader range of full Electronic Warfare. There are just a handful of officers worth listening to on this score.

CHAPTER I

Introduction

Since WW II, the nature of combat has changed, the modern battlefield is more lethal than ever before. Losses to both sides may well be horrendous, and the United States can for the first time expect to fight outnumbered—outnumbered in tanks, artillery, aircraft, virtually all equipment, ships, and troops. If there is a next war, it may be a nuclear war, it may be a chemical war, but it will certainly be an electronic war. If a unit can be seen on this battlefield, either visually or *electronically,* it can most likely be hit, hit with first-round fires. Given the lethality of modern weapons, if a unit can be hit, it will most likely be destroyed.[1]

To fight and win in this environment, the United States armed forces must depend on superb command and control communication systems to see the battlefield more quickly and clearly than the enemy, and to respond with the best mix of technologically superior weapons at the best time and place against a numerically superior enemy. Unless we are prepared, any future war against a major opponent is likely to find our front-line military electronic systems—including communication systems—severely crippled and totally shutdown for periods of time when they are critically needed. They will be shut-down by the weapons and methods of electronic warfare—Radioelectronic combat as it is referred to by the Soviets. The enemy will attempt to knock out our electronic emitters and sensors with massive jamming, electronic deception, and suppressive fires.[2]

The United States armed forces are dedicating expensive resources of both men and equipment to fight the electronic battle in the fourth dimension of the modern battlefield. There are billions of Army dollars at stake and similar amounts of money to be spent by the Air Force and Navy. Before these resources are dedicated, we had best insure that we are preparing to fight the right war at the right time. To do this, it is necessary to understand the development of electronic warfare—not in a technical sense—as an element of strategy and multiplier of combat power.

The origin of "electronic warfare" can be traced to the use of electronic systems to detect and protect aircraft by both sides in the European Theater early in WW II; however, the use of electronic warfare as an offensive element of ground combat is relatively new. Electronic warfare first emerged as a serious threat to ground force tactical communication systems when the British mounted a jammer in a Lancaster type bomber to be used against Rommel's Afrika Korps in 1941. This first attempt at airborne jamming of ground forces was successful; it was also short-lived, however, as the Germans spared no effort to destroy the bomber. Today, analyses of the 1973 Mideast War and the Soviet radioelectronic combat capability indicate that electronic warfare will be a decisive element in future battles. Unfortunately, our national security strategy may be preparing to fight the wrong war at the wrong time. A strong case is made within the Department of Defense that the Allies gained a decisive advantage over the enemy during WW II by listening to the enemy—signals intelligence—listening to his secret radio messages. This is referred to as Ultra. We need to understand more than has so far been told if we are to understand that chiefly listening to the enemy on the modern battlefield will not be satisfactory. If we do not want to lose a next war, we had best be prepared to fight the electronic battle and this includes a great deal more than listening in on the electromagnetic spectrum in which that battle will be fought. The United States and NATO must control that electromagnetic spectrum. To do this, we must thoroughly understand the relationship of signals intelligence—cryptology—within electronic warfare and accept that signals intelligence may most likely have to be part of and subordinate to electronic warfare. This is not widely understood or believed today.

During the past forty years, signals intelligence has remained separate and distinct from and predominant to other aspects of electronic warfare. That relationship was suitable for WW II, of proven value again in Korea, it began to break down in Vietnam, and is totally unsuitable for the modern battlefield of which the 1973 Mideast War serves as an example in miniature. That battlefield has become so lethal that commanders on both sides will attempt to disrupt the entire electromagnetic spectrum in order to increase or reduce the lethality of modern weapons dependent upon electromagnetic energy. If the United States is to fight and win on that battlefield, it needs a sound strategic electronic warfare policy, a policy based on war fighting and not entombed in security.

A generation of silence was broken in 1974 with the open publication of first-person and institutional reports describing the effect of electronic warfare and cryptology during WW II. Material pertaining to cryptanalysis is now popularly referred to as Ultra and Magic. Material pertaining to the use of radar and other electronic detection, disruption, and deception techniques is referred to as electronic warfare in those reports. The dichotomy is convenient for the technocrat and the historian but not for the strategist or the commander. Today, all forms of cryptology and manipulation of electromagnetic energy are so thoroughly woven together that one can no longer distinguish one from the other when measuring their cause and effect or when developing strategy. Though cryptanalysis was singularly distinguishable within cryptology and from other forms of electronic warfare during WW II, the advent of modern electromagnetic systems is so complex that there will most likely never again be the opportunity for opposing forces, fighting on a modern battlefield, to read the secret messages of the other to the extent that this was done during WW II by both sides. The ability to manipulate the opposing force by controlling the electromagnetic spectrum has the potential to provide the winning side with an even greater advantage than provided by "code breaking" during WW II.

By modern standards the WW II method of encrypting messages was primitive, but, fortunately for the Allies, it was barely within the human ability of cryptanalysis when aided by calculating machines. Without in any way intending to detract from the contribution of Allied cryptologists during WW II, it must be understood that a great deal of good fortune on the part of the Allies and almost unbelievable naivete on the part of the Germans were as responsible for the Allied success as was cryptologic skill. While the success achieved in actually reading the secret messages of the enemy was important, the use that the Allies made of that information was the crux of the success. Nothing further should be said without acknowledging the great debt owed by the Allies to the Polish cryptologists for their skill, perseverance, and special courage. As is seen in Chapter III, the Polish cryptologists provided the foundation for cryptanalyzing the German Enigma cipher system.

From the time of the Czars, the Russians have demonstrated considerable sophistication and skill in protecting their communications. There is no indication that the Soviets have paid any less attention to the security of their important electronic data during the intervening years.[3]

If there is a next war, a modern battlefield will include not only the customary three dimensions of depth, width, and airspace of previous wars, but an added dimension as well. The fourth dimension, the electromagnetic spectrum, is a mostly invisible medium which will saturate the entire battlefield upon which the use of all electromagnetic devices will depend.[4]

On 15 February 1980, the Associated Press reported that Soviet missile coding may have prevented monitoring by the United States when the Soviet Union test fired a new strategic missile which radioed key information in code. The use of the code was assumed to have prevented the United States from fully monitoring the performance of the missile according to unidentified administration officials. The missile is designed for use in the advanced Soviet Typhoon submarine.[5]

Consider a battlefield so thoroughly saturated with electromagnetic radiation of every type that commanders of fighting forces may well have to transmit continuous wave radio transmissions to bounce off the ionized trails of meteors—perhaps manmade meteors.[6]

It will be a battlefield on which not only the command and control of armies, navies, and air forces and weapons in space will depend upon tens of thousands of emitters conveying messages, digital firing data, imagery, intelligence, logistics, and detection information, but one which may very well be controlled to the extent that it can manipulate human behavior by the manipulation of radio frequency energy or the polarization of the ions contained in the very air we breathe. [Investigation involving the control of aberrant behavior among emotionally disturbed children in a drug-free environment has been continuing for several years outside the military.] Each opposing military force will make every effort to control the full range of the electromagnetic environment by detecting, deceiving, and disrupting the electromagnetic energy used by his foe.

We already know that even the slight polarity emitted by digital watch batteries influences the accuracy of hand-held lensatic compasses by several degrees. Radio-controlled garage doors are mistakenly opened by interference from electrical devices. Consider the potential for an enemy to transmit the right combination of electronic data at the right time to cause all attacking pilots to prematurely eject from their aircraft before firing the first missile or dropping the first bomb. New aircraft ejection systems are controlled by digital systems not manual levers. As another example, consider the potential with the advent of new digital speech security devices used with tactical radios for an enemy to broadcast, at relatively low power, a continuous digital signal which succeeds in locking all radios used by a defending force into the receive-only mode, preventing communication, as the radio attempts unsuccessfully to authenticate the bogus digital security bits. One may presume that no military force could possibly attempt to deliver equipment to its field units before faults similar to those just described are detected in operational and developmental testing.

As one last example, consider a situation in which one adversary saturates the battlefield with positively charged ions while protecting his own forces with negatively charged ion fields. One familiar with the subject may reply that should an adversary do this he would increase the vulnerability of his own forces to chemical weapons because the negative ion field will increase the persistence of chemical droplets and vapor; that this would be too great a risk to assume in order to modify the behavior of the opponent with positive ion fields. That is exactly the point, the battlefield will be manipulated in the fourth dimension in ways never before considered in the Geneva Conventions of Land Warfare, by Clausewitz, Mahan, or Sun Tzu Wu. It isn't so much that our war colleges do not believe this to be true as that their faculties do not understand it; and not understanding it, they do not make the effort to integrate electronic warfare as an element of strategy and multiplier of combat power.

To fight and win in the electronic environment, on and above both land and sea, the United States must depend upon electronic warfare as a weapon to prevent the enemy from controlling the electromagnetic spectrum. First, we must understand the characteristics of electronic warfare. Electronic equipment has changed greatly during the period between WW I and the present day, but sound fundamental principles governing its use have stood the test of time and remain valid for electromagnetic devices of any sophistication and technology. Decisions that led to strategic errors during WW I predictably caused the same type of errors during WW II and can be expected to cause similar errors in a next war on the modern battlefield.

First, it is necessary to understand those basic fundamental principles. These are explained in succeeding chapters by tracing events during WW II which are illustrative and now unclassified. Secondly, it is necessary to understand that intelligence and electronic warfare must be thoroughly interwoven if either is to serve as an element of strategy and multiplier of combat power. Together they can win battles. The Battle of the Atlantic presents this case clearly. Thirdly, if electronic warfare is indeed to serve as an element of strategy and multiplier of combat power, then examples must be provided of this application. Finally, a definition of electronic warfare which is adaptable to both the technocrat, the strategist, and the commander is required. Our present understanding of the term electronic warfare does not suffice.

CHANGING THE DEFINITION OF ELECTRONIC WARFARE

In the past, electronic warfare has meant mostly jamming, techniques to counter jamming, and electronic deception. Explanations of the most commonly related terms follow:

Cryptology: The science of deriving information from the electromagnetic spectrum. Cryptology includes signals intercepting, identifying, recording, direction finding, fingerprinting of transmitter characteristics, cryptanalysis, and the analysis of electromagnetic signal parameters in order to provide intelligence. Cryptology also includes the protection of friendly signals from manipulation by unintended recipients. Cryptology is usually restricted in its application to the use of the radio frequencies of the electromagnetic spectrum.

Decryption and Encryption: Decryption is the transforming of the ciphertext of a message back to plaintext using the original version of the cipher or code key. Encryption is the transforming of the plaintext of a message to ciphertext using the original version of a cipher or code key.

Cipher and Code: Both are methods used to transform the original text, called the plaintext, of a message to a form unintelligible to all except those possessing the original version of the cipher or code key, called the keylist or code book. Ciphers are used to transform plaintext units of *regular* length; codes to transform units of *variable* length.

Cryptanalyze or Cryptanalysis: Transforming an intercepted message from ciphertext to plaintext without having possession of the original version of the cipher key unless it was obtained surreptitiously. Referred to as "code breaking" in the popular literature.

Enigma: A German-manufactured cipher machine built in several models, each with a different capability, used during WW II to encipher German and Japanese radio messages before their transmission. Both the United States and Britain were able to reconstruct the Enigma based on valuable help from Polish cryptanalysts and information provided by a member of the German military, through the French Intelligence Service to the Polish Secret Service. It was still necessary to determine the cipher key before the Allied Enigma machines could be used to decipher (in the cryptanalyze sense) an intercepted radio message.

Ultra and Magic: Code words arbitrarily selected to distinguish Allied Cryptologic intelligence derived from cryptanalysis in the European and Pacific Theaters, respectively, from other intelligence. The code words signified that special security was required to protect cryptologic material. Ultra and Magic compartmented intelligence limited access to those with a need to know; they were not a security classification like Top Secret, Secret, and Confidential, but rather indicated that access was limited only to those individuals having a definite need to know specific information gained by cryptanalysis. The same information was provided to others, protected by a security classification, but the source of the intelligence was attributed to other than cryptanalysis.

It is in the environment of the definitions explained above that the term electronic warfare must compete. Previously electronic warfare was separate and distinct from the other aspects of cryptology and used mostly to describe the jamming and deception of radar devices during WW II. Those who argue for the expansion of the more traditional definition of electronic warfare beyond the customary scope of jamming and deception into an entirely new domain advocating control of the entire electromagnetic spectrum as a strategic imperative, acknowledge the scope of the modern battlefield. While the components of electronic warfare retain their traditional definitions, electronic warfare itself emerges not as a technology or a component of cryptology but as a science in which cryptology is included. Chart I il-

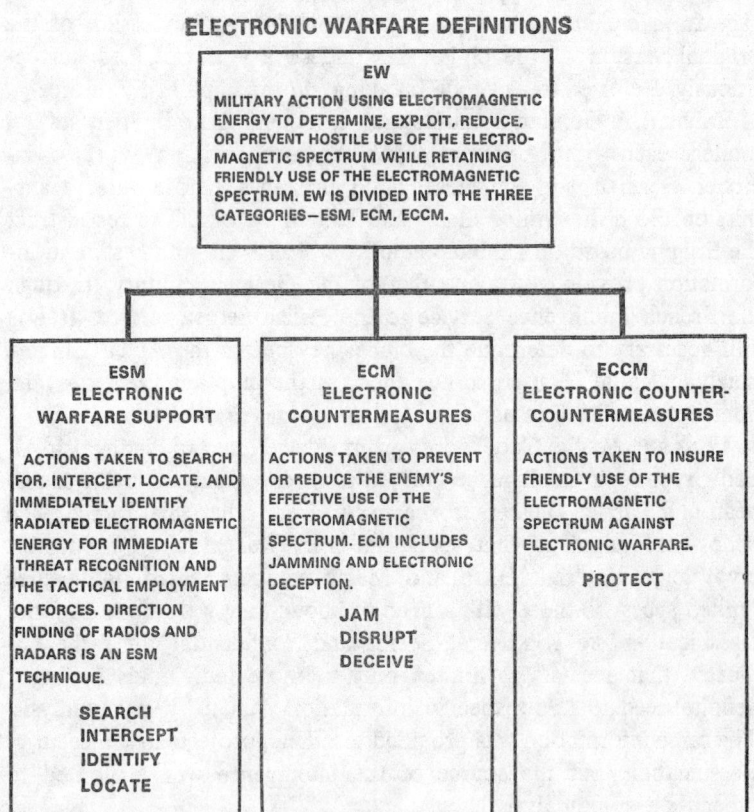

TABLE 1
ELECTRONIC WARFARE DEFINITIONS

EW

MILITARY ACTION USING ELECTROMAGNETIC ENERGY TO DETERMINE, EXPLOIT, REDUCE, OR PREVENT HOSTILE USE OF THE ELECTROMAGNETIC SPECTRUM WHILE RETAINING FRIENDLY USE OF THE ELECTROMAGNETIC SPECTRUM. EW IS DIVIDED INTO THE THREE CATEGORIES—ESM, ECM, ECCM.

ESM ELECTRONIC WARFARE SUPPORT	ECM ELECTRONIC COUNTERMEASURES	ECCM ELECTRONIC COUNTER-COUNTERMEASURES
ACTIONS TAKEN TO SEARCH FOR, INTERCEPT, LOCATE, AND IMMEDIATELY IDENTIFY RADIATED ELECTROMAGNETIC ENERGY FOR IMMEDIATE THREAT RECOGNITION AND THE TACTICAL EMPLOYMENT OF FORCES. DIRECTION FINDING OF RADIOS AND RADARS IS AN ESM TECHNIQUE. SEARCH INTERCEPT IDENTIFY LOCATE	ACTIONS TAKEN TO PREVENT OR REDUCE THE ENEMY'S EFFECTIVE USE OF THE ELECTROMAGNETIC SPECTRUM. ECM INCLUDES JAMMING AND ELECTRONIC DECEPTION. JAM DISRUPT DECEIVE	ACTIONS TAKEN TO INSURE FRIENDLY USE OF THE ELECTROMAGNETIC SPECTRUM AGAINST ELECTRONIC WARFARE. PROTECT

lustrates that the military has dedicated some very awkward terms and acronyms to convey these definitions—they do so poorly and do not convey the syntax of modern military application. The chart provides a "Rosetta stone" for current military terminology. (See Chart I)

A NEW DEFINITION OF ELECTRONIC WARFARE

Electronic warfare includes all actions in the entire electromagnetic spectrum to intercept, analyze, manipulate, or suppress the enemy's use of the spectrum as well as to protect friendly use of the spectrum from similar attack by an enemy—to be considered an element of the technological aspect of strategy and an element of the combat power of the United States armed forces. The electromagnetic spectrum includes both the visible and invisible ranges, measured in megahertz, of the spectrum. The use of signals intercepting, locating, identifying, detecting, jamming, disrupting, deceiving, protecting, analyzing, and cryptanalyzing is electronic warfare. Electronic warfare can be used to provide intelligence or combat power like jamming, disruption, or deception.

BACKGROUND

There are parallels between the conditions which existed prior to the outbreak of WW II and the pre-1986 military planning posture that the United States and NATO now find themselves preparing to use. There are simplistic comparisons in which the United States still underestimates the lethality of the Soviet submarine fleet, overestimates its ability to reinforce Western Europe if invaded by the Soviet Union, and depends on grandiose technology to overcome Soviet perseverance and orthodoxy. More complex are the subtle similarities in which we may misjudge the determination of the enemy. Empirical evidence observed during the past ten years suggests that the Soviets have studied the errors of both sides during WW II and are committed to not repeating them while the West seems oblivious to those lessons and careless of the vital time available. During the past several years, beginning in 1978, reports have come to public attention explaining the effect of both strategic and tactical electronic warfare [using the new definition] on the major battles of WW II. It can be concluded that electronic warfare contributed decisively to Allied victories in North Africa, Western Europe, at Coral Sea and Midway, and during the Battle of the Atlantic and the air Battle of Britain, as well as to the tragic Allied losses at Pearl Harbor, Tobruk, and Anzio. Any of these battles [except Tobruk] could have proven decisive to the outcome of WW II. Some historians contend that they are astonished by these revelations; others argue that the ability to look inside the enemy's plans did not significantly alter the overall outcome of a battle in which capabilities, rather than intentions, were the decisive factor. The latter argument is bolstered by the consideration that the Germans were able to break many Allied codes and ciphers and, though this often resulted in a tactical advantage for generals like Rommel, it did not help the Germans win the war. The argument is also introduced that eventually the overall war would have been won by the superior resources of the United States even at the expense of delaying the war in the Pacific by five or more years. This research reveals that the Allies certainly enjoyed superiority in manpower and resources but that they were unable to bring that superiority to bear on the enemy until they first learned how to apply electronic warfare to accomplish strategic objectives and to multiply combat power. The Allies did not have a superior technological capability (they were about even with the Germans) but they did learn how to use it to their advantage. Germany understood the technological aspects of electronic warfare but they did not use electronic warfare to complement strategy or to multiply combat power. This distinction was decisive.

To make this case, a single campaign—The Battle of the Atlantic—from the volumes of WW II military history serves as an analytical study to support the hypothesis that electronic warfare, a technological element of strategy, was decisive for Allied victory in WW II.

The works of the naval historians S. W. Roskill, Samuel Eliot Morison, and C. D. Bekker among others are reviewed to portray the conventional perspective of that battle. Revelations from current investigations into the impact of Ultra during WW II have been integrated into this historical perspective to examine a revisionist view of WW II strategy. In this context, strategy is defined as the art or science of employing the economic, military, psychological, and technological forces of a nation to afford maximum support to national policies. It follows that strategy should be supported by subordinate economic, military, political, psychological, and technological policies intended to implement the overall national strategic policy. It will be seen that at the beginning of WW II, the Allies did not have a deliberate electronic warfare, cryptologic, or technological policy suitable for integration with the strategic decision making process. Rather electronic warfare appeared to shine as a single ray of sunshine through an otherwise darkening sky, a sky which had become increasingly dark the longer the war continued into 1942. Fortunately, that single ray of sunlight was absorbed by Allied leaders much like vitamin D. Surprisingly, electronic warfare, especially by the end of WW II, clearly emerged as a method of permitting the selection of the best course of strategic action. This was especially true when requirements for strategic resources exceeded their availability. Electronic warfare permitted the Allies to multiply combat power. Because more current examples of the use of electronic warfare to multiply combat power remain highly classified, it is necessary to resort to the Battle of the Atlantic as a classical example to convey an understanding of the basic fundamentals of electronic warfare and the magnitude of its contribution. One does not have to be clairvoyant to understand the similarities between the Battle of the Atlantic in 1943 and a Battle of the Atlantic in 1986.

An understanding of the decision-making environment created by both senior Allied and German leaders during WW II is helpful to place electronic warfare in proper perspective. For reasons of security, the use of electronic warfare information, especially the cryptologic component or Ultra, was restricted to small cadres. Their decisions, Montgomery is one example, were often explained to outsiders as resulting from individual intuitive judgement on the part of many senior Allied leaders at the national and theater levels of command. In many cases these men were very comfortable with that unearned credit and not anxious to dispel false conclusions mistakenly made by historians in the absence of reliable information to the contrary.[7]

Further, leaders who made decisive errors after being afforded the benefit of cryptologic insight have not been anxious to bear special criticism for failure. A study of the Anzio battle [Anzio, Italy, 22 January 1944] reveals that senior officers like General Mark Clark were unduly harsh to subordinate commanders like General Lucas. Lucas, with access only to local intelligence and denied access to Ultra presumably because he lacked the "need to know", did not want to feed his troops into a "meat grinder". Clark had access to Ultra, made the wrong decisions and Lucas, the commander who needed the intelligence to fight the battle, was denied access, fought the battle incorrectly and lost 2,000 men per week needlessly. Lucas was relieved, Clark promoted.[8]

It can be argued that General Patton's allusions to divine intuition and presumed reincarnation—"I have seen this battlefield before at an earlier time"—were most likely used as a successful method to protect his cryptologic sources. Patton did this well and effectively, Clark did not. Consider the inconsistency with Patton. He was, after all, a Fundamentalist Christian, not a believer in the occult. General

Patton, like Rommel, is thought by this writer to have had the rare and exceptional ability to use cryptologic intelligence to see and anticipate the enemy at a time when that technique was not taught in Army service schools.[9]

Among all of WW II history, the Battle of the Atlantic was selected for analysis for several reasons. First, the use of cryptologic intelligence, radar, and the integration of both with other sources of intelligence, in conjunction with operations intended to support strategy, was more thoroughly demonstrated in the British Navy's Operational Intelligence Center during the Battle of the Atlantic Campaign than any similar function in the Allied military forces. Even the most current book on this topic, *Ultra in the West,* does not provide a better example.[10] Secondly, the British Operational Intelligence Center of WW II more closely resembles the present day Allied intelligence system focused on all-sources-of-intelligence centers than any other WW II model. It has stood the test of time and emerged as an operant model with considerable flexibility for strategic and tactical operations.

Every other Allied campaign in the WW II European Theater including Stalingrad, depended directly upon the Allies first defeating the German Navy in the Atlantic. It was a campaign which the Allies barely won and which according to the hypothesis, if it had been lost, would most likely have extended the length of WW II by several years with untold consequences as the Germans completed delivery of their new submarine fleet.

The hypothesis must stand to several tests. First, is it reasonable to judge that the Allies would not have won a decisive victory without the advantage of electronic warfare? Secondly, can that judgement be based on substantive information? Third, can any aspect of electronic warfare, like cryptanalysis or radar, stand alone as the single most decisive influence, or do all several aspects of electronic warfare fit better alongside other elements of intelligence and technology to provide a decisive factor in the outcome of WW II?

David Kahn, the noted author in the field of cryptology, reported that a remarkable conference took place at a German university in November 1978. Surviving Allied and German "code breakers" met to discuss thirty-five years later and under friendlier circumstances, the importance of cryptologic revelations during WW II. The British representatives explained how the Allies had outwitted the Germans for six years, detailing success after success. A German questioned, "If the Allies could read it all, why didn't they win the war sooner?" An American historian replied, "They did." Kahn also noted that the United States Army Chief of Staff, General George C. Marshall, reported that cryptanalysis became ". . . our chief basis for information regarding Hitler's intentions in Europe."[11] But there was more.

Electronic Warfare: Element of Strategy and Multiplier of Combat Power is not a technical analysis of the Allied success in cryptanalyzing the German Enigma cipher system. It is not a technical report explaining electronic wizardry. Those explanations are thoroughly explained by Beesly, Garlinski, Jones, Kahn, Lewin, and Winterbotham among others.[12] Rather this is an analysis of how the application of electronic warfare allowed the Allies to multiply combat power during WW II in order to accomplish strategic objectives and how the United States had best prepare a strategy to fight on the modern battlefield with electronic warfare.

CHAPTER II

The Strategy

The Treaty of Versailles prevented Germany from building submarines. The 1935 Anglo-German Naval Agreement limited German naval strength to thirty-five percent of that of Great Britain. The agreement did, however—in contrast with the Treaty of Versailles—permit Germany to achieve one hundred percent parity in submarines by 1938. The numbers were not large. Neither the British nor German submarine fleets exceeded fifty-seven boats before the war began. Nevertheless, in retrospect—considering the damage that Germany's submarines inflicted upon the British, in particular during WW I—it is difficult to understand why the British would ever agree to permit the Germans to possess even a single submarine. Submarines, regardless of their mission, are intended chiefly to serve as offensive weapons. The British benevolence involving Germany's acquisition of submarines is attributed to harshness of the other treaty conditions imposed upon Germany after its surrender in WW I.

Apparently, many members of the British government came to feel that the Versailles Treaty was so harsh that the Anglo-German Naval Agreement was intended to show reasonableness toward the Germans in an attempt to assure peace by conciliation. Permitting Germany to build submarines was an attempt to be "reasonable" in that regard but it was evidence of a lack of strategic understanding of the potential of that weapon.[1]

The issue is of interest, but probably not significant, when it is understood that Germany blatantly exceeded the limitations in some areas of naval construction and masked their violation in other areas in an attempt to build a major naval power. As one example, though the Germans were prevented from building submarines prior to 1935, it was widely known that before 1935 the German government heavily subsidized a naval architectural and design company in Holland. The Dutch company, paid by the Germans, designed U-boats for Germany while building submarines for other nations. The Allied Control Commission [of the Versailles Treaty] certainly did not serve as an effective deterrent to German Navy expansion prohibited by the Versailles Treaty. The British position on the issue reflected the British conciliatory attitude of the time and their lack of understanding about the use of the submarine as a strategic weapon despite popular literature available on the subject by both Bauer and Doenitz.[2]

Nevertheless, during the period between WW I and WW II, the Royal Navy was generally acknowledged by both British and German naval authorities to be totally superior to the German Navy when measured in conventional terms of strength common to that period. The British fleet was superior in numbers, type, tonnage, and the size of main guns in spite of the fact that British ships were for the most part aged, even obsolete. Of the Royal Navy's 150 destroyers, fifty were built for WW I. The Royal Navy was the most powerful fleet, but power by itself cannot ensure success. Power must be utilized at the time and place where it can be strategically decisive.[3]

The first indication that Britain subordinated strategy for budget occurred when the "Ten Year Rule" was established in 1919 and made self-perpetuating by Churchill in 1928. The Rule, a budget decision, directed the military departments to plan their annual budgets on the basis that Britain would not be involved in a war with a major power for ten years. The Rule remained in effect until 1937.[4]

Though the Royal Navy was smaller in size in September 1939 than it had been at the beginning of WW I in August 1914, it continued to be superior to the German fleet with respect to a measurement of combat power and by an even greater degree than it had been in 1914.[5]

The second indication that the British Navy had lost sight of strategic objectives occurred when the Admiralty reported to the Parliament in 1936 that the convoy system which had been used effectively during the First World War would not be necessary or used again. That evaluation was prompted by several considerations. First, during WW I, convoys created considerable delays for shipping and it was at first believed that steam ships would waste valuable time and fuel trying to maintain uniform convoy speeds and positions. Secondly, the Admiralty was over-confident in the ability of asdic (sonar) to detect submarines. Third, the Admiralty had not applied the study of statistics—a science introduced to the Royal Navy during WW I—to an examination of the convoy system to discover the statistical efficiency of convoys. Fourth, the Royal Air Force insisted that convoys provided good targets for enemy bombers and should therefore not be used. During the intervening years between WW I and WW II, the United States and British Navies concentrated exclusively on the study of massive fleet engagements and the use of battleships at the expense of developing tactics to protect trade. By 1937, signs of a major war were evident to many. The ensuing controversy resulted in the Admiralty reversing its decision by late 1937 so that the battle-proven convoy system was at least resurrected and available for use by September 1939. During WW I, [David] Lloyd George, the Prime Minister, also had to make that same decision for the Admiralty under similar circumstances. Ironically, by 1939 England, with forty-six million people, was no longer self-sufficient with respect to food and fuel as it had been during WW I.[6]

Prime Minister Churchill eloquently described the major aspect of British strategy after the war when he wrote:[7]

> Amid the torrent of violent events one anxiety reigned supreme. Battles might be won or lost, enterprises might succeed or miscarry, territories might be gained or quitted, but dominating all our powers to carry on the war or to keep ourselves alive, lay our mastery of the ocean routes and the free approach and entry to our ports.

Churchill emphasized that not only victory but the national survival of England in WW II was totally dependent upon protecting her sea routes and trade.[8] Though this judgement was evident after the war, and to some in 1937, that strategy was opaque to many during the intervening years between the two wars. The failure of England to consider its national interest when drafting its strategy and foreign policy may have resulted in England acceding to Germany's plea for a restoration of limited naval power. It was a compromise made entirely for an intangible purpose—Germany agreed not to contest Britain for hegemony of the seas when, in fact, Germany lacked the power to do so in the first place. Memories had apparently dimmed.

When war began on 3 September 1939, England was equipped with an obsolescent Navy intended for offensive strategic operations but faced with fighting a defensive campaign to protect its vital trade.

Having ignored strategy, England had the wrong Navy. Roskill explained that the Royal Navy misused its resources initially by immediately assuming the offensive to hunt U-boats rather than to defend convoys. The result was heavy losses to convoys.[9]

From war's beginning until January 1943, German U-boats sank an average of three British ships a day, day after day, quickly depleting England's merchant fleet and exhausting its warships.[10]

Imports to England, excluding oil, arrived at about 1,200,000 tons per week until June 1940 when the full force of the U-boat fleet began to take effect. By June, England's imports were reduced by about half to 750,000 tons per week. Though imports increased slightly to 800,000 tons per week throughout the following three months, July to September 1940, the cost was excessive as many more merchant ships were sunk in a desperate attempt to increase imports. The situation had become so serious by December 1940 that Churchill proposed laying an antisubmarine mine field, three by sixty miles wide, and consisting of 180,000 mines. The mine field would have cost in 1940 over fifty million dollars and monopolized all of Britain's explosives in order to protect only the Atlantic approaches to the ports on the Mersey and Clyde Rivers.[11]

By early 1941, England was exhausting its reserve supplies rapidly. Oil imports had been reduced by fifty percent and provided only two-thirds of peacetime consumption. The reduction was caused not only by the sinking of merchant ships but by the increased turn-around time now required in British ports, a consequence of the overcrowding of those few ports which remained open after German bombing.[12] By December 1942, only 300,000 tons of commercial oil remained in Britain, while rationed consumption continued at 130,000 tons per month. The German stranglehold was taking effect.[13]

With benefit of retrospect, ten years after the war's end, Roskill explained that England's grand strategy passed through several traditional phases: the defensive, the period of balance, and the offensive.

The defensive phase involved at least six steps. First, a new continental coalition had to be formed. In this case, it became a trans-ocean coalition. Previous British strategy had been shaped by an appraisal that the continental coalition formed after WW I was superior to any threat. That assumption proved to be incorrect. Second, the Navy had to defend the Island Empire from invasion. Third, the

Navy had to sever the enemy's access to world markets. Fourth, key strategic locations like Gibraltar had to be held by the Navy. Fifth, the Navy had to be able to assume a tactical offensive when necessary for short periods of time. Sixth and last, the Navy had to force the enemy to expose his forces when attacking England or its colonies.

The second phase occurred when England was able to gain control of selected maritime zones essential to supplying England and her forces overseas.

Finally, once resupply was assured, the Navy assumed the third phase—the offense and exploitation of the enemy.

This strategy formed the premise for separating warships into three classes: cruisers were intended to control sea communications, battleships to protect cruisers when they were engaged by a superior enemy force, and flotilla ships like destroyers to scout and escort. The aircraft carrier, relatively new as a tactical concept, was initially restricted to the flotilla role to scout and escort. During the pursuit of the *Bismarck* and during the Battle of Coral Sea, aircraft carriers were employed in the role of battleships, using their aircraft as an extension of deadly fire. Aircraft were used as substitutes for long-range cannon fire adding the advantages of versatility.[14]

Predominant naval thought before WW II considered the combat power of a warship as a function of how far away a warship could be from an enemy ship and still be able to hit and damage the enemy while remaining far enough away so as not to be seriously damaged itself. The fastest ship with the largest guns and most armor was considered the most powerful. If substitution was necessary, speed was most often substituted for armor. Using this criterion the small, unarmored submarine did not count for much.

Forty years later, in 1982, the force and range of modern weapons negates the value of massive armor. The most powerful ship is that one which can detect and hit the enemy first from the greatest distance. Given the lethality of modern weapons a first round hit usually means a first round destruction. Speed, maneuverability, and electronic detection and deception have become the key. The submarine was largely responsible for this change in concept during the past forty years.

It was not until 1942 that Roskill considered the military strategy of the Allies depended on defeating the U-boat. Prior to that time, primary emphasis was placed on strategic bombing—particularly by the British—as an essential preliminary to victory. It now appears that strategic bombing was motivated more by retaliation than by strategy. It was a concept of attrition rather than strategy. The Admiralty argued that the act of grand strategy required employment of all forces to further a common aim which it held was control of the seas with a superior surface fleet. The air force maintained that the destruction of the enemy homeland was the essential first ingredient.

When the examination is completed the Allied strategy emerges as: Defeat Germany first by an offensive into Europe resulting in unconditional surrender by the enemy. This can only be done if we can first mount superior forces on England's soil. To do this we must control the seas. To control the seas we must first destroy the German surface and U-boat fleets. In 1982 that strategy is very clear. It was not clear in 1939 and it did not develop because of superior strategic planning; it developed through evolution as the Allies solved a continuous list of crises. It is a credit to democratic institutions that in wartime they are better able to accommodate crises than are less flexible types of authoritarian government.[15]

THE GERMAN STRATEGY

By contrast with the Allied strategy, the German Navy planned to achieve naval parity with Britain by 1943 as outlined in the German Z-Plan (thought to be named after Admiral Zenker, commander of the German Navy prior to Admiral Raeder), and to achieve naval superiority by 1944. The Z-Plan was an ambitious design for fleet construction promulgated at the end of 1938 and provided for a fleet of modern battleships, aircraft carriers, pocket battleships, cruisers, and 350 modern submarines—U-boats. Hitler had assured Admiral Raeder, the Chief of Staff of the German Navy, that Germany would not be at war before 1944.[16] German strategy developed from an illusion that the nation could become a major sea power without benefit of tradition or experience. In the past, attempts to do this were not successful for Germany. German strategy was not developed from a foundation of purposeful military, economic, and political goals.

Speer, Hitler's Minister of Armaments and War Production, advised after the war that Hitler never intended to accelerate his strategic political objectives in such a manner as to be forced to confront England in combat prior to 1944. According to Speer, war with England was a miscalculated and premature consequence of Hitler's unexpected rapid success against Poland. Hitler had not expected Britain to risk war for Poland in 1939.[17]

Speer also advocated that Hitler had not intended to engage in war with Britain until at least the German U-boat fleet was capable of achieving the strategic objective of severely limiting England's economic and military capability.[18]

Shirer reported that on 23 May 1939, Hitler summoned his military chiefs, including Admiral Raeder, to the Chancellery in Berlin to discuss his military strategy. During these discussions, Hitler revealed his personal concept of sea power. He explained (though he was in error on the facts) that if Germany had only two more battleships and two more cruisers—and the battle had begun earlier in the morning—the German fleet would have won the decisive naval battle at Jutland during WW I. The British fleet would have been destroyed and the war ended in Germany's favor. Despite that misconception, Hitler continued by recognizing that it was not necessary to invade England to defeat that nation and acknowledged that air attacks would not end in England's surrender. In fact it was later estimated by German authorities that in order to defeat England, the imported supplies of food and fuel upon which the nation depended for sustenance and survival must be reduced by the amount of 700,000 tons per month and those losses continued for a year or longer; it was an amount about twenty-five percent of England's peace-time consumption. Actually, experience gained by 1943 indicated that almost twice that amount, a loss of 1,250,000 tons per month, would be required. That larger amount was actually being lost before the U-boat fleet was finally defeated.[19]

The German national strategic policy, Hitler implied, was to force England to capitulate by cutting off her supplies. To do this, Germany must first obtain army, air force, and naval bases from which to effect and support a blockade. But Germany needed more than bases; it also needed more U-boats—there were only fifty-six available. Of those fifty-six U-boats, about twenty-eight were suitable for combat duty.[20]

Admiral Raeder's diary of 3 September 1939 reveals the German

Navy was not prepared to engage the British Navy at the outset of WW II. Both the surface and submarine fleets were inferior to the task.[21] The British Merchant Marine consisted of more than 5,600 ships of which 2,600 were at sea on a typical day, ships steaming principally in the Atlantic and Indian Oceans and the North Sea, but over 1,000 smaller ships were also involved in European coastal trade. To destroy British shipping, the German Navy had four battleships, of which two were still under construction, six cruisers, five light cruisers, seventeen destroyers, twelve merchant raiders, and fifty-six U-boats. Most of the U-boats were of WW I design.[22]

Germany neglected the development of a sound defensive navy befitting a major land power in order to build a surface fleet of prestige but of little strategic value. Admiral Doenitz reported after the war as the German Navy Commander-in-Chief that Germany was not prepared for war at sea. As the former commander of the U-boat fleet, his judgement is considered authoritative.[23]

A popular concept which persists to this day is that Germany began WW II with several hundred submarines. It was an impression that was easy to develop considering that U-boats sank more than 2,800 merchant ships at 15 million tons during the war, most during the first few years.

Despite reports from some sources which have led to a popular conclusion that Admiral Raeder did not appreciate the combat power of the submarine, and that the submarine fleet commander Admiral Doenitz appreciated *only* the power of the submarine, that conclusion is in error. The German historian, C. D. Bekker, reports that at the initial war meeting on 3 September 1939 at Supreme Command of the German Navy, Oberkommando der Marine (OKM), the German Admiralty, Raeder acknowledged that the German Navy was unprepared to attack, let alone destroy the British Navy. Raeder stressed that the submarine was to be the chief weapon to harass the British merchant fleet. He agreed that many more submarines were needed and directed that submarine construction be increased from about two to thirty boats per month and that this be done at the expense of constructing new capital warships. It was the right decision, but one made too late; the political strategy had changed—Hitler was faced with war with Great Britain four years too soon.[24]

STRATEGIC TASKS

And so the strategic arena of the war was set, the tasks formidable for both sides. Prior to the war, England depended on 5,600 merchant ships, hundreds of foreign vessels, and 1,000 coastal vessels steaming unmolested throughout the sea lanes to deliver 60 million tons of supplies annually—five million tons a month—during peacetime. England could survive with 3,750,000 tons per month, but at least 6 million tons were required to shift the fighting to the enemy's territories.[25] When war was declared, the magnitude of the problem increased exponentially because more ships were required to carry the tremendous increase in imports of raw material and oil necessary to fuel the war effort. The steaming area was increased in width and length, not only to seek the protection afforded by a vast ocean, but to seek new markets and supplies as the enemy captured and dominated England's traditional sources of supply in Africa, Europe, and the Pacific.[26]

The inferior German Navy forced the world's largest and most powerful navy from an intended offensive role into a defensive, strategic role for which it was ill suited and untrained. The Royal Navy was forced to use major warships as substitutes for antisubmarine corvettes and to guard against German warships that seldom left their moorings. Germany maintained the strategic initiative until mid-1943.

Though the British Navy was superior in size, it was confronted with implementing a national maritime strategy of unprecedented magnitude with strategic resources insufficient for the task. The task on 3 September 1939 was:[27]

- Blockade Germany to prevent ships from leaving or entering German-controlled areas and exercise "belligerent rights" to prevent delivery of war materials by neutral ships which included, at this time, those of the United States and Italy.
- Protect British and neutral merchant ships from attack by enemy surface ships, submarines, or aircraft on all oceans and seas used to supply England and its forces.
- Protect England from invasion.
- Protect against enemy mining of seaways and ports.
- Later, as a top priority, protect troop convoys.

The British Navy may have had *numerical* superiority when compared to the German Navy, but the German Navy had *strategic* superiority when combat power was compared to strategic objectives. What neither Navy had was strategic adequacy when compared to the tasks confronting each. Initially, neither the Royal nor German Navies considered that intelligence was a strategic objective.

The Allies won WW II by finally multiplying the combat power of existing resources and destroying the resources of the enemy. The Allies did not learn how to do this quickly; it took until mid-1943, and required that intelligence be considered as a strategic objective.

During the period September 1939 to May 1943, German U-boats and warships, as well as merchant ship raiders, inflicted far greater damage on Allied shipping than Britain, its Commonwealth, the United States, and other Allies could absorb or replace. On the other hand, the risk to Germany, though often painful, was acceptable and easily sustainable.[28]

There are several factors which should be considered in a comparison of German and Allied strategy. First, the Allied Navies lacked an adequate number of ships capable of accomplishing the vital strategic tasks previously cited. Secondly, most of the ships were obsolescent. Finally, though the Admiralty had been instructed to revise convoy planning, a review of the literature does not provide evidence that either the British Navy or the United States Navy had a strategic plan for the protection of trade prior to the beginning of the war in 1939. Both navies had failed to understand and appreciate the extent of the threat to their merchant shipping in the event of war. Beesly related that the Admiralty could not conceive that sea battles would spread not only throughout the entire Atlantic but throughout all the oceans.[29] Despite the memory of the German U-boat campaign of WW I—memories which had apparently dimmed considerably in twenty years—the British naval tactics in early 1939 were intended chiefly to counter a threat from enemy surface vessels, not submarines. Admiral Samuel Eliot Morison, the United States Navy historian, judged that neither the British Navy nor the United States Navy were prepared for antisubmarine warfare despite their losses of WW I. The United States Navy lacked an intelligence and operations center for an effort against U-boats until March 1942. They certainly did not know how to use air patrols off the east coast of the United States to search for submarines during the bitter turkey-shoot period beginning in January 1942. According to Morison, the United States Navy did not know how to hunt submarines. The best way to protect merchant ships during WW II was to shepherd them into convoys while hunting and killing submarines.[30]

Aside from submarines, the German Navy also had a surface Navy composed primarily of the most technologically advanced ships afloat. The German naval strategy retained the initiative and advantage so long as the British could not find and destroy the German ships and submarines at a time and place of advantage to the British. Not having that capability in late 1939, the Royal Navy was forced by its own strategy to simultaneously protect all merchant ships, blockade the German fleet, chase the submarine fleet, and stand as pickets against invasion. During the first year of the war, the tactics and strategy of the Royal Navy was defensive; their strategy was reduced to reacting to German tactics and strategy. Beesly explains that by April 1940, both the Germans and British had both severely limited the capability of their respective fleets by mutual errors in estimating the strategic situation. Admiral Raeder is criticized by Roskill for lacking the moral courage to press his strategic convictions against Hitler's and Goering's opinions. Raeder was judged to have suffered the failure of excessive veneration for authority.[31]

When a nation designs a war policy and an implementing strategy, it must determine if it has the necessary military and economic resources required to support the strategy and hence enforce the policy. The cost of national defense, especially in the period following WW I, required an extensive capability at enormous expense, not only to fight with armies on fields of battle and with ships at sea, but to control large resources, markets, and routes of trade. Though technological resources are not always recognized as an element of the definition of strategy, recent experience—especially during WW II—indicates that a nation's technological resources may be as important as military, economic and psychological resources. In effect, technology must serve as a combat power multiplier. Despite the lessons of WW I, Britain and the United States had observed, but not learned, how to multiply strategic combat power by using technology, specifically intelligence, as one factor. Both simply reduced forces and expenses without compensating for the reduction of combat power by improving technological intelligence.

The literature is replete with examples of Britain, Japan, and Germany recognizing the decisive importance of new weapons before and during WW II and of the ability of the United States to mass produce weapons in order to achieve a technological advantage. Invariably, weapons were considered exclusively in terms of destruction. It followed that weapons that could cause the most destruction were considered to be the best weapons rather than to consider those weapons which could destroy key strategic targets with the least risk to be the best weapons. A major deficiency which emerges from a study of WW II strategy is the failure of leaders to understand and judge the importance of using technological resources early in the war in conjunction with intelligence and strategic planning for decision-making. The case in point is cryptologic intelligence. Despite their superiority in the field of cryptologic intelligence during WW I, especially naval cryptology, the British failed to devote the resources or attention deserved and earned by this national resource in WW I. The irony is that during WW II cryptology cost less than a single ship of the line, but it was chiefly responsible for leading to the destruction of many enemy ships and submarines.

*****

Radar is an example. The British did not distinguish between strategic bombing of German-occupied territory and the German homeland and the defeat of the German Navy, and assign the highest priority to the latter. Coastal Command, which shouldered much of the responsibility for hunting and killing submarines, did not receive the priority for aircraft and radar commensurate with its role of achieving the major British military objective. A misunderstanding of strategic goals in an atmosphere of emotion led Britain instead to place priority on strategic bombing. It was an emotional response to a strategic issue. Had strategic bombing been effective—and it is generally agreed that it was more retaliatory than effective—in reducing production it still was not directed at targets designed to reduce the German impact on British shipping. The amount of bombs dropped on submarine pens and yards was too small by comparison to other targets, and was too late. British strategic bombing is a policy better described as retaliatory bombing.

Hitler, on the other hand, responded to his perceived concept of British capabilities. During April of 1940, Hitler had become convinced that the British were intending to invade Norway in force. A closer examination of the facts would have revealed that the capability was lacking. There were other factors. The Royal Navy was mining the Norwegian Leads and interdicting the shipment of vital iron ore from Sweden, and Admiral Raeder had been pleading for Norwegian ports to service his surface and submarine fleets. But chiefly, Hitler recalled the submarine fleet from its primary strategic task—attacking British merchant shipping—to support the invasion. It was a serious blunder that gave the British time to recover from high losses. Hitler also used almost the entire surface fleet to support the invasion and so arose an opportunity for the British to engage the German Navy in what could have been a time and place of advantage to the British—a decisive battle at sea. The Royal Navy was to be provided with an opportunity to destroy the German Navy. In an overall explanation of the basic strategy involved, suffice to say that Britain failed to discover the operation in an incident having a remarkable similarity to the WW I Battle of Jutland. Hitler successfully completed yet another high-risk strategic gamble and won at little cost. To understand why Britain failed to develop this battle, it is necessary to study a little about British Naval Intelligence in the following chapter.[32]

CHAPTER III

Cryptology

AN ELECTRONIC WARFARE WEAPON

Twice, during WW I and then again during WW II, the British had the exceptional good fortune to gain special insight into the German cryptographic process. The British were able to read secret German radio messages during wartime. During WW I, the British were provided by the Russians with a captured code book from the German cruiser *Magdeburg* and during WW II they were provided with vital cryptographic research about the German electro-mechanical Enigma enciphering machine by the Polish General Staff and French Intelligence. A German army cipher clerk, the brother of a German Army general, provided the French Intelligence with critical cryptographic material essential to determining the Enigma keylist. Additionally, shortly after the war began, the British twice captured vital Enigma material, first from *U-111* in late 1939 and later from *U-110*. The details are explained in this chapter.

BRITISH CRYPTOLOGY

British cryptology, a function of the British Secret Service, began its military contribution during WW I in Room 40 of the Old Block Building of the British Admiralty. As a consequence, cryptologic operations were traditionally referred to as Room 40 Operations during WW I. Room 40 achieved the status of a cryptanalysis bureau after they were able to exploit a German code book that had been recovered from the sunken cruiser *Magdeburg* by the Russians. The Russians sank the *Magdeburg* in the Baltic Sea, recovered the code book and provided it to the British in 1914. It was a lucky break. With that benefit, Room 40 subsequently became an integral part of the Naval Intelligence Division of the Admiralty in 1917. Without access to the German Navy code book, it is expected that Room 40 would have become subordinate instead to the British Foreign Office. In any event, Room 40 personnel learned their work well; they masterminded the Zimmerman Telegram, an achievement which helped to manipulate the United States into WW I.[1]

THE BATTLE OF JUTLAND

We go back to an earlier time—the Battle of Jutland, 13 May 1916, when British Admiral Jellicoe was chasing German Admiral Scheer and the German fleet across the North Sea—to find the foundation on which electronic warfare rests as an element of strategy. It was during that battle that a series of errors by Room 40 personnel created an undeserved reputation for ineptness that was to pervade British Naval Intelligence for many years to come and directly into WW II. The Battle of Jutland is important to a study of WW II strategy because the errors of intelligence and tactics are symptomatic of similar errors in WW II and precursory of errors on the modern battlefield.[2]

There were errors during the production and dissemination of intelligence during the battle. The errors are traced to excessive secrecy as well as to capability. Room 40 activities were so secret during the war that very few senior officers in either the Admiralty or aboard the fleet were aware of cryptologic intelligence, the capture of the German code book, or the reliability of the intelligence. Secondly, those that were aware of cryptology were not familiar with either its limitations or capabilities to the extent required to make decisions when confronted with conflicting information. Similarly, the cryptanalysts working in Room 40 were not trained in either intelligence or naval operations and lacked an appreciation of what information was vital to those at sea. The British fleet did not know what to ask of Room 40, and Room 40 did not know or appreciate what the fleet needed. Seemingly all concerned knew just enough to be dangerous.[3]

To understand the tactics involved in the Battle of Jutland, it is necessary to realize that the British had to determine precisely the right combination of time and distance factors required to set a course from their home base at Scapa Flow on the northern tip of Scotland. A course was required which would permit the British fleet to avoid German U-boats and still permit them to engage the German fleet when it steamed from the safety of its Baltic Sea home waters. The British fleet could not afford to linger in the area and thus preclude the element of surprise or to become submarine targets; it could not steam into battle either too soon or too late. That was the crux of the tactical decision upon which naval strategy depended in May 1916. The British Navy needed to know precisely when the German fleet left its moorings—they needed intelligence.

The circumstances leading to Room 40's involvement in the Battle of Jutland began when the Director of the Admiralty's Operation Division asked Room 40 personnel for the direction finding plot of German naval callsign [DK]. This was the callsign used by the German Commander-in-Chief of the Navy, Admiral Scheer. At his request, the director was advised of the most recent location of the radio station that last used that callsign; it was the headquarters located at Wilhelmshaven, Germany, on the Baltic Sea. The callsign had not changed locations. The director, satisfied, departed Room 40. He had not told Room 40 personnel, "We want to engage the German fleet, we expect it to steam to sea shortly, and we believe that the ship using callsign [DK] will provide the location of Admiral Scheer and hence the location of the fleet." Nor did he say, "Where is Admiral Scheer because we believe he will be with the German fleet?" The director had developed the correct premise: Admiral Scheer would, of course, lead his fleet into battle, and his callsign would reveal the location of the fleet once a direction finding fix was obtained on the radio station transmitting Scheer's callsign. But the director was asking the wrong questions. Room 40 personnel could have provided the answer to either question, and the answer would have been entirely different than the answer given to the director in response to his inquiry. An inquiry shaped by his attitude of: give me the facts, I'll do the analysis.[4]

Room 40 personnel were well aware that when Admiral Scheer went to sea with the fleet, he changed callsigns. Callsign [DK] was only used when at his headquarters at Wilhelmshaven. Armed with only the answer to his question, the Director of Operations incorrectly advised Admiral Jellicoe that the German fleet remained in port. Actually, Scheer and his fleet had been moving toward the Atlantic for about ten hours. One can imagine the surprise when Jellicoe ran into the German fleet only four hours later in the North Sea. Jellicoe was not impressed with either intelligence or cryptology.[5]

After the ensuing battle, the outnumbered and battered fleet attempted to disengage. There were four routes to safety for the Germans. German fleet communications were intercepted and, with benefit of the captured code book, cryptanalyzed. Admiral Jellicoe was provided a report that a German warship had transmitted a message in which it revealed its own location. Unfortunately, German seamanship, lacking in tradition and experience, was such that the ship had actually miscalculated its own location and its report was greatly in error. This was not an attempt to deceive. However, all other information contained in that ship's radio message was correct and provided considerable insight into the German course of action.[6] Jellicoe knew the correct location of that German warship, knew that the reported location was in error and, therefore, discounted the entire intelligence report, relying instead on his own judgement in the matter. He counted this as his second experience with naval and cryptologic intelligence. He had not been favorably impressed.[7]

The issue of asking wrong questions and receiving wrong answers has been discussed. This was the first error; the inexperienced naval personnel associated with Room 40 had lacked the impertinence to ask the director of the Operations Division why it was that he needed that information pertaining to the callsign. Additionally, Room 40 had not correlated the cryptanalyzed message with radio direction finding, a standard cryptologic technique, especially at sea, to distinguish reported locations from near-actual locations. That was the second error.

Finally, Room 40 personnel cryptanalyzed another German radio message and reported, through the Admiralty to Jellicoe, that the German fleet was ordered back to its Baltic Sea bases; Jellicoe was provided with the enemy fleet's actual course. Based on his previous experience, Jellicoe ignored the intelligence, thinking it was incorrect, though it was totally correct as was later additional intelligence. Jellicoe lost the opportunity to destroy the German fleet in 1916, and the legacy of Room 40 and naval intelligence in general endured right into WW II.[8]

Two of the errors have been cited, there were others. Cryptology was not integrated with general naval intelligence. Cryptologic intelligence, with protection for its source, was not disseminated widely to those who needed to study it. Most importantly, operations and intelligence were not integrated at the Admiralty staff level. After the study of the Battle of Jutland was completed, the Navy Staff determined that secrecy had become an obsession. Cryptologic intelligence was provided only by direction of the Chief of the Navy Staff and the

Director of the Operations Division of the Navy Staff. The function of disseminating intelligence was withheld from the Director of the Intelligence Division and left instead to the discretion of the Chief of Operations. A chief lesson learned from Jutland was that cryptology must be integrated with other intelligence information, like direction finding reports, at a consolidated intelligence and operations center. Operations, plans, and intelligence are inseparable functions of the strategic or tactical process. As a consequence, the British implemented a strategic operations and intelligence center within the Admiralty in mid-1917, drawing a blueprint for the essential integration of a technological resource to be used to multiply strategic combat power. The center served the Royal Navy well for the remainder of the war, then it was deactivated.[9]

BETWEEN WARS

At the end of WW I, there were lapses. Manpower cutbacks, as well as a reduction in all resources caused by economic constraints and intergovernmental rivalry, considerably reduced the cryptologic capability of the British government. The Foreign Office placed great pressure on the government and succeeded in separating Room 40 from the military. The Foreign Office contended that the Director of Naval Intelligence had developed unparalleled and important powers and more influence outside naval operations than the Foreign Office. By 1936, cryptology was relegated to a position of inactivity, Room 40 disbanded, and intelligence collection—what little survived—was concerned mainly with naval construction and coastal defense. After 1936, naval intelligence could not respond with an analysis of foreign naval fleets, their organization, dispositions, or movement. The Navy could not estimate the threat to British trade or to the Royal Navy. Only five radio direction finding stations remained, when previously the number had exceeded one hundred. What little naval intelligence was available was provided almost exclusively from defense attache reports.[10]

During this period, from 1936 to 1940, many European Navies and the United States Navy were beginning to replace medium range naval communication systems with longer range high frequency radio communications. While naval communications had previously been limited to a range of only several hundred miles, high frequency communications allowed any Admiralty to now communicate with fleets or ships around the world. The potential to exploit these communications with radio intercept and radio direction finding stations was great. Instead the world's largest and most powerful navy was forced to neglect this considerable potential for relatively low-cost intelligence.[11] The world's largest and most powerful navy, the Royal Navy, lacked an effective intelligence capability.

By 1936, the now very limited cryptologic capability of the British government was organized as the Government Code and Cipher School; its effectiveness as a military organization or an organization which could support military operations had been lost. Great Britain was unable to estimate the enemy military threat by cryptanalyzing secret military radio messages.[12]

The Admiralty had not ascended to higher perspective during the intervening years either. The British Staff system had been forced on a reluctant navy by the First Sea Lord of the Admiralty, Winston Churchill, just prior to WW II. The prevailing organizational attitude was that any naval officer not trained and developed as a ship's officer could not be trusted with responsibility of interpreting and disseminating intelligence upon which tactics and strategy depended. The Battle of Jutland was a case in point. Interpreted another way, the Navy Staff 'incestuously' selected from among senior ship's officers had not yet learned how to determine and prescribe essential elements of information needed by a commander to fight. They did not know how to task military intelligence. Presumably, only those few selected Regular Navy officers of the executive branch had been ordained with the insight necessary to interpret and disseminate intelligence. Ordained perhaps, but not trained or refreshed in the lessons of WW I and, specifically, the Battle of Jutland and the U-boat war that followed. In fact, Admiral of the Fleet, Sir A. Dudley P. R. Pound, First Sea Lord and Chief of the Naval Staff—a leader of exceptional integrity—has been considered by naval historians such as Roskill[13] to have carried centralization inside the Admiralty too far. That appraisal is an understatement.

During the Abyssinian Crisis of 1936, a conflict which nearly involved war between Italy and Great Britain, there was virtually no intelligence available to the Admiralty. By the summer of 1937, Admiral Sir William James, the Deputy Chief of Naval Staff, initiated an intelligence and operations center modeled on the post-1917, WW

I model but one which would now depend on the Government Code and Cipher School, an entity of the Foreign Office, for cryptanalysis. The Spanish Civil War was already a year old by 1937. The Code and Cipher School had initial success against some Italian Navy and Spanish Nationalist ciphers, codes, and callsign analysis by mid-1937, but it had not yet begun to integrate naval radio direction finding reports to determine the source and location of the encrypted signals.[14]

TWO VITAL DECISIONS

Two critically important operational decisions were made during this period by the British Admiralty. First, an agreement was reached between the Code and Cipher School and the Admiralty that *all* signals which were intercepted—encrypted or otherwise—would be sent to the Code and Cipher School by the Navy and that *all* information derived by the Code and Cipher School would be provided directly to Naval Intelligence after exploitation. The Code and Cipher School would not determine what information they thought the Admiralty needed, they would provide all information. This decision was an outgrowth of a situation referred to as the "Pirate Submarine Case" in which the lack of coordination—that is, a charitable evaluation—between the Code and Cipher School and Naval Intelligence resulted in wrong conclusions being formed because neither party shared all the information each possessed. A two-man Naval Intelligence Division team was granted authority to coordinate all naval intelligence, regardless of its source, and was provided full responsibility for analysis and evaluation. The team activated an operational intelligence center which became a principal function of the Naval Intelligence Division and referred to by its abbreviation, the "OIC."[15]

Secondly, in 1938, the OIC was permitted to disseminate intelligence evaluation and analysis under the authority of the Director of the Naval Intelligence Division directly to authorities having a need to know—both inside and outside the Admiralty to ships at sea, and to the Commander-in-Chief of the Navy. They could do this without needing special authority from the Chief of Naval Operations, as had been the case in the past. Intelligence was at last recognized as a principal staff function. As will be seen in the next chapter, during the chase of the *Bismarck,* despite the wisdom demonstrated in reaching these two decisions, the Admiralty had overlooked a circumstance not foreseen by those unfamiliar with the traditions of the sea. The commander of the Home Fleet could refuse to accept intelligence analysis provided by the OIC.[16]

Nevertheless, these two decisions, born of British experience during WW I, probably allowed the British Navy to accomplish a significant jump of perhaps two to three years, vital years, ahead of the German Navy. The dissemination of Ultra material was markedly different in the Navy using the system just described than the system used by Allied armies and air forces in which a special Ultra distribution system using Special Liaison Units (SLU)—described thoroughly by Winterbotham—were used. The Navy system has stood the test of time; the SLU system became too cumbersome for use on the modern battlefield. This was not an issue of security—both systems used one-time encryption pads exclusively to protect Ultra—it was an issue of disseminating intelligence directly from the intelligence center to the commander without an intermediary, it was the Reformation.

At the beginning of WW II, the OIC had placed emphasis on increasing the number of radio intercept and high-frequency radio direction finding stations, on the design of a secure Ultra dissemination system, and on other cryptographic techniques to protect friendly communications. By 30 October 1940, the Admiralty expected the OIC to use intelligence to compensate for a shortage of combat power needed to accomplish strategic objectives and tasks, and to serve as a multiplier of combat power.[17] During this period, 1926 to 1939, however, a very secret attempt was being conducted by the Polish General Staff to cryptanalyze the newly introduced [1926] German electro-mechanical Enigma enciphering machine. The problem was that between 1926 and 1932 the branches of the German Military gradually introduced the Enigma and the British were unable to break the cipher system.[18]

POLISH CRYPTOLOGY

Jozef Garlinski, greatly assisted by Colonel Tadeusz Lisicki, in his 1979 book, *Intercept,* thoroughly explains the Allied success with Enigma. *Intercept* is rated by this researcher as the most complete explanation of Ultra written to date. Garlinski's work eliminates remaining mysteries, considerable speculation, and assigns credit where it rightfully belongs.[19]

After reading Garlinski, Lewin writing in *Ultra Goes to War* and Beesly in *Very Special Intelligence* provide an exceptionally clear insight into the Allied accomplishment with the German Enigma family of cipher systems used by the German Navy during WW II. It is not within the scope of this report to repeat a detailed analysis of how Enigma was broken. That information is provided in complete detail in the appendix to Garlinski's work. However, a general description of how Enigma worked and a chronology of events leading to the Allied success with Enigma is important because the technological policy directing that effort pertains equally to technological considerations peculiar to the present time as well. One needs to understand Enigma not as an enciphering machine but as a technological device to see how the Battle of the Atlantic was won by the Allies rather than by the Germans.[20]

ENIGMA

The earliest version of the Enigma electro-mechanical enciphering machine was first demonstrated in Berlin as a commercial security device by the Scherbius manufacturing company in 1923.[21] The German Navy adopted the Enigma after ordering additional security modifications in 1926. The Army adopted the device in 1929 and the Air Force in 1934. Copies of the civilian-model Enigma, a model using three enciphering wheels of twenty-six points each, were available to purchasers outside Germany at a cost of $144.00 each until 1933 when it was removed from the market. Representatives from England, Japan, Poland, and the United States among others purchased Enigma machines. The first United States model arrived in 1928 and, with refinement, was later used to successfully break Japanese versions of the Enigma cipher. The Japanese too modified their Enigma, a device referred to as the Model 97 or Purple Cipher machine.[22] The noted American cryptologist William Friedman also arranged for the purchase of an Enigma in 1929.[23]

The Polish government was reading manually encrypted German Army messages in the Double Cassette Cipher, a double transposition system, through cryptanalysis from 1920 to 1926. This advantage was lost as Enigma was gradually introduced by the Germans between 1926 and 1929.[24]

By 15 January 1930, the previously separate functions of radio intercept and cryptanalysis were combined in the Second Bureau of the Intelligence Department (also referred to as the Polish Secret Service) of the Polish General Staff.[25]

Confronted with historical enemies, the Germans to the west and the Russians to the east, Poland well understood the strategic implications of cryptology, the ability to read the secret military messages of their enemies. The Polish General Staff made every effort to recruit, train, and sponsor a strong national cryptologic effort against both Germany and the Soviet Union. Until the defeat of Poland in 1939, Polish cryptanalysts surpassed all others in Europe.

In January 1929, Polish intelligence organizations successfully gained access to a commercial-model German Enigma enciphering machine passed through the Polish Customs Office in Warsaw. The device was surreptitiously examined and photographed. Though the device was obviously an enciphering machine, it was not at that time recognized as an Enigma machine. Later, those photographs and notes would provide the first insight of Enigma. When the connection between the device and Enigma was discovered, Polish intelligence purchased a commercial-model Enigma through the Polish AVA electrical firm, a civilian enterprise.[26]

During the period 1926 to 1932 British, French, and Polish intelligence all tried independently to cryptanalyze Enigma radio messages. They were unsuccessful.

Possession of the commercial-model Enigma enciphering machine revealed its basic operating principles but did not reveal the special security modifications performed for German military models of Enigma.

By considerable good fortune, French Intelligence had been contacted by a cipher clerk in the German Army. The soldier was the younger brother of a General in the German Army; more importantly, the soldier was employed in the German General Staff Cryptographic Branch and later in the Communications Intelligence section [Forschungsamt] of the German Air Force. He was motivated, it was speculated, primarily by expenses incurred by a compulsion to gamble and a feeling that his government did not fully appreciate his capabilities for a higher station in the military. He was willing to sell

Enigma material to French Intelligence in 1931.[27] The soldier, his name was Hans-Thilo Schmidt, was codenamed Asche. He was executed for treason in July 1943 after his case officer [Lemoine, a.k.a. Stelmann] was captured by the Germans and revealed the identity of Asche among others in return for his own life. Lemoine died in a French prison in 1946.[28] It is remarkable that the arrest and subsequent torture of Schmidt did not result in the Germans concluding that Enigma had been compromised in July 1943.

Schmidt provided operating instructions, keying instructions, details of Enigma's military modifications, technical drawings, and the keylists for September and October 1932. This information along with the intensive cryptanalytic training previously completed by the Polish cryptanalysts permitted them to systematically reconstruct future keylists until September 1939.[29]

The Polish cryptanalysts were initially confronted with about sixty different Enigma keylists, one for each of the sixty military nets used by Germany between 1932 and 1938.[30]

During the period 1932 to 1938, Polish success in reading Enigma enciphered messages gradually increased until by 1938, all German ciphers except naval ciphers could be read in near real-time of intercept.[31] Because the Germans began to change cipher wheel settings more frequently and to rotate one cipher wheel with another more frequently (thereby considerably increasing the possible permutations, as well as increasing the number of military radio nets), the Polish cryptanalysts were being overwhelmed by the sheer volume of German ciphers. To meet this challenge the Polish cryptanalysts developed a high speed calculating device called a bombe. It was a machine composed of six Enigmas, electrically powered, and used to solve the settings of Enigma machines, to provide a keylist.[32] Garlinski provides an excellent description of how the bombe worked.[33] Polish cryptanalysts were able to recover a complete Enigma keylist in less than two hours using the bombe.[34]

All this changed on 15 September 1939 when the German Army introduced a second improved version of Enigma; a model using two additional twenty-six point enciphering wheels which served as spares. When Germany invaded Poland in October 1939, the Polish General Staff was not able to cryptanalyze enciphered text from the newer model German Enigma cipher machines.[35]

FRENCH CRYPTOLOGY

French Intelligence did not provide cryptology deserving examination. French Intelligence, by good fortune, had soldier Schmidt contact them to sell Enigma information and they took advantage of the opportunity. This information was later traded to the Poles for cryptologic intelligence. After Poland was captured by Germany, many Polish cryptanalysts escaped to France and continued the cryptologic effort there until France was captured; many then escaped again to substantially assist the British.[36]

THE POLISH GIFT

The British, French, and Polish intelligence agencies concerned with cryptology maintained a loose affiliation between cryptologists beginning in about 1929. On 24 and 25 July 1939, representatives of the Second Bureau of the Polish General Staff, the British Code and Cipher School, and French Intelligence met in the Pyry Forest, ten kilometers south of Warsaw. Polish cryptanalysts revealed their success in cryptanalyzing all German ciphers except naval ciphers. They revealed about fifteen Enigma machines which had been built for them by the Polish AVA electric company, Polish copies of the Enigma. They revealed the bombe which could determine Enigma keylists in less than two hours. More importantly, the Poles volunteered to give one copy of the Polish Enigma machine to France and one to Britain along with technical drawings of the bombe and copies of the perforated sheets critical to the use of the bombe. The British copy of Enigma and the technical drawings arrived in England on 16 August 1939. Based on this information, the popularly repeated story accredited by Winterbotham, indicating that a Polish worker in the German Enigma factory smuggled parts of the complete Enigma machine to Britain to be reconstructed, is believed to be an error.[37] Other important information pertaining to the German naval Enigma was to be recovered from the captured *U-111* later in 1939.[38]

HOW ENIGMA WORKED

The Enigma electro-mechanical enciphering machine, as explained by Lewin in *Ultra Goes to War,* is a device resembling a typewriter in appearance. The most thorough explanations of how Enigma worked are believed to be best presented by Hinsley and Garlinski in their separate works on the subject.[39] An Enigma operator used a 26-letter (A to Z inclusively) alphabetical keyboard to type each plaintext letter of a message to be encrypted. As each plaintext letter was typed on the keyboard an electrical impulse was transmitted through wiring to an entry switch, then to and through three enciphering wheels which rotated inside the Enigma machine. The impulse travelled through the enciphering wheel circuitry (also called a rotor or drum) to contact a reflector which returned the impulse through wiring by a different route to the enciphering wheels and then through a circuit connected to a lightbulb on top of the Enigma case. Instead of typewriter keys which could be used to print a message, the Enigma contained a second alphabet, the cipher-alphabet also consisting of 26 letters which lighted as the impulse hit any one bulb. The operator transcribed the letters as each lighted to compose the enciphered text of the message. As each letter on the plaintext keyboard was depressed, another letter on the ciphertext lightboard was lighted. The lighted letter represented but was different than the letter pressed on the keyboard. Hence the plaintext message was encrypted letter by letter. It was a slow process. To this point, the impulse passed through only seven permutations—the three enciphering wheels, the single reflector, then back through the three enciphering wheels.[40] In some explanations the entry switch and the reflector are considered to be rotors hence the Enigma is referred to by Polish cryptanalysts as a five rotor machine. The British consider only the enciphering wheels to be rotors, the entrance switch and reflectors to be switches, hence they refer to Enigma as a three rotor machine. This is important mostly to understand that the naval Enigma possessed extra security primarily because it used one more enciphering wheel, and more spare wheels than did the Army and Air Force models. This applies whether the machine is referred to as a three or five rotor enciphering machine.[41]

Each enciphering wheel was a distinct electric circuit with twenty-six contact points located equidistant around the wheel, each point corresponded to one of the twenty-six letters of the alphabet. Each of the three wheels in the same Enigma machine had a different circuit than the other two wheels; however, the number one wheel in all Enigmas was the same. Similarly all number two and three, and numbered spare wheels were identical.[42] The enciphering wheels could be interchanged one with the other to provide six combinations. Additionally, the German Army and Navy also issued from two to five spare enciphering wheels so that a total of five to eight wheels could be interchanged in the same Enigma. The use of a set of five enciphering wheels, as an example, of which only three were in the Enigma at any one time, provided sixty variations.[43]

Additionally, connected to the back of the Enigma case was an add-on box with a third alphabet with electrically connecting female sockets which corresponded to each of the 26 letters of the alphabet. The sockets could be connected with a patch cord having a male plug at each end to add circuitry variations between the enciphering wheels and the lighted ciphertext alphabet.[44]

Considering the variations which could be provided by the number of enciphering wheels, the interchangeability of the enciphering wheels with one another, the spare enciphering wheels, the twenty-six contact points on each enciphering wheel and the seven permutations inherent in the basic Enigma circuitry, the possible total permutations amount by one calculation to between 3×10^8 for the Army version of Enigma to 4×10^{20} for the Navy, Model M [der Marine] Enigma, the latest model introduced on 8 March 1940 with four rather than three primary enciphering wheels.[45] Garlinski's research, however, reports that the possible permutations for the Army Enigma was 5 and 87 zeroes.[46]

All enciphering wheels were made in sets so that all enciphering wheels of the same number were identical in all Enigma machines and were interchangeable from one machine to another. It is important to understand that the enciphering wheels did not rotate in a manner dependent upon striking a particular key on the plaintext keyboard. As an example, whenever the letter [K] was pressed, the same cipher letter did not continuously light. It was not a simple substitution. Instead, the enciphering wheels rotated in exactly the same manner whenever any plaintext letter was depressed and the enciphered letter corresponding to the plaintext was always different. There would be no similarity between the word [headquarters] enciphered the first time [kighyrmnfrqs] and the second time [thkqkoudmpry]. Since the word would also be broken down into consistent five letter groups for transmission, it would not resemble the twelve letter word [headquarters] but rather [thkqk] [oudmp] [ryvdj] pickingup three letters [vdj] from the next word in the message.[47]

Both the sending and receiving cryptographic operators, called cipher clerks, had to ensure that both Enigma machines had all enciphering wheels with their twenty-six points aligned identically in order to make the enciphered text correspond to the plaintext. To do this, all cipher clerks used a keylist which instructed them how to set the enciphering wheels and when to rotate enciphering wheels. The keylist was published periodically by the headquarters controlling the radio net. Each keylist provided a separate and distinct cipher system. The Triton cipher system was used by the headquarters of the U-boat fleet; the U.d.B. Merchant raiders communicated using the Tibet and One Hundred ciphers. The surface fleet used yet another cipher. Unless a cryptographic operator had access to more than one cipher system, and it was rare that he would, he could not use his Enigma machine to read the messages encrypted in an Enigma cipher system other than his own. U-boat cipher clerks, as an example, could not read surface fleet radio messages. This was intended primarily to increase security.[48]

Since several hundred radio stations used the same cipher system, and since these stations were frequently at sea at different times, keylists had to be distributed well in advance of their intended use and covered periods of several months. The keylists captured from *U-110,* as an example, were effective for six months.[49]

Similarly, a cryptanalyst, though in possession of an Enigma machine and all the enciphering wheels, could not read any Enigma cipher unless he had access to the keylist. If able to obtain one keylist, the cryptanalyst still could not read messages encrypted in other cipher systems using different keylists.

There are two ways to obtain a keylist: obtain it directly from the enemy by capture or stealth, or reconstitute the keylist by cryptanalysis. In either event, if the enemy determined that a keylist had been compromised, he would simply change to a new keylist and the cryptanalyst would start again from the beginning. Consequently, as it can be appreciated, cryptanalytic information is considered to be highly classified by both sides.

The fastest way to obtain a keylist of the type used for Enigma is to steal it from the enemy without his knowledge. A sophisticated enemy uses strict accounting procedures to prevent the loss of a keylist. The opportunity presented by a cipher clerk like Schmidt is also very rare. Cipher clerks are selected because they are dependable; they are not randomly selected from the conscripts. Garlinski estimates that the Germans used about 30,000 Enigma machines during WW II; the number of compromises was exceptionally small and only one soldier, Schmidt, has surfaced to date.[50] Keylists can also be captured if cipher clerks are unable to destroy the list quickly enough. Enigma material, enciphering wheels for certain, possibly keylists, were captured first from *U-111* in the Dover Strait in late 1939, then from *U-33* in February 1940, and in May 1941 *U-110* provided significant Enigma information.[51] Another way to obtain a keylist was to use a bombe calculating machine to compare the billions upon billions of possible permutations one at a time but at high speed. Even a machine with relatively high speed took a lot of time to do this. It may be recalled that the first Polish bombe working against the earlier Enigma machines limited to only several million permutations required two hours to solve the keylist against a single cipher system. In some cases, poor cryptographic security by German radio or cipher operators could be used to expedite the calculations. This occurred most frequently when German cipher clerks lazily aligned their Enigmas using repetitious procedures, aligning all enciphering wheels to AAA as an example.[52]

Once a keylist was recovered all messages sent in that cipher system could be read in near real-time. Each cipher used by the German Navy required a different keylist and there were thirteen primary cipher systems.[53] Each time a keylist changed, a new solution had to be achieved. Minor keylist changes were conducted at least every twenty-four hours and frequently more often. Major keylist changes, like the exchange of enciphering wheels, were conducted every month with a corresponding major impact on cryptanalysis.[54]

The German operators changed cipher variations by simply rearranging the position of the enciphering wheels. The Allies had to determine the setting of the three wheels in order to perform cryptanalysis. The bombe played a key role in cryptanalysis. The bombe was designed to mechanically try each potential permutation at a rate much faster than the speed achievable by a human mathematician in his entire lifetime. Bombe and its subsequent variations of increased complexity and higher rates of calculation was to become known as the Turing Machine because of basic logic improvements added by the British mathematician Alan Turing during WW II. Bombe was the forerunner of modern computers.[55]

By late 1939, after the introduction of the second version of Enigma, Polish cryptologists working for the French were able to read some German Air Force radio messages due to heavy use of gratuitous plaintext revelations provided in Air Force messages; however, the Air Force messages could not be read in real-time. As the German Army advanced into France and increased its coordination with the German Air Force by radio, Polish cryptologists working with the French also began to cryptanalyze some German Army Enigma encrypted radio messages as well. By April 1940, British cryptanalysts were also able to read small amounts of German Air Force Enigma. After the capture of the *U-110* keylist, the British were finally able to cryptanalyze the U-boat Triton cipher in near real-time until the keylist expired in July 1941. The British gradually began to break through the new keylist based on their experience with the *U-110* material until, by May 1943, the British were adept at cryptanalyzing several German Navy cipher systems to include Triton.[56]

The limited success against German Enigma during late 1939 and early 1940 cannot be attributed to mastery of Enigma cryptanalysis by the British, French, and Poles. To this point, Allied success was due more to poor communications security by the German Air Force than to any other factor.[57] German naval Enigma remained very secure during this period because of exceptional communications security in which Enigma keylists were changed consistently and because large amounts of routine administrative traffic was transmitted over landline ashore rather than by radio as was the Air Force practice.[58]

It can be concluded that throughout WW II, the German Air Force dependence on Enigma enciphered radio messages to transmit large volumes of administrative radio traffic combined with a high incidence of poor communications security practices often led to successful cryptanalysis not only of German Air Force radio messages but to the compromise of classified Army and Navy information as well as breakthrough into Army and Navy Enigma cipher systems as well.

Though it is not conclusive, there is a strong suggestion in the review of the literature that a major British breakthrough occurred when in the autumn of 1939, *U-111* forced by mechanical problems to travel on the surface through the Dover Strait, was surprised and captured by a British destroyer. The crew, stunned and overwhelmed by superior fire, abandoned the U-boat without completely destroying the Enigma enciphering wheels and other classified Enigma material. Official commentary on this incident by the British government is silence.[59]

On 23 February 1941, the Royal Navy captured spare German naval Enigma ciphering wheels from the armed trawler *Kerbs*. Though the capture itself was of no major value, it prompted a plan to capture other German cryptographic material. On 7 March 1941, the armed weather trawler *Munchen* was captured after radio direction finding bearings revealed its approximate location between Iceland and Jan Mayen Island. The trawler *Lauenberg* was next, captured on 25 June 1941. Keying instructions and a keylist were recovered.[60]

Earlier on 8 May 1941, *U-110* was blown to the surface by escort ships of convoy OB 318 and the entire naval Enigma machine and the Triton U-boat cipher keylist for the period February through June 1941 were captured.[61]

With this material the British broke the German Navy Triton U-boat cipher until the keylist expired on 1 July.[62]

Throughout WW II the Allies intercepted and cryptanalyzed between 75,000 and 80,000 individual messages encrypted in Enigma cipher systems.[63]

The success against Enigma's mechanical capability by bombe was previously explained but there was more. The German penchant for centralized control, detailed record keeping, and the methodical exchange of information, actually trivia, is believed to have been significantly responsible for the Allied success not only in cryptanalyzing the U-boat Triton cipher beginning in January 1942 but also in being able to make such damaging use of the information. The nature and tempo of the war, and the centralized methodology of the U-boat command, U.d.B., encouraged by the German way of doing things created a reliance on radio communication that was otherwise unnecessary. The wide scope of information, literally every scrap of information, provided a surprisingly wide background for judging German anxieties, suspicions, fears, misconceptions, intentions, countermeasures, and capabilities.[64]

The centralized control of U-boat operations by U.d.B. required the transmittal of large volumes of bookkeeping and administrative data by proforma message. Proforma messages often provide one of the easiest and quickest methods of breaking into a cipher because the same type of information, the same words, are transmitted time and time again in the same order. The Germans provided heading points of their U-boats, operational plans, passage reports, patrol lines defined by hour and day, position and location reports, fuel reports, detailed damage reports, expected times of arrival and departure, and detailed reports of new equipment used by the U-boats. All of this was provided in agonizing detail. Virtually no deviation from the routine was permitted. As an example: there was the Hundred Fathom Report; a U-boat had to transmit a short message every time it passed the hundred fathom line when heading to sea. Even before the messages could be cryptanalyzed, the intercept and direction finding of those messages allowed the OIC to detect and track each U-boat as it entered the killing area.[65]

If these criticisms sound suspiciously like the pattern of the United States Army in Vietnam and its attendant communications security problems, it should come as no surprise.

As any wife learns, it is easy to predict and control habitual and routine behavior of a single opposing mind. Rather than be required to predict the operational behavior of hundreds of U-boat commanders operating as circumstances dictated, the British OIC had to contend chiefly only with the single mind of the U.d.B. control center. The Germans insisted on centralized control to increase efficiency; what they accomplished was the efficient destruction of their U-boat fleet.

By the winter of 1943-1944, the Allies were reading almost every message the German Navy transmitted and doing so in real-time. By using radio direction finding fixes and reports of German intercepts of Allied radio messages, the Allies were able to conduct improved training designed from German reports of Allied naval weaknesses.[66]

Because Allied bombing and the French Resistance destroyed much of the German landline system toward the end of the war, all three German military services placed exceptional reliance on the naval high frequency radio system. As a result, the British Navy was provided with considerable information on the enemy's plans across Europe and in other theaters.[67]

By 1944, the German communication system had become so efficient, that the British and United States Navy command centers, located near the center of the German Radio net, frequently knew more about German submarine operations than did the U.d.B. When *U-505* was captured, the Commander-in-Chief, Atlantic, had more up-to-date information on the U-boat's mission than the boat commander had yet received, a situation which led to its capture intact and its present position outside the Museum of Science and Industry in Chicago as a tourist attraction. The U.d.B. radio communication system was rated by the United States Navy [Security Group, formerly OP-G-20], part of the predecessor units now comprising the National Security Agency, as the best, most flexible, and efficient communication system used by any branch of any military service during WW II. It provided Allied cryptologists with the very best intelligence available.[68]

On occasion, intelligence provides a specific time, date, location, and perhaps describes a future activity or an enemy weakness. More often, intelligence provides large volumes of data to offer a sound appreciation of enemy operating procedures and routines which enable analysts to intuitively predict enemy behavior. From this accumulated knowledge in which the analyst learns to think like the enemy free of many of the enemy's distractions, the analyst predicts behavior. Intelligence analysts establish norms against which deviations can be measured.[69]

Intelligence was not derived solely or even mostly from cryptanalysis during WW II or during any part of that war. Rather, intelligence was derived from a continuous and patient evaluation of countless pieces of information from photographic material, reconnaissance, agent reports, captured material, interrogation, open publication, scientific deduction, and intuition.

Importantly, it should be understood that Enigma provided a cipher at a stage of sophistication just barely within the limits of human ingenuity to cryptanalyze—to break the code.[70]

The Allies gradually applied cryptology and radar together as a technology to multiply combat power in order to achieve strategic objectives so that by mid-1943, the Allied navies had become a projection of offensive strategic power rather than a defensive picket line.

To do this, the Allies not only had to multiply their own combat power but to deprive the enemy, Germany, of the ability to do the same thing. The German B. Dienst had considerable success cryptanalyzing Allied naval communications and they were able to use this advantage to multiply combat power but not to project offensive strategic power.

GERMAN CRYPTOLOGY

The German Admiralty, referred to as the Naval High Command, abbreviated to OKM in German, was comprised of the naval staff and six war staffs: Operations, Submarine Operations, Intelligence, Communications, Radar Research, and Hydrography and Meteorology. The first four staffs listed, the principal staffs, were headed by admirals.[71]

German naval cryptologic intelligence was performed by the Naval Communications Intelligence Division, the Funkaufklaerung, of the Naval Communications Staff. It was referred to popularly as the Beobachter Dienst meaning observation service but construed to mean radio intelligence service and usually written as the B. Dienst.[72]

Radio intelligence was *not* part of the Intelligence Staff in the German Navy. By 1944, at its peak, the B. Dienst consisted of about fifty intercept and radio direction finding stations and about 1,600 personnel. It was much smaller than similar Allied functions which consisted of about 20,000 personnel. The operations of the B. Dienst was separated into two sections—evaluations and cryptanalysis. German radio intelligence was different from its Allied counterpart by one important distinction—the Germans considered radio message analysis [traffic analysis] to be as important as cryptanalysis. The B. Dienst centralized the correlation of intercept results and integrated radio direction finding, message analysis, and low grade radio intercept in the evaluation section before disseminating the cryptologic product to the intelligence staff. Unlike the Allied cryptologic system, the Germans did not pass direction finding bearings, cuts, or fixes to their ships and U-boats until after the second U-boat offensive began in September 1943. Even the direction finding information was considered to be of little utility by the German Navy. Direction finding information was for the most part incorporated with other intelligence and disseminated as all-source intelligence. In effect, the Germans used direction finding principally as an aid to analysis not as target acquisition as the British frequently did.[73]

Radio intelligence was disseminated to commanders and other users by the *Radio Intelligence Bulletin* which reported results of traffic analysis, cryptanalysis, and translations of plaintext messages without distinguishing the source. The *Bulletin* rated intelligence for probability of correctness. Dissemination of the *Bulletin* was restricted by "need to know" and was generally distributed to all who needed to know that information. Toward the end of the war, as Germany became more desperate, the dissemination of *Radio Intelligence Bulletin* items was sent by encrypted radio message [which the Allies were able to cryptanalyze] rather than by one-time pad systems used earlier in the war and which the Allies were not able to read. This attempt to expedite critical intelligence to U-boats compromised the intercept effort but was an understandable calculated risk under the circumstances. Overall, the B. Dienst certainly understood the sensitivity of cryptology. The *Radio Intelligence Bulletin* of 23 June 1944 reminded its subscribers: "Should the enemy learn that [these] reports are obtained by deciphering of his radio messages . . . one of the most important sources of information for the execution of the Naval war would be destroyed."[74]

Both the German and Allied conclusions were that the B. Dienst furnished the U-boats with the essential requisite for successful prosecution of the war in the Atlantic. In fact, the German High Command felt that radio intelligence was so successful that by 1944 the already crowded U-boats were provided with two-man voice intercept and radio direction finding teams from B. Dienst to take advantage of inter-convoy communications. It was one of these teams that most likely exploited the intercepted communications from the Canadian corvette *Spikenard* leading to the sinking of the *Spikenard,* several ships in the convoy, and the diverting of other ships back to Newport, Rhode Island, by imitative communications deception messages during 10 to 12 December 1942.[75]

As of this date (1980), there is no evidence that the Germans, Italians, or Japanese were able to cryptanalyze the high grade cipher systems used by the United States or British naval forces. The cipher system used to protect Allied amphibious task force operations during Operation Torch, the Normandy landings, and the Market Garden operations was not cryptanalyzed by the enemy.[76] However, the collection of cipher and code systems referred to as the Allied Combined Convoy Cipher was easily cryptanalyzed by the B. Dienst.[77]

During the period January to March 1943, the Battle of the Atlantic was truly a contest of cryptology. Initially, the B. Dienst was able to read the Allied Combined Convoy Cipher and locate Allied convoys and ships for its U-boats to attack. The B. Dienst could do this better during this period than the Allies could cryptanalyze German Navy radio messages to find and sink U-boats. The turning point occurred in May 1943 when, as the United States Navy [Security Group] reports, "Decryption intelligence held its own but even when the [U-boats] made contact the strengthened surface defense attacked with a force the [U-boat] could not withstand." Interpreted this means that Allied aircraft and ships recently equipped with the new H2S microwave radar were homing directly to and bombing U-boats before they could submerge to safety. At the same time, the Allies changed to a more secure cipher of their own after learning that the B. Dienst was regularly reading most convoy related radio messages, thus denying the U-boats an advantage they had enjoyed since the beginning of the war.[78]

The Allied Combined Convoy Cipher had several weaknesses. First, the cipher key was seldom changed early in the war; when it was changed, the actual transfer between ciphers took so long that often identical messages were transmitted in both old and new cipher key on different radio nets at the same time. The Allied Combined Convoy Cipher was overused and abused to protect both high and low priority operational traffic much of which was unclassified, administrative traffic most of which was unclassified, and traffic of no consequence. Proforma text was common and, frequently, the same proforma message was sent several times after the keylist had changed. Callsigns were usually not changed and frequently used interchangeably between different radio nets thus linking the user from net to net.[79]

The Germans consistently possessed a clear picture of Atlantic convoys; they were aware of convoy departures, speed, route, escort composition, lanes, and diversions. They also frequently knew the zones of patrol of aircraft carrier launched patrols based on nothing more than bits of seemingly unimportant information.[80]

The British Navy Intelligence Division suspected the compromise of the Combined Convoy Cipher prior to May 1943 but was unable to provide sufficient information to cause the Admiralty to change the cipher system.[81]

The first strong, substantive indication, by the United States Navy Security Group, referred to as OP-G-20, hereafter referred to as the Security Group, that the B. Dienst was reading the Allied Combined Convoy Cipher occurred on 18 February 1943. Two U-boat attack groups of twenty-six boats were shifted and a third group formed to attack convoy ON 166 in response to an attempt, detected by the B. Dienst, by the convoy to clear the original U-boat attack area by a diversion to the south. The original U-boat attack area had previously been determined by the Allied cryptanalysis of German U.d.B. to U-boat radio messages. By 26 February, twenty-two merchant ships had been sunk and seven more damaged when the U-boat attack groups maneuvered against the diversion.[82]

In this case, the B. Dienst had not been directly identified as the source of the German intelligence, but intuitive correlation of convoy radio messages, German intelligence messages, and a firm understanding of the operational area and German U-boat operational techniques, as well as the techniques used by the U.d.B. (information acquired after months of studying decrypted messages), led to the very strong suspicion that only radio intercept and rapid cryptanalysis could have provided the information to the German U-boat attack groups in so timely a manner. Neither the United States nor British Navies felt that "strong suspicion" warranted the expense and complication of changing the Allied Combined Convoy Cipher. The irony is that the British remained convinced that the Germans were unable to cryptanalyze their cipher despite the fact that the British and United States Navies were at the time cryptanalyzing the more complex German ciphers within twenty-four hours of intercept in most cases.[83]

It was not until mid-1943 that the United States Navy Security Group could demonstrate, using three radio messages from U.d.B. to U-boat groups, pertaining to Allied convoys HX 237 and SC 129 that the Allied Combined Convoy Cipher was beyond any doubt compromised.[84]

The Allies introduced a new cipher on 10 June 1943. By September 1943, it was again strongly suspected that this cipher too had been compromised. Again, the United States Navy Security Group could not substantively demonstrate, beyond a reasonable doubt, that the Germans were reading the cipher until late 1943. At that time, the cipher was again changed with the quick concurrence of both the United States and British Navies. The new cipher remained secure throughout the remainder of the war but the B. Dienst continued to read lesser ciphers and to derive considerable intelligence from message analysis.[85]

The United States Navy Security Group suspected that German U-boats had access to a unique and highly reliable source of intelligence as soon as they were able to cryptanalyze German U-boat radio messages, about December 1942. U-boats were obviously using a specific source of intelligence besides their own collective reconnaissance efforts to detect and locate convoys and to design their group attack tactics in order to defeat the convoy system used to protect merchant ships. By early 1943, probably January 1943, B. Dienst was appearing with increasing frequency as the source of the most reliable intelligence messages sent to U-boats in the North Atlantic. For the most part, these reports were extracts from the *Radio Intelligence Bulletin* with sources added and special B. Dienst reports sent directly from the B. Dienst through the U.d.B. to U-boats.[86]

The British did not recognize early enough the decisive difference between the tactics used by the German U-boats of WW I and those of WW II. This insight was available in 1931 when Admiral Bauer, the WW I, German U-boat fleet commander, published his book, *Das Unterseeboot,* and explained that convoys succeeded during WW I because their routes could not be determined early enough to group U-boats (Wolf Packs) for mass attacks. He suggested the use of radio intelligence to provide this information explaining that Germany had had no difficulty reading the simple codes and ciphers used by the Allied convoys and enhanced by the large volume of convoy radio messages, most of which were unnecessary, during that war. Despite that warning, Allied convoy communications were generally unchanged from the period of WW I until early 1944 and the United States Merchant Marine was the worst offender.[87]

German cryptanalysts were not confronted with an Allied electromechanical enciphering device like Enigma. Instead, the B. Dienst had to contend with Allied code and cipher books prepared by cryptographic techniques designed to provide excellent security provided that the codes and ciphers were not saturated by overuse. That is exactly what happened; codes and ciphers designed for limited use and the protection of highly classified information were routinely used in the Allied Combined Convoy Cipher to pass large volumes of administrative traffic and often totally unnecessary information. The large volumes of proforma messages provided enemy cryptanalysts ample opportunity to find entry points into the Allied ciphers. As Morison reports, the communication system that had been adequate for a small peacetime Navy with experienced radio operators became strangled with the tremendous increase in volume, the constant repeating of radio messages for inexperienced radio operators, and the slower speed required of manual Morse radio nets for inexperienced radio operators.[88] When ciphers of increased security were recommended for combined use, the United States Navy consistently replied that they thought those ciphers were too complicated for junior officers. This was especially true since too many United States Navy commanders required cipher clerks and cipher officers to decrypt not only the traffic for their ship but *all traffic* in order that they may become aware of the wider scope of naval operations.[89]

The B. Dienst, with no more than fifty cryptanalysts compared to about 500 for the Code and Cipher School of Great Britain, had studied the Royal Navy communication system and its ciphers since 1936. They were well aware that Allied ciphers used consistent repetition, like 7761 was used for new paragraph, 4834 for stop. The B. Dienst earned every pfennig spent on them.[90]

UNITED STATES CRYPTOLOGY

To this date, there is insufficient information to judge the contribution of the United States Navy cryptologic effort in the Battle of the Atlantic. It appears as though the British government provided the United States with adequate material and assistance to permit the United States to conduct separate cryptanalysis of the Enigma system. Presumably, the British Code and Cipher School exchanged keylist information with its American counterpart. It also appears evident from the small amount of material released by the United States National Security Agency since 1977, most of it fragmented, that after mid-1943, the United States Navy was able to perform cryptanalysis of Enigma radio messages about as fast and competently as the British; the major United States contribution, however, was provided in cryptanalyzing the Japanese Purple Cipher.

Cryptanalysis provided an important part of the Allied cryptologic effort, a critical part of the Allied overall technological effort, but radar was equally as valuable. The following chapter illustrates the tremendous advantage the Allies also achieved in the development and application of radar.

CHAPTER IV

Microwave Radar

AN ELECTRONIC WARFARE WEAPON

Radar changed night into day. An aircraft equipped for antisubmarine duty with the model H2S Microwave radar could detect a surface U-boat about ten miles away on a smooth sea. Radar could do this in darkness or in fog. Once the U-boat was locked-on the radar scope, located with an accuracy of fifty feet or less, the aircraft raced at a speed of 350 miles per hour to attack the boat. An exchange of antiaircraft and strafing fire erupted as the aircraft approached at an altitude of only 250 feet. Directly over the U-boat, the aircraft released a string of shallow-firing depth charges. The U-boat crash dived as the water erupted in geysers forty feet high; more often than not, the boat would never again surface. The German Navy reported that it lost about 250 U-boats in the last eighteen months of WW II to this tactic.[1]

Despite the advantages of radar, the Allies lacked adequate numbers of aircraft and radar sets necessary to blanket the sea lanes of the world. Radar was so successful during WW II because, by 1943, the Allies were able to cryptanalyze significant portions of German naval radio messages. Those messages transmitted between U.d.B. and its U-boats also allowed U-boats to be located within a circle having a radius of ten miles by radio direction finding.

HOW RADAR WORKS

It is important to understand the basic fundamentals of how radar works in order to understand the decision-making steps that distinguished Allied and German technological policy during WW II.

Radar is an acronym for *ra*dio *d*etection *a*nd *r*anging, the use of radio waves to determine the range to an object. Radar is the radio transmitting and receiving of a signal that emits either a succession or constant flow of sharp, short bursts of radio frequency energy called pulses. When transmissions are short, successive pulses they are referred to as pulse radar. By contrast a continuous wave radar transmits radio energy continuously. The Allied model H2S radar was a pulse radar.

The pulses are transmitted only along a line-of-sight path. This means there must be an unobstructed path from the radar antenna to its target. Radar is able to penetrate darkness, and most fog and clouds. Heavy rain, however, can interfere with radar. The pulses are reflected by dense objects like mountains, hills, buildings, bridges, ships, aircraft, and surfaced submarines in the path of the transmitted radio wave. The manner in which the radar pulse is reflected enables an operator to distinguish between land and water.

The reflected pulse returns to the radar receiver as an echo. The larger and closer the object, the louder the echo. Under most circumstances, the radar receiver should then retrieve the pulse and measure the time required for the pulse to travel from the transmitter back to the receiver. Since radio frequency energy travels at the speed of light, the elapsed time is very short. Radar can also measure direction to and velocity of the target.

To do this, the transmitting component of the antenna concentrates and focuses the radio frequency energy, the pulse, into a beam. The antenna is rotated so that its position at the instant the reflected pulse is received in the receiving element of the antenna provides the azimuth of the object from the antenna. In this manner, radar is capable of determining both the direction to and distance of the object from the radar each time the antenna rotates. By measuring the time between rotations, the velocity of the object can also be calculated. An explanation of the doppler effect is omitted for simplicity. Current model radars usually operate at radio frequency ranges from 100 MHz to 60,000 MHz, perhaps 100,000 MHz. During WW II, radars operated in the shorter-wave, X-band of 5,200 to 10,900 MHz and the longer-wave S-band, microwave, of 1,550 to 5,200 MHz.[2]

Prior to 1943, radio messages between U.d.B. and U-boats could not be cryptanalyzed to reveal a significant portion of their text, but they could be analyzed to an extent that the messages revealed important routing and identification clues. These clues are referred to as message externals by cryptologists. When these clues were applied in conjunction with radio direction finding, they provided reliable indications of general operating procedures and locations of U-boats. The use of cryptology and radar enabled the Allies to apply economy of force to direct antisubmarine aircraft and ships against German U-boats. Antisubmarine capability was multiplied by this use of electronic warfare; a single aircraft guided by electronic warfare was able to perform the work of ten or more aircraft conducting routine patrols without assistance from electronic warfare information.

THE DEVELOPMENT OF RADAR
STRATEGIC TECHNOLOGICAL POLICIES COMPARED

The development of radar provides a case study for the examination of strategic technological policies applied by Germany, Great Britain, and the United States during WW II. The policy of each nation practically reflected the perceived character of its people more so than it did a deliberate, rational, policy-making process.

Germany characteristically pursued development within a highly structured bureaucratic system guided by the constraints of fundamental laws of physics as they were understood at the time. England, ever anxious to prove its scientific institutions the equal of German fundamental science, methodically examined Germany's research. England, quick to take advantage of expanding the limits of fundamental laws, discovered more from the English perspective by the inquiring mind than by an apostolic compliance to absolute laws governing nature. The Americans, with a healthy belief that all fundamental laws are half right and half wrong, pragmatically searched to find the right half. Americans characteristically sacrificed pure research in favor of using ancillary discoveries for mass consumption in the market place.

Hertz, the German physicist, is credited with proving that radio waves could be reflected from solid objects as early as 1886. Marconi followed with similar but more practical observations, in 1922. During the intervening years, Hulsmeyer, a German engineer, patented the proposed use of radio wave echoes to detect obstacles to ship navigation in 1904. Two United States Navy scientists, Taylor and Young, in 1922, recorded the first practical use of radio energy to detect ships in any weather. The British Signal School reached a similar conclusion in 1923. Breit and Tuve, United States scientists, conducted the first scientific range finding in 1925 when they measured the distance to the ionosphere. By 1931, the British postal service noted that disturbances with their radio receivers were caused by low flying aircraft. Simultaneously, collateral research conducted by France, Germany, and Great Britain applied the pulse technique used by Breit and Tuve to military application in detecting aircraft. All this is reported to explain that by 1934 both the Allies and Germany understood the scientific application of radar. Each nation understood the scientific application and practical potential of manipulating the electromagnetic spectrum with radio waves to measure range and detect objects beyond the range of human observation. A concerted effort to actually use radar for practical application emerged a year later, in 1935. By this time, scientists from all three nations had completed the necessary prerequisite research to begin practical application by reflecting transmitted radio waves to detect and measure the range, direction, and velocity of solid objects in their path.

Based on initial research conducted during the period 1934 to 1939, German scientists favored the use of longer-wave, referred to as decimeter wave, radar and dismissed the shorter-wave, referred to as centimeter wave or microwave, radar as impractical. The decision was based on the commonly-held but limited grasp of a fundamental law advocating, at that time, that microwaves could not be generated by electronic valves because the time taken by the electron to travel through the valve was too great. The interpretation was incorrect but readily accepted by most German and British scientists working in this field. After a series of short experiments in 1934 involving a small ship and a coastal radar station, German scientists eventually determined that microwave radar was possible but that its range was less than that of human observation. Germany, its scientific institutions and authorities speaking in this instance, concluded that microwave radar was not practical and that continued research in the area was not of military advantage.[3]

R. V. Jones, one of Churchill's senior scientific advisors during WW II, has explained in his book, *The Wizard War,* that a country may know how to build but not develop a particular weapon because it is not needed. In other instances, a new weapon is not developed because conclusions about its feasibility and utility are derived from careless analysis and a lack of insight. When ideas occur before their time, the failure to develop the idea into a practical application is often attributed to limitation of a fundamental law—better described as a lack of imagination. Jones commented that British and German scientists had "become almost congenitally inclined to accept postulates of impotence in basic science." It was in this environment, prior to 1934, that it was commonly believed by British and German scientists that microwaves could not be used for radar.[4]

The case can be made that British scientists stumbled into the discovery of microwave radar. Jones explained that during a demonstration for the British Air Staff in 1934, the fallacy of the fundamental law became apparent in a totally unexpected manner. A very powerful loudspeaker system developed for the British Frontier Police in India was being demonstrated at an airfield in England. The loudspeaker was intended to be installed in an aircraft and used to broadcast to marauding tribesmen that their continued raids would result in the destruction of their villages. It was intended that, by broadcasting the warnings from an airplane, the tribesmen might be convinced that it was the voice of God speaking. During the demonstration—conducted on a field, not in an aircraft—the microphone was accidentally placed in such a manner as to inadvertently create a two-second, delayed-echo. The echo was rebroadcast through the microphone. Human voice oscillations that were transmitted occurred at about 1/1,000 cycles per second and were faithfully generated by a loudspeaker system separated from the microphone by about 2,000 feet. In effect, electrons travelled across the valve, the microphone, at uniform speeds. With that accidental demonstration, it was observed that electrons could also be made to generate oscillations of shorter period and wavelength than the limits that had been established by previous experiments. What was now required was the construction of a device that could provide a regular stream of electrons. The British developed a cavity magnetron to do this. A cavity magnetron is an oscillator that provides a large quantity of radio frequency power at radio frequencies required for microwave radar, frequencies above 1,000 MHz. It was an accidental discovery but one the British put to advantage. In effect, microwave radar was possible.[5]

Even after microwave radar was demonstrated to be feasible, many British scientists predicted that radar microwaves would reflect too strongly and be unuseable. There are seemingly more learned individuals willing to advocate the failure of a new idea than there are those with enthusiasm for its success. What really happened, after the development of the cavity magnetron, was that microwave radar produced a better and more useable signal, virtually a terrain map of the area scanned by the radar beam.[6]

Germany appeared to be at a distinct advantage in the development of radar when the war began in September 1939. By 1939, German industry had produced the Seetakt model radar. It was totally superior to any radar yet manufactured by either the United States or Britain. The chief disadvantage of German radar was that it had been developed into a scientific instrument rather than a practical weapon. Further, the German military was reluctant to use a glass-encased cathode ray tube in aircraft or small ships for fear that it was too fragile.[7]

A COMPARISON OF TECHNOLOGICAL POLICIES

On the German side, radar was judged to be of practical value in late 1934, only a few months before the British derived a similar conclusion in February 1935. At this point, the German government followed a decision-making process distinguished by two major errors. First, the German military dictated scientific requirements rather than allow the German scientific community to explain technology and match technology to military needs. Secondly, the Germans sacrificed research and development in order to concentrate on the development of weapons of known technology with which to execute and win a short war.

Germany did not have a coordinated technological policy, written or expressed, which in some manner could consistently guide the coordination of scientific and military objectives with national strategy. Instead, the scientific community responded, in the mood of the times, to military dictates. The military prescribed scientific requirements, not technological needs. German scientists, engineers, and industrialists responded by attempting to apply technology known to be available. When the military dictated that they needed radar to detect enemy aircraft and ships before the enemy was within range of their guns, German science and industry responded by building radars that could do exactly that. The contradiction was that the radars were precise, but they were also very large, sensitive, and unsuitable for use where they would provide the best advantage. Despite the dominant influence of the military, German radar was not designed to be small, light-weight, rugged, or simple to operate. The military would not trade accuracy for durability within accepted limits.[8]

The Germans could not conceive that radar could be reduced in size to fit inside an aircraft because they were deprived of the resources to search the fringes of fundamental science. The development of German military radar was hampered by a misguided policy that minimized research in favor of concentrating all available manpower and other resources on a short, powerful attack to defeat the enemy.[9]

Germany maintained active interest in the progress of British research in the development of radar throughout the prewar period. In August 1939, less than a month before WW II began, the German airship *Graf Zeppelin* paid a 'ceremonial' visit to England. One of the chief purposes of the visit was to search for and identify British radar signals. The British foresaw the real intent of the *Graf Zeppelin* visit and insured that all radar sets, at stations and in laboratories, were turned off. It was not until June 1940, after the Germans occupied the French Coast, that they first detected longer-wave British radar signals. By then, the German decision-making hierarchy, especially Goering and Keitel, were convinced the war was won. Their well known contempt for British technology reinforced their lack of insight and strategy. In any event, Hitler had personally directed that no scientific research be initiated for the war effort which could not be completed by the war's end in [sic] a year.[10]

Despite previous German experiments in the 14-to-48 centimeter range and the development of the forerunner of the cathode ray tube, the [Karl Ferdinand] Braun tube, microwave radar eluded the Germans.[11]

Not only the development but also the application of radar, was left to the military. There was no evidence that the German military evaluated the threat to their military capability and strategy when deciding how to best employ radar. The German Air Force in particular focused on the wrong objective when considering the application of radar. The German military considered radar only as a technological extension of the capabilities of human observers. Since radar could "see" farther than a human during darkness and in fog, it was used chiefly to replace observers on shore and at sea. By December 1942, U-boat commanders were advised by message to disregard their radar detection devices (equipment used to warn of approaching enemy aircraft by detecting the enemy aircraft's radar signals before the radar detected the U-boat) because Allied radar was presumed to be ineffective and also because it was incorrectly thought that the Allies could locate the U-boat radar detectors because of oscillator radiation.[12] The situation became increasingly confusing.

German radar was produced in a variety of models during the war, but all were dependent on outdated research conducted before 1939. German technological policy was founded more on the dictates of the military than on a cogent and sound effort developed from a premise founded on a comparison of threat and objectivity. Consequently, Germany produced a radar that was too large and fragile to work effectively aboard aircraft and small ships and boats; radar was relegated to use at ground stations and aboard large warships that spent more time tied to their moorings than at sea. The Germans failed to multiply combat power with this technological resource.

The Allies on the other hand recognized their vulnerability to air attack well before the war began. They did not immediately associate the potential of radar with the antisubmarine effort or the U-boat threat, but they did recognize the potential of radar for use against the air threat.

In early 1935, the British government established the Committee for Scientific Survey of Air Defense—afterwards known as the Tizard Committee—named for its chairman. The committee assigned a high priority to the development of radar and a communications system necessary to report radar data between radar stations and the control station. Consequently, the British had at least a rudimentary (one-and-one-half meter) air defense radar system that, by the beginning of WW II, provided limited air defense protection.

The Tizard Committee guided the further development of the pulse-type radar innovated by the British scientist, Watson-Watt. By 1939, a rudimentary air defense system had been constructed, the entire system completed by 1941. In conjunction with this effort, the Tizard Committee led British science and industry through the development of a shorter-wave one meter, airborne radar, the ASV model. By 1939, thirty airborne intercept radar sets were mounted in British aircraft. The British Microwave [radar] Committee was formed in 1940 to explore the substitution of microwave for the longer-wave radars used by the British. The cavity magnetron was a consequence of research sponsored by the Committee in an environment now characterized as one in which scientists were able to advise the military of potential technology and in an environment in which it was understood that electrons could be made to travel at uniform speeds, and be generated at shorter periods and wavelength.[13]

As a result, the British emerged with a decisive weapon. The Germans unaware of the significant British breakthrough in radar had failed to develop electronic countermeasures to the threat or to develop an improved microwave radar of their own. In addition to developing radar, the British also developed radar as a device of tactical-size that could be mounted side by side with cannon inside bombers and aboard small antisubmarine boats; also radar proximity fuzes which followed from this basic research turned near misses into direct hits multiplying combat power.[14]

The British were not able to do this because they began from a position of technological advantage over the Germans. To the contrary, research in the radar field was at about the same level in Germany, Great Britain, and the United States before the war. The Germans may have been a year more advanced, but no more. Instead the British applied a sound technological policy. Working together with national leadership at the cabinet level, British scientists first defined the threat, then recommended national strategic priorities for the development of technological resources. Representatives of both the military and scientific communities reached agreement on the best way to beat the threat.

The British applied military, economic, and technological policies to achieve a strategic objective—multiply the combat power of its outnumbered Royal Air Force to defeat German Air Force bombing attacks. Do this by allowing the Royal Air Force to apply their aircraft and pilots with economy of force to take maximum advantage of a force inferior to the Germans in numbers of aircraft and pilots. Next, attack German U-boats with the limited antisubmarine aircraft and ships available by multiplying their combat power as well.

The policy was not quite that clearly expressed. For a brief interlude of about a year, the British confused the benefit of strategic bombing with the necessity to destroy the German U-boat fleet. They placed their strategic priorities in the wrong order. The error was eventually corrected and the U-boat fleet destroyed barely in time.

Contrary to their strategic objective which placed protection of British sea routes, their lifeline, as the top priority, the British equipped Bomber Command before they equipped the antisubmarine aircraft of Coastal Command with the new microwave radar and medium-range aircraft essential to the effective hunting of U-boats. Roskill writes that the Allies narrowly escaped defeat in the Battle of the Atlantic. Had the Allies lost the battle it would have been for want of only two squadrons of medium-range, radar, equipped aircraft.

On the other hand, had the microwave radar sets been provided to Coastal Command before Bomber Command, the U-boat fleet operating in the North Atlantic could most likely have been destroyed six months earlier. Beesly reports that radar was probably the most decisive single British development in the U-boat war. The German submarine fleet commander, Admiral Doenitz, reported without benefit of the knowledge that the British had broken into the U-boat Enigma system, that radar was the weapon that changed the balance of the war in the Atlantic. In truth, the success of radar was also very dependent upon radio direction finding and success in cryptanalyzing the U-boat Triton cipher and that did not begin in earnest until January 1943.[15]

The Anglo-American agreement on exchange of scientific data conducted in September 1940 resulted in the exchange of a cavity magnetron that had been developed at the University of Birmingham [England] between Britain and the United States. Techniques developed in the United States were used to massproduce microwave radar for both the United States and Great Britain. The alliance of British and American technological policy, resource, and temperament resulted in a superior weapon used to multiply combat power.[16]

German U-boats were destroying Allied shipping twice as fast as ships and supplies could be replaced. By late 1942, England had less than ninety days of rationed consumption for her people of food and fuel. Despite the lessons learned from WW I, the Allies had neglected to consider the full impact of the U-boat threat. The development of radar, though based on a sound technological policy which integrated military, economic and technological objectives in most areas, had not adequately weighed the U-boat threat. Priority for both radar and aircraft was assigned to Bomber Command for strategic bombing, not to Coastal Command to fulfill its antisubmarine responsibilities.

There were several other considerations which needed to be

weighed before the effectiveness of radar could be measured in determining priority between Bomber and Coastal Commands. It can be shown that the loss of Allied bombers and crewmen may not have been worth the damage inflicted upon Germany. German war production actually increased during the period of strategic bombing. Certainly, of the 11,000 tons of high explosives and 8,000 tons of incendiaries dropped on U-boat pens in France, not a single bomb penetrated the concrete structures or caused serious damage to the U-boats.[17] By contrast radar-equipped bombers of Coastal Command sank thirty-seven U-boats in the first six months of 1943 without the loss of a single aircraft to enemy action.[18] Bombing did impact, as was learned after the war, on the production of new-design equipment which included new types of German radar and U-boats. The British referred to that effect as the 'German technical distress.'[19] It can also be argued that nothing like precision bombing of German industry could have been accomplished without the use of the microwave radar used by Allied bombers. Because the Allies defeated the U-boat fleet in time, the argument—whether or not priority should have been assigned to Coastal Command before Bomber Command—will continue despite the decision in early 1943 to change that priority from Bomber Command to Coastal Command. One thing is certain: even after the priority was changed, the effectiveness of the microwave radar against U-boats was not fully realized until the Triton cipher used by U-boats was broken in April 1943. Eventually, the air ministry diverted the first forty H2S radars from Bomber to Coastal Command. Number 19 Group of Coastal Command was equipped with the new H2S microwave radar sets, but six months later than necessary.[20]

A very real danger was the threat of losing a microwave radar from an aircraft crashed in German controlled territory. Once the Germans recovered a microwave radar set, it was reasonable to expect them to examine it in great detail, build a countermeasure device to jam it, and duplicate the radar for their own use.

R. V. Jones, the scientific advisor, informed the Vice Chief of the Air Staff that the probability of losing a radar equipped bomber over Europe was much higher than from a Coastal Command aircraft over the sea. This was yet another argument for priority use of the new radar sets by Coastal Command.[21]

When the Germans eventually captured enough pieces of a model H2S radar from a downed Bomber Command aircraft they were able to build radar detection devices. The radar detectors enabled the Germans to detect Allied bomber formations assembling over England from as far away as Berlin solely on the testing of the H2S and SCR radars by Allied bomber crews before they crossed the English Channel to attack targets in Europe. The Germans used this warning to alert their fighter aircraft. Even after the German Kammhuber Air Defense Radar System had been neutralized by the Allies, this tip-off enabled the Germans to inflict serious damage on Allied bomber formations. This breach of signals security by the Allies allowed the enemy to multiply its combat power.[22]

A POLICY TO PROTECT THE ELECTRONIC WARFARE CAPABILITY

As important as losing the radar design to Germany, perhaps more important, was the consideration that the Allies needed a good cover story to protect their success in breaking the German Triton U-boat cipher. By January 1943 the British were able to determine the approximate location of U-boats after cryptanalyzing Triton—one of the most complex of all the ciphers used with the Enigma system—and with the help of direction finding. (The German Navy used four rather than three cipher rotors as did the other services thus multiplying the potential cryptanalytic solutions exponentially.) In order to preclude the Germans from correctly deducing either British success with Enigma or with microwave radar, the British had initiated a deception plan. The plan was intended to cause the Germans to incorrectly deduce that the British were using infrared detection to find U-boats. The objective was not only to protect British success with Enigma and radar but to direct German countermeasures down the wrong path. The model H2S radar provided a capability that made infrared detection seem highly likely since the H2S was so accurate that the radar-equipped aircraft could fly directly at the target as though homing-in on the heat source of the boat's diesel engines.[23]

In fact the Germans spent considerable effort developing an infrared camouflage paint using a suspension of powdered glass to provide a refractive index allowing the hull of a surfaced U-boat to blend with the sea when viewed through an infrared-viewing device.

Unknown to the Germans, the paint actually created a more distinctive target when viewed with radar.[24]

There were other cover stories used to impede German discovery of the use of microwave radar. As one example, a downed British aircraft crewman, apparently of his own volition, explained to his German captors that British aircraft could locate German submarines easily because of unintentional radiations emitting from the submarine. The Allied cover story was an unsolicited initiative, perhaps locally contrived within his squadron, but resulted in the Germans expending considerable resources and time. The Germans knew that the oscillator of the Metox radar detector mounted aboard their U-boats did in fact inadvertently transmit signal pulses. Despite the cover story, the British did not know at this time, however, of the actual Metox weakness and did not capitalize on this German U-boat vulnerability during the war. Upon further experimentation the Germans discovered that the Metox radiation could indeed be detected by special equipment carried aboard an aircraft. In fact a U-boat could be detected by an aircraft flying at an altitude of 6,000 feet from a distance of seventy miles. [As an aside, this discovery did eventually lead to the development after the war of radio direction finding equipment used to locate radio receivers. The German Bundespost applied the technique to finding owners of commercial-band radio and television sets who failed to purchase the German commercial radio and television tax stamps.][25]

In any event, the Germans replaced all the Metox model 600 radar detectors with newer German designed and manufactured Wanz, model G1 and Hagenuk, model G2, radar detectors which operated between 120 and 180 centimeters. These later devices were able to detect an approaching aircraft flying at an altitude of 1,000 feet at a distance of about one mile, the U-boat could now detect the aircraft at a range of thirty miles. Had the Germans applied the same inventiveness to find the microwave signal used by the British, model H2S microwave radar, both a radar detector and a jammer could probably have been built in the same amount of time. As it was, the leading German radio scientists and engineers remained baffled by the British innovation. Additionally, the cryptanalysis of German naval radio messages permitted the Allies to know daily whether the Germans were close to solving the problem, reserving to the Allies an ability to react accordingly.[26]

Cover stories helped to provide six months of use with H2S/SCR model radars before German submarines again began to dive when approached by radar-equipped aircraft in September 1943. By September the Germans, fortunately for the Allies, concluded that radar was the *sole* culprit for the detection of all U-boats. The security of the Enigma cipher system was examined but its vulnerability dismissed by the Germans.[27]

THE DYNAMIC ELECTRONIC WARFARE DUO

With the release, beginning in 1974, of previously classified special communications intelligence—referred to by the Allies as Ultra—the interrelated roles of radar and cryptology can now be placed in their proper perspective. Hinsley, editing the British government's *British Intelligence in the Second World War* in 1979, provided a rare official insight into the interrelationship of radar and cryptology.[28]

The coordinated use of radio intercept, cryptanalysis, radio direction finding, and radar, in conjunction with reliable analysis and superb dissemination of the findings and conclusions through a consolidated intelligence, operations, and plans center to aid decisionmakers, cost the Germans at least half of their U-boats operating in the North Atlantic. This finding is also expressed as a loss of most of their boats operating in-shore and a total of thirty percent of the entire German U-boat fleet in a single month—May 1943.[29]

This did not occur because thousands of radar-equipped aircraft and ships blanketed the Atlantic Ocean. It occurred because the Allies could send their very limited number of radar-equipped aircraft (two squadrons) to the right place and at the right time to catch individual U-boats on the surface.

Beginning gradually in January 1943, though limited success had preceded this start, communications intelligence derived from cryptanalysis and radio direction finding enabled the Allies to predict the departure, course and killing zones of German U-boats. With the exception of a sixty boat wolf pack attack on two convoys simultaneously in March 1943, most convoys were routed away from killing zones at this time. By May 1943, whenever U-boats surfaced to replenish or to travel faster at best speed, they were more likely than not detected by radar and destroyed. The situation had deteriorated so badly by 24 May 1943 that Admiral Doenitz withdrew all U-boats from the convoy lanes to safer operating areas. By June 1944, U.d.B. message 230212JUN44 ordered all U-boats in the Bay of Biscay, the most important killing zone, to return to their pens or to sanctuary west of the Azores. The U-boats were advised in that message that they would most likely be sunk whenever they surfaced because of their vulnerability to Allied radar.[30]

As explained previously in Chapter IV, the Allies gradually gained insight into German naval communications. They did this after using cipher solutions, derived by cryptanalysis, in British copies of German Enigma cipher machines. The Germans compounded the cryptanalytic revelations by the wealth of information provided by the steady flow of detailed reports characteristic of the strong, centralized control imposed by the U.d.B. on their boat commanders. The British OIC used intercepted and cryptanalyzed German naval radio messages to determine departure times of German submarines from their respective bases in Germany, Norway, and France. Daily information reporting fuel remaining in submarine tanks, weather reports and U-boat operating ranges and speed were so methodically monitored by the U.d.B. that it was easy to predict the operations, courses and attack areas of the German U-boat fleet. From this information the Allies were able to establish patrol missions for their limited number of radar-equipped antisubmarine aircraft and ships and to divert convoys to safety.[31]

It had not always been so easy. The earliest models of Allied radar were limited to a range of about one mile. The U-boat crews could usually see the approaching aircraft before the aircraft detected the surfaced U-boat on its radar. At night the situation favored the U-boat completely. As a result most U-boats surfaced with total impunity at night. In June 1942, British airmen connected a searchlight —called a Leigh-light after its innovator—to their ASV-radar-equipped aircraft. Aircraft equipped in this manner flew far enough away from the surfaced U-boat to avoid audible detection, were immune to visual detection by darkness and searched for the radar with the ASV radar. Once the U-boat was detected, the aircraft raced toward the boat, flashing its searchlight as it approached to pinpoint the target for bombing and strafing. Twelve U-boats were sunk in July 1942; fifteen were sunk in August.[32]

The Germans correctly attributed the detection technique to the British ASV, model Mark II, radar. Detailed knowledge about the

Mark II had been gained after the Germans captured a working model of the radar from a downed aircraft in April 1942. There were no surprises. The Mark II was a variation of the shorter-wave radar used by Germany. The Germans were impressed that the British had reduced the set to a size small enough to fit into an aircraft but doubted that its limited range was worth the expense and effort.[33]

The German solution was prompt and simple. The U.d.B. equipped its U-boats with the French-manufactured Metox, model 600R, radar detector. The Metox could detect an airborne radar as much as ten to fifteen miles away, plenty of time to crash dive to safety. By September 1942 most U-boats were equipped with Metox. Several hundred of the Metox sets had been captured at a radio factory near Paris earlier in the war. Once Metox was in use, radar had little effect on the U-boats. Though U-boat activity was increasing rapidly, the sighting of U-boats by Allied aircraft was the lowest ever from October 1942 to January 1943, despite an increase in the use of ASV-type radar with the Leigh-light. Metox was so successful, in fact, that later—in 1943—German U-boat commanders were reluctant to use their own GEMA (980 centimeter) and Hohentweil (50 to 55 centimeter) radars to search for Allied aircraft. They feared that Allied aircraft might be equipped with radar detectors similar to Metox that could locate the U-boat radar signal before the U-boat could detect the aircraft. (Allied aircraft were not equipped with radar detectors.) U.d.B. reports indicated that the aircraft-detection radar used by the U-boats had a range of eight to ten miles.[34]

In late January 1943, U-boat commanders began to report surprise attacks by Allied aircraft. *U-519* was located and sunk by a United States Army Air Force B-17 bomber equipped with the British SCR microwave (the United States variation of the British H2S) radar on 10 February 1943. *U-333* was then attacked by a British Wellington antisubmarine bomber equipped with the British H2S microwave radar in late February. *U-333* survived and reported that the new radar detectors did not pick up the British radar signal. It should be remembered from an earlier discussion of the Metox in this chapter, that the Metox radar detectors had been replaced with German models because the Metox was found to radiate a signal that could be detected by a specially-equipped aircraft flying seventy miles away. The Metox could not have detected the microwave radar signals anyway because they were of a different frequency, but the

German U-boat crews were not aware of all this. The U-boat crews knew only that Metox was used to detect Allied antisubmarine aircraft radar and that the new German equipment could not detect the approaching aircraft. They surely must have wondered if the U.d.B. knew what it was doing. *U-333* reported that there was no indication of enemy radar on their detector and that the aircraft did not use a searchlight. The aircraft dived out of the darkness directly at the boat and dropped a string of depth charges. *U-156* was attacked in March, the commander specifically stating in his message of 010507MAR43 that he expected a new type of radar was being used by the Allies.[35]

After microwave radar was introduced in January, a total of twenty-eight U-boats was destroyed by Allied aircraft. About half of those airplanes were equipped with the new microwave radar. During the previous four months, Allied aircraft had destroyed twenty-two U-boats. To this point the introduction of microwave radar had not yet made a big impact. During the four-month period from 1 September to 31 December 1942, Allied aircraft equipped with the older radar destroyed about fifty-one percent of the U-boats destroyed by Allied forces. During a similar four-month period from 1 January to 30 April 1943, after the microwave radar was introduced, aircraft destroyed about fifty percent of all U-boats destroyed by Allied forces.[36]

However, by late April cryptanalysis of German U-boat messages had reached a peak. The Triton cipher was broken, and radio direction finding was superb. The OIC was now able to predict and report U-boat operating areas and schedules with timely accuracy. During May 1943, radar-equipped aircraft destroyed twenty-two U-boats in a single month—destroyed as many U-boats in one month as had previously been destroyed in four months. However, aircraft continued to destroy only about fifty percent of all U-boats destroyed by Allied forces in May 1943.[37]

The case is made that the integration of cryptology with radar—the application of electronic warfare—allowed the Allies to multiply combat power by a factor of four. This was done before the tremendous increase of other Allied resources such as aircraft, warships, and cargo ships after mid-1943. It occurred at a time when the Allies could not replace the losses taken by U-boats.

German U-boats continued to operate but at exceptional risk to individual boats and with a tremendous reduction in their activity and effect. After May 1943, the U-boat fleet operated entirely in a strategic defensive role. The advent of the schnorchel early in 1944 provided the U-boat with capability to operate underwater for extended periods, but even schnorchel was detectable by radar, though with considerable difficulty due to the small size of the protruding trunk. Schnorchel-equipped U-boats were sunk because electronic warfare was used to direct radar-equipped aircraft to the right place at the right time.

The full impact of Allied microwave radar became evident to German scientists in August 1943. It was not until August that the Germans recovered enough pieces from downed Allied aircraft to reconstruct a working model of the H2A radar. The reconstructed radar was installed on the Humboldt-Hain flak tower in Berlin. When the radar was turned on for the first time it exposed all Berlin with such clarity on its cathode ray tube that buildings, the zoo, all could be clearly distinguished. It was like a terrain map. It was obvious to those Germans in attendance that surfaced submarines could easily be detected at sea at ranges in excess of fifty miles by searching aircraft. By September 1943, the Germans began to provide their U-boats with Naxos microwave radar detectors. The detectors assisted the U-boats in averting surprise, but by then it was too little, too late. Antisubmarine aircraft and ships were chasing the U-boat fleet from every sanctuary.[38]

Errors were committed by both sides but Germany's errors lost her the battle. Germans failed to understand how to use technology. Germany did not, as a premise to a strategic technological policy consider this question: Does the military say, "We need this; do it"— or does the scientific community say, "This is what can be done and how it can be used"?

Rather than assume that the British may have developed a better radar, German scientists had for too long been directed toward other possibilities—deduced more from believing British deception about infrared and Metox emissions than from scientific observation. Valuable time was wasted by not attempting to search the electromagnetic spectrum through portions other than the conventional wavelengths. The Germans were prejudiced by a belief in "fundamental law" at the expense of imagination. Not until early 1944 were a few U-boats finally equipped to search large portions of the electromagnetic spectrum to detect microwave radar signals.[39]

By 1943 British radar was decisively superior to German radar as a technological weapon. That conclusion can be measured and demonstrated. More importantly, the British used the decisive advantage radar provided for strategic advantage and as a multiplier of combat power. As significantly, the British fully integrated the use of radar with intelligence and combat power.[40]

Radar was used as an extension and multiplier of combat power of their naval fleet to compensate for a navy not fully able to meet the strategic objectives by conventional combat power alone. The British also used radar to multiply the effect of their defensive aircraft fighters during the air Battle of Britain when the air force was considerably outnumbered. Britain used radar to help achieve the specific national policy of protecting trade. All scientific applications were carefully integrated with the overall strategic military policy to increase combat power. British technological policy was founded on the premise that scientists can best direct the military to properly *use* technology, whereas the Germans followed the premise that scientists should produce new devices needed by the military. There is a fundamental difference. Chiefly, the British system was and remains superior because it systematically required the collection and analyzing of operational data, combining operational knowledge of past use with predicted performance, evaluating performance, and then improving design. The technique is now referred to as quantitative analysis.[41]

The irony is that the British were led by desperate necessity, the mother of invention, to select a design approach to defend against the German aircraft threat. In the meantime, Germany concentrated on radio direction beams as a technical aid to guide German bombers to targets in Great Britain. This resulted in the British producing the best offensive radar. The Germans mounting a major offensive campaign developed a defensive radar.

CHAPTER V

The German Surface Fleet

THE FIRST TARGET

Prior to WW II, Germany had set course to rapidly build modern warships because of an illusion that the nation could become a major sea power in less than ten years without benefit of tradition or experience. The German Z-Plan, initiated at the end of 1938, defined German naval ambition and construction objectives. The Z-Plan was the embodiment of an offensive strategic policy founded upon strategic illusion. The illusion misdirected Germany's strategic effort and cost that nation resources and human energy necessary to build a defensive and formidable U-boat fleet, a navy more suitable for the strategic objectives of a major European land power.[1]

An introduction to the German Navy's ten new warships, the battleships *Graf Spee, Bismarck, Tirpitz,* and *Deutschland* and the cruisers *Scharnhorst, Blucher, Gneisenau, Hipper, Scheer,* and *Prinz Eugen* provides a list of the most technologically advanced warships of their time. What was to be the strategic purpose of such a navy? Admiral Raeder, its Commander-in-Chief, thought he knew the answer: Use the navy chiefly as a threat against British shipping until 1944 when the German Navy, it was hoped and intended, would have completed its construction and would then be superior in strength to the Royal Navy. Hitler had assured Raeder that there would be no war with England before 1944. Once superiority was achieved, Germany would deploy the new navy to contest the British for strategic naval superiority. But the war started in late 1939, not 1944. The German Navy was not prepared. Nevertheless, without ever leaving port, Admiral Raeder demonstrated that he could tie the British Navy to picket duty, forcing the British into a defensive strategic role until mid-1943.[2]

By 1943 half the German fleet had been destroyed, but not because the British Navy outnumbered or outfought the Germans in the hot exchange of shot and shell. To the contrary—relatively few warships were sunk by warships of the adversary. For the most part enemy submarines and aircraft did the damage. In order to destroy the German Navy, the Allies had to first find the German warships. The British were not very good at this when the war began.

At the beginning of the war, most German warships were secure in their home waters of the Baltic Sea; only the battleships *Graf Spee* and *Deutschland* were at sea. Both were able to roam undetected, sinking British commerce at will for almost a month.

The Royal Navy was assigned several major strategic objectives explained in the preceding chapters. None was more important than the protection of British shipping. The Royal Navy was directed to destroy or contain German warships, to prevent them from raiding the lifeline to the island nation. It was necessary to find the enemy at the right time and right place to fight with an advantage—to do this intelligence should have been considered as a strategic objective. This was not the case before the war began.

There was very little British naval intelligence available at the beginning of WW II. The world's largest and most powerful navy, as judged by the standards of that day, had an intelligence division as part of its Naval Staff but virtually no intelligence. The Navy was blind. The United States Navy was in no better condition. The British Navy lacked an adequate number of radio communication intercept and direction-finding stations, and it lacked an ability to perform effective photographic reconnaissance. Both arts had been mostly lost after war's end in 1918. Britain decided it was too expensive to maintain an intelligence organization of the quality developed to support its fleet during WW I. Britain also lacked an effective network of agents required to maintain observation of German naval bases. Even six months after WW II began, the British had very little idea as to where German warships were located on a timely basis.[3]

Though the Royal Navy was superior in a measure of combat power, the strategic requirements placed upon the Navy were so consuming of the fleet that the German Navy actually achieved and maintained the strategic advantage until mid-1943 with an inferior fleet. By simply remaining in port and doing nothing, the German surface fleet and a small number of U-boats provided a threat to strategic mastery of the seas, a threat that was previously unparalleled in Britain's history as a major sea power. It was a threat that came close to exhausting Britain's naval forces.

Without intelligence the Royal Navy could not fight with economy of force. Some may be quick to point out that the Royal Navy found and sunk the *Graf Spee* shortly after the war had begun. *Graf Spee*, after sinking the merchant ship *Doric Star,* had been discovered by the intuitive judgment of the pursuing Commodore Hardwood, not because of intelligence. The *Graf Spee* was eventually trapped and forced to scuttle off the Platte River Estuary, Uruguay, South America. Most of the Royal Navy had been searching for the marauding battleship before it had been found. In the meantime, U-boats were sinking unescorted merchant ships in large numbers. It was an expensive way to find and sink German warships—too expensive. The loss of *Graf Spee* was an embarrassment to Hitler, a loss that Hitler would not soon forget or forgive the German Navy and an event that did more to contribute to the emasculation of the German fleet than the Royal Navy and all its ships.[4]

As a taste of things to come, the German cruisers *Scharnhorst* and *Gneisenau* had broken out to the Atlantic by the end of November 1939. They raided British shipping at will to sink twenty-two ships at 116,000 tons. Additionally, the *Deutschland* had returned safely after its foray with *Graf Spee*. German warships were able to leave their Baltic Sea ports without interference. The chief constraint was a lack of German aggressiveness, not the Royal Navy. As late as November 1943, the cruisers *Scheer* and *Hipper* were able to operate in the Atlantic and Indian Oceans, sinking the British merchant cruiser *Jervis Bay,* and five merchant ships from convoy HX84, while taking 100,000 tons and over two hundred lives in a six-month period.[5] The very presence of *Scheer* and *Hipper,* roaming the shipping lanes at will, severely reduced imports to England by several times the amount actually sunk by those warships.

INVASION OF NORWAY

German warships had to be found before they could be sunk. This conclusion became an axiom. A major opportunity to do just that occurred in April 1940 during the German invasion of Norway and the Low Countries. To understand the opportunity to destroy a large portion of the German fleet, October 1939 is reviewed.

Shortly after Britain declared war on Germany, Admiral Raeder convinced Hitler that the German Navy needed bases in Norway to insure egress and to improve freedom of action for its warships in the

Atlantic. Raeder wanted the Norwegian ports prior to the occupation of France and, most importantly, before the British Home Fleet had an opportunity to consolidate and deploy to the waters adjacent to Norway. Hitler concurred in principle with Raeder's strategic objective in December 1939 and directed that necessary planning be completed. But other events were to move too rapidly. The Norwegian invasion was postponed continuously until finally the date of 9 April 1940 was selected only a few days prior.[6]

Though the British were very concerned that a Soviet victory against Finland in the ongoing Russo-Finnish War of 1939-40 would result in a Russo-German expansion (the Soviet Union and Germany were allied at that time as a consequence of the nonaggression pact both had signed) into Norway, that fear was relieved by the Russo-Finnish false peace of 1940. Subsequent to the peace, the British did not anticipate the invasion of Norway by the German Army. Roskill, writing as the British Navy historian for WW II, explained in 1954 that the Admiralty and Home Fleet both concentrated exclusively on the possibility of a breakout by German warships intent on destroying British shipping. The Admiralty was not thinking; it was not planning for the German invasion of Norway. It was instead consumed by the threat to British shipping.[7]

There were several reasons the British did not consider more than a single enemy course of action. First, though there was a lot of information, there was little that could pass for intelligence. Secondly, it was considered foolhardy for an enemy to attempt an amphibious invasion in the face of a superior British fleet. At the time, an invasion of Norway was considered by both the British and German war staffs to be foolhardy if conducted as late as April when the British fleet demonstrated superiority in the North Sea. Both Roskill in his after-the-war analysis and Raeder in his before-the-invasion estimate, concurred that the German invasion could succeed only if total surprise was assured. Raeder advised Hitler that the operation in the face of a superior British fleet was contrary to all principles of naval warfare. Nevertheless, Hitler risked almost the entire German surface fleet, defying British naval power.[8]

There was another reason the British did not anticipate the German invasion of Norway, and it was the reason that caused Hitler to insist on the invasion in spite of the local British naval advantage. Hitler was convinced that Britain also intended to invade Norway.

Actually, Britain did have a plan to do that, but only if Germany were to invade Norway first. It was a paradox. But more importantly, the British were mining the Norwegian Leads (Operation Wilfred) in an attempt to halt the shipment of twenty-two million tons of Swedish iron ore—a 1938 figure—from Narvik, Norway to Germany, as well as to disrupt the free run of German coastal shipping up and down the Norwegian Leads. It was Hitler's reaction to the mining and the threat of a British invasion of Norway, rather than Raeder's request for bases, that finally led to the invasion of Norway in April 1940.[9]

The invasion of Norway was a major operation. Virtually every available merchant ship in the Baltic, 200,000 tons of shipping, was required to transport the six participating German army divisions. It was a force of about 80,000 troops. One thousand aircraft were assembled at Baltic airfields. The invasion involved two landings of 2,500 and 3,000 paratroopers respectively and the deployment of six separate naval landing groups at Oslo, Kristiansand, Egersund, Bergen, Trondheim, and Narvik, Norway. In most cases the landings had to be completed inland, at the end of fjords. Surprise was not easy.

Landing Groups one and two, comprised of three cruisers and ten destroyers between them, were intended to disembark their troops, join together as a single division and steam toward the North Atlantic so as to create a diversion and draw the main British forces away from the Norwegian coast.[10] The question which arises now is, how did the Germans conceal the purpose of so many ships and aircraft crammed into the limited facilities of the Baltic ports of Kiel, Rostock, Stettin, and Swinemunde? How did the Germans conceal the assembly of 80,000 troops, 1,000 aircraft, and the communication required to support an operation of that magnitude?

Part of the answer lies in the British preoccupation with its retreat in France. Churchill described the time as the ". . . dense and baffling veil of the unknown."[11]

There were intelligence indicators, clear indicators of German capabilities and intentions. The absence of British aerial photographic reconnaissance and a cryptologic intelligence capability equal to the task precluded a clear insight into German capabilities and intentions. Additionally, firmly held and preconceived ideas of the British war staff and Prime Minister Churchill regarding German plans, capabilities, and intentions hindered an objective consideration of a reliable estimate of the enemy situation provided by the Chief of the Naval Intelligence Division, Admiral Denning.[12]

This is what the British did know: On 4 April 1940, five days before the invasion, British agents in Copenhagen provided the first warning of an impending invasion of both Denmark and Norway. A German naval chart was captured; it showed the disposition of twenty-eight U-boats deployed to protect the Norwegian coast from Narvik to Oslo. By 5 April the Admiralty received reports from its military attaches in Oslo which advised that the Great and Little Belts, crucial passageways from the Baltic to the North Sea, were now free of winter ice. On 6 April there were intelligence reports of increased and nonroutine naval activity and large-scale movements of German troops and merchant ships to the German west Baltic Sea ports of Kiel, Rostock, Stettin, and Swinemunde. In fact German troops began embarcation on 6 April. Intercepting and direction finding of German naval radio messages (but not cryptanalysis) during 6 to 8 April revealed unusually heavy radio traffic on the German Baltic Fleet main command and control frequencies. On 7 April British reconnaissance reported German cruiser and destroyer groups moving toward Norway. Beesly reports that on 7 April, two days before the invasion of Norway, the very first British aerial photographs of the principal German naval base at Kiel revealed a harbor filled with [invasion] shipping and adjacent airfields crowded with aircraft.[13]

Without previous photography of the area, the British photo-interpreters were unable to conclusively demonstrate that crowded port and airfield conditions were a deviation from the norm. They were unable to prove that the ships and aircraft stuffed into those facilities had only recently been collected for the invasion.

When exceptionally heavy radio traffic was reported on the main German Baltic Fleet radio frequency on 8 April, only a day prior to the invasion, it was dismissed by both the Admiralty and Home Fleet as no consequence. But no wonder, messages reporting this indication of a pending major enemy activity were prefaced with the comment, ". . . these reports are of doubtful value."[14]

At 1200 hours, 8 April, the Polish submarine *Orzel* sank the German troop ship *Rio de Janeiro*. German soldiers rescued from the *Rio de Janeiro* reported they were bound to occupy Oslo and Bergen. The six German naval landing groups, accompanied by merchant ships, were detected by aerial reconnaissance moving toward Trondheim and Narvik. As was the German intention, the British assumed these ships were a naval battlegroup attempting to breakout to the Atlantic. The Home Fleet responded accordingly and departed with four battleships, eight cruisers, and forty destroyers from its Scapa Flow base on a course intended to intercept the German battlegroup. By doing this the Royal Navy left the central North Sea, the invasion route to Norway, unprotected. At a time and place when a large portion of the German Navy would be very vulnerable to destruction, when the troop transports moved through the Skagerrak separating Norway, Sweden, and Denmark on the night of 7-8 April, and later when the troop transports were unloading troops and equipment ashore, the British were unable to develop the clue. The opportunity was lost.[15]

Roskill judged, "There was a complete failure to realize the significance of the available intelligence—let alone to translate it into a vigorous and early counteraction."[16]

In retrospect there was a failure to correlate cryptologic information with photographic information. Taken together an analysis of communication intelligence, especially radio message analysis and aerial reconnaissance, could have revealed the German intention and capability to invade Norway as early as 4 April and no later than 6 April. There would have been adequate time to react to the threat.

Information was abundant. It was translated into intelligence by Admiral Denning and his staff but it was not adequate to overcome both Churchill's and the Admiralty's predisposition to believe that Hitler would not invade Norway. As a result the Home Fleet was not deployed to strike the German invasion force when it was most vulnerable, with cargo ships filled with troops and supplies.

It was unfortunate for the British that there was little reconnaissance available. Bad weather was a factor. The lack of suitable equipment was also a chief factor. But ultimately it was the failure to weigh alternative courses of action available to the enemy that was the major error. The Admiralty had convinced itself that the Germans were capable of and intended only to breakout to the Atlantic. They neglected to consider a logical German reaction to the British mining of the German supply route through the Norwegian Leads.

Those who argue that the British were prepared for the German invasion of Norway refer to the British Plan R-4, alternatively referred to as Plan III by the Germans. However, the British plan to occupy Norwegian ports in the event Germany attempted to violate Norwegian neutrality was little more than a statement of British intent. The plan gave little consideration to German air superiority in the area. When Franco-British Army forces finally did respond to the German invasion, arriving on 14 April, they were overwhelmed by superior German forces and by 13 May forced to either surrender, withdraw, or be interned in Sweden. Most were withdrawn.[17]

It was not until 9 April, after German forces began to land, that the British understood the real threat—the invasion of Norway. But once they understood the situation, the Royal Navy spared no effort to pursue German naval forces right into the narrow confines of the fjords at considerable risk. The Royal Navy exacted a deadly toll of German troopships—most empty by now—and destroyers, but by then it was too late. The troops had been landed and the German fleet had escaped.

THE SECOND TARGET—BISMARCK

By October 1940—now free of Hitler's plan to invade England—the German Navy was able to concentrate its capability to disrupt British shipping. The plan, some were later to contend, was a deception effort to permit Germany to concentrate its effort in Russia. The new battleship *Bismarck* and the cruiser *Prinz Eugen* were nearing completion. The cruisers *Scheer, Scharnhorst, Gneisenau,* and *Hipper* along with twenty-six attack submarines were poised to disrupt British shipping. *Scheer,* six merchant raiders, and a fleet of coastal motor torpedo boats took 103 Allied ships at 443,000 tons in October alone. The cruisers *Scharnhorst* and *Gneisenau* continued attacks on British shipping taking twenty-two merchant ships out of convoys, sinking 115,000 tons by March 1941. To counter the threat, the British had to tie a battleship to every convoy. The Royal Navy remained on the defensive.[18]

The deployment of the new *Bismarck* and *Prinz Eugen,* escorted by destroyers on 18 May 1941, was to be a test. The orders, written with memory of *Graf Spee*'s loss and Hitler's direction, instructed the squadron to raid British commerce but *avoid battle.* It was the kind of order given more to a fox raiding chicken coops than to the world's most powerful battleship. *Bismarck* was employed as a strategic weapon with the chief objective of forcing the Royal Navy to continue a defensive role. *Bismarck* was worth more running from British warships than fighting them.[19]

Almost forty years later, in 1980, it is interesting to review an account of the battle between the British and German adversaries. The *Bismarck* first sank the British battleship *Hood* when forced to fight, then *Bismarck* was sunk just before the pride of the German Navy almost escaped. Previously, popular literature and the motion picture portraying the *Bismarck* exclusively credited a reconnaissance aircraft from the carrier *Ark Royal* with finding the *Bismarck* just in time, before the battleship escaped. The complete story, publicly available only after the declassification of relevant cryptologic information in 1976, is not only revealing of intelligence capabilities but of mistakes by commanders. Writing in 1954, the British naval historian, Roskill, first distorted the role of intelligence in the destruction of the *Bismarck* while, secondly, compensating for poor operational decisions made by the British commander.[20]

The magnitude of the threat is easily measured in this case. If the German squadron led by *Bismarck* brokeout to the Atlantic, the effect on British shipping would have been disastrous. The impact would be felt not only by the constriction of vital supplies for England but for the supply of British troops in North Africa as well. To meet this threat the Royal Navy first pitted the twenty-year-old veteran battleship *Hood*—at 46,000 tons the largest battleship in the world, carrying eight 15-inch guns—against the new 43,000 to 45,000 ton (figures differ) German flagship, *Bismarck,* with eight 15-inch guns.[21]

The collection and analysis of information which revealed *Bismarck*'s attempt to breakout to the Atlantic was the first successful attempt by the Admiralty to integrate plans, operations, and intelligence with strategy since WW II had begun. The example illustrates the strategic implication of coordinating a national level electronic warfare resource like cryptology with tactical intelligence in the decision-making process to develop sound conclusions and courses of action. The reader will find that much of the battle proved to be a fiasco, but the fiasco must be separated from the decisive advantage which electronic warfare proved capable.

The German Navy intended to employ *Bismarck* with its superior fire power and faster speed to tie down British battleships used to escort convoys, while the *Prinz Eugen* was employed to attack merchant ships within the convoy. Since both German ships individually outclassed their British equivalents, the threat which they posed to British shipping could be devastating once they gained the expanse of the Atlantic Ocean. The best chance afforded the Royal Navy depended on its ability to confine the *Bismarck* and *Prinz Eugen* to a battle in which the aggregate British fleet could be thrust at the right time and right place.[22]

To this point the Admiralty's Operational Intelligence Center, the OIC, had kept track of the 43,000-ton *Bismarck* as it steamed back and forth from Kiel to Hamburg and through the Eastern Baltic, finally departing Gdynia on 18 May 1941. Most information had been provided by an agent in the German naval post office able to observe the changing destination points for *Bismarck*'s mail.[23]

In early April, the OIC was provided with information from the British Code and Cipher School which had most likely been cryptanalyzed from German Air Force Enigma enciphered radio messages. The Air Force messages indicated that *Bismarck* had been provided new charts. This clue, of itself unrevealing and unspecific, was the first hint that *Bismarck* would attempt a breakout in the near future. The suspicion was not developed by application of deductive logic alone. Issuing new charts to a battleship could have meant many things. A clue of this type is called an intelligence indicator. Good analysts detect and use clues like this one while others either ignore or fail to understand them. The men in the OIC intuitively judged it meant a breakout, and they were right.

Next the British detected an increase in German Air Force reconnaissance flights over the British Home Fleet base at Scapa Flow and the Strait of Denmark. The latter was a logical breakout point. The increase in reconnaissance was also linked by radio message analysis (but not by cryptanalysis) to reveal communication links between the air reconnaissance units and the *Bismarck*. The Germans wanted to know for certain that the British fleet was not yet lying in wait for the *Bismarck* at the Strait of Denmark.

The coordination of national level cryptologic intelligence and tactical naval intelligence within the OIC when used with sound judgment and analysis provided the second clue of *Bismarck*'s run for the sea.[24]

Air reconnaissance and photographic interpretation by the Royal Air Force also revealed that the Germans were preparing new moorings suitable for a battleship at Brest, France. Finally, Major Tornberg, the Chief-of-Staff to the Swedish Secret Service and a passionate British and Norwegian sympathizer, conveyed a Swedish Navy report of 20 May. The Swedish cruiser *Gotland* had observed both *Bismarck* and *Prinz Eugen* with their squadron north of Gothenburg heading for the southern coast of Norway. The report was provided to the British Defense Attache through the Norwegian Defense Attache in Stockholm. The Embassy relayed the report back to England by radio. Suspicions of the breakout were now confirmed.[25]

Next, Norwegian resistance members, at Kristiansand, Norway, reported at great risk by radio that *Bismarck* and squadron were passing the southern tip of Norway.[26]

By now the Royal Navy was fully alerted and prepared by the flow of reliable information. An extensive naval and air reconnaissance was mounted to pinpoint *Bismarck*.

Because of good intelligence, cost-effective reconnaissance with limited resources was possible. *Bismarck* was located on 21 May at Korsfjord, Norway, near Bergen where *Prinz Eugen* had stopped to top-off with fuel. *Bismarck*'s squadron departed for the open sea on 22 May, a fact established by a near-suicidal air reconnaissance mission conducted through nearly impenetrable weather by two older British naval flying officers, Captain Fancourt and Commander Rotherham, flying an obsolete, twin-engine, Maryland aircraft intended primarily for target towing.[27]

The Royal Navy, individually outclassed by *Bismarck* and *Prinz Eugen,* needed every advantage which could be provided by intelligence if they were to win. The new battleship *King George V,* the *Repulse,* and the aircraft carrier *Victorious* in one squadron and the *Hood,* and the new battleship *Prince of Wales* in a second squadron set course to intercept *Bismarck* and *Prinz Eugen.* On 23 May *Bismarck* and *Prinz Eugen* encountered the British cruisers *Norfolk* and *Suffolk* steaming in the Denmark Strait. The Germans were surprised; the British were not. Initially the Germans were bewildered by the ease with which the *Norfolk* and *Suffolk,* hiding in the fog, continued to shadow them throughout the night. The new British radar had been detected by the radar detectors used by both German ships. Though the *Bismarck* and *Prinz Eugen* were both equipped with radar, the Germans were unaware that the British, too, had mounted a new search-type radar on the *Suffolk*. This was not yet a microwave radar, rather it was the older, long-wave type radar, but it was capable of searching all angles except across the *Suffolk*'s own stern. It was an excellent radar with which to shadow the *Bismarck* and remain out of range of the *Bismarck*'s 15-inch guns. Though an exact comparison cannot be provided, it is believed that the new search radar mounted on *Suffolk* was superior to the German radar. The range of *Suffolk*'s radar was twelve to thirteen miles. The longer-wave German radar's range probably did not exceed eight miles. To understand the following events it is necessary to know that the German commander concluded that the British radar had a greater range than did German radar. It was an assumption and an error that later contributed significantly to a fatal German mistake.[28]

The battleships *Hood* and *Prince of Wales* were to intercept *Bismarck* and *Prinz Eugen* the next morning, 24 May. *Hood* blew up and sank with only three survivors. *Prince of Wales* was damaged. *Hood* had wasted valuable time and ammunition firing at the wrong German ship—the *Prinz Eugen*—while both *Prinz Eugen* and *Bismarck* together fired on the *Hood*. The *Prince of Wales* required six salvos to hit *Bismarck,* but *Bismarck* and *Prinz Eugen* hit the *Hood* with their first salvos. These were not only superior German ships but it was superior German gunnery directed by radar operators who knew well their business. The British radar operators, using better radar, actually hindered the battle by their inexperience and lack of training. There were other considerations. The *Hood* did not have a search radar like *Suffolk* or *King George V,* only a gunnery radar with a range of about six miles. The *Hood* had been fitted with its gunnery radar only the previous March. Because *Hood* and *Prince of Wales* were attempting to close on the *Bismarck* through the fog with surprise, they intentionally turned their gunnery radar off until only minutes before the battle to prevent the *Bismarck* from detecting their presence by their radar pulses. The radar pulses were detectable at a range of thirty miles or more. As a result the *Hood*'s radar operators were also deprived of those vital minutes to adjust their radar sets before the firing began.[29]

Bismarck, too, had been hit by *Prince of Wales* and was losing and contaminating fuel at an alarming rate. The second British squadron with *King George V, Repulse,* and *Victorious* was closing from the north, 330 miles and about twenty-four hours away. *Victorious* launched an attack with its aircraft at midnight 24-25 May but caused only minor damage with a single torpedo. *Bismarck,* now short of fuel, transmitted radio messages to German Navy Headquarters in Wilhelmshaven to report damage and to advise that *Bismarck* was heading for Brest after first detaching *Prinz Eugen* to operate independently. The British intercepted the radio transmission but were not able to cryptanalyze the German Neptun cipher used by the surface fleet. Neptun was used for the first time during *Bismarck*'s foray. The British, ignorant of the text of the message, presumed *Bismarck* would head for her home port at Hamburg for repairs. At 0300 hours on 25 May, contact with *Bismarck* was lost by *Norfolk* and *Suffolk* which had been shadowing for the past several days. The British were unable to reestablish contact with visual reconnaissance.[30]

The British cruisers had been using radar to shadow *Bismarck* and their radar signals were constantly detected by the *Bismarck*'s radar detection equipment. A radar detector is able to report a radar signal two to three times as far away as a radar can detect a ship. It is necessary to understand a little about radar to understand the significance of the error that next occurred.

A radar signal must use enough power to travel from the radar's transmitting antenna to the target and return to the antenna by reflection. *Suffolk* had to remain within about twelve miles of *Bismarck* to detect the German battleship, but *Bismarck*'s radar detectors could detect the radar signals from the two cruisers at two to three times that distance, well beyond the range of *Bismarck*'s own radar. The British cruisers had a careful game to play. They had to remain close enough to *Bismarck* to shadow the ship with their radar but far enough away to remain beyond the range of *Bismarck*'s 15-inch guns. The range of a warship's guns depends not only upon how far the shell can be fired but whether it can penetrate the armor of the enemy ship when it hits. *Bismarck* could cause serious damage to cruisers like *Norfolk* and *Suffolk* at a range of about eight miles and to battleships like *Hood* at six miles. The radar equipment used by *Norfolk* provided consistent ranges to about five miles while *Suffolk*'s radar extended twelve to thirteen miles. In high seas all radar range was seriously reduced. Playing this careful game, hiding in the fog, the log reveals that *Suffolk* lost *Bismarck* at 0306 hours, 25 May, while conducting an anti-submarine zigzag course and at extreme limit of its radar range. *Norfolk* had remained well out of radar range during this time. *Bismarck* slipped through the hundred-mile-wide net of closing British warships.[31]

At the same time *Bismarck*'s commander, Admiral Lutjens, knew the British radar signals were still reflecting off his ship because the radar detector screen showed the presence of the British radar signals. Either Lutjens was not aware of the principles of radar [radio] wave propagation or mistakenly thought that the British cruisers were still close enough to shadow his ship. He thought the British still had contact and saw no reason to initiate radio silence since he presumed the British knew exactly where he was. They did not. The *Bismarck* was beyond the range of British radar.[32]

At this point in the saga, the *Bismarck* could most likely have reached safety in Brest. Instead Lutjens committed a fatal error. He transmitted the first of three long radio messages at about 0700 hours, 25 May, to the naval base at Wilhelmshaven. When he did this the *Bismarck,* with its powerful radios, became a British radio direction-finding target. To understand the importance of what happened next the reader should also understand a little of how radio direction-finding works.[33]

RADIO DIRECTION FINDING

In this case, *Bismarck* was transmitting with a powerful, high frequency radio—standard equipment for naval forces. To be able to provide the location of the *Bismarck* inside a circle with a 50-mile radius and a fifty-percent probability of being right, it is usually best to use at least four radio direction-finding stations. Each station is typically located with respect to one another along a concave baseline. Each station is separated from the station to either side by a distance of about one-third the distance of the target from the closest point on the baseline. Hence naval radio direction-finding stations are frequently separated from one another by hundreds of miles to compensate for the long distances involved in naval communications. These stations require excellent and instantaneous communication with one another. They must flash data from the outstations back and forth with the control station where plotting and analysis are completed.

A single direction-finding station can provide only an azimuth, called a line bearing, from the station to the target along a straight line. A bearing provides the direction to the target but not the distance. Two direction-finding stations sighting on the same target can provide intersecting line bearings called a "cut" which provide direction and an approximate distance from the point of intersection back to the baseline. Three, preferably four, direction-finding stations can provide three or more intersecting bearings called a "fix" which usually form a triangle of intersecting lines. Naval direction finding at the high frequency ranges, during WW II, provided an average accuracy when circumscribing the intersecting points of a triangle to form a circle with a radius of about fifty miles. That is, there was a fifty-percent chance that the target was within a circle having a radius of fifty miles. Admiral Doenitz judged direction-finding accuracy to be about seventy miles, and the British usually reported direction-finding plots allowing for an error of one hundred miles. The use of analysis and intuitive judgment by direction finding plotters could reduce the size of the circle considerably, depending upon the ability of the plotter and the availability of other information relative to the situation. The more the analyst understood about the operational considerations of the situation, the better his chances of reducing the size of the circle. It was yet another case requiring the full cooperation of intelligence and operational personnel.

This was exactly the case during the chase of *Bismarck*. The British direction-finding plotting of twenty-two radio transmissions made by *Bismarck*, before she was lost to observation, had been analyzed. The location of *Bismarck* reported by radio direction-finding had been compared to the battleship's location determined by observation by British ships and radar; direction-finding errors were recorded. British intercept stations had also radio-fingerprinted the distinctive signal from *Bismarck*'s radio oscillator, no two of which are alike even when mass-produced, on photographic film. *Bismarck*'s manual Morse radio operators, each of whom had a distinctive sending characteristic caused by the peculiarity in which he used the transmitting key, called a "fist," were also recorded.[34]

Bismarck was 1,200 miles west of Edinburgh, Scotland, at 0700 hours, 25 May, when the ship transmitted its first radio message. During the previous four hours, the British could not find the battleship. Only two British radio direction-finding stations, both located in England, were operational at the time *Bismarck* transmitted the long message to Wilhelmshaven. The remaining stations—one located in Iceland and the other at Gibraltar—were not operational at the time. All four stations were required to form the necessary concave baseline explained previously. Consequently, the two adjacent radio direction-finding stations located in England were able only to provide bearings with very acute intersections. That kind of information requires a lot of professional interpretation and the use of special Gnomonic charts. Those inexperienced with radio direction finding could draw the wrong conclusions from this information if it were provided without benefit of analysis. The inexperienced could easily conclude that *Bismarck* was located where in fact it was not located and they did exactly that.

INTELLIGENCE MUST BE DISSEMINATED

Prior to receiving the direction finding reports, Admiral Tovey, Commander-in-Chief of the Home Fleet—his pennant carried by the new British battleship, *King George V* which was southwest of and chasing *Bismarck*—had reached the erroneous conclusion that *Bismarck* was heading northeast to the Denmark Strait and back to Germany, or to the Iceland-Faeroes Passage and on to Norway for repairs. It was a conclusion based on seafaring tradition and experience but not on intelligence. Once a senior admiral in the British Navy developed a conclusion, it was not easily changed.[35]

Among the "Old Navy," intelligence was used to determine how long an enemy ship was, how large its guns, how much water it displaced, and how fast it steamed. Intelligence was used to collect facts, not to determine capabilities or intentions. It was a bookkeeper's skill.

The senior direction finding plotter, an analyst at the OIC—Lieutenant Commander Kemp—was not of the "Old Navy." He was a reservist, but he knew his business well enough to know that the bearings and their acute intersection indicated that *Bismarck* was not heading northeast. To the contrary, *Bismarck,* he judged, was heading southeast. The conclusion was more clear when the almost parallel bearings were plotted at 55 degrees, 30 minutes north and 30 to 32 degrees west on a Gnomonic chart depicting Great Circle lines used by direction finding plotters. Still, the information was not conclusive. When the same parallel lines were plotted on a Mercator navigational chart—like those used aboard the *King George V*—they were found to depict 57 degrees north and 30 degrees west, a difference of about ninety miles. There was not sufficient data to reach any conclusion about *Bismarck*'s actual location. Nevertheless, the bearings were plotted on a Mercator navigational chart aboard the *King George V* and interpreted to fit the situation—the preconceived conclusion that *Bismarck* was heading northeast. It is suspected after this research that those aboard the *King George V* made the bearings support the preconceived conclusion that *Bismarck* was heading northeast.[36]

Kemp tied all this together because, after working for twenty months using innate intelligence, intuition, deductive logic, analysis of radio-fingerprinting and radio operator characteristics, along with radio wave propagation theory, he had a "gut" feeling that enabled him to discern between aberration and the unexplained. Further, *Bismarck*'s net control station had been transferred from Wilhelmshaven to Paris at about 1200 hours the day prior, 24 May, also indicating a course toward Brest, rather than Germany or Norway. Intuitively, Kemp knew he was right; he just could not explain why in a manner acceptable to operational or executive officers. One could sympathize with a decision-maker first confronted with Kemp, but Kemp had been doing this work for several years. During this time, he had been mostly right but senior officers had seldom gone "below decks" to learn of this intelligence effort.

This was not an issue of whether anyone could be found to believe Kemp. This was an issue of whether a senior analyst of proven dependability should be allowed to state his case. Neither Kemp nor the officer in charge of the OIC had the authority to disseminate analytical conclusions to the fleet. It was a repetition of 1916—the Battle of Jutland. Again intelligence officers did not have the authority to disseminate intelligence.[37]

Admiral Tovey, the commander directing the chase of the *Bismarck* aboard *King George V*, was not interested in analysis. Tovey had previously directed that only direction finding bearings, not analysis, be transmitted by the OIC to his fleet so that he could draw his own conclusions. He advised that he would be aided by the information gained from the direction-finding equipment that usually accompanied his fleet aboard two specially-equipped destroyers. Unfortunately, on this mission both the destroyers and their direction-finding equipment and experts were absent from the chase. The situation was further complicated because the direction-finding plotting center aboard *King George V* lacked the special Gnomonic charts used to manipulate the parallelograms formed by the bearings provided by the two adjacent direction-finding stations. The Gnomonic charts were needed to understand the acute intersection those bearings formed. Instead, the plotting center used a Mercator navigational chart to plot the bearings and the result, though inconclusive, was used to reinforce Tovey's original erroneous conclusion that *Bismarck* was returning northeast to Germany or Norway.[38]

King George V pursued a shadow—pursued it in the wrong direction, northeast—while the *Bismarck* was gaining valuable time heading in the opposite direction.[39]

Admiral Tovey's decision was an error. The error resulted not so much because he made the wrong choice, but because he did not allow all choices to be considered. Wrong decisions are inevitable in combat, especially under the stress emerging in this action. It is precisely because of the factors affecting judgment in combat that military decision-making came to rely on a process which places great emphasis upon consideration of alternative courses of action. It is the weighing of each course of action in consideration of both the enemy and the friendly capability and intention that hopefully will lead to the selection of the best course of action. Tovey precluded the penetration of new ideas and the presentation of alternatives. He precluded choice by his directive which prevented the forwarding of intelligence analysis to the fleet from the center of all Admiralty intelligence operations, the OIC. The decision-making process upon which Tovey insisted eliminated the advantages of fully-integrated operations, plans, and intelligence. This integration is an integral part of a rational process required in combat decision-making.[40]

The Admiralty was aware of Tovey's arbitrary practice and also erred when allowing the commander of the Home Fleet to persist in using an operational procedure which inhibited the dissemination of analysis and precluded the best chance of accomplishing the strategic objective. The errors were compounded by the consideration that up to this point in the saga, it was the very system of integrated operations, plans and intelligence that had proven successful in finding *Bismarck* and alerting the fleet.[41]

In any event, more delay was incurred as Kemp and his superiors decided upon a technique to circumvent Tovey's obstruction to the dissemination of vital intelligence. Kemp and his superiors were confronted with the necessity of having to overcome restrictions to what should have been routine operating procedures. Kemp's data was rechecked to eliminate the slightest chance of error. This procedure always seems to occur when an individual with the right answer also happens to hold the minority position on an issue. After all, the Intelligence Division now bore the burden of deviating from established procedure.[42]

Kemp and his superiors urged that the analysis of the direction-finding "cut", which indicated a southeasterly course by *Bismarck*, be sent to Tovey at once. Senior officers were hesitant; they did not want to interfere with the commander on the scene. Finally, the directors of both the Operations and Plans Divisions agreed with the Intelligence Division director and Kemp from the OIC and sent the analysis to Tovey. Three hours had passed since the analysis had first become available. *Bismarck* had gained seventy miles.[43]

The Admiralty advised Tovey that *Bismarck* was probably heading to Brest. Two better direction-finding "cuts" locating *Bismarck* at 55 degrees, 15 minutes north and 30 to 31 degrees west and 55 degrees north and 31 degrees west, respectively, were made at 0948 and 1054 hours. Those "cuts" confirmed a southeasterly course from the 0700 hours "cut" made on *Bismarck*'s first transmission. That information was sent to Tovey without delay at about 1100 hours, 25 May. But more delay occurred aboard the *King George V*, however, resulting in the loss of another three and one-half hours. At 1530 hours, eight hours after Kemp first detected that *Bismarck* had turned southeast, *King George V* finally turned to an intercepting course. By now *Bismarck*, faster than *King George V*, was two hundred miles away.[44]

A classical mystery of the sea now emerges. The British battleship *Rodney*, approaching from the south, was on a course and at a distance which would have permitted the interception of *Bismarck* the next day. Instead, *Rodney* received a radio message, enciphered by the British naval cipher system, ordering the battleship to change course toward the Iceland-Faeroes Passage to join with *King George V*.[45]

Some were later to suspect that Prime Minister Churchill himself ordered this movement, interfering with military operations because he could not resist the temptation as the former First Sea Lord to reinforce *King George V*. In the coming duel, the British battleship would be the weaker of the adversaries. Advocates of that theory explain that both *Repulse* and *Victorious* had been previously detached from *King George V* in order to refuel. The official British military history of intelligence during WW II leaves the mystery unexplained.[46]

Research suggests another theory. Since the German B. Dienst could cryptanalyze some British naval ciphers at this time, the German Navy may have transmitted an imitative deception message, purportedly from the British Admiralty, with the intention of preventing *Rodney* from intercepting the damaged *Bismarck*. The message could have been transmitted from a B. Dienst station or from a U-boat. U-boats regularly carried two-man B. Dienst teams to cryptanalyze Allied radio messages. The potential for deception was certainly high. The Admiralty was now "interfering" with the conduct of the battle. Tovey did not consider Kemp's direction finding analysis to be intelligence. He most likely regarded it as Admiralty interference. The use of communications deception thrives in an atmosphere of conflicting directions sent by radio message. The use of communication deception of this type was certainly not without precedent. Later—in February, 1941—in a better documented example, a German U-boat sank the Canadian corvette *Spikenard*. The U-boat next imitated *Spikenard*'s communication to learn the location of the convoy the corvette was escorting and then sank several merchant ships in the convoy. After exhausting all torpedoes, the U-boat used a deceptive message and successfully directed other ships in the convoy back to Newport.[47]

The suggestion of deception involving the *Rodney* provides a sound reason for using radio direction-finding to locate friendly as well as enemy radio transmitters at sea. The British did not routinely do this during WW II and we still do not routinely follow this sound practice today. There is no other substantive evidence to explain why *Rodney* was diverted or by whom. Copies of the incoming message were received by both the *King Georve V* and *Rodney* but there is no known record of the original authority for the outgoing message; at least such information has not been released. Additionally, the text of the message though obviously in English language, was not worded typically like British naval language. Opponents of this theory argue that if the Germans had successfully diverted *Rodney* that they would now be anxious to tell of that success forty years after the war. However, considering the loss of the *Bismarck* with most of her crew the following day, Hitler's reaction, and the implication of an initiative of this type, it is not unlikely that the entire subject may deliberately not have been recorded by some German station.[48]

One thing is clear from the record: Admiral Tovey was confused when he received the information copy of the message directing the *Rodney* to join with *King George V*. Tovey's interpretation of the message was that the Admiralty had again changed its mind and thought that *Bismarck* was indeed heading northeasterly as Tovey had originally assumed. Tovey again changed course.[49]

By this time the OIC was receiving cryptanalyzed German Air Force radio messages confirming that *Bismarck* was heading southeasterly toward Brest. The Air Force messages alerted German air units to protect the battleship once it reached the limits of the protective German air umbrella.[50]

Interestingly, *Bismarck*'s general destination was also provided at 1812 hours, 25 May, in a German Air Force radio message Red cipher used by general officers for personal messages. A German general, the Chief-of-staff of the Air Force—then in Athens, Greece—enquired of Berlin about the *Bismarck*. His son was serving aboard the battleship. Berlin was only too happy to reply that *Bismarck* had sunk the *Hood* and was safely proceeding to Brest. This information substantively confirmed a whole new set of radio direction-finding "fixes" providing the same conclusion. The potential to derive critically important intelligence from unnecessary communication is obvious.[51]

The Royal Navy had one last chance to sink *Bismarck* as the *King George V* seemingly steamed in circles. The antique battleship *Renown* and the aircraft carrier *Ark Royal* were approaching from the south. If the *King George V* and *Rodney* changed course and approached *Bismarck* from the north they could intercept the German battleship, but only if *Bismarck* could be slowed or halted. Air and sea reconnaissance were increased and directed to the area indicated by plotting the two radio direction-finding "cuts" in conjunction with calculating the estimated speed of *Bismarck*. Then at 1030 hours, 26

May, as correctly reported in the popular literature and the motion picture, a British air reconnaissance plane pinpointed the *Bismarck* about 700 miles west of Brest and barely beyond the protection of the German air umbrella.[52]

The fiasco continued. British aircraft comprising the first assault against *Bismarck* mistakenly launched fourteen torpedoes against their own cruiser, the *Sheffield*. To the credit of British seamanship and inferior torpedoes, they all failed to hit or explode. Aircraft from the *Ark Royal* finally struck the damaged *Bismarck* during the second assault. A torpedo from a single Swordfish bi-plane torpedo bomber wrecked the battleship's steering mechanism causing it to steam in circles while almost out of fuel. *King George V, Rodney,* cruisers, and destroyers closed on *Bismarck* for the kill. The battleship sank between 1027 and 1036 hours, 27 May, with the loss of 1,900 of her crew. Only 110 survived.[53]

It is now the prevailing authoritative judgement that if *Bismarck* had won the open sea, the British would not have located *Bismarck* for this battle without the remarkably timely and reliable cryptologic intelligence provided by the OIC. Radio direction-finding was chiefly responsible for providing critical information when it was needed most. There was more. It was consistent and reliable collection, collation, and analysis of intelligence from agents in Sweden, Norway, and France, as well as reconnaissance, which enabled the British Navy to catch and sink the *Bismarck*. It is true that most messages in the Neptun cipher to and from the *Bismarck* were not read [cryptanalyzed] until twenty-four hours after the *Bismarck* was sunk. Agent reports were accurate but slow. Nevertheless, cryptology—especially good solid radio direction and radio message analysis along with radio-fingerprinting and "fist" analysis—were chiefly responsible for pinpointing the *Bismarck* for destruction.[54]

THE LOSS OF BISMARCK
A DECISIVE STRATEGIC FACTOR

In an Apologia, Roskill explained that Tovey had set after the *Bismarck* on the wrong course because he had gained the impression from direction-finding bearings sent to him by the Admiralty that the *Bismarck* was heading northeast. Roskill concluded that Tovey's deduction was incorrect because of a mistake by ". . . the Admiralty's method of signalling the bearings." Roskill as late as 1954 chose not to pursue the discrepancy further. That analysis by Roskill is an understatement that prevailed until the release of previously classified material explained earlier in this chapter. Hinsley, writing in an official British government history in 1979, also chose to "softly" ignore the controversy involving the dissemination of the direction-finding analysis to Tovcy. If we are to learn from our mistakes we must first understand them.[55]

Roskill, again writing in the official British Navy history, made it clear that he had little idea why the *Bismarck* evaded the *King George V* and the rest of the Home Fleet for three days. He attributed the final defeat of the German Navy to the inferiority of the German 8-inch cruisers like the *Prinz Eugen* and *Hipper*. An evaluation of naval armaments is beyond the competency of this research, but one thing is clear: The role of the German 8-inch cruisers had nothing to do with this battle, and it was this battle that defeated the German surface Navy. The defeat of *Bismarck* was the result of good electronic intelligence which permitted the British to strike, if not swiftly, at least with economy of force and with adequate protection for convoys against the U-boat threat. Electronic intelligence permitted the British Navy, briefly, to assume the role of an offensive, strategic force when that role was vital. *Scharnhorst* and *Tirpitz* were yet to be destroyed in 1943, but despite the British fiasco with the *Bismarck* the sinking of the pride of the German Navy was the end of the serious and strategic German naval surface threat.[56]

The loss of *Bismarck* was not of itself a decisive loss to the overall German war effort. The battleship *Tirpitz* and the new German cruisers remained untouched at this time. It was Hitler's reaction to the loss of *Bismarck* that was decisive. First, there had been the stigma caused by the loss of *Graf Spee*. Now the loss of *Bismarck*, the most modern battleship in the world, resulted in Hitler confining the German surface fleet. He threatened seriously to dismantle the warships and to use their guns for coastal defense. His edict of "take no risk" along with his subsequent illusion of the continued threat of a British invasion of Norway, resulted in his ordering the German Navy to protect against the imagined invasion threat. It was the German Navy that would now stand picket duty. Hitler did more to negate the strategic value of the German Navy than the entire Allied navies could do before 1944.[57]

Hitler committed the classical strategic error of responding to the perceived intention of his enemy rather than to the threat of his enemy's capability. The Allies lacked the resources to invade Norway in strength before 1944.

The British, too, committed a classical strategic error. They repeated history because they did not understand it when they fought the Battle of Jutland in 1916. The significance of Jutland to the Admiralty was that it resulted in changes to internal gun-turret design to prevent chain-reaction explosions among cordite charges stored in the turret. They studied the tactical lessons of that battle but not the strategic lessons. They did not recognize the tremendous impact that electronic intelligence had upon that battle. By not using electronic intelligence correctly the British lost the opportunity to destroy the German fleet. The intelligence lessons of Jutland could have precluded unnecessary loss of Allied blood and treasure during the early years of WW II.[58]

If employed with skill and in concert with the growing U-boat fleet, the German warships had the capability to cause havoc to Allied shipping. The Germans had the capability to deprive the Soviets of North Atlantic supply convoys and to either double the loss to Allied shipping or to tie down escort ships so as to delay the resupply by a factor of about eight and postpone Allied operations in the Pacific—the Germans could have starved England. The Allies lacked sufficient warships to escort either more or larger convoys. The German Navy could have caused a delay in the Allied November 1942 landings in North Africa from Morocco to Cairo, through the Middle East, the Suez Canal, and to the Balkans where German Eastern Front forces could have linked and severed the remaining entry point for supplies to the Soviet Union.

Operation Torch, fortunately for the Allies, was a model of secrecy. There is no evidence, even after the recent declassification of WW II cryptologic documents, to indicate that the Germans were aware of the Allied operation to land in North Africa in November 1942 until after the landings had commenced. Convoys began to assemble as early as 20 October. Over six hundred ships completed time-dependent rendezvous without detection. The flotillas participated in multiple landings on the beaches off Algiers, Oran, and the west coast of Morocco without being detected. The first indication of Torch was received by the German High Command at 0630 hours, Berlin time, 8 November 1942. The notification occurred after the landings had commenced the night before. It was not until this time that the German U.d.B. dispatched fifteen U-boats in an unsuccessful attempt to disrupt the operation. By then it was too late.[59]

With the sinking of the *Bismarck* and as a result of Hitler's strategic decisions pertaining to the German surface fleet, Germany was forced to rely totally on the U-boat fleet and a small number of merchant raiders to accomplish the strategic objective of disrupting British shipping to the extent that it prevented Britain from conducting an offensive campaign against the Germans in Europe until 1944.

In the following chapters it will be seen that Germany came very, very close to achieving an important strategic objective—the total disruption of Allied merchant shipping by the end of 1942. Again, intelligence and electronic warfare intelligence in particular permitted the Allies to multiply their combat power and to assume an offensive strategic role.

CHAPTER VI

A Unique Trilogy: *Tirpitz*, Convoy PQ 17, and Raiders

TIRPITZ, THE THIRD TARGET

Though the destruction of the *Bismarck* signalled the end of the German surface fleet, that consequence was not as readily apparent in 1942 as it was after the war. In mid-1942, the Allies continued to guard against the severe weather of the Arctic routes, German U-boats, and the threatening breakout of the new German battleship, *Tirpitz*, and the new cruisers, *Scheer, Lutzow, Hipper,* and *Prinz Eugen*. The largest part of the Royal Navy was standing picket duty against their breakout. Additionally, the Royal Navy needed warships to escort convoys. Each convoy required an accompanying escort of destroyers and corvettes to protect against U-boats, a close-in covering force of cruisers and destroyers to protect against German warships and a distant covering force of battleships and aircraft carriers to reinforce close-in covering forces which might become engaged with a superior and concentrated force of German warships. All of this consumed large numbers of British warships. Convoy protection was expensive and constantly placed the Royal Navy on the defensive from October 1939 until mid-1943. The strategic limitation which these circumstances imposed sapped the offensive capability of the Allies. By mid-1942, the numerically inferior German Navy continued to keep the world's largest and most powerful navies on the defensive with only five capital warships and 196 U-boats. The heavy toll taken of Allied shipping was so dismal by mid-1942—with the loss of 4,244 merchant ships carrying a total of 17 million tons—that there was a major movement within the Admiralty to postpone all convoys until the next period of prolonged Arctic darkness—six months later, in January 1943.[1] There were political considerations to the matter as well. President Roosevelt insisted, and Prime Minister Churchill agreed, upon a policy of continuing material support to the Soviet war effort in order to placate Stalin's insistence on an immediate second front despite the conspiracy of Roosevelt and Churchill to delay that effort until at least 1943. Stalin pleaded to

Churchill and Roosevelt for food, material, and munitions in his message of August 1942. The Soviet situation was so dire when the British temporarily halted convoys after the loss of convoy PQ 17, that a task force of United States and British warships led by the cruiser *Tuscaloosa* brought sixty tons of emergency supplies to Vaengna Bay on 23 August 1942.[2] Though the Soviets subsequently contended that Allied supplies were not vital to their victory in WW II, the German Oberkommando der Wehrmacht (OKW), German Army Headquarters certainly felt otherwise. The OKW implored the German Navy in late 1942, during the Battle for Stalingrad, to make every effort to cut off the supply of war materials to Soviet Forces.[3]

Confronted with the political policy, the Admiralty was able to reinforce the Home Fleet with the addition of a United States Navy task force comprising the battleship *Washington* and the cruisers *Tuscaloosa* and *Wichita,* but no more.[4]

There were three principal routes to ship war supplies to the Soviet Union. The Trans-Pacific route was confined exclusively to Soviet ships which carried forty-six percent of all war supplies from the United States to the Soviet Union. The Japanese did not attack those Soviet ships with an understanding that the Soviet Army would not attack Japanese troops in China. The second route introduced supplies destined for the Soviet Union sent via the Atlantic and Pacific Oceans into the Persian Gulf ports by ship and then transshipped by rail through the Caucasus. Twenty-three percent of war supplies from the United States to the Soviet Union were shipped via this long and slow route. The third route—the Arctic route, from the east coast of the United States and from Britain to the North Russian ports of Murmansk and Archangel—was the shortest, quickest, and most dangerous. Thirty-one percent of the supplies from the United States and most of the war supplies from Great Britain to the Soviet Union were shipped via the Arctic route until 15 February 1942 when the Soviets halted the German offensive in Russia. About twenty-one percent of all cargo sent via the Arctic route was sunk versus only eight percent shipped via the other two routes. Additionally, the most critically needed war material was shipped via the Arctic route. Despite horrendous losses, gross mismanagement of shipping, bottlenecks of many kinds which resulted in some shipments arriving *two years* later on a fourteen-day trip, the Allies persisted in using the Arctic route to assuage Stalin's insistence on a second front in 1942. They did this to demonstrate that the Allies were taking every risk to support the Soviets and to prevent an accusation that the Anglo-Americans were fighting to the last Soviet soldier. One thing is certain: The Allies were taking every risk. During the three-month period of April to June 1942, the United States lost one-fourth of the eighty-four ships sent to the Soviet Union. During only twenty days in March 1943, the Allies lost ninety-seven ships, one of every four United States Merchant seamen was lost on the Arctic run.[5]

The confrontation between Allied and German strategic goals is illustrated in a study of the factors preceding the destruction of Allied convoy PQ 17 outward bound to North Russia via the Arctic route in July 1942. The letters P and Q were arbitrarily selected to designate the convoy as outward bound to North Russia. The number 17 indicated the serial number of the convoy. It was an infamous combination that served as a time of horror for those who served aboard the thirty-six ships and a source of many allegations as to whom or what was to blame for the destruction of most of the convoy.[6] Reviewing more facts in 1980 than were available in 1942, it may appear as though the British Navy tried to sink the *Tirpitz* by destroying convoy PQ 17. It is not contended that this was a conscious or deliberate decision but rather the consequence of decisions made at the time.

CONVOY PQ 17

Convoy PQ 17 was one of a series of convoys transporting war material from the United States and Great Britain to the Soviet Union by the Arctic route. Admiral Morison, the United States Navy historian, described a convoy as a supply train comprised of merchant and troop ships under the protection of warships to ward off attack by enemy submarines, warships, and aircraft. The merchant ships, usually thirty to forty in 1942, were formed inside a protective envelope with a separation between ships in all directions of about 1,000 yards. By 1944 hundreds of ships comprised a convoy. Naval escorts patrolled around the circumference of the convoy as it proceeded to its destination at the speed of the slowest ships.[7]

Considerable dependence was placed on the Arctic route because of Stalin's refusal to permit the Allies, the British in particular, to establish a greatly expanded Persia-Caucasus land route to Russia. The land route, beginning at the terminus of a safer ocean convoy route, was more efficient and far safer. The route was also considerably longer, but that was not why Stalin refused. The British advocated the stationing of Allied troops and airmen in the North Persia and Caucasus area to support and protect the lines of transportation. It was this last suggestion of Churchill's to which Stalin was unbending. Stalin would have none of it.[8]

The Arctic route, on the other hand, usually resulted in bad conditions for a ten-to-fourteen-day trip through ferocious gales, ice, fog, and six month cycles of alternating perpetual daylight and darkness to Murmansk and Archangel. The prolonged darkness offered protection to the merchant ships, but prolonged daylight made the ships better U-boat targets twenty-four hours a day. Convoy duty to North Russia during the first years of WW II was probably the most dangerous duty of the war. The ships' crews did little to improve their chances by persisting in what was probably the very worst communications security practices used during WW II.[9]

The scene was set. The Allies (to include the Soviet Union) concurred in the political policy and strategy which specified the reinforcement of the Soviet Union with war materials despite the intransigence of the Soviet Union to permit expanding the use of the Trans-Caucasus Convoy route and despite over-extending the Royal Navy to accomplish these strategic tasks. The Germans played their part well using economy of force. They took every opportunity to take advantage of the Allied vulnerability. In early 1942, the German Navy initiated Operation Rosselsprung—Knight's Move—intended to select and destroy an entire Allied convoy. PQ-17 was to become the victim.[10]

Morison contended that the war staff in Berlin, not the Navy, ordered the annihilation of the next convoy to North Russia. This just happened to be PQ-17. Actually, information now available indicates that by January 1942, the German Navy, especially Admiral Raeder, wanted to force a breakout of its warships to raid Allied commerce and finally succeeded in obtaining Hitler's reluctant approval. The memories of *Graf Spee* and *Bismarck* were fresh in Hitler's mind, as well as his overall contempt of the surface fleet earned by the lack of understanding of strategic sea power as well as the destruction of Germany's two battleships. The battleship *Tirpitz*—new, technologically advanced, the remaining pride of the German

Navy—steamed from sanctuary in Wilhelmshaven to Trondheim, Norway. *Tirpitz* arrived at Trondheim 15 January 1942 and was joined by *Scheer, Lutzow,* and *Prinz Eugen.* All departed through the fjords on 6 March with the mission to attack outward bound convoy PQ-12. Cryptologic intelligence obtained by the British enabled the Admiralty to move the aircraft carrier *Victorious* to within striking distance of *Tirpitz* and its squadron. When the Germans detected the British move, *Tirpitz* and its squadron of three cruisers and eleven destroyers were returned to Trondheim and PQ-12 passed safely. Nevertheless, the attempted breakout by *Tirpitz* clearly demonstrated the vulnerability to disaster of the convoys bound for the Soviet Union if German warships were able to attack on the open ocean. The First Sea Lord, Admiral Sir Dudley Pound, as he was to explain after the war, could feel an impending disaster.[11]

Admiral Tovey, commander of the Home Fleet, has since written that the strategic situation was most favorable to the enemy.[12]

Writing in 1948, Morison lacked many of the details explaining why the British Navy, charged with protecting PQ-17, withdrew the covering and escort forces. Morison concluded, in the absence of all the pertinent information, that the British could not risk engaging the German surface fleet while the convoy remained assembled. The combat power of the *Tirpitz* squadron was superior in a local action. Instead, the covering force was withdrawn to engage the German fleet which was thought incorrectly to be the way to attack PQ-17. The convoy was ordered to scatter based on an overestimate of the enemy situation. There is now much more to the story after the release of previously classified Ultra material.[12]

Convoy PQ 17 consisted of thirty-six merchant ships of which twenty-two were United States merchantmen. The remainder were British and Soviet, three rescue ships, and an oiler. The merchant ships carried 160,000 tons of oil, war supplies, tanks, and aircraft from the United States for the armed forces of the Soviet Union. The study of PQ 17 is important because with its loss, and after the arrival of PQ 18 in September, all convoys to North Russia were halted for about five months until convoy JW 51 resumed the convoy of supplies in January 1943.

A small convoy of Allied warships transported about sixty tons of supplies during this period, convoy PQ 18 delivered a small amount of supplies in September and individual or small groups of ships were able to deliver limited supplies during this period. But as a general consideration, the convoy system was temporarily halted by the loss of PQ 17.[13]

On 14 June, thirteen days before PQ 17 left port, the British Code and Cipher School constructed an outline of Operation Rosselsprung from cryptanalysis of German radio messages. The information was provided to the Admiralty's Operational Intelligence Center, the OIC, and from there to the Admiralty's Operations and Plans Divisions. On 14 June the Admiralty was given the location of the forthcoming German attack on the convoy, PQ 17 was identified as the victim and the disposition of the German warships and U-boats designated to participate in the operation was identified.[14]

Convoy PQ 17 sailed on 27 June 1942 escorted by six destroyers, four corvettes, nine mine sweepers, a trawler, two antiaircraft gun ships, and two submarines. The distant covering force was comprised of the battleships *Duke of York* and *Washington,* the aircraft carrier *Victorious,* and four destroyers.[15]

The question which arises is, why did PQ 17 steam-on in the face of a major attack planned by the enemy? Was it to trap *Tirpitz*? If that was the purpose, why not set a better trap using heavily armed merchant ships? It appears more reasonable to believe, however, that there was no plan to cope with the German threat except for a crudely conceived decoy convoy of a few empty ships.

German Air Force reconnaissance sighted PQ 17 on 1 July 1942 while homeward-bound QP 13 was observed passing in the opposite direction. By now U-boats had been alerted and were shadowing PQ 17. Events moved quickly. The *Tirpitz*'s squadron departed Trondheim on 2 July but as the squadron passed through the fjords, three of the four accompanying destroyers hit rocks and were put out of action. The cruiser *Lutzow* also ran aground. On 3 July as PQ 17 approached Bear Island, it was attacked by German aircraft; one merchant ship was sunk. Early on 4 July, twenty-four German torpedo-bomber aircraft sank two more merchant ships and damaged a third. The battle was so heated that the United States Navy armed guard aboard the merchant ship *Troubadour* loaded and fired the main guns of two army tanks carried on the deck as cargo and succeeded in destroying a German aircraft.[16]

Later on 4 July, the Admiralty ordered the covering force to withdraw westward. The escort commander misunderstood the intention of the order and mistakenly joined the covering force in what was presumed to be an engagement with a superior German fleet. The mistake left PQ 17 defenseless in a sea filled with U-boats. By 5 July, after the convoy had been ordered to scatter, the widely-dispersed ships of PQ 17 were continuously attacked by German U-boats and aircraft from all quarters. Twenty-three more of the thirty-six merchant ships and one rescue ship were sunk. In all 99,000 tons of cargo plus 3,350 vehicles, 430 tanks, and 210 aircraft intended for the Soviet war effort were lost.[17]

During the past thirty-five years, the PQ 17 disaster has been attributed to a variety of reasons ranging from poor intelligence to poor leadership. With the recent revelations pertaining to Ultra communications intelligence, one myth is corrected. PQ 17 was not lost due to poor intelligence work, nor did the British Navy cower as some have accused.

INTELLIGENCE WORK WAS GOOD

The British Navy's Intelligence Division OIC reported the following intelligence gained by cryptology to the Admiralty on 18 June. This occurred only four days after the Germans officially released Operation Rosselsprung on 14 June and nine days before PQ 17 steamed from port on 27 June:[18]

- The German Navy intends to attack the next convoy outward bound or homeward bound from the Soviet Union on the Arctic convoy route. It was determined that PQ 17 or QP 13, the latter homeward bound, were the targets. The attack would occur near Bear Island about 2 July.

- The German Air Force will use air reconnaissance to locate the convoy once it passes Jan Mayen; the convoy will be bombed after it is located.

- Two groups of German warships including *Tirpitz, Scheer, Hipper, Lutzow,* ten destroyers, submarines, and aircraft will simultaneously attack the convoy at six degrees east of Bear Island.

- The 18 June disposition of participating German ships and aircraft units stationed in Norway was provided.

Access to this type of knowledge about enemy intentions and capability provided a decisive advantage to the commander. The Admiralty passed this intelligence to the commander of the Home Fleet, the protector of convoy PQ 17. On 1 July the British OIC, again from cryptology, was aware that the German Air Force had sighted PQ 17 and so advised the commander of the Home Fleet. Similarly, British intelligence apprised the Home Fleet of the German reports pertaining to aircraft and U-boat attacks on the convoy. They also advised the Home Fleet in a timely and accurate manner as soon as the German squadron moved from its anchorages down the fjords and into coastal waters to rendezvous.[19]

To this point the British Code and Cipher School was able to penetrate the German naval cipher with cryptanalysis. The delay from time of intercept to time of solution took about twenty-four hours. The bombe had to find the solutions to the daily-changing keylists. This process usually took twelve to twenty-four hours. However, during the night of 3-4 July, the German fleet routinely changed its Enigma keylist, but this change caused a delay in solution beyond the normal twelve to twenty-four hour cryptanalysis cycle. As the German fleet was thought to be approaching the sea, the OIC was unable to receive cryptanalyzed information reporting on its location. The ships themselves were on radio silence so direction finding was of no use. Nevertheless, an examination of unencrypted German naval radio message routing and procedures, referred to as message externals, made it clear that *Tirpitz*'s squadron was *preparing* to breakout to the open sea. The OIC also confirmed, based on the cryptanalysis of German Air Force radio messages, that the Germans did not know where the British Home Fleet was located. The presumption of the OIC was that an inferior force does not steam into the home waters of a superior enemy force when the location of the superior force is not known.[20]

The British, on the other hand, were reasonably certain what the German Navy intended to do. Cryptanalysis had provided the Admiralty with the German Navy battle plan and its capabilities. The British knew that the Germans had been unable to find the Home Fleet by reconnaissance. Though the British did not know that Hitler had strictly instructed the German Navy not to risk its capital ships, an evaluation of the past performance of the German fleet strongly indicated that the German Navy would not stand to fight gun-to-gun battles with the superior British fleet.[21]

There was more. Allied submarines stationed as pickets at the Altenfjord entrance to the Atlantic had not yet reported the movement of the German squadron through this front door to the Barents Sea. It was also known that German U-boats, shadowing and lying across the route of PQ 17, had not yet been alerted that the German surface squadron had departed for the killing zone. This last procedure was routine in the German Navy and intended to prevent its U-boats from mistakenly torpedoing its own ships. In short, there was no evidence to indicate that the German squadron had entered either the Barents Sea or the Atlantic; there was good reason to believe that it had not.[22]

At 1800 hours, 4 July, the British covering force signaled to the Home Fleet that in accordance with its standing instructions the covering force was preparing to reverse course once PQ 17 reached 25 degrees east at about 2200 hours, 4 July.

At 1900 hours the new German naval Enigma keylist was broken, and the Code and Cipher School reported that cryptanalyzed messages based on the new keylist could be expected momentarily. Hopefully, the cryptanalyzed messages would provide a timely insight into the location of the *Tirpitz,* and its squadron. In the interim, the covering force was ordered to remain with the convoy.[23]

During the period 1900 to 2200 hours, 4 July, the OIC continued to counsel their estimate of the situation indicating that the *Tirpitz* and its squadron had not yet departed the Altenfjord. Cryptanalyzed radio messages had still not been received by 2200 hours. OIC personnel built their case on the factors previously cited, the absence of friendly submarine sightings of the *Tirpitz* near Altenfjord, the absence of an alert to the U-boats, and the inability of the Germans to locate the British Home Fleet. In addition, German naval radio messages did not show routing procedures indicating that German Naval Group North was yet communicating with *Tirpitz* directly, a procedure that would have revealed that *Tirpitz* was at sea.[24]

It is necessary at this point in the examination to introduce the personality of the key decision-maker in this event—First Sea Lord Admiral Pound. Admiral Pound was noted for his autocratic manner and insistence on centralized control of the Admiralty. He would not permit an intelligence briefing to be given on the matter of PQ 17. There was a need here for Pound to at least listen to a premise drawn from the facts as they were then known, to consider assumptions and to judge conclusions and recommendations accordingly. Instead Pound preferred to ask short questions. The dialogue of this event is recorded by Beesly and McLachian. He wanted short answers.[25]

Pound would not consider a null hypothesis: The German ships are not yet at sea because there are no indications that they are at sea. Instead Pound presumed that because intelligence could not demonstrate that the German ships were still in the fjords they must be at sea. It was a dilemma and an interesting corollary when men's lives are at risk.

Two key points are at issue: First, why did Pound order the covering force to withdraw and secondly, why did Pound order the convoy to scatter? When the covering force and, by mistake, the escort as well, withdrew, the implications were clear. The convoy was left unprotected. But when the convoy was next ordered to scatter, it abandoned its self-protection. When a convoy scatters, it abandons its close and disciplined formation. Scattering is a recognized tactic of last resort when a convoy is attacked by a superior surface force in a broad expanse of sea, but scattering deprives a convoy of mutually supporting antiaircraft fire and escort protection against U-boats. The real threat was a combination of enemy aircraft and U-boats, not a surface threat.[26]

At 2000 hours, 4 July, a meeting of the Navy staff was held to decide the issue of whether convoy PQ 17 should be ordered to scatter before the convoy ran out of sea room required to execute the maneuver. There was still no cryptanalytic intelligence. There was not complete staff agreement on the issue either. Beesly reports that Pound made the decision for the convoy to scatter after hearing short arguments on the question. Pound, it will be remembered, liked short answers. Some have considered that Pound may have been influenced in his decision to order the convoy to scatter because the ships in the convoy lacked sufficient fuel to conduct an alternative action—to change course and head back to the United States, as an example. There is not sufficient information available at this date to judge whether the supply of fuel was a consideration but it appears that it was not. There is also no evidence that Admiral Clayton, the Deputy Director of the Naval Intelligence Division, took a strong, decisive, nonconcurring stand on what the OIC personnel felt was an error by Pound to scatter the convoy. Clayton was a man widely respected for his experience, calmness, and shrewd judgment, a retired rear admiral recalled to active duty for the war. He may have been too calm in this situation. The OIC firmly held that the *Tirpitz* squadron had not yet left the fjords and they wanted that opinion solidly presented at the meeting.[27]

At 2100 hours, 4 July, the covering force of cruisers was ordered to withdraw at high speed by the Admiralty. At 2115 hours, Beesly reports that the order was amended to read—due to the threat of enemy surface ships, the convoy was to disperse and proceed to Russian ports. The covering force and escort force interpreted the message to mean that German warships were about to appear at once or at least shortly. The commodore of the convoy did not have any information about the "German squadron" but under no circumstances could he see the advantage of scattering his convoy in the area of the worst U-boat and aircraft threat. The commodore requested a verification of the order. It was provided. Once the convoy scattered, beginning at 2120 hours, the escort commander could see no alternative but to join the covering force which was weaker than the German squadron it was expecting to momentarily face. The commander of the escort force had the mission of protecting the convoy and he was willing to steam head-on into a superior German fleet if necessary in order to give the convoy more time to scatter. The fault in this plan was that there was no German threat; there was no German squadron steaming into battle over the horizon. But one thing is certain: The British escort did not, for its own safety, abandon the convoy.[28]

Finally, at 2200 hours, 4 July, Admiral Clayton returned to Pound with a timely cryptanalyzed German radio message indicating that the German squadron was not at sea. Specifically, German U-boats were advised that German warships were not in their area near PQ 17. Still, Admiral Pound would not change his order for the convoy to scatter and ordered that the ships regroup.[29]

ANATOMY OF A DISASTER

Roskill, writing after the war, attributed much of the problem in this situation to poor intelligence work. Despite Roskill's analysis, intelligence personnel did not fail in providing accurate and timely information. In retrospect there was adequate information to make a sound decision. Few commanders ever enjoyed more sound intelligence before a battle. Pound made the wrong decision; he recalled the covering force prematurely. The escort force mistakenly accompanied the covering force, leaving the convoy defenseless. The worst mistake was that Pound ordered the convoy to scatter precluding any chance that the escort force and covering force could rejoin the convoy at a later time. All this was done on the presumption that the German fleet was at sea. But worst of all, senior officers felt the decision was an error but were denied the freedom of access to their commander required to present their case.[80]

Stalin's analysis of the situation was harsh. In his 23 July 1942 message to Churchill he advised that he found it "incomprehensible and inexplicable" that Allied warships abandoned PQ 17.[81]

An analysis of what went wrong may be too quick. It is easier to judge thirty-five years later, free of the pressure of combat and survival, not to mention the years of accumulated stress and fatigue that had burdened Pound and others. The biggest error was that Admiral Pound did not understand the limits and capabilities of his chief combat multiplier in this battle—the cryptologic facet of electronic warfare. Pound did not know how to use the intelligence process nor did he take the opportunity, despite his other demanding duties, to learn of these things. He imposed his own deficiency upon the commanders of the forces at sea by interfering with the judgment of their commanders.

Benefactors of Admiral Pound may argue that he could not be expected to place absolute confidence in naval intelligence. That argument has additional considerations, however. The Germans had conformed precisely to the plan briefed by the OIC on 18 June. The OIC had established a record of sound judgment demonstrated repeatedly. The OIC clearly distinguished fact from assumption. The OIC had also been right when the *Bismarck* was the target earlier in the year. But again the OIC had been ignored by the First Sea Lord. That error had almost cost the British the opportunity to sink the *Bismarck;* it was not to cost convoy PQ 17. The OIC could not find all the answers to questions asked by Pound, but what they did report was correct and adequate to make sound decisions in this deployment. The OIC advised that the departure of the German squadron could be detected by observing radio message routing and message procedures from German naval shore stations even if the warships maintained radio silence. One thinks that Pound did not understand any of this, it was mysticism to him.[82]

The withdrawal of the covering force was later judged by the Admiralty to be a sound decision but the order to scatter the convoy was based on the threat of German warships without sufficient consideration afforded the enemy U-boat and aircraft threat. A more candid judgment would have clearly explained that the decision was made without considering all the information available with the experience expected of the senior officer in the Royal Navy. The Admiralty order to withdraw the covering force of cruisers was also considered to be confusing. Too frequently battle messages are written based on the objectives of the writer rather than with an appreciation of the objectives of the commander receiving the message. The vagueness of some messages from the Admiralty and the overstatement in the last message which implied that the German fleet was actually steaming toward the convoy resulted in the conclusion that contact with the enemy fleet was imminent when in fact the German warships were still anchored off Norway.[33]

Roskill, writing as the British naval historian, at a time after many of these facts were known, advised that Pound reported the Admiralty possessed intelligence which had indicated the *Tirpitz* had eluded the British submarine pickets on the night of 3-4 July. There is no evidence that this information is correct.[34]

Convoys to North Russia were halted by the Allies until January 1943. The halt was due chiefly to the loss of PQ 17, though PQ 18 steamed to North Russia in September 1942, most of its cargo was also lost.

After the Admiralty investigation of the loss of PQ 17, the Intelligence Division was finally provided the spirit as well as the letter of the regulation which provided the authority and responsibility to convey information of importance to commanders and staff at every echelon—the *authority* and *responsibility* to disseminate intelligence.

MERCHANT RAIDERS, THE FOURTH TARGET

A transition is made at this point to introduce the German merchant raider. During the early stages of WW II, the German Navy reinstituted the WW I tactic of using raiders disguised as merchant ships to conduct piracy against Allied commerce. It was an extension of the strategic objective intended to disrupt supplies to Great Britain and its forces elsewhere. Twelve raiders, ranging in size from 4,000 to 9,000 tons—frequently referred to as Q-Ships because the Morse code signal QQQ indicating distress, was transmitted by victims—were commissioned. (The QQQ signal eventually had universal application to indicate an attack by a raider.) Nine raiders eventually went to sea in two deployments. The first deployment occurred in the winter of 1939-40, the second deployment in 1942. At a speed of eighteen knots, the raiders were relatively fast; most merchant ships steamed at seven to thirteen knots. The raiders were also well armed; one sank the cruiser *Sydney*.[35]

Admiral Raeder, Commander-in-Chief of the German Navy provided three strategic missions to the raider task force:[36]
- Destroy or capture Allied merchant ships.
- Dislocate Allied shipping movements.
- Disperse Allied warships.

During the period September 1939 to April 1940, five of the raiders sank 600,000 tons of Allied shipping in eighty-seven ships.[37] The raider *Pinguin* alone sank twenty-eight Allied ships at 136,000 tons. The seven raiders in the first deployment sank one-fifth of all British tonnage sunk during the period 1939-1941, over three million tons in one and a half years.[38]

Prior to 1941, German warships and raiders came and went at will and without being detected. By May 1941 material captured from German U-boats *111* and *110* permitted the British Code and Cipher School to cryptanalyze and read a lot of German U-boat radio traffic. Usually the delay required by cryptanalysis consumed twelve to twenty-four hours as explained earlier; radio messages were therefore usually valuable only in a historical perspective. This insight, however, provided the OIC with a comprehensive and accurate picture of the U-boat fleet, its operations, dispositions, and movements. *U-110* carried keylists needed to set the Enigma rotors during the period February 1941 to July 1941. Since the U-boat was captured in May 1941, unknown to the U.d.B., the keylists were of immediate use only from May to July, but the Allies were able also to read all the older messages from February to May. Though that information was historical it provided extensive insight into U-boat operations. With keylists in hand, the Allies were then able to read current U-boat radio messages from June to July 1941. From these revelations the OIC was able to track and capture, or sink, in only twelve days, the six German tankers intended to supply the battleship

Bismarck and the cruiser *Prinz Eugen* when they broke out to sea.[39]

Having gained advantage of techniques gleaned from the material captured from *U-110*, the British eventually broke the Triton cipher used exclusively by the U-boat fleet. Raider *Atlantis* was found and destroyed when *U-126* was instructed in a Triton enciphered message by the U.d.B. to meet and refuel from the *Atlantis*. The British cruiser *Devonshire* was advised of *Atlantis*' location, closed with the raider and sank her. *U-126* later surfaced to pick up survivors from *Atlantis* and was instructed by U.d.B., again using the Triton cipher, to meet raider *Python* and transfer the survivors. Again the British intercepted and cryptanalyzed the message and ordered the cruiser *Dorsetshire* to close with and sink *Python*. It did. By now there were more than four hundred survivors. In what is rated as a major accomplishment, the survivors were picked up by other U-boats, transferred in mid-ocean to Italian submarines and returned to safety in France. The raider *Komoran* and the cruiser *Sydney* sank one another after the cruiser foolishly approached within 2,000 yards of the heavily armed raider. By December 1941, three of the seven raiders and eight supply ships had been sunk, most as a direct result of cryptologic intelligence. Though the Allies were never able to cryptanalyze the One Hundred and Tibet ciphers used by the raider fleet, the British were able to pursue the raiders by reading the Triton cipher, the Hydra fleet cipher, and the German Military Attache in Tokyo Bertox cipher—all of which provided considerable information pertaining to the operation and location of the German raiders.[40]

After the sinking of the battleship *Bismarck* and later the destruction of *Scharnhorst* and *Tirpitz,* the Germans abandoned all attempts to use capital warships to raid Allied commerce, relying instead on U-boats and raiders. Between November 1941 and July 1942, the Triton cipher keylist changed to an extent that the Allies were unable to immediately recover the system and hence were unable to read U-boat radio messages or locate raiders during their second offensive in 1942.[41]

When raider *Komet* operated in the German home waters of the Baltic Sea using the Hydra fleet cipher, rather than the One Hundred cipher used by the raiders in the Atlantic Ocean, the OIC was able to detect the attempted breakout of *Komet* from the Baltic to the Atlantic. The British could read Hydra. Cryptanalysis provided by the Code and Cipher School provided a route map as *Komet* steamed from Kiel to Swinemunde to Bremen to Dunkirk to Le Havre, with dates of arrival known well in advance.[42]

This information about *Komet* permitted the British to initiate air reconnaissance, and the location of the raider was easily pinpointed when she arrived on schedule in the Seine Bay. *Komet* was intercepted and sunk off Cap De La Hague on 13 October 1942 as a direct result of cryptologic intelligence.[43]

In January 1943, the raider *Togo,* also in the Baltic, was advised by a Hydra-enciphered message, to breakout to the Atlantic. *Togo,* too, was intercepted and damaged by the Royal Air Force. She returned to her Baltic port to remain until war's end.[44]

By the beginning of 1943, the intercepting and cryptanalyzing of U-boat and Hydra fleet cipher radio messages not only resulted in the destruction of the raider fleet but the destruction of about half of the German surface blockade runners as well, when messages sent to U-boats advising them of the passage of the blockade runners were read by the British Navy. In the same manner Norwegian and British blockade runners were protected from German interception because cryptology revealed the location and patterns of German air and sea patrols. Cryptologic intelligence also insured the successful delivery of 348 tons of vital Swedish ball bearings delivered by Allied motor torpedo boats during a series of nine trips through German controlled coastal waters. The Swedish government was not particular in these matters. It provided ball bearings to Germany as well as adopted a benevolent attitude toward England, but after 1943 when the Allies were, if not winning, certainly no longer losing the war.[45]

The defeat of the German U-boat fleet, explained in the next chapter, ended the strategic German naval threat, but it was a considerable threat while it lasted.

CHAPTER VII

U-Boats

THE U-BOAT, A STRATEGIC WEAPON, THE FIFTH TARGET

If an intelligence analyst had reported in 1938 that half of the 5,600 merchant ships then steaming back and forth across the world's trade routes would be sunk by U-boats before May 1943, very few would have taken him seriously. But, that is exactly what happened. It can be argued that the Allies could have lost WW II if the U-boat had not been defeated by mid-1943. The Allies certainly would not have decisively won the war.

When measured in numbers, the U-boat threat was comparatively small; there were never more than 434 U-boats, and of those not more than 188 and usually only sixty or so were operating at sea at the same time. During the first year of the war only about fifteen were at sea at the same time.[1]

In the vastness of the ocean, a single U-boat is as inconsequential as a grain of sand upon the beach and about as hard to distinguish. During WW II, a U-boat could be found only when it surfaced, when preparing to attack, or when it transmitted an encrypted radio message. The first was rare, the second too late, and the third required superb intelligence. The Allies used intelligence to take advantage of revelations from German radio messages protected by the Enigma machine-cipher. The radio messages were a rich source of information in which U-boats reported their locations with exceptional precision to Flag Officer, U-boats and the Befehlshaber der U. Boote, abbreviated here as B.d.U., the headquarters of U-boat operations, located first in Germany and then in France.

There have been popular misunderstandings, perpetuated until 1977 by a lack of information, explaining the defeat of the U-boat as a strategic weapon. Credit for the defeat is usually shared between the convoy system and radar.

The convoy system deservedly earned credit for the protection of merchant ships. However, in only twenty days during 1 to 20 March 1943, ninety-seven ships were lost. Two-thirds of these ships were in convoy. After mid-1943 when microwave radar was introduced and the German Air Force was deployed from the Atlantic convoy routes to North Africa against Allied operations in Torch, convoy escorts sank U-boats. However, the escorts did not defeat the U-boat fleet. Convoys were successful and comparatively few merchant ships were sunk after mid-1943 when protected by convoy but the use of radar was a major factor. Unfortunately, the use of convoys also required the commitment of large numbers of warships, forcing the world's largest and most powerful navy to become a defensive navy. The convoy system severely limited the use of the Royal Navy as an element of offensive strategic power when it was most needed in that role.

Radar is also rightfully afforded an important role in the defeat of the U-boat. Radar could pinpoint the location of U-boats with such accuracy that they were easily sunk by antisubmarine aircraft and ships. Radar could be used to "see" through darkness and fog. But, radar could do all this only when the U-boat was surfaced; it could not detect the submarine underwater. To be detected the U-boat also had to be within range of the radar set, usually one to twenty-five miles depending on the type radar and altitude of the aircraft. The newer model radar sets had longer ranges and the higher an aircraft flew the longer the range of the radar set. However, there were neither sufficient aircraft, ships, fuel, radar sets, nor ordnance available to blanket the oceans with radar-equipped antisubmarine aircraft and ships. Radar was effective only because specially-equipped aircraft and ships could be sent to the right place at the right time to detect a U-boat when it was most likely to surface. Only then was the effect devastating. When this technique was first mastered by the Allies in May 1943—forty-three U-boats, a third of the operational fleet, were sunk in one month. It was cryptologic intelligence that provided this highly effective multiplier of combat power when used in conjunction with radar. It was also intelligence that alerted convoys to forthcoming U-boat attacks, permitting their timely diversions to safety.

Some have confused the cryptanalysis of radio messages between U-boats and U.d.B. as the chief reason the Allies were able to break the stranglehold of the U-boat fleet so soundly during WW II. The cryptanalysis of these and other German radio messages is referred to as Ultra. Though Ultra played a significant role, it was no more effective than radar. Rather it was the total integration of all aspects of cryptology with the use of radar, the convoy system and good antisubmarine weapons, applied with sound judgment, that beat the U-boat. It was the productive use of a solid intelligence system that allowed the Allies to find the grain of sand in the vast oceans. It was the consolidation of intelligence with operations and plans, three separate and distinct divisions within the British Naval Staff, that established the model by which good intelligence came from behind the 'green door', symbolic of secrecy and limited access, to serve as a combat multiplier for the Allied navies.

A DESCRIPTION OF THE WEAPON

The submarine was first introduced as a strategic weapon by Germany in WW I. It was intended to achieve a strategic objective—the disruption of the economic and military capabilities of Germany's enemies. During that war Germany employed submarines to sink eleven million tons of Allied merchant shipping despite the overall inferiority of the German Navy. During WW II, the submarine served as an even more important strategic weapon because the disruption of England's economic and military capabilities pertinent to merchant shipping was more vital to the success of Germany under the conditions that occurred between WW I and WW II.

Identified by the Germans as a "Torpedo Attack Underwater Boat", the submarine, called unterseeboot in German, was abbreviated to and most commonly referred to as a U-boat.[2]

The battle which ensued during WW II between the Allies in their attempt to protect the Allied merchant shipping lifeline and the Germans in their attempt to destroy it was referred to as the Battle of the Atlantic. It was a major campaign of WW II and more colloquially referred to as the U-boat war. It is probably the first time that military history refers to a campaign named after a technological weapon. The campaign took place chiefly in the Atlantic Ocean but also included the Baltic, Caribbean, Mediterranean, and North Seas, the English Channel, and the Bay of Biscay.[3]

The submarine was, by comparison to other warships, small, rugged, cheap to build, simple to maintain, and ugly; the German model was primitive, using mostly WW I technology. However, the submarine was not yet considered to be a "true underwater boat" because of its limitations. It is necessary to understand the U-boat's capabilities and limitations in order to understand its impact on strategy.

Generally, the WW II model U-boat could submerge only to a

depth of about four hundred feet—five hundred feet in exceptional circumstances—and was limited to a submerged time of about forty-eight hours. Toward the end of WW II the Germans adapted many of their U-boats with the Dutch-invented schnorchel device permitting U-boats to remain underwater for much longer periods and to operate diesel engines while submerged. When submerged, the U-boat could travel at speeds of about two knots for prolonged periods by using its storage batteries, slightly faster when running on diesel engines with schnorchel. The boat could travel at about nine knots for one hour in an emergency. When surfaced and using its diesel engines, the U-boat could travel at about seventeen knots. By comparison, a typical destroyer could steam at about twenty-five knots and the mass-produced Liberty merchant ships at about nine knots. The U-boat had to surface to breathe and to travel fast; these were its most important weaknesses, or so the Germans thought. Because of its slower speed the U-boat had to leave to chance that a merchant ship would blunder into its path. This was an inefficient tactic. The U-boat could also be advised of the course and speed of an individual ship or convoy, arrive well ahead of time at a point where both the ship and the U-boat's courses could intersect and wait in ambush. This was the efficient tactic, but it depended upon superb intelligence and communications.

The German type VII U-boat could remain at sea for about forty-two days unless replenished with fuel and other supplies at sea. In 1942 and 1943, twenty-eight of those forty-two days were consumed in travelling to and from killing areas. As a result, only one third of the U-boat fleet was stationed to attack merchant ships at any one time.[4]

The design and construction of the United States Navy submarines in 1939 provided submarine crews with habitation comforts similar to those provided to destroyer crews. This was not to be the case aboard the approximately 700 German type VII U-boats built during WW II. The German U-boat was appropriately named a pig boat by its crews. It was not a term of endearment. Despite conditions of exceptional privation, U-boat crews were considered to be the most dedicated and highly motivated personnel in all the German military. All were hand picked. Their fleet commander, Admiral Doenitz, took special interest in every commander and every crew. Personal leadership was extraordinary at every level and, most important, success or failure was immediately observable to every crew member. For the most part German U-boat crews, especially their officers, avoided many of the psychological problems reported among United States Navy crews and officers serving in more modern submarines in the Pacific Theater.[5]

The poor ventilation used by the U-boat caused constant exposure to unpleasant and toxic levels of battery gases and diesel fumes. Excessive carbon dioxide was routine. High humidity in combination with both excessively hot and cold temperatures was uncomfortable. German U-boats did not have provisions for fresh meat or vegetables and few facilities for personal hygiene. The operating characteristics and capabilities of the U-boat resulted in a primitive submarine about half as capable as the United States Navy fleet model submarine used during WW II. The United States Navy model was twice as large, ran faster and more quietly—both submerged and surfaced—cruised fifty percent farther, fired twice as many torpedoes in a salvo, carried twice as many torpedoes, had larger caliber deck guns and twice the crew size of the German type VII U-boat.[6]

A comparison of the United States Navy and the German type VII submarines is illustrated in Table 1 below.[7]

Table 1
Performance Characteristics of USN and German
Type VII Submarines Used During WW II

Characteristic	USN	German
Displacement	1525 Tons	720-750 Tons
Length	311 Feet	220 Feet
Surface speed	20 Knots	17 Knots
Submerged speed	9 Knots	2-3 Knots
Maximum speed when submerged	11 Knots	7-9 Knots
Range	15,000 Miles	8,500 Miles
Torpedoes	24	14
Torpedo tubes	10	5
Guns	5-Inch (127 mm)	37 mm
Crew size	90	44

The contrast between the United States Navy and German model submarine is important because the United States Navy, despite its numerical inferiority after the Japanese attack on Pearl Harbor, was able to destroy the Japanese merchant fleet with its submarine force. The United States Navy achieved its strategic objective with the submarine. The German Navy could not accomplish this though it used many more submarines (1,000 German submarines versus 200 United States submarines) than did the United States Navy and over a smaller operating area. When Germany finally began to build larger and more sophisticated type IX U-boats, it was discovered that the new boats could not stand the stress of combat as well as the smaller boats and were retired to safer operating areas. The older type VII U-boats absorbed the brunt of combat in the North Atlantic.[8]

Germany began WW II with about fifty-six U-boats—mostly small, 250-ton model II boats of WW I design the first of which had been built at Kiel on 29 June 1935 and the rest after 1936. Fifty-six additional type II, larger 600- to 740-ton type VII and 750-ton type IX boats were in advanced stages of construction. [Numbers and type differ according to source and authority.[9]] When the war began on 3 September 1939, forty-three of the fifty-six U-boats were operational; but since the small, 250-ton type II boats were only practical for in-shore operations, the German Navy was limited to an effective strategic force of eighteen type VII and ten type IX boats for extended patrols in the Atlantic. The remaining boats were confined to coastal and Baltic operations. Germany commenced its strategic attacks with only twenty-eight U-boats. Twenty-eight U-boats confronted the world's largest and most powerful navy. The U-boats came very, very close to winning.

Of the twenty-eight U-boats, eighteen were at sea when the war started. Within only a few weeks the number of operational U-boats available for sustained operation at sea was reduced to about twelve. Six U-boats had been sunk the first week of the war. As late as January 1942, only sixteen U-boats would be available for stationing off the eastern shore of the United States. This was not a large threat measured by numbers. Further, at war's beginning, Germany was delivering only about one or two new U-boats each month.[10]

Though Italy added about one hundred additional submarines to the Axis force by 1942, only about sixty of these were capable of fighting in the North Atlantic. Of that number, thirty-seven were sunk or captured during the first year of the war. Italy's contribution did not add appreciably to German combat power. The drain which the Italian boats placed on limited German fuel and supplies was not warranted by the quality of their crews or boats, certainly not by their effectiveness or accomplishment.[11] Most Italian submarines were relegated to operations in the South Atlantic and the Caribbean and Mediterranean Seas. The Germans eventually integrated all Italian boats into the German fleet to be manned by German crews.[12]

There were several important distinctions between the U-boat confrontations of WW I and those of WW II, distinctions which explain the relative impact of the U-boat on the strategy of both wars. During WW I, the Allies were able to close most German submarine exits to the Atlantic. In WW II the situation had changed markedly. After Germany occupied Denmark, Norway, the Netherlands, and France early in the war, the Allies were confronted with practically unlimited access by German U-boats to the Atlantic. During WW I, England was virtually self-sufficient. During WW II, England—now a nation of forty-six million people—could neither feed nor fuel its nation without significant imports. Importantly, British armies dispersed widely overseas could not survive on the WW II battlefields without consistent supplies and modern weapons. Finally, there were many more Allied and neutral merchant ships to serve as U-boat targets than during WW I. However, there were fewer German U-boats available when WW II began than during WW I.[13] Despite the intervening twenty years between the wars, the German-built submarines had not changed significantly, and the British had not materially improved their technique in finding and destroying them. The German U-boat was designed to attack on the surface whenever possible. This tactic, apparently unread in Britain and the United States, was clearly advocated by both Bauer and Doenitz. The U-boat submerged only to hide, when pursued, to escape, or to gain surprise. The U-boat's capability was severely reduced when submerged. In fact, about eight percent of U-boat attacks and U-boat losses during the first two years of WW II occurred when the U-boats were surfaced.[14]

Germany had several tactical advantages to be sure. Prior to 1943 the submarine, for the most part, was able to maintain the element of surprise so essential to a weaker adversary. The German Navy radio intercept intelligence service, referred to as the Beobachtung-Dienst, abbreviated to B. Dienst, was able to determine departure dates, ports, routes, present locations, and diversions of most Allied convoys by easily reading the Allied Combined Convoy cipher, a collection of WW I model encryption systems. Though keylists were changed on occasion, this simple-to-cryptanalyze system was used continually by the Allies with only minor modifications until finally changed to provide total security in November 1943.[15]

This advantage enabled the Germans to practice economy of force in the deployment of its very limited U-boat fleet. Cryptology probably increased the relative combat power of the small U-boat fleet by a factor of three to four. Admiral Doenitz reported after the war that he considered the B. Dienst equal to at least fifty additional U-boats, an increase of his fleet size by one hundred percent. There is no doubt that the German Navy used cryptology to multiply combat power.[16]

At the same time, the Royal Navy had become over-extended in attempting to achieve the several strategic objectives it had been assigned to include the exhausting demand of protecting convoys. The Royal Navy quickly became a defensive navy.

To add to the problem, pre-war and continued emphasis on U-boat construction enabled the German Navy to replace U-boats and crews at least twice as fast as the Allies could destroy them until May 1943.

The advantage gained by the primitive U-boat was a direct consequence of the inability of Allied naval forces to locate U-boats in the vast expanse of the Atlantic Ocean and adjacent waters. They were like a grain of sand upon the beach. If a U-boat could be found it could usually be destroyed. The acoustic sound ranging and direction of submarine device—called asdic by the British and sound navigation ranging or sonar in the United States Navy—was used to detect the echo of sound waves transmitted underwater. Asdic did this by using a chemical discharge to create bubbles which returned an echo, detectable by an operator using hydrophones, from a submerged U-boat. Asdic was a product of pre-1935 technology in which the British placed too much faith as being practically a total submarine detection device. The British did this at the expense of developing sound antisubmarine tactics and weapons. As it was, asdic was of limited effectiveness until an additional innovation called doppler detection was added in 1942.[17] U-boats were usually successful in foiling asdic by releasing air bubbles (pillenwerfer) to distort the echo created by their submarine hull. Asdic was also useless when a U-boat had surfaced to attack, usually during darkness when it also evaded visual detection.[18]

As this study explains, the U-boat war turned in favor of the Allies between May and July 1943. But even then, Germany had the potential to return with larger numbers and greatly improved U-boats. By May 1944, Germany could, but did not, commit 150 U-boats against the Allied landings in France. By late 1944, most U-boats were being equipped with the schnorchel air intake and exhaust device which allowed U-boats to submerge just below the surface and operate for extended periods while continuing to operate their diesel engines. Though the schnorchel was much more difficult to detect by radar or observation, two of every three U-boats equipped with schnorchel that attacked cross-channel shipping in support of the 1944 Allied landings were reported to have been sunk.

The operating location of the U-boat had to be much more closely defined after the introduction of schnorchel because the radar image produced by its small surface, the only part of the U-boat actually above the surface, required radar-equipped aircraft to fly directly into the U-boat's operating area with an error of no more than a mile or so. Again, it was electronic intelligence that earned credit for ferreting out U-boats.

Allied success against the U-boat came none too soon. Though only fifty U-boats were actually operating at sea by mid-1944, Germany had finally developed an improved U-boat similar to the United States Navy fleet class submarine.[19]

The new type XXI and XXIII U-boats, respectively 1,600 and 232-ton U-boats, were close to true submarines. The new boats were equipped with silent-running motors, improved torpedoes, radar detectors, improved radar, improved detection plotters, and capable of greatly increased ranges, up to 20,000 miles. The type XXI U-boat carried twenty torpedoes, could travel submerged at eighteen knots for one hour or twelve knots for ten continuous hours. The new boats were virtually undetectable when their technology and tactics were compared to the technology and tactics of Allied antisubmarine forces. They were undetectable in every respect but one—cryptology. Had the 189 new German U-boats which were constructed before the end of the war put to sea as early as May 1943, the losses to Allied shipping would have been horrendous.[20]

The Germans were consistently five to ten years behind their capability in the development of many weapon systems, and too late in the development of what should have become one of their major strategic weapons, the submarine. Much of the responsibility rests with German economic policy, and blame can be shared among those who failed to coordinate military and economic strategy at a time when it was vital to Germany.[21]

It is difficult to analyze the effect and relationship of German economic policy with that nation's strategic policy. The constant manipulation of policy and strategy by Party Secretary Borman, State Secretary Lammars, and Chief-of-Staff Kietel in their attempt to block the expansion of Speer's increasing power as the Minister of Armaments and War Production seriously distorted national strategy. Nevertheless, the inability of Germany to support a major strategic weapon with its economic policy shared responsibility for the destruction of the U-boat fleet. Hitler's own unpredictability further confounds the examination.

In January 1943, Hitler classified the expanded Panther Tank Program, a tactical weapon system, as the highest national priority. In effect he incongruously designated a tactical weapon program to a higher priority than a major strategic weapon program. In so doing Hitler disregarded the strategic military policy which he was instrumental in designing—the destruction of British shipping. Later, in April 1943, on the advice of Speer and Doenitz, Hitler reconsidered his decision and designated the submarine program [Naval Armament Program] as the highest priority. But because of bureaucratic competition the decision still did not clearly define U-boat construction as the highest priority. The decision only allowed Doenitz to compete equally with the Panther Tank Program for resources and production. Speer and Doenitz (by 1943 the Commander-in-Chief of the Navy) worked out a compromise with Army procurement officials to prevent delays caused by additional controversy and a contest for Germany's limited resources and production capacity.[22]

Speer, the manufacturing and production mastermind, devised an assembly-line method for construction of the new submarines beginning in July of 1944. The first models were completed in December

1944. The new boats were built inland in sections then assembled at shipyards—a technique to eliminate the delay of having to undertake shipyard expansion. The production system was designed to provide forty new U-boats each month in full production. By early 1945, twenty-five boats a month were being constructed. Other wartime demands on the economy and Allied bombing prevented the full production capacity of the U-boat construction system from being attained. The construction of U-boats peaked in the winter of 1944-45, a year too late. By war's end a third of all surviving U-boats were destroyed in their pens by Allied bombing; but this was not to be the case during the first four years of the war. The Allies had dropped ton upon ton of high explosive bombs on the U-boat pens in France and not a single bomb penetrated the reinforced concrete. Not a single U-boat was seriously damaged. The Commander-in-Chief, British Coastal Command, had proposed early in the war that Bomber Command should attack new U-boat pens while they were undergoing construction behind watertight caissons and were highly vulnerable to air attack. Bomber Command disagreed, carried the argument and, instead, placed bombing priority on industrial targets in Germany—it was retaliatory bombing versus strategic bombing. The *Strategic Bombing Survey* completed after the war clearly indicated that that decision was an error. Once the bombproof concrete roofs were in place the pens remained protected from Allied bombing.[23]

At the end of the war, the predominant thought among German naval historians like C. D. Bekker, unaware of Allied cryptologic success, was that the U-boats were most likely lost in large numbers because of increased Allied convoy security, superior radar, and large numbers of antisubmarine aircraft. It has been reported that 785 U-boats were sunk (all causes), 196 scuttled, and 189 captured by the end of the war. By the end of 1943, the German Navy had lost 237 of their most experienced crews and commanders. The German and Allied records together accounted for every U-boat. It was estimated that 28,000 of the 39,000 U-boat crewmen were killed during WW II.[24]

There were other factors as well. As explained previously in this report, Hitler interfered decisively with the rational operation of the surface and U-boat fleets. Hitler deployed the U-boat fleet off Norway and later into the Mediterranean when U-boats were needed to achieve *decisive* strategic objectives in the Atlantic Battle. At a time when U-boats were achieving their maximum losses against Allied shipping, Hitler withdrew the boats for battles of less importance. Hitler failed to provide a decisive policy for the use of this major strategic weapon. The German Navy fought with outdated U-boats—submarines not much improved from their WW I predecessors—without consistent strategic direction. Yet, as Morison wrote as early as 1947, "No one accomplished so much with so little [as did the U-boat crews]."[25]

THE BATTLE

At 2100 hours, 3 September 1939, twelve hours after war was declared, U-boat number 30, a type VII boat, achieved the distinction of torpedoing the British liner *Athenia* two hundred miles west of the Hebrides. The *Athenia* was the first ship sunk by a U-boat during the war. Of the 1,400 passengers aboard, 112 lost their lives. On 12 September 1942, three years later, *U-156* sank the *Laconia,* unknown at the time by the Germans to be carrying 1,500 Italian prisoners of war from the battles in North Africa. As a humane gesture *U-156* attempted to rescue all aboard by taking lifeboats in tow. A United States Army Air Force bomber approaching the scene attacked U-boat and lifeboats alike with depth charges from an altitude of 2,500 feet. The depth charges sank the lifeboats but *U-156* escaped undamaged. That event resulted in U.d.B. directing all U-boats not to lend assistance during any future attacks on merchant or passenger ships. It was probably the beginning of unrestricted submarine warfare in WW II.[26]

On this note the U-boat war began in earnest; it was to become a campaign in which the Allies lost at least 15 million tons of shipping, more than 2,800 merchant ships, and a host of escorting warships. It was to be a battle in which one of every four United States merchant seamen would be killed. The toll would be even higher for Great Britain.[27]

The campaign reached its apex in spring 1943. By the end of 1942, the Allies were losing over one million tons and 140 ships a month. It was an amount of shipping that was too large to replace. In perspective, the amount of loss during a single month was equal to the amount of supplies required by sixty-two infantry divisions for a month in combat. Even worse, the losses were outpacing construction at a rate of two million tons for the first year. The Allies were losing twice as many ships as they could build.[28]

Germany, on the other hand, was completing construction of twenty to twenty-five new U-boats a month and far outpacing their losses during 1942. By the end of 1942, Germany increased its U-boat fleet from eighteen to 400 type VII U-boats, as well as increasing the number of smaller type II and the larger type IX boats. Germany eventually built almost 800 U-boats of the types II, VII, and IX. Constant losses after mid-1943 restricted the average fleet size to less than 400 U-boats. The typical type VII U-boats, depending upon the shipyard, required between thirty-six to fifty-two weeks to construct.[29]

The final tabulation of ships lost to U-boats is, of itself, impressive but it was the creeping terror that truly explains the horror of these primitive German machines. Germany sank 65,000 tons per week during the first four months until losses finally peaked at an average of 153,000 tons per week during 1942. Essentially, the amount of material required to supply nine divisions for thirty days in combat was being sunk each week. Obviously much more vital supplies were also being shipped and lost, but the use of an infantry division's supply rate provides an example of the magnitude of the loss. (see note 28)

During the first seven months of 1942 U-boats, of which only sixty to sixty-five were at sea, sank 681 Allied ships at 3,600,000 tons. Five hundred and eighty-nine of those ships were lost in the Atlantic. The Germans did this with less than fifteen percent of their U-boat fleet at sea.[30]

Overall, during the period September 1939 to May 1943, the German U-boat fleet destroyed about 12,500,000 tons of Allied cargo and almost 2,500 merchant ships. Allied ships were sunk at an average rate of three ships per day.[31]

The U-boat fleet sought targets other than merchant ships. U-boats sank three aircraft carriers—*Courageous, Glorious* and *Ark Royal*—the battleship *Royal Oak* inside the British Home Fleet base at Scapa Flow and several cruisers and destroyers.[32]

Both cargo and warships were being destroyed about twice as fast as they could be replaced. The terrible drain on supplies caused England to consume its reserve stores of food and fuel. The Germans were able to accomplish these heavy losses to British commerce with typical losses of one U-boat per 100,000 tons of Allied shipping sunk by U-boats. The statistically-average U-boat sank twenty Allied ships before it was sunk. In human dimensions, the German Navy lost about 500 sailors to destroy one million tons of war material. This loss was insignificant compared to German losses on the Eastern Front. It was also only a small fraction of the blood and treasure paid by the Royal Air Force during its strategic bombing raids over Germany to accomplish a small fraction of the damage in comparison to the damage caused by U-boats.[33]

By October 1943, Allied convoy practices, used in conjunction with intelligence analysis of radio messages to and from U-boats, and microwave radar finally resulted in conscious strategy to beat the U-boat.

The apotheosis of British intelligence collection, analysis, production, and dissemination was the naval Operational Intelligence Center, a control and analysis function of the Naval Staff's Intelligence Division. The Center, abbreviated and referred to as the OIC, acquired the skills, techniques, savvy, and operational insight required to understand both the limitations and capabilities of the U-boat. The OIC applied its expertise to take advantage of the enemy's vulnerabilities and to avoid his advantages. The small staff of the OIC was eventually able to determine the actual locations of U-boats, their routes and operational procedures, or to at least reliably predict these items of information based on intuitive judgment developed from hundreds of bits of seemingly irrelevant information. Signals intelligence, including decryption of enemy air force and navy radio messages by cryptanalysis, message analysis, and direction finding provided vital pieces to the daily puzzle. Agent reports and reconnaissance were also vital. It is important to understand that it was the collection of information from many sources, and the exceptionally capable analysis of that information, that enabled the British to see U-boat operations as clearly as did the German U.d.B. see their own operations.

Even those German radio messages which were cryptanalyzed long after their interception, often a month or more later, may not have provided timely intelligence, but they provided basic and detailed information necessary to construct a case study of U-boat operations. This was all the more valuable because many U-boat operational procedures were repetitious. Information gleaned from daily fuel reports, weather observations, contact reports, and other routine matters allowed the OIC to understand general U-boat operating procedures which served to outline future operations of U-boats. Consequently, when only fragmentary information was available, this occurred especially after a keylist change to the cipher, considerable basic information was available to fill in the gaps. Most of the unknown aspects of the operation could be reliably predicted. One could almost read the mind of the commander of the U-boat fleet and of individual U-boat commanders.[34]

After the war Admiral Doenitz was asked if he was aware that someone was practically reading his mind during the war. He replied that he was not. Actually, Commander Winn, an analyst in the Submarine Tracking Room of the OIC, was doing exactly that. Winn emerges from recent studies, after the declassification of Ultra material, as a hero of sorts—not a hero with accolades for valor, but one who, despite a serious physical handicap, used his gifts of good judgment and perseverance to silently save the lives of many of his countrymen and other Allied sailors.[35]

Winn had subconsciously, one supposes, trained himself to reach decisions in the same manner that Doenitz and his U.d.B. staff did when Winn had access through cryptanalysis to the same information made available to Doenitz and U.d.B. Winn frequently received the information before Doenitz since his channel of communication ran directly from the radio intercept site to the British Code and Cipher School to his desk. Doenitz was the victim of staff layering. Winn was also spared the need to attend to the multitude of operational and support requirements that burdened the commander of the German U-boat fleet. Winn was able to concentrate exclusively on U-boat operations.[36]

Winn was at his best in July 1943 when of his own volition he produced an assessment of the U-boat situation for the Assistant Chief of Naval Staff, Admiral Edelsten. The assessment was intended to provide the Prime Minister with an outline of the options available to Admiral Doenitz who had lost thirty percent of his U-boat fleet in May and withdrawn the remaining boats to safer operating areas.

Winn's basic conclusion was that though the U-boat force had been withdrawn from the Allied convoy routes due to unacceptable losses, the potential to attack with 150 U-boats still remained. The Allies were dependent for men, food and war supplies based on a guarantee of safe convoy routes if the landings in Europe were to succeed. A single troop ship like the *Queen Mary* speeding at twenty-eight knots, carried 15,000 troops—the equivalent of one and a half infantry divisions. When the smaller troop ship, *Dorchester* was sunk by *U-456* on 3 February 1942, the equivalent of an entire infantry battalion was lost. The risk of losing a single of the larger troop ships like the *Queen Elizabeth, Queen Mary, Aquitania, Mauretania, Ile de France,* or *Nieuw Amsterdam* to a 750 ton boat crewed by only forty-four men would not only have been a disaster in terms of lost human life but would have had a considerable impact on the morale of soldiers and populace alike. These ships transported some 60,000 troops per month between the United States and England.[37]

Winn predicted renewed enemy U-boat attacks, a last stand so to speak, by U-boats armed with a wide variety of new weapons. He concluded by recommending that a major strategic objective of the Allied effort should be the dedication of major naval forces to continue aggressive, offensive, measures to hunt the dispersed U-boat fleet wherever it could be found. Winn submitted the paper for review by the commander of the OIC and the Deputy Director of the Intelligence Division. Both senior officers were sympathetic to his judgment but were concerned that Winn may have overstepped his responsibility by preparing an unsolicited assessment. Tradition in the Royal Navy was often more an impediment to ideas than a stalwart to sustain men in times of stress. It was not chiefly an issue of whether Winn was right or wrong; it was, instead, the older issue of who had authority to disseminate intelligence analysis. It was the Battle of Jutland, the chase of *Bismarck,* the same scenario, played again to the tune of authority matched with position rather than authority matched with the right answer. Apparently, one could derive a right answer only by virtue of one's position. In the overall scheme of things, Winn did not occupy a high position in the decision-making chain. Nevertheless, he convinced his superiors to send the estimate forward and accommodated their counsel by respectfully penning, "A purely personal view."[38]

Admiral Edelsten incorporated many of Winn's recommendations in an Appreciation Paper submitted to the Naval Staff in August 1943. As predicted, the German Navy did launch a new U-boat offensive. U-boats were, as predicted, equipped with new weapons including a new radar search detector and the acoustic torpedo.

Fortunately neither worked very well. The Battle of the Atlantic resumed on 20 September 1943 with more U-boats at sea than ever before. The Allies were ready. With the advantage of the intelligence provided by the OIC, and its United States Navy counterpart, Group 20, an effective Allied convoy strategy was employed. The strategy was not easily negotiated. The British not only had to fight the German Navy in a war of depth charges and torpedoes but had to fight the United States Navy in a war of ideas and experience as well. Many were later to wonder which of the two battles was the more exhausting. The United States Navy, as reported by Roskill and clearly evident in the reports of Morison, was not quick or inclined to learn from British experience paid for dearly during the first two years.[39]

There is little indication to be found in the professional literature to suggest that the United States Merchant Marine fleet had trained in antisubmarine measures so painfully learned by the British during WW I and the first years of WW II. Though the United States Navy had full access to the British OIC since the war began, it did not have an equivalent to the OIC despite considerable effort on the part of the Admiralty to encourage Americans to establish the necessary function. The judgment is made, not because the United States Navy lacked an intelligence function, but because it lacked an *integrated* operations, plans, and intelligence function.[40]

When German U-boats first moved into the Western Atlantic, off the eastern coast of the United States in 1942, their commanders were open in their criticism of the inexperienced antisubmarine tactics used by the United States Navy and the Merchant Marine. U-boat commanders considered their attacks on shipping off the North American coast like a step back to their easier hunting of 1939. The lack of training for United States Merchant Marine crews resulted in more deaths than were necessary. By March 1943, every convoy was losing six to twelve ships to U-boats during the Atlantic crossing. Losses were so high that a decision to halt the convoys—to stop shipping—was almost made and most likely would have resulted in a one- or two-year extension of the war.[41]

Instead the Allies won the Battle of the Atlantic. The Allies definitely were on the defensive until early in 1943. A period of balance, as Roskill refers to the period, existed from early 1943 until the Allied offensive began in earnest in the fall of that year. The roles were reversed by about May and assured by July, though those turning points were not so evident at the time. By July 1943, Admiral Doenitz temporarily withdrew most of the U-boats from the North Atlantic killing areas. A number of factors contributed to the Allied campaign victory.[42]

First, the British and United States navies eventually perfected a convoy strategy and complementary antisubmarine tactics guided by intelligence rather than intuition. During the period 1941 to May 1945, the Allies deployed about 250 convoys with an average size early in the war of about forty ships and about 100 ships later in the war. In all, 9,481 ships were reported to have crossed the Atlantic in one direction or the other by convoy; only 132 ships were sunk and most of those before 1943.[43]

Secondly, the Allies introduced a combination of antisubmarine technical devices including high-frequency radio direction-finding, S-band radar (microwave radar), improved sonar with doppler, sono-radio buoys, radar-directed Leigh floodlights, magnetic detectors, Loran-type navigation, improved multiple-depth charges, shallow-firing depth charges for use by aircraft and electronic torpedoes. All these devices were available in large numbers after May 1943 as a result of mass production in the United States.[44]

Third, Allied ship construction outpaced losses due to the mass production of the Liberty model cargo ships in the United States. This accomplishment did not occur until after May 1943.[45]

Fourth, by the end of 1943, the entire convoy system was protected by air patrol, additional escort vessels were becoming available and radar permitted both air and ship escorts to detect U-boats with greater efficiency.[46]

Finally, and perhaps most importantly, radio direction-finding provided the approximate locations of U-boats whenever their radio transmissions were longer than about thirty seconds and intercepted by Allied stations. Direction-finding provided fixes, an intersection of converging lines from the direction-finding stations to the target transmitter, with a probability of fifty percent that the U-boat was within a circle having a radius of fifty nautical miles. More accurate fixes were available after the Allies began mounting direction-finding sets on convoy escort ships and warships and then used that data in conjunction with shore station data.

Once a U-boat's approximate location was determined, radar

equipped aircraft or ships were dispatched to patrol the general area. On many occasions the cryptanalysis of all or part of U-boat radio messages, or an understanding of the boat's routine procedures derived from cryptanalysis of a large volume of its previous radio traffic, could reveal the approximate time the boat would surface to replenish or to meet with supply boats. Typically, patrolling aircraft would loiter outside the U-boat's operating area to avoid detection. Once the aircraft's radar locked on a surfaced U-boat it raced in for the kill. It could do this in daylight, darkness, or fog. As it approached the U-boat at an altitude of only a few hundred feet the aircraft suppressed the U-boat's antiaircraft fire with strafing fire and dropped its shallow-firing depth charges as the boat began its crash dive. Later in the war—equipped with better antiaircraft weapons—the U-boats remained on the surface to fight it out, but the consequences were usually the same. The U-boats were seldom a match for aircraft in these battles. Many U-boats were sunk in this manner; those that were not were left stuttering.[47]

The S-band radar has been singled out in the past as the most important weapon used to defeat the U-boat. As late as 1978, Beesly writing in his book, *Very Special Intelligence,* and having benefit of a working knowledge inside the OIC, ranked radar as the most important weapon used in the defeat of the U-boat. Beesly certainly acknowledged the importance of communication cryptanalysis and other aspects of cryptology, but he still rated radar as number one. Others like Winterbotham in his work, *The Ultra Secret,* allude that cryptanalysis, called Ultra, was number one.[48]

Actually radar would have been of limited effectiveness and of excessive cost without benefit of radio direction finding, communications analysis, and the ability to cryptanalyze the Triton cipher used by the U.d.B. and U-boats. The Allies could have used every aircraft and radar available in every theater during WW II and they still would be searching for German U-boats had cryptology not been available to refine U-boat operating areas into manageable search areas. Conversely, cryptology would have been of little utility without radar, magnetic detection, improved sonar, and multiple depth charges like Hedgehog. All forms of cryptologic intelligence were like groins of stone in the defensive brickwork of the Allied antisubmarine campaign.

GERMAN VULNERABILITY

By August 1943, the German Navy attributed the Allied ability to locate U-boats to an unidentified airborne locating device which was thought to be an infrared detector. Though the Germans considered the possibility of the compromise of their naval Enigma systems they never seriously credited the British with the ability to break their ciphers. There had been strong suspicion within the U.d.B. that the U-boat Triton cipher used with the Enigma enciphering machine was not secure. Time after time, the conclusion was reached that Triton could not, had not, been compromised. These findings were supportable after reviewing the results of communication deception operations conducted by the U.d.B. following Germany's declaration of war against the United States in December 1942. Previously, Hitler had mandated that United States ships and the Western Atlantic be off-limits to U-boats. Operation Paukenschlag (Drumbeat) moved the U-boat offensive to the coast of North America in December. Germany intended that Paukenschlag come as a complete surprise to the Americans. All U-boats were to attack simultaneously to demonstrate the greatest effect. To accomplish this tactic, U.d.B. instructed some U-boats remaining in the North Atlantic off England to simulate the radio transmissions of other U-boats which were moving undetected to North American coastal waters. Winn, the analyst in the OIC, had seen enough bits and pieces of largely undecrypted German U-boat radio traffic to put the German plan together; he identified seventeen participating U-boats and provided ample warning to the United States Navy. The warning did little good.[49]

Upon arriving off the North American coast, U-boat commanders reported peacetime conditions, bright lights ashore and on ships, total lack of radio security by merchant ships and inexperienced antisubmarine patrols. All this five weeks after war had been declared. The only sound conclusion one could expect the German Navy to derive under these circumstances was that Paukenschlag was uncompromised and their cipher system totally secure. Otherwise, the United States Navy and Merchant Marine would not have been so totally surprised. The conclusion was correct but the premise was an error.[50]

Nevertheless, the possible compromise of the U-boat cipher should not have been a surprise to Doenitz. The German B. Dienst was reading Allied convoy messages until 18 November 1943, when the vintage WW I code and cipher systems were finally changed to a secure system. But then the British Admiralty had also been convinced that their codes and ciphers could not be read by the Germans until the United States Navy [Security Group] proved otherwise in mid-1943.[51] Both sides were reading the codes and ciphers of the other, but none believed their own codes and ciphers were vulnerable.

Likewise, the Germans could not believe the Allies were capable of building a microwave radar small enough to fit into an aircraft and still work. Instead the U.d.B. persisted in believing that the Allies were using an infrared detection device to locate their U-boats. They went so far as to paint the U-boats with a special infrared camouflage paint made with powdered glass to provide concealment from infrared detectors. What this countermeasure really did was to make the U-boat more detectable by radar.[52]

U.d.B. equipped twenty-eight late model, type VII U-boats with Naxos S-band radar detectors, acoustic torpedoes, and other internal improvements but neglected elementary signals security. U.d.B. insisted that U-boats transmit large volumes of operational data by radio, rather than providing general orders to U-boats before sailing and then relying on standard operating procedures for routine operation. The nature of submarine operations did not prevent decentralized control of this nature; centralized control resulted mostly from an insistence and penchant by Admiral Doenitz that his boats operate in that manner. In so doing he neglected to take advantage of the exceptional capability of his U-boat commanders. By comparison, both the United States and Japanese Navies issued operational orders to submarines prior to their departure and relied upon the boat commanders to make day-to-day decisions. The German penchant for dogmatic, centralized control probably contributed as much to the loss of individual U-boats than any technical weakness inherent in the boats. This syndrome is not particular to the German U-boat command; a study of the Vietnam War and preparations for the modern battlefield reveal similar command and control constraints contemplated by commanders.[53]

CRYPTOLOGIC REVELATIONS

There were rare instances of extraordinary information gleaned directly from cryptanalysis of U-boat radio messages to and from U.d.B. The British learned the Germans had evacuated the pro-Japanese Indian Nationalist leader, Subhas Chandra Bhose—the fomenter of riots and sabotage—and transferred him to a Japanese submarine. This event signaled the temporary end to a major internal problem in India allowing the British to devote their resources to fighting the invading Japanese armies. The readiness report of every U-boat in the German fleet was intercepted and available to the British OIC by mid-1943. The British were able to learn the names of boat commanders, crews, and their training status. The value of communications intelligence was demonstrated when the U-boats began to report on the performance of their new acoustic torpedoes. It was again illustrated when U.d.B. directed a major change in U-boat tactics to their boats at sea—attack escort ships, not merchant ships, as top priority.[54]

When information gained from communications intelligence was fitted with pieces of intelligence from other sources and with observations of enemy activity by British naval units, the British were able to develop counter-weapons before newly introduced German weapons gained the effect of surprise.[55]

The German acoustic torpedo provides a good example. The application of German data acquired by communications intelligence was combined with information collected by British ships observing torpedo runs aimed at their hulls. Analysis resulting from that information permitted the development of the Foxer anti-acoustic torpedo device—a contraption which caused acoustic torpedoes to explode harmlessly. The Germans had become so convinced that the new torpedo was exceptionally accurate and lethal that they continued to manufacture what was actually a defective weapon and one easily avoided. The British on their side gave the Germans every indication that the acoustic torpedo was causing considerable damage.[56,57]

The survival of U-boats at sea also depended upon clandestine refueling and replenishment from large supply submarines and merchant raiders. The elusive supply submarines *Charlotte Schliemann* and *Brake,* as well as many merchant raiders, were sunk as a direct result of revealing their rendezvous points in encrypted radio messages. The loss of both supply submarines, in particular, severely restricted U-boat operations in the Indian Ocean for six months.[58]

There was more. The United States Navy documents released by the United States National Security Agency in 1978 revealed that Ultra provided information of "vital significance" about enemy radar, anti-radar devices, weapons, underwater diesel propulsion using schnorchel, U-boat antiaircraft weapons, radar deception devices like Aphrodite (a small balloon designed to deceive radar by suspending metal strips cut to a length harmonious with the length of the U-boat hull—the metal strips created a U-boat-like image on a radar screen causing aircraft to race to attack a small balloon instead of the U-boat), and the use of pressure-activated mines.[59]

Most importantly, the United States Navy learned from Ultra revelations beginning in January 1943, and conclusively demonstrated in May 1943, that the Germans were reading the Allied Combined Convoy cipher and other codes and ciphers. This insight eventually led to the development of a secure Allied convoy cipher by November 1943. The delay occurred because the British were as reluctant to follow the advice of the United States Navy in cryptographic matters as the United States Navy had been to follow the antisubmarine-warfare advice of their British allies.[60]

The German U-boat fleet accomplished several important strategic objectives before its defeat. First, as intended, it restricted the economic and military capability of the Allies to a degree totally out of proportion to the cost in manpower and resources required to maintain the U-boat fleet. Captain Francis D. Walker, Jr., editing for the *Encyclopedia Americana,* reported that 800,000 Allied sailors and airmen were assigned principally to antisubmarine duties versus only 39,000 U-boat crewmen. The Allies committed thirty warships and a host of smaller boats against every U-boat at sea.[61]

The cryptanalysis of radio messages from U-boats at sea to U.d.B. clearly revealed that U-boat commanders had identified two chief factors for their defeat. First, the inability of the U-boat to cope with surprise from the air [by radar-equipped antisubmarine aircraft directed to their operational areas by radio direction-finding and cryptanalyzed U-boat radio messages]. Secondly, because of the increasing intimidation of U-boat crews as they began to appreciate the visibility and vulnerability of the U-boat.[62]

One thing is now clear after forty years. The Allies were not winning the battle until cryptology and radar were used as a multiplier of combat power to defeat the U-boat as a strategic weapon. If we do not learn that lesson now we may not again win the battle at sea, on land, or in the air.

CHAPTER VIII

Can the United States Win the Next War?

A study of WW II or of a single campaign like the Battle of the Atlantic cannot provide a solution to all the problems of a strategic defense which our nation faces today or which we will face in the years ahead. There are, however, similarities and insights provided by the study which serve as examples of cause and effect having equal application in 1939 and 1980. These are issues of preparedness, the cost of defense, the role of technology, political and economic appraisal, and the need to multiply combat power quickly and inexpensively when the cost of meeting multiple strategic tasks in wartime exceeds the practical availability of resources during periods of peace. This research provides six findings in conjunction with the investigation of the hypothesis cited in Chapter I.

- The Allies could not mount a military offensive in Europe during WW II with the combat power available in 1943 or estimated to be available in the foreseeable future so long as the Germans destroyed Allied ships and supplies twice as fast as they could be replaced. By 1943 England was consuming its last ninety days of reserve supplies.
- If the Allies could not have conducted a successful European Campaign, the enemy could not have been defeated decisively. Technology and combat power gained the Allies a decisive advantage. By contrast, the Germans did not coordinate electronic warfare to multiply combat power.

The single most important lesson discovered by this examination is not only that technology is an important aspect of strategy, but that the application of modern technology used to multiply combat power directed at achieving strategic tasks is vital and decisive. The Allies learned how to do this during WW II; the Germans did not. The Soviet Union is learning how to do this now while the Allies are steadily losing their advantage in the field of electronic technology to the Soviet Union. This is occurring for several reasons. First, there is practically unrestricted exchange of technological data to other nations, data which eventually finds its way to the Soviet Union. Second, we are giving away our technological advantage to the Soviets. As an example consider the comparison of the exchange of students between the United States and the Soviet Union. While American students studied languages, socio-economic development, psychiatry, marriage patterns, economy, criminal law, and medicine in the Soviet Union, their students were studying digital automatic control, ferroelectric ceramics, computer application for machine-tool control, passage of shock waves through heterogenous materials, conversion of hydraulic signals to electric signals, photoelectric phenomena in semi-conductors, and solid state electrochemical thermodynamics in the United States.[1] Third, there is virtually no incentive to invest considerable time and money into research and development by American industry. This statement is supported by the declining application for United States patents by United States citizens in contrast to the increasing application for United States patents by foreigners.[2]

Dr. Simon Ramo—a founder of TRW Inc. and former chairman of the President's Committee on Science and Technology—has cautioned that national security is being threatened by the severely weakening technological base of the United States. He noted that the technological productivity rate of the United States is now the lowest of any industrialized nation.[3] This problem is of an entirely new dimension than that which confronted the Allies in 1939. We have the ability to maintain technological superiority in the field of electronic warfare at this time but we are gradually surrendering that capability to the Soviet Union.

The application of cryptanalysis in particular played a critical role during WW II but it may have little or no impact on the modern battlefield. The American Civil War and the Franco-Prussian Wars were wars of the telegraph; the Russo-Japanese War saw the introduction of naval radio in combat and the interception of radio messages by the adversary. The First World War revealed the impact of basic cryptology against simple encoding by both sides. World War II was fought to a decisive conclusion largely because of the impact of electro-mechanical encipherment and cryptanalysis devices, radio direction-finding radar, and counter-radar devices. The Vietnam War introduced sophisticated electronic targeting devices and techniques. The 1973 Mid-East War, a battlefield miniature of the modern battlefield expected in a Third World War, demonstrated the lethality of electronic warfare.

IS THE U.S. NAVY PREPARED TO FIGHT
AN ELECTRONIC BATTLE OF THE ATLANTIC?

Vice Admiral W. J. Crowe, Deputy Chief of Naval Operations for Plans, Policy, and Operations, testified before the Seapower Subcommittee of the House Armed Services Committee on 13 November 1979 to explain the strategic impact of seapower. Crowe explained that in 1939 Great Britain had the strongest Navy and Merchant Marine in the world. He noted that British offensive naval strategy completely collapsed and in its place a defensive strategy was assigned to the Royal Navy. The world's largest and most powerful navy was relegated to protecting England's economic lifeline. The Royal Navy, at the time, was unable to control even the Mediterranean Sea, a task upon which the British Middle East Command was dependent for its supplies and war materials. Instead Rommel, with a force only about one-third the size of the British force came very close to winning the North African Campaign. The Royal Navy maintained a defensive posture until mid-1943, the exception being the landings in North Africa in November 1942 which caught the Germans totally by surprise because the Allies changed naval ciphers for the operation. Crowe continued by explaining that the Battle of the Atlantic was the dominating strategic factor throughout all WW II. Until the Allies regained control of the Mediterranean Sea as well, the German southern flank remained impenetrable. Crowe's summary was consistent with the research presented in this paper, but he did not explain how the British or United States Navies were able to assume an offensive role only months after suffering their worst losses of the war. We did not equate the lessons learned from that experience to today's problem of numerical inferiority and overwhelming strategic naval tasks.[4] The intensity and lethality of modern weapons will not again afford the United States the opportunity to build a navy required to accomplish strategic tasks after a war has begun.

As Crowe proceeded he developed an analogy which he purported illustrated that seapower was the cornerstone of our nation's global strategy. It is a strategy, he contended, that is dependent upon ascendancy at sea, not parity or margin.[5] Crowe supported his premise with two cases explaining that naval supremacy during both the Korean and Vietnam Wars prevented the Soviets, Chinese, North

Vietnamese, and North Koreans respectively from attacking our supply lines. He stated the enemy would have vastly preferred to fight at sea rather than on Asian Soil [sic]. The Subcommittee may have entertained those thoughts but they would have strained Von Clausewitz and Sun Tzu Wu and Vo Nguyen Giap probably could not conceive of seapower that was not rowed, poled, or sailed.[6]

In any event Crowe fortunately expanded his analogy with a second case to predict that the Soviet Union will use its Navy to protect its shores and to isolate the United States from its Allies and economic interests.[7] The first is obvious, the latter is logically assumable and a point thoroughly endorsed by the construction and employment of the Soviet fleet and by the International Institute for Strategic Studies in a 1977 paper, "Sea Power and Western Security: The Next Decade."[8] Crowe very accurately pointed out that the United States has acquired many of the resource problems which plagued the United Kingdom in 1940 and assessed that the Soviet Union is striving for a worldwide coalition of political, economic, and military forces in the Middle East, Southeast Asia, and the Caribbean directed at securing petroleum resources and strategic waterways.[9]

Crowe applied his premise by explaining that the chief United States naval strategic objective must be to keep the Soviet Union on the defensive. In war, he explained, the United States Navy must be able to seek out Soviet surface ships and submarines and destroy them. It follows, as it did during WW II, that to do this the United States Navy must first be able to find Soviet warships and submarines and then destroy them within the first days of a war. The enthusiasm for the ability of the United States Navy to be able to do this is no less today than in 1939 when the Royal Navy was equally convinced that asdic (sonar) would enable it to find German submarines whenever and wherever they were employed. This did not work. The hard fact is that neither Admiral Crowe nor other admirals testifying later on the same subject explained how the United States Navy and its allies would defeat both the Soviet surface Navy and the submarine fleet of 300 and 400 first class submarines simultaneously. Without a convincing explanation, our nation remains tied to an ineffective 1939 naval strategy and will not be able to reinforce the United States Army in Europe or our NATO allies until after it is too late to win.

In this day of modern weapons of unprecedented range and lethality one does not envision a contest between flotillas, not even distant flotillas like those that fought one another, totally out of one another's view at the battles of Coral Sea and at Midway. It will most likely be a ship-on-ship fight in which both ships appear to one another as only a bit of electronic data on a luminiferous scope. There will be battles primarily to protect trade not to maneuver great battlegroups at sea. We are probably studying to fight the wrong tactics. There may be nuclear weapons used in these battles but there will certainly be electronic weapons used.

Crowe judged the Soviet Union to be an adversary far more lethal than the enemy in WW II.[10] Crowe was counting ships, aircraft, missiles, and submarines. He was not comparing electronic technology, nor did he later make such a comparison for the House members. He most likely did not do this because the United States Navy understands very little about how to use electronic warfare as a weapon. In a major 1979 training exercise, Northern Wedding, the details of which are available in classified reports, a NATO naval force destroyed about thirty-five of its own aircraft while allowing a similar number of enemy aircraft to attack and seriously damage the fleet. These are simulated destruction and damage. It was evaluated that those aircraft would have destroyed much of the fleet.[11] It was an electronic battle and participating United States Navy ships did not know how to win it. Ships of other NATO participants did not provide an example of how to do it right either.

Faced with a Soviet Navy approaching if not already achieving parity with the NATO navies and confronted with exhausting strategic naval tasks not unlike those of WW II, the United States Navy may engage an enemy which has studied the German mistakes of WW II and is determined not to repeat them. The Soviets have taken decisive steps by building a large and modern submarine fleet, a surface fleet based more on utility than prestige, a naval air arm, and is steadily improving technologically. The Germans required three years to begin sinking Allied ships and supplies twice as fast as they could be replaced. The Soviets can probably accomplish the same feat in thirty days.

COMPARISON OF TWO WORLD WARS—
WW II AND WW III

The Allies could not have won WW II without the ability to dominate the seas. Whether a next world war occurs in Central Europe, The Middle East, both places, elsewhere, or everywhere, we cannot win a next war unless we again dominate the seas. Additionally, though we may eventually defeat our enemy, unless we do it quickly, the expenditure of resources and the lethality resulting from a protracted war would most likely relegate all participants to exhausted nations no longer able to compete as major powers.[12]

The United States is by necessity now involved in a more economically and politically complex world into which it has been gradually forced by fortune and history, more so than by design, to serve as a world leader among nations.[13] Maritime superiority is a basic element of any nation finding itself separated from its coalition by the two major oceans; it is a basic element of the defensive posture of the United States. According to Admiral Hayward, Chief of Naval Operations, maritime superiority has three chief characteristics:[14]

• The Navy must have the flexibility to maintain maritime supremacy wherever a threat to the vital interests of the United States occurs.

• The Navy must be able to convincingly demonstrate that it has the capability to support its allies.

• The Navy must be able to protect freedom of the seas.

On 20 December 1979, Admiral Hayward testified before the House Subcommittee Seapower and Strategic and Critical Materials. The CNO presented a statement intended to express naval force requirements.[15] Twice during his testimony, sprinkled liberally with reference to going in harm's way, Admiral Hayward advised that analysis and strategy have in the past been confused [inferring] by the Department of Defense.[16] He explained in his discussion of the Soviet naval threat.

THE THREAT

Admiral Hayward explained that during the last ten years the Soviets have built a capability to challenge United States supremacy of the seas.[17] He emphasized that the Soviets are constructing four new cruisers including a 27,000-ton nuclear ship, and already have the largest submarine fleet of any nation in peacetime or immediately preceding any war. There are about 240 Soviet submarines [versus the United States goal of 90 submarines] some of which are capable of speeds of forty knots and able to submerge to depths in the vicinity of 2,000 feet. The Soviet submarine fleet is increasing in size not only with new diesel boats but with an addition of six or eight new nuclear boats each year to sustain a force of 240 to 300 submarines.[18] The Soviets have thirty percent more combatant ships than the United States, the best mine warfare capability, strong and redundant command and control communications, and excellent electronic warfare and counter-electronic warfare capability.[19]

THE STRATEGY

Hayward continued by explaining that the chief strategic objectives of the Navy have remained relatively consistent since WW II:[20]
- Supply allies of the United States [during war].
- Protect United States markets [freedom of the seas].
- Be prepared to fight sequential campaigns rather than to fight simultaneously wherever threatened.
- Destroy the enemy's control of the seas.
- Fight with a smaller number of but superior weapons compared to those used by the enemy. This objective was introduced after WW II.
- Support SALT so as not to use general purpose funds to compensate for increased strategic purchases.

CAPABILITIES

To accomplish these strategic tasks the Navy must have the following capabilities listed by Admiral Hayward:[21]
- Steam wherever and whenever necessary, with adequate combat power, to protect the vital interests of the United States.
- Commit a minimum of 130 submarines to control the under-the-sea battle.
- Deploy tactical naval aviation at sea as a major source of strength.
- Employ a strong antisubmarine capability.
- Be able to rapidly reinforce United States and allied land forces

overseas [ninety percent of reinforcement requires delivery by sea].

However, when evaluating the capabilities of the United States Navy for the period of the '80's, Admiral Hayward candidly made the following appraisal:[22]

- The Navy has only one-half the number of air wings it had fifteen years ago [and inferring that it needs now].
- The Navy has only one-half the number of combatant ships it had ten years ago [and inferring that it needs now].
- The Navy has only 90 of the 130 submarines that it needs to win the under-the-sea battle.
- The Navy now has the absolute minimum number, twelve, of aircraft carrier battlegroups necessary to convincingly project strategic combat power in a manner necessary to protect the vital interests of the United States. This is interpreted to mean that the United States has the minimum number of battlegroups necessary to fight a defensive campaign but not an offensive campaign against the Soviet Union. Here is why that interpretation is made: The Navy lacks, according to Admiral Hayward, the manpower required to appreciably increase the number of ships now on line and may lack the qualified manpower to sustain the present size of the fleet if the loss of experienced noncommissioned officers, seamen, and aviators continues at the 1978-79 rate.[23]

Additionally, the Navy cannot meet the present Indian Ocean commitments without reducing forces in the Mediterranean or the Far East. There are no Indian Ocean bases from which to project a major show of power in that area.[24] If faced with multiple major contingencies, as an example in the Middle East and Korea, the Navy could not support the commitment unless the United States mobilized.[25] Admiral Hayward emphasized that the United States Navy today, without war, is overworked and over deployed. It is short ships, but even worse it is short the men required to man additional ships. It may soon be short an adequate number of personnel to man even the present fleet adequately.[26]

The United States Navy, according to Admiral Hayward, does not have the ships or aircraft necessary to totally protect troop or economic convoys.[27] The Navy must depend on the Naval Reserve to escort convoys, a force largely without modern antisubmarine ships or aircraft or adequate numbers of personnel. Further, the Navy can support the deployment and sustenance of only a single Marine Corps Brigade.[28]

After an examination of the readiness of the United States Navy and a review of Admiral Hayward's testimony, it is my opinion that the United States Navy cannot both defend the Atlantic lifeline to Europe or the Middle East and simultaneously fight an offensive naval war against the Soviet surface fleet while protecting the flanks of NATO and the Middle East oil markets. If we cannot do this as a nation we should prepare for a vastly different lifestyle, reexamine our commitment to national defense and redirect our priorities more toward vital national interests than social pacification, or quickly develop a relatively inexpensive multiplier of combat power—electronic warfare. Though it is cautioned that the best technology will never serve as a substitute for adequate numbers of well-trained military and naval personnel, technology can substitute for shortages of other resources.

IS THE U.S. ARMY PREPARED TO FIGHT THE ELECTRONIC BATTLE?

A single United States Army division fighting on the modern battlefield can have more and better combat intelligence and electronic warfare support than the British Eighth Army and the Afrika Korps had combined at Tobruk in June 1942. A brigade commander in the 82d Airborne Division can see the battlefield more quickly and clearly than Field Marshal Rommel ever saw the battlefield in Africa. Even today, the study of Tobruk, referred to as the battle of Gazala-Bir Hacheim, is an important tactical study because the U.S. Army cannot afford to make the mistakes on the modern battlefield that were made by both the British and Germans at Tobruk.[29]

June 1942 was a bad month for the Allies. The Soviets had lost Sevastopol and Kharkov, the Caucasus oil fields were threatened and the British, though numerically superior to the Germans in Africa by a ratio of 3 to 1, lost Tobruk and almost lost Africa.[30]

The British lost Tobruk though they were advised in detail weeks ahead of time of Rommel's intentions, objectives, capabilities, the date of the attack, and knowing that Rommel had only three courses of action available to him. (He could penetrate, turn the southern flank, or do both.) Tobruk should have been a major disaster for

Rommel, the end of the Afrika Korps, and the end of German-Italian aspirations in Africa. Instead Tobruk most likely prolonged WW II by as much as a year.[31]

The British had very good theater-level intelligence. Recent revelations in the popular literature report that the British were reading Rommel's exceptionally detailed reports to the Italian Headquarters in Africa and the Italian High Command in Rome on a daily basis. Since these reports were encoded in a lesser code, the British were able to use their solution of the lesser codes to read similar messages sent in higher codes to the German signal base in Rome and then on to the High Command of the German Armed Forces (OKW) in Berlin. The British were also intercepting and sinking Axis ships bringing Rommel's replacements and supplies because they were reading German and Italian naval codes.[32]

It is true that the Italians were reading Cairo-based U.S. Army Attache's telegrams to Washington in which he detailed the British plans and capabilities, but the British knew far more about Rommel than Rommel learned from German and Italian military intelligence.[33]

Why, then, did the British lose Tobruk? They had adequate theater-level intelligence, but they did not know how Rommel would fight. They knew Rommel's plans, but they did not know where he was. In short, the British lacked tactical intelligence at the brigade level. They also neglected to disseminate the information they were receiving at their higher headquarters to their division and brigade commanders.[34]

The major error, historians tell us, was that the British did not form a concentrated reserve (using the 1st and 7th Armored Divisions of the XXX Corps) to hit Rommel as soon as his forces appeared and he had selected a particular course of action.[35]

By contrast, Rommel not only knew of British plans and of their numerical superiority in a general way, he also knew—thanks to his signal intelligence company [Fernmelddeaufklarung]—exactly where the British fighting units were deployed. British low-level tactical communications, sent mostly in plaintext, provided the location, strengths, deployment, and readiness of their units. Rommel probably knew there was no concentrated reserve poised to strike his numerically inferior force, and while he, himself, lacked the forces to provide his own reserve, he managed to win the battle by first luring the British into an ambush by enveloping tactics (that aspect of the battle referred to as the "iron cauldron") and turning the British southern flank. The British responded to Rommel's moves by feeding 200 of their 500 to 600 tanks piecemeal into the mouths of Rommel's dug-in 88mm antiaircraft guns used in this battle as antitank guns. The British tried to fight an active defense without good combat intelligence. They lost. The Germans won, resupplied themselves from the stores captured at Tobruk, and came close to pushing the British out of Africa. If Rommel had had the capability to jam the British tactical communication systems during that battle, the consequences could have been expected to be even more terrible during the British withdrawal.[36]

The British learned fast, and we are indebted to them because their help evolved into our present day Communications-Electronics Operations Instructions (CEOI). These field instructions require the random selection of callsigns and frequencies and other essential electronic security procedures. Those lessons are also responsible for the United States Army using signal security units to monitor our own radio traffic during training and combat to preclude providing an enemy with free targets.[37]

Almost 30 years after Tobruk, the Israelis suffered severe casualties in the Sinai Peninsula during the 1973 Mid-East War because they either had forgotten or had never learned the lessons of Tobruk. At first, it was thought that the exceptional accuracy of the Egyptians' artillery against Israeli command posts was because of their very accurate radio direction-finding equipment. That was hard to believe considering the physical behavior of VHF radio waves. The reason became clear when it was discovered that the Iraelis had lost a truck-load of maps that had grids overprinted on them to their enemy. The Israelis used those grids as a low-level field code. When this error was combined with an abundance of radio chatter, the explanation became clear. Radio DF is not a target acquisition device unless radio operators provide free targets by sloppy procedures.[38] Just as importantly, the Israelis encountered extensive jamming of their ground and air force communication and radar systems. A black cloud of electronic interference did not descend on the battlefield and prevent communication, but jamming did cause significant interruption with command, control, and weapon systems.

Though the Israelis were unprepared, the Soviet-designed electronic warfare effort was fortunately crude. A better orchestrated electronic warfare plan by the Arab armies could have cost the Israelis a heavy price, perhaps the war. Both sides, especially the Israelis, learned well from the mistakes of all.

Prior to the 1973 Mid-East War, the Army tactical intelligence system was comprised of the United States Army Security Agency (referred to as the ASA) and units from other military intelligence commands. ASA units responded directly to that agency. Some intelligence units responded to the Army Chief of Staff for Intelligence, and a few intelligence units were assigned to divisions and corps. A division commander frequently had several military intelligence units assigned. Operational control was retained by the parent intelligence command often located a thousand miles or more away. The result was a lack of centralized control, a lack of coordinated intelligence product, duplication and needless competition between overworked intelligence units.[39]

To the dismay of many tactical commanders, they were tasked to provide logistic and administrative support to intelligence units, but were unable to establish inspection standards or to evaluate intelligence product. Intelligence units were known to take the path of least resistance and complied with administrative and maintenance standards of their own choosing.[40]

Intelligence functions were often needlessly compartmented, sequestered, and not integrated into a usable all-source product needed by brigades and divisions. Intelligence was frequently so well-protected that those who needed access did not know where to find it. In short, military intelligence, especially the United States Army Security Agency, was perceived as an army within an army. The situation was further complicated because military intelligence did not become a branch of the Army until 1964. It previously had been a corps of the Reserve forces. The Army did not have a foundation of noncommissioned and commissioned intelligence officers who had gained experience in military intelligence platoons, companies, and battalions. This process is essential to the development of individuals for positions of executive responsibility for doctrine, training, and concept development. However, the process only began with the officer classes of 1960.[41]

Management of resources during and immediately after the Vietnam War caused military intelligence units to be left understrength and with antiquated equipment. Most dollars which were available were being spent for strategic intelligence equipment. Giant strides were made in electronic technology during the 1960s and early 1970s. Tactical intelligence units, however, were left with 1950 technology equipment.[42]

A U.S. Army analysis of the 1973 Mid-East war indicated that a revival of military intelligence and electronic warfare was desperately needed. Inspection and audit reports during 1973 and 1974 confirmed deficiencies in equipment and in combat, material, and training development. There was an absence of standard procedures and a demonstrated need to reorganize Army intelligence. There was also a need to design equipment to confront the threat. Technology, simply for the sake of modernization, was counterproductive. Research and development rather than tactics had been driving equipment design for too long.[43]

In late 1974, the Army chief of staff directed a study to consider ways to improve Army intelligence organizations and operations. This was the Intelligence Organization and Stationing Study referred to by its acronym as IOSS. The IOSS group was tasked to provide a road map for the integration of all military intelligence and the electronic warfare functions and units of the Army Security Agency. Their recommendations served as the implementing decision for the augmentation of electronic warfare and intelligence units to combat forces—battalions at division and groups at corps.[44]

IOSS came at a time when many middle-level and junior officers were discouraged with military intelligence. For some, IOSS presented the first opportunity to contribute to U.S. Army tactical military intelligence.[45]

IOSS was not welcomed with open arms by the entire intelligence community. There were many within the military intelligence branch who seriously objected to the concept. They also objected to changes in the existing structure and to the way the very term used to describe the new Combat Electronic Warfare and Intelligence units—CEWI—sounded. The blend of soft consonants and vowels provides a sound which sounds more like a shoe polish than a military unit. The term is not crisp and sharp like "Ranger!" or "Airborne!" It was observed that any unit referred to as a CEWI battalion would be forced to make a strong and vigorous effort for acceptance in a tactical unit.

That was good. The goal should be to ram electronic warfare and intelligence into the battle plan and not to expect the commander to ask for it.[46]

For that reason alone, the CEWI title was appropriate, but there are better reasons. The fact is that these units are not military intelligence battalions. These units are combat electronic warfare *and* intelligence battalions and so designated by their military table of organization and equipment with the numerical preface of 34. They are not type 30 or 32 military intelligence units. The Army's military heraldry office opposes the term CEWI because it lacks lineage. Many others prefer the title Military Intelligence battalion because it designates alignment with a branch as do Infantry Battalions. True, these units cannot trace their lineage to the War of 1812. But, if there is ever a modern battlefield, a next major war, there will be no doubt as to who or what a CEWI—pronounced 'see wee'—unit is. We are preparing for that war, not for the War of 1812.[47]

Why is CEWI better?[48]

- CEWI is a more cost-effective use of personnel and equipment than its predecessor.
- All intelligence personnel live and work together in the same battalion—they routinely talk to one another and exchange ideas.
- The intelligence unit is supported by the division to which it is assigned. It trains with the division with which it will fight in combat.
- Individual soldier skills, equipment maintenance and field training have improved at least 20 percent—CEWI units are manned by soldiers rather than technicians. They can provide intelligence and electronic warfare and still survive on the battlefield.
- The CEWI battalion communication system supports the entire divisional area and can be further tailored to make certain that intelligence is delivered directly to commanders who need it.
- CEWI places all intelligence and electronic warfare troops in a battalion with their own commander; they don't work for a staff officer.
- Because CEWI units train with divisions with which they will fight, an increasing number of commanders and staff at every level learn how to integrate both intelligence and electronic warfare with the battle plan.
- CEWI provides brigade and division commanders far more responsive and more thorough battlefield information and intelligence

and electronic warfare than before. CEWI does this chiefly by consolidating all intelligence from all sources directly to the combat force which requires knowledge, and they do it well.

The CEWI concept certainly has its detractors. There are three chief criticisms of CEWI. First, it is argued that the previous vertical command structure provided direct control by the intelligence infrastructure and hence better intelligence. That argument presumes that direction of battlefield intelligence can be performed more effectively at echelons beyond the battlefield. This contradicts the overriding theme of Field Manual 100-5, the Army's operational bible: The commander operates his battlefield and everything on it or above it.[49]

The second argument is an apologia which presumes that soldiers with intelligence skills should be technicians first and soldiers second, and then only if soldiering does not seriously interfere with technical duties. It is argued that CEWI places too much emphasis on soldier skills. Technicians won't survive the lethality of the modern battlefield; only well-trained soldiers will return and all those soldiers will be technicians to some degree.[50]

The third criticism directed at CEWI is that it does not go far enough in separating tactical intelligence from its affiliation with strategic intelligence. These critics would prefer a system which returns ground surveillance radars to infantry battalions and which places radio and radar direction-finding equipment with target acquisition units. They want immediate targeting data provided directly to firing elements without the delay incurred by intelligence analysis or processing of the information.[51]

This recommendation is little more than a mirror image of the cumbersome system used by a numerically superior but technologically inept enemy. It is a system which uses mass and barrage fires as a substitute for command and control. The U.S. Army will have neither the ammunition nor the transportation to support a targeting concept so wasteful of limited ammunition. In fact, one of the most important reasons the U.S. Army considers that electronic warfare is an element of combat power is to recognize that jamming can relieve artillery of some of its burden to neutralize enemy command and control.[52] But to do this will require an ability to filter thousands of emitter signals, both enemy and friendly, to determine when to best listen, when to jam, when to fire, and when to do nothing. The information overload will be overwhelming if we do not effectively filter from among the mass of signals those which are vital to winning the battle and take the best action.

The purpose of electronic warfare and especially jamming in the United States Army is to confuse or delay the enemy. It is mutually supportive of communication intelligence. Electronic warfare tactics advocate the surgical application of spot jamming rather than barrage jamming. Jamming is considered a weapon system for selective use. It can be a highly effective combat multiplier. By turning on a noise jammer for a long time to prevent communication by an enemy, we endanger the jammer by increasing its vulnerability to direction finding and subsequent suppressive fires. U.S. Army jamming is like an electronic piranha, short and vicious; it attacks the guts of the message. It is the electronic key that can unlock communications security.[53]

In contrast, Soviet forces and some of our allies attempt to prevent communications by overwhelming barrage jamming. This can be overcome by good protective techniques, by good radio operators. Jammers in these armies are assigned to signal or electronic warfare units and are separate and distinct from military intelligence units. The purpose of barrage jamming is to make the electronic spectrum so dirty that a numerically inferior force—The United States Army—is unable to coordinate technologically superior weapons and command and control systems. The enemy does this by using large numbers of cheap, rugged, high power (1500 to 3000 watts) jammers. When barrage jamming is combined and coordinated with direction finding and massive suppressive fires against friendly command and communication centers, the effect can be devastating. The enemy calls this radioelectronic combat or REC. Unless the U.S. Army trains to fight on a dirty electronic battlefield, it can lose to REC.[54]

In March of 1977, the United States Army conducted the largest electronic warfare exercise in peace or war. The Army's 1st Cavalry Division played the role of the aggressor reinforced with the electronic warfare assets normally assigned to an entire corps of four divisions. The 2d Armored Division with its new CEWI Battalion trained to fight on an intensive EW battlefield.[55] The conclusions were startling:[56]

- Jamming increased and improved signals intelligence because most operators were not trained to recognize jamming and usually

turned-off their speech security equipment in which case jamming was stopped. The obvious but wrong conclusion by radio operators was that speech security equipment hampered their communication.
- Jamming seriously disrupted artillery fires by disrupting the control of those fires.
- Jamming equipment needs to be rugged, protected from the lethality of the battlefield, and of comparable mobility to the force it supports. The U.S. Army is now putting much of its divisional EW equipment in tracked vehicles and using antennas that go up quickly.
- If jamming is to be cost effective a lot of different types of equipment should be consolidated in a single vehicle—a CEWI fighting vehicle. This equipment will deploy well forward.
- CEWI units can be effective on the battlefield when manned with soldiers, noncommissioned officers, and officers like any other combat or combat support battalion; it cannot be effective if technical control is considered more important than operational control. This means that CEWI units should be commanded by commanders not staff officers.

This analysis of the Army's ability to fight on an electronic battlefield is not intended to compare the electronic warfare posture of the Army to the Navy. I leave to the sea service the challenge of determining the adequacy of the Navy's electronic warfare capability and similarly to the Air Force responsibility to judge its electronic warfare capability; I do this knowing that ultimately we must depend on a joint Army-Navy-Air Force electronic warfare capability if the United States armed forces are to win a next war. We lack the resources to do otherwise.

Throughout this analysis it has been difficult to carry a thread between army and naval operations, from WW II to the present, to derive conclusions which are meaningful to either. This technique was necessary because of the unorthodox subject material and the need to use points of reference that were understandable.

I can report that the Army as an institution is now seriously preparing to fight the electronic battle, but it is not yet ready to do this well. For its part the Army is putting "its money where its mouth is." It is sacrificing tank battalions for CEWI battalions in the overall cost of things. It is sacrificing badly needed equipment purchases in other areas to purchase the very best electronic warfare equipment as soon as feasible. But I must also report that the Army is not moving forward in this area as far as we must or as fast as we should. This results not from a lack of motivation or intent, rather it is a question of resources. Of one thing I am certain, the U.S. Army is contributing to CEWI a fair share of resources but it actively competes with the National Security Agency as well as the general purpose forces for badly needed dollars and quality personnel. While the Army struggles against uneven odds to keep an all-volunteer Army afloat, it is judged by sophomoric reports and prophets of failure to be losing ground in the reformation of electronic warfare and intelligence. While the evidence is mostly correct—the Army is indeed in very bad shape—it is the entire Army and not only CEWI. If they were implemented, the recommendations typically provided by the sophomorists would not solve the problem. The Army does not need to divert more soldiers and dollars to strategic intelligence; it needs the resources to implement the billion dollar CEWI program and the quality of soldiers required to run sophisticated equipment as well as meaningful programs to retain those soldiers. Some within the Department of Defense now question whether the U.S. Army can afford both CEWI and strategic intelligence. One thing is certain, a commander may or may not win with CEWI, but he will surely lose without it.

The United States Army also needs a substantive electronic warfare concept for its current equipment; instead we are wasting our best talent on designing concepts for the future that few will ever see at the expense of building a solid training and tactics base for today's CEWI.

The United States Army can fight on the electronic battlefield and it can win in this electronic battle, given the resources. Those resources are available once it is grasped that control of the electromagnetic spectrum will be more important in a Third World War than listening to that spectrum as we did during WW II.

AN ELECTRONIC WARFARE POLICY RECOMMENDATION

The following electronic warfare policy for the United States is recommended:

• To win on the modern battlefield, electronic warfare—defined to include all actions conducted in the entire electro-magnetic spectrum to intercept, analyze, manipulate, or suppress enemy use of the spectrum as well as to protect friendly use of the spectrum from similar attack by an enemy—to be considered an element of the combat power of the United States armed forces.

- An Under-Secretary of Defense for Electronic Warfare to be appointed to insure coordination of electronic warfare with science and technology and to coordinate readiness, combat and training development, electronic intelligence, and related matters among the services and within the Department of Defense.
- The National Security Agency to be redesignated the Defense Electronic Warfare Agency to be assigned the mission of integrating signals intelligence with and subordinate to electronic warfare in all its facets so that at every echelon commanders will establish procedures and directives specifying whether to listen to, manipulate, or suppress enemy electronic systems in a manner determined by their impact on the battle.
- Signals intelligence to support electronic combat at the direction of the battle commander.

This policy's intention—that the United States have an electronic warfare capability absolutely superior to any other nation.

NOTES

Chapter I

1. Don E. Gordon, Army CEWI Battalions, "Journal of Electronic Defense, Vol. 3, No. 1, Jan-Feb, 1980, p. 40.
2. Ibid.
3. Wilhelm F. Flicke, *War Secrets in the Ether*, United States Army Training and Doctrine Command, 1977, single volume reprinted from three original volumes first printed by the United States National Security Agency, 1953, same title, declassified 1977, *passim; Historical Background of the Signal Security Agency*, United States Army Security Agency, 1946, declassified by United States National Security Agency, 1977, SRH-001, p. 296, hereafter known as *SRH-001;* and R. A. Haldane, *The Hidden War*, St. Martin's Press, 1978, p. 69.
4. Gordon, p. 40.
5. "Soviet Missile Coding May Have Prevented Monitoring by U.S.," Associated Press, 15 February 1980.
6. "Science Worldwide," *Popular Mechanics*, March 1980, p. 87.
7. Haldane, p. 18 and Jozef Garlinski, *Intercept*, Dent, London, 1979, p. xx.
8. Anthony Cave Brown, *Bodyguard of Lies*, Bantam, 1976, pp. 418-22; F. W. Winterbotham, *The Ultra Secret*, Harper and Row, 1974, pp. 111-17; Ronald Lewin, *Ultra Goes to War*, McGraw Hill, 1978, pp. 285-86.
9. Don E. Gordon, "The CEWI Battalion, A Tactical Concept That Works," *Military Review*, Jan, 1980, p. 3.
10. Ralph Bennett, *Ultra in the West*, Hutchinson, 1979, *passim.*
11. David Kahn, "Cryptology Goes Public," *Foreign Affairs*, Fall, 1979, p. 141.
12. Patrick Beesly, *Very Special Intelligence*, Doubleday, 1978; Jozef Garlinski, *Intercept*, Dent, London, 1979; R. V. Jones, *The Wizard War*, Coward, McCann, Geoghegan, 1978; David Kahn, *The Code Breakers*, MacMillan, 1967; Ronald Lewin, *Ultra Goes to War*, McGraw Hill, 1978; F. W. Winterbotham, *The Ultra Secret*, Harper and Row, 1974.

Chapter II

1. Don E. Gordon, personal notes of conversation with Patrick Beesly, author of *Very Special Intelligence*, Doubleday, 1978, on 18 March 1980, Lymington, England. Hereafter referred to as Gordon notes on Beesly.
2. C. D. Bekker, *Defeat at Sea*, Ballantine, 1955. pp. 6-7; Patrick Beesly, *Very Special Intelligence*, Doubleday, 1978, *passim;* Gordon notes on Beesly (Germans design U-boats in Holland).
3. Beesly, p. 25, and Bekker, p. 8.
4. Beesly, p. 11n.
5. Beesly, p. 25 and Bekker, p. 8.
6. *Encyclopedia Americana*, Vol. 25, pp. 780-81.

7. Winston S. Churchill, *The Second World War*, Houghton Mifflin, 1948, Vol. II, p. xxx.
8. Ibid., p. 601.
9. S. W. Roskill, *The War at Sea, 1939-1945*, HMSO, 1954, Vol. I, p. 11.
10. Samuel Eliot Morison, *The Battle of the Atlantic, September 1939-May 1945*, Atlantic, Little, Brown, 1947, Vol. I, pp. 312, 315.
11. Churchill, Vol. II, pp. 602, 607, and S. W. Roskill, Vol. I, p. 97.
12. Churchill, Vol. II, pp. 602-3.
13. Roskill, Vol. II, p. 217.
14. Ibid., Vol. I, pp. 1-12.
15. Ibid., Vol. III/II, p. 370.
16. Beesly, pp. 25, 35; William L. Shirer, *The Rise and Fall of the Third Reich*, Simon and Schuster, 1960, 3d Ed., p. 487; and Albert Speer, *Inside the Third Reich*, Memoirs, MacMillan, 1970, 4th Ed., p. 166.
17. Speer, p. 166.
18. Ibid.
19. Shirer, pp. 486-87; Roskill, Vol. II, p. 94; and *Allied Naval Communications Intelligence and the Battle of the Atlantic*, United States National Security Agency, 1945, declassified 1977, from United States Navy OP-G-20, SRH-009, pp. 9-10. Hereafter known as *SRH-009*.
20. Ibid.
21. Shirer, p. 622, and Erich Raeder, "Fuehrer Conference on Matters Dealing with the German Navy, 1939," *Reflections on the Outbreak of War, 3 September 1939*, personal paper, 1946.
22. Roskill, Vol. I, Appendix G.
23. Morison, Vol. I, p. 4, and Roskill, Vol. I, p. 22.
24. Bekker, pp. 9-10.
25. Roskill, Vol. I, p. 25.
26. *SRH-009*, p. 10.
27. Churchill, Vol. II, p. 598.
28. *SRH-009*, p. 10.
29. Beesly, p. 27, and Gordon notes on Beesly.
30. Morison, Vol. I, pp. 131, 205, and 303.
31. Roskill, Vol. III/II, p. 354 and *Proceedings of the International Military Tribunal Sitting at Nuremberg*, "The Trial of German Major War Criminals," Part 14, HMSO, 1947, pp. 162, 210.
32. Beesly, p. 123.

Chapter III

1. Patrick Beesly, *Very Special Intelligence*, Doubleday, 1978, pp. 1-2.
2. Ibid., pp. 3-5.
3. Ibid.
4. Ibid.

5. Ibid.
6. Ibid.
7. Ibid., p. 7.
8. Ibid.
9. Ibid.
10. Ibid., p. 10.
11. Don E. Gordon, personal notes of conversation with Patrick Beesly, author of *Very Special Intelligence,* cited above, on 18 March 1980, Lymington, England. Hereafter referred to as Gordon notes on Beesly.
12. Beesly, p. 9.
13. S. W. Roskill, *The War at Sea, 1939-1945*, HMSO, 1954, Vol. I, p. 17.
14. Beesly, p. 10.
15. Ibid., p. 14.
16. Ibid., p. 15.
17. Ibid., p. 46.
18. Jozef Garlinski, *Intercept,* Dent, London, 1979, p. 18.
19. Ibid., pp. 14-15.
20. Beesly, pp. 63-75; Garlinski, Appendix, pp. 192-204; F. W. Hinsley, *British Intelligence in the Second World War,* HMSO, 1979, pp. 487-99; Ronald Lewin, *Ultra Goes to War,* McGraw Hill, 1976, pp. 25-50.
21. Lewin, p. 25.
22. Ibid., pp. 26-27, 29, and 33; Beesly, p. 64; Hinsley, p. 487; and Garlinski, pp. 10, 14.
23. Garlinski, p. 10.
24. Ibid., p. 18.
25. Ibid., pp. 18-19.
26. Ibid., pp. 2-3, 19.
27. Ibid., pp. 14-16.
28. Ibid., pp. 16, 26n (10).
29. Ibid., pp. 12, 16.
30. Ibid., p. 32.
31. Ibid., pp. 32-35.
32. Ibid., p. 35.
33. Ibid., pp. 35-37.
34. Ibid., p. 44.
35. Lewin, pp. 39, 41 and Hinsley, pp. 488, 494.
36. Garlinski, *passim.*
37. Garlinski, pp. 42-45; Lewin, pp. 36-37, 40-41, 44-45; Hinsley, pp. 488-90, 494; Beesly, p. 65; and Winterbotham, p. 10.
38. Garlinski, pp. 1-2 and R. A. Haldane, *The Hidden War,* St. Martin's Press, 1978, p. 27. Supplemental reference: Peter Gretton, *Crisis Convoy,* Peter Davies, London, 1974, p. 171.
39. Hinsley, Appendix G, pp. 487-95.
40. Lewin, pp. 30-33.

41. Garlinski, pp. 31, 32.
42. Lewin, pp. 30-33.
43. Ibid.
44. Ibid.
45. Lewin, p. 33; Beesly, p. 184; and Hinsley, p. 487.
46. Garlinski, p. 23.
47. Lewin, pp. 30-33.
48. Ibid.
49. Beesly, p. 68.
50. Garlinski, p. 33.
51. Beesly, p. 74; Lewin, pp. 30-33; and Hinsley, p. 494.
52. Garlinski, p. 28.
53. Ibid., p. 75.
54. Beesly, p. 68.
55. Lewin, p. 58.
56. Beesly, p. 66.
57. Ibid., p. 65.
58. Ibid., p. 66n.
59. Garlinski, pp. 1-2; Gretton, p. 171; and Haldane, p. 27.
60. Beesly, p. 73.
61. Beesly, p. 74. Note: Beesly, p. 69n reports that the Soviets raised U-250 on 30 July 1944 after it sank in the Gulf of Finland and recovered an Enigma machine. The disposition of the keylist is unknown.
62. Ibid., p. 74.
63. Don E. Gordon, personal notes on lecture by Ronald Lewin at Smithsonian Institute, Washington, D.C., 1 November 1979, subject: *Ultra*. Hereafter referred to as Gordon notes on Lewin.
64. *German Naval Communications Intelligence*, United States National Security Agency, 1945, declassified 1978, *SRH-024*, p. 13. Hereafter referred to as *SRH-024*. *Allied Naval Communications Intelligence and the Battle of the Atlantic*, United States National Security Agency, 1945, declassified 1977, *SRH-009*, Vol. I, pp. 9-10. Hereafter known as *SRH-009*.
65. *SRH-024*, passim.
66. Ibid., pp. 15-16.
67. Beesly, p. 240.
68. *SRH-009*, pp. 27-28.
69. Beesly, *passim*.
70. R. V. Jones, *The Wizard War*, Coward, McCann Geoghegan, 1978, p. 530.
71. *SRH-024*, p. 3.
72. Ibid.
73. Ibid., pp. 5, 9, 21, and 22.
74. Ibid., p. 9.
75. Ibid.
76. Ibid., pp. 90, 97, and 99.

77. *SRH-009*, pp. 89-91.
78. Ibid., p. 34.
79. Ibid., p. 87.
80. *SRH-024*, pp. 24-40.
81. *SRH-009*, p. 87.
82. *Battle of the Atlantic*, United States National Security Agency, 1945, declassified 1978, *SRH-008*, p. 29. Hereafter referred to as *SRH-008*.
83. *SRH-009*, p. 85.
84. Ibid.
85. Ibid., pp. 83-91.
86. Ibid., pp. 80, 82.
87. Bauer, *Das Unterseeboot*, Mittler and Son, Berlin, translated by United States Navy, cited in *SRH-009*, pp. 80-81.
88. Samuel Eliot Morison, *The Battle of the Atlantic, September 1939-May 1943*, Atlantic, Little, Brown, 1948, Vol. I, p. 102.
89. Haldane, pp. 42-43.
90. Haldane, pp. 42-43 and Garlinski, p. 51.

Chapter IV

1. S. W. Roskill, *The War at Sea, 1939-1945*, Her Majesty's Stationery Office, Vols. I, II, III/I and III/II, Vol. III/II, p. 472, Appendix Y. The model designation H2S, also the formula of hydrogen sulfide, a stink bomb, was selected as the code name because when the microwave radar was initially demonstrated as a device to map terrain from the air, the Scientific Advisor to Churchill, a man of little encouragement, is reported to have said, "it stinks." Hence the malapropism—H2S. Reported by R. V. Jones, *The Wizard War*, Coward, McCann, Geoghegan, 1978, p. 318. The United States model of the same basic radar design was called the SCR-517 as reported by Samuel Eliot Morison, *The Battle of the Atlantic, September 1939-May 1943*, Atlantic, Little, & Brown, 1948, p. 247n.
2. *Encyclopedia Americana*, Vol. 23, p. 115t.
3. C. D. Bekker, *Defeat at Sea*, Ballantine, 1955, pp. 87-88.
4. Jones, p. 75.
5. Ibid., p. 76.
6. *Americana*, Vol. 23, p. 115u.
7. Bekker, p. 87.
8. Ibid., p. 77.
9. *Americana*, Vol. 23, p. 115u (1).
10. Bekker, pp. 87-88.
11. Bekker, p. 85 and *Americana*, Vol. 4, p. 421.
12. *Allied Communications Intelligence and the Battle of the Atlantic*, United States National Security Agency, 1945, declassified 1977, *SRH-009*, p. 67, hereafter known as *SRH-009*.
13. *Americana*, Vol. 23, p. 115s-t and Jones, pp. 16, 17 and 35.
14. *Americana*, Vol. 23, p. 115n.

15. Roskill, Vol. III/II, p. 370; Vol. II, p. 205, Patrick Beesly, *Very Special Intelligence*, Doubleday, 1978, p. 152; Jones, p. 322; and Bekker, p. 152.

16. *Americana*, Vol. 23, p. 115t.

17. Roskill, Vol. III/II, p. 352.

18. Ibid., p. 348.

19. Jones, p. 303.

20. Jones, p. 303; Roskill, Vol. II, p. 205; and Vol. III/II, p. 370.

21. Jones, pp. 319-20.

22. Ibid., p. 502.

23. Ibid., pp. 319-20.

24. Ibid., p. 321.

25. Jones, pp. 319-20 and Bekker, p. 82.

26. *Allied Naval Communication Intelligence: Technical Intelligence From Allied Communication Intelligence*, United States National Security Agency, 1945, declassified 1978, *SRH-025*, p. 13; hereafter known as *SRH-025*. *SRH-009*, p. 65.

27. Jones, p. 321.

28. Patrick Beesly, *Very Special Intelligence*, Doubleday, 1978; Ronald Lewin, *Ultra Goes to War*, McGraw Hill, 1978; F. W. Winterbotham, *The Ultra Secret*, Harper and Row, 1974; R. V. Jones, *The Wizard War*, Coward, McCann & Geoghegan, 1978; and F. H. Hinsley, *British Intelligence in the Second World War*, Her Majesty's Stationery Office, 1979.

29. Bekker, p. 84 and Beesly, p. 255.

30. *SRH-025*, p. 31; Beesly, p. 190; and Bekker, pp. 80-81.

31. *SRH-025*, p. 58.

32. Alfred Price, "That Damned Light," *Journal of Electronic Defense*, Vol. 3, No. 1, p. 19; Bekker, pp. 76-77; and *SRH-025*, p. 5.

33. Bekker, pp. 78-79 and Roskill, Vol. II, p. 205.

34. Roskill, Vol. II, p. 369; Bekker, pp. 78-79; and *SRH-025*.

35. Roskill, Vol. II, p. 369.

36. Ibid.

37. Roskill, Vol. II, p. 467, Appendix J; *SRH-025*, p. 7; and Bekker, p. 80.

38. Bekker, pp. 85-86 and Jones, pp. 319-21, 392.

39. *German Naval Communication Intelligence*, United States National Security Agency, 1945, declassified 1978, *SRH-024*, Vol. III, p. 33. Hereafter known as *SRH-024*.

40. Bekker, p. 40.

41. Morison, Vol. I, p. 22.

Chapter V

1. William L. Shirer, *The Rise and Fall of the Third Reich*, Simon and Schuster, 1960, 3d. Ed., p. 487.

2. Patrick Beesly, *Very Special Intelligence*, Doubleday, 1978, p. 32 and S. W. Roskill, *The War at Sea, 1939-1945*, HMSO, London, 1954, Vols. I, II, III/I, and

III/II, Vols. I and III, Appendix G. Note: German pocket battleships are referred to as cruisers in this manuscript.

3. Beesly, pp. 30-32.

4. Beesly, pp. 32 and 96; Roskill, Vol. I, p. 118; and R. A. Haldane, *The Hidden War*, St. Martin's Press, 1978, p. 36.

5. Beesly, pp. 49-50; Roskill, Vol. I, pp. 287-92; and C. D. Bekker, *Defeat at Sea*, Ballantine, 1955, p. 22.

6. Beesly, pp. 39-40 and Roskill, Vol. I, pp. 156-63.

7. Ibid. and Don E. Gordon, personal notes of conversation with Patrick Beesly, author of *Very Special Intelligence*, cited, on 18 March 1980, Lymington, England. Hereafter referred to as Gordon notes on Beesly.

8. Only the cruisers *Scheer* and *Prinz Eugen* along with two light cruisers would not be deployed. The battleships *Bismarck* and *Tirpitz* had not yet been commissioned.

9. Beesly, pp. 39-40 and Roskill, Vol. I, pp. 156-63.

10. Roskill, Vol. I, pp. 158-67 and *The West Point Atlas of American Wars*, Praeger, 1959, Vol. II, Map 11.

11. Winston S. Churchill, *The Second World War*, Houghton, Mifflin Co., 1949, Vol. II, p. 161.

12. Patrick Beesly, *Very Special Admiral*, Typescript, to be published by Hammish Hamilton, June 1980.

13. Beesly, *Very Special Intelligence*, pp. 31, 38-40.

14. Ibid., p. 45.

15. Roskill, Vol. I, pp. 156-57 and Churchill, Vol. II, p. 589.

16. Roskill, Vol. I, pp. 156-57 and Churchill, Vol. II, p. 592.

17. *The West Point Atlas of American Wars*, Vol. II, Map 11.

18. Roskill, Vol. I, pp. 156-67 and Beesly, pp. 44 and 51.

19. Beesly, pp. 44, 81 and Bekker, p. 24.

20. Roskill, Vol. I, p. 415.

21. Beesly, p. 45.

22. Beesly, p. 28 and Roskill, Vol. I, p. 395.

23. Beesly, p. 28.

24. Roskill, Vol. I, p. 395 and Beesly, p. 78.

25. Beesly, pp. 78-79.

26. Ibid., pp. 79-80.

27. Ibid., pp. 80-81.

28. Beesly, pp. 80-81; Roskill, Vol. I, p. 404; and Ernle Bradford, *The Mighty Hood*, Hodder and Stoughton, London, 1959, p. 165.

29. Roskill, Vol. I, p. 404; Beesly, pp. 81-82; F. H. Hinsley, et al., *British Intelligence in the Second World War*, HMSO, London, 1979, Vol. I, p. 342; and Bradford, pp. 147, 164-65, 174-75.

30. Roskill, Vol. I, p. 407; Beesly, p. 81; and Hinsley, p. 342.

31. Beesly, p. 82 and Roskill, Vol. I, p. 409.

32. Bradford, pp. 167-69 reports that the German radar on *Prinz Eugen* did not detect *Suffolk* at 14,000 yards (7.7 miles) at 0722 hours, 23 May but did detect *Norfolk* later at 6,000 yards (3.4 miles) at 0830 hours, 23 May in the Denmark Strait.

33. Hinsley, pp. 342-43.
34. Beesly, pp. 56 and 83-84. Note Gnomonic charts follow the Great Circle lines of the earth rather than the Mercator projection lines of the earth.
35. Beesly, p. 83.
36. Beesly, pp. 84-85 and Hinsley, p. 343.
37. Beesly, p. 84.
38. Beesly, p. 85; Roskill, Vol. I, pp. 410-11; and Hinsley, p. 344.
39. Beesly, p. 85.
40. Roskill, Vol. I, pp. 410-11 and Beesly, p. 85.
41. Roskill, Vol. I, pp. 410-11.
42. Beesly, p. 84.
43. Ibid., p. 86.
44. Ibid.
45. Beesly, p. 86; Roskill, Vol. I, pp. 411-12; and Hinsley, p. 343.
46. Beesly, p. 86.
47. Samuel Eliot Morison, *The Battle of the Atlantic, September 1939-May 1945*, Atlantic, Little, Brown, Vol. I, p. 128.
48. Beesly, p. 87.
49. Ibid.
50. Ibid.
51. Beesly, p. 88 and Hinsley, pp. 344-45.
52. Beesly, p. 89.
53. Roskill, Vol. I, pp. 410-13 and Bradford, p. 194.
54. Beesly, p. 90.
55. Roskill, Vol. I, p. 410 and Hinsley, p. 343.
56. Roskill, Vol. I, p. 418 and Bekker, p. 60.
57. Bekker, p. 46.
58. Roskill, Vol. III/II, p. 289 and Bradford, p. 68.
59. Roskill, Vol. II, p. 333.

Chapter VI

1. S. W. Roskill, *The War at Sea, 1939-1945*, Her Majesty's Stationery Office, 1954, Vols. I, II, III/I and III/II, Vol. II, pp. 130, 134, 475 (Appendix K), 485 (Appendix O), Vol. III/II, p. 615.
2. Samuel Eliot Morison, *History of U.S. Naval Operations in WW II, Sep 1939-May 1943*, Atlantic, Little, Brown, 1947, Vol. I, pp. 358-60; Patrick Beesly, *Very Special Intelligence*, Doubleday, 1978, p. 136; and Roskill, Vol. II, pp. 278-79.
3. C. D. Bekker, *Defeat at Sea*, Ballantine, 1955, p. 56 and Beesly, p. 45.
4. Roskill, Vol. II, p. 136 and Morison, Vol. I, pp. 180-81.
5. E. G. Schumacher, "Letter to the Editor," *Washington Star*, 17 October 1979 and Roskill, Vol. II, p. 367.
6. Morison, Vol. I, p. 179 and Beesly, p. 138.

7. Morison, Vol. I, p. 17.
8. Francis L. Loewenheim, Harold D. Langley, and Manfred Jonas, Eds., *Roosevelt and Churchill, Their Secret Wartime Correspondence,* Saturday Review Press-Dutton, 1975, pp. 256-57; Walter Kerr, *The Secret of Stalingrad,* Doubleday, 1978, pp. 194-95; and Beesly, p. 131.
9. Morison, Vol. I, p. 159.
10. Beesly, p. 137.
11. Morison, Vol. I, p. 179 and Beesly, pp. 130-47.
12. Roskill, Vol. II, p. 135 and Morison, Vol. I, p. 185.
13. Beesly, p. 138; Morison, Vol. I, p. 179 and Roskill, Vol. II, p. 288.
14. Beesly, p. 137.
15. Ibid., p. 139.
16. Morison, Vol. I, p. 191.
17. Roskill, Vol. II, p. 143.
18. Beesly, pp. 137-38.
19. Ibid., pp. 138-39.
20. Ibid., pp. 141-42.
21. Ibid., pp. 142-47.
22. Ibid., pp. 142, 145.
23. Roskill, Vol. II, p. 138 and Beesly, p. 142.
24. Beesly, pp. 144-45.
25. Roskill, Vol. II, p. 145, Vol. I, p. 17 and Beesly, p. 144.
26. Beesly, p. 145.
27. Ibid., pp. 145-46.
28. Ibid., pp. 140-45.
29. Ibid.
30. Roskill, Vol. II, p. 139.
31. Kerr, p. 81.
32. Beesly, p. 141 and Roskill, Vol. II, pp. 140-41.
33. Beesly, pp. 130-47 and Morison, Vol. I, pp. 179-92.
34. Roskill, Vol. II, p. 144.
35. Roskill, Vol. I, p. 279. Note: The United States Navy also used the term Q-boat or Q-Ship to refer to heavily armed merchant ships disguised to decoy U-boats. Three were used by the United States Navy during WW II. The German raiders were identified as: *Atlantis, Orior, Widder, Thor, Pinguin, Komet, Kormoran, Togo,* and *Michel.*
36. Winston S. Churchill, *The Second World War,* Houghton, Mifflin Company, 1949, Vol. II, p. 595 and C. D. Bekker, *Defeat at Sea,* Ballantine, 1955, p. 49.
37. Churchill, Vol. II, p. 595.
38. Beesly, p. 49.
39. Ibid., pp. 92-93.
40. Ibid., pp. 95-97, 229-44.
41. Ibid., pp. 230-31.
42. Ibid.

43. Ibid.
44. Ibid., p. 232.
45. Ibid., p. 234.

Chapter VII

1. R. A. Haldane, *The Hidden War*, St. Martin's Press, 1978, p. 38 and Barrie Pitt, *The Battle of the Atlantic*, Time-Life Books, 1977, p. 186.

2. *Handbook for U-boat Commanders*, (translated title) Oberkommando ker Kriegsmarine (OKM), (Supreme Naval Command), 1942, p. 71, primary source, translation by United States Navy in secondary source: *Allied Naval Communications Intelligence and the Battle of the Atlantic*, United States National Security Agency for United States Navy, 1945, 2 Vols., declassified 1977, SRH-008 is Vol. II, SRH-009 is Vol. I, SRH-009, p. 16, secondary source. Both Vols. hereafter known respectively as *SRH-008* and *SRH-009*.

3. *Encyclopedia Americana*, 1962, Vol. 25, p. 781 and *SRH-009*, pp. 16-17.

4. Samuel Eliot Morison, *The Battle of the Atlantic, September 1939-May 1945*, Vols. I and II, Atlantic, Little, Brown, 1947, Vol. I, pp. 26, 129.

5. Patrick Beesly, *Very Special Intelligence*, Doubleday, 1977, pp. 201-2; *SRH-009*, p. 17; and *Americana*, Vol. 25, p. 770.

6. *Americana*, Vol. 25, p. 770 and Erminio Bagnasco, *Submarines of WW II*, Arms and Armor Press, London, 1977, p. 54.

7. *Americana*, Vol. 25, p. 770.

8. Ibid.

9. Numbers and type differ according to authority and source: *SRH-009* reports 50 U-boats; S. W. Roskill, *The War at Sea, 1939-1945*, 4 Vols., Vol. I, p. 59 reports 56 U-boats; Morison, Vol. I reports 43 U-boats; Haldane, p. 38 reports 57 U-boats; and Beesly reports with best information, having worked inside OIC during the war, 56 U-boats.

10. *Americana*, Vol. 25, p. 780; C. D. Bekker, *Defeat at Sea*, Ballantine, 1955, p. 7; United States Army Air Force, *United States Strategic Bombing Survey*, "German Submarine Industry Report," Exhibit B-1, 1946; Morison, Vol. I, p. 4; Beesly, p. 35; Roskill, Vol. I, p. 59; and *SRH-009*, p. 9. Roskill contends that thirty-nine U-boats were actually at sea when war began, Bekker reports twenty-two fit for sea duty at this time.

11. *Americana*, Vol. 25, p. 781.

12. Roskill, Vol. I, pp. 293, 295, 347, and 538.

13. *Americana*, Vol. 25, p. 781.

14. Bekker, p. 174, Roskill, Vol. 1, p. 130; Hermann Bauer, *Das Unterseeboot*, Mittler and Son, Berlin, 1931; and Karl Doenitz, Die Fahrtender, "Breslau M Schwazen Meer", Ullstein, Berlin, 1917 and *Die U-Bootswaffe*, Mittler and Son, Berlin, 1939.

15. Morison, Vol. I, p. 128 and Roskill, Vol. I, p. 469.

16. Beesly, p. 55.

17. Beesly, pp. 26, 57; Bekker, p. 177; Morison, Vol. I, p. 213; and Don E. Gordon, personal notes on conversation with Patrick Beesly, author of *Very Special Intelligence*, cited, on 18 March 1980, Lymington, England. Hereafter referred to as Gordon notes on Beesly.

18. Morison, Vol. I, p. 322 and Roskill, Vol. I, pp. 57, 130.
19. Beesly, p. 255 and *SRH-009*, p. 74.
20. *Americana*, Vol. 25, p. 782.
21. Beesly, pp. 181-82; Bekker, p. 183; and *SRH-009*, p. 36.
22. *SRH-009*, p. 36; Morison, Vol. I, p. 134; and Albert Speer, *Inside the Third Reich*, Memoirs, MacMillan, 1970, p. 274.
23. Morison, Vol. III, p. 352 reports that the Allies flew 6,982 sorties against the Biscay U-boat pens at Lorient, La Pallice, Brest, St. Nazaire, and Bourdeaux dropping 11,000 tons of high explosives and 8,000 tons of incendiaries at a loss of 266 bombers. Not a single bomb penetrated the U-boat pens. *United States Strategic Bombing Survey*, Exhibit B-1, Roskill, Vol. I, p. 459.
24. Bekker, pp. 10-11, 183; Beesly, p. 202; *Americana*, Vol. 25, p. 782; and Roskill, Vol. III/II, Appendix Y. Beesly reports 1,170 boats built, Roskill accounts for 785 boats sunk, Bekker accounts for 189 boats captured after the war (8 type XVII, 61 type XXIII, 120 type XXI), 196 scuttled. *Americana* using different reports: 1,179 boats built, 781 sunk, 82 lost at sea, 181 captured after the end of WW II, mostly in their pens, and 217 scuttled. The difference of eight boats is accounted for by one boat sunk twice and seven boats reported as lost at sea accounted for by British records.
25. *German Naval Communication Intelligence*, United States National Security Agency, 1945, declassified 1977, *SRH-024*, p. 16. Hereafter known as *SRH-024* and Morison, Vol. I, p. 204.
26. Morison, Vol. I, p. 9; *Americana*, Vol. 25, p. 780; and Bekker, pp. 12-18.
27. E. G. Schumacher, "Letter to the Editor," *Washington Star*, 17 October 1979. See addendum this fn. fol. fn. 61.
28. Bekker, p. 10 and United States Army, *Staff Officers' Field Manual, Organization, Technical and Logistics Data*, FM 101-10-1, July 1976, pp. 3-1 to 3-4. Consumption computed for WW II infantry division of 10,000 men consuming daily: 6.7 pounds, class I (rations); 3.26 pounds, class II (clothing); 47.8 pounds, class III (POL); 8.5 pounds, class IV (personal items); 4.2 pounds, class VII (end items); .35 pounds, class VIII (medical supplies); and 1.52 pounds, class IX (spare parts). Total consumption per man per day equals 106.83 pounds. Formula is short tons = 10,000 men × 107 pounds per man per day × 30 days divided by 2,000 = 16,000 tons required to support consumption of one 10,000-man infantry division. Loss of one million tons per month divided by 16,000 tons equals loss for 62 infantry divisions.
29. *Americana*, Vol. 25, p. 770 and Morison, Vol. I, pp. 6-7.
30. *Americana*, Vol. 25, pp. 780-81; *SRH-009*, p. 11; and Roskill, Vol. I, pp. 111, 485.
31. Roskill, Vol. III/II, Appendix ZZ and *Americana*, Vol. 25, Table 4 and p. 781. Of 23 million tons and 5,151 ships sunk by the enemy during WW II, 15 million tons and 2,828 Allied ships were sunk by German U-boats.
32. *Americana*, Vol. 25, p. 782.
33. *Americana*, Vol. 25, p. 781; Roskill, Vol. II, pp. 110-13; and *SRH-009*, pp. 10-11.
34. Roskill, Vol. I, pp. 18-21.
35. Roskill, Vol. I, pp. 18-21 and Beesly, pp. 151, 182-83.
36. Roskill, Vol. I, pp. 18-21.
37. Morison, Vol. I, p. 334 and Roskill, Vol. II, p. 212.
38. Beesly, pp. 200-2.

39. Ibid.

40. Beesly, p. 111; *Americana*, Vol. 25, p. 782; Morison, Vol. II, pp. 119-20; and Roskill, Vol. II, p. 96.

41. Ibid.

42. Beesly, pp. 110, 180-92 and Roskill, Vol. II, pp. 376-77.

43. *Americana*, Vol. 25, pp. 780-81; *SRH-009*, p. 34; Beesly, p. 130; and Morison, Vol. I, p. 315.

44. *Americana*, Vol. 25, pp. 781-82; Roskill, Vol. II, pp. 205, 364-65, 369; Morison, Vol. I, pp. 26, 93-4, 220, 224-26, 244, 247n, 251, 316, 357, and 401; Beesly, pp. 81, 111, 151-52, 181, 197, 206, 219, and 265; and Haldane, p. 41.

45. *Americana*, Vol. 25, Table 4 and pp. 781-82.

46. *Americana*, Vol. 25, pp. 781-82 and Beesly, p. 206.

47. Roskill, Vol. II, p. 112 and Beesly, pp. 151-52, 198.

48. Beesly, p. 265 and F. W. Winterbotham, *The Ultra Secret*, Harper and Row, 1974, in context and D. Macintyre, *U-boat Killer*, Corgi, London, 1976, p. 56.

49. Beesly, pp. 107-15.

50. Ibid.

51. Ibid., pp. 169, 153.

52. R. V. Jones, *The Wizard War*, Coward et al., 1978, p. 321.

53. *Americana*, Vol. 25, p. 784.

54. Beesly, pp. 198, 203-8.

55. Ibid.

56. Beesly, pp. 198, 203-8 and *SRH-009*, pp. 52, 60-62.

57. Beesly, p. 247. In one instance *U-377* and *U-972* both fired acoustic torpedoes at the same merchant ship at about the same moment. The torpedoes missed the ship but hit and sank the other U-boat. The U-boats radioed that they had successfully hit their target [sic] but that their boats were sinking. Many of the torpedoes exploded harmlessly at the end of their run or in wakes but were reported by harassed U-boat commanders as successful hits. The Germans convinced themselves that the acoustic torpedo hit its intended target at least sixty percent of the time and that it was responsible for sinking about fifty ships in only a few months. In fact, relatively few, perhaps three or four hits were made. The British did all they could to encourage the Germans to believe their own reports of success and to continue manufacturing and firing defective torpedoes during 1944.

58. Beesly, pp. 198-200, and *SRH-024*, p. 136.

59. *Allied Naval Communications Intelligence: Technical Intelligence from Allied Communication Intelligence*, United States National Security Agency, 1945, declassified 1979, SRH-025, pp. 29, 33. Hereafter known as *SRH-025; SRH-009*, pp. 64, 75; and R. V. Jones, *The Wizard War*, Coward, McCann, and Geoghegan, 1978, p. 508. The schnorchel was first developed by the Dutch Navy prior to WW II. Two Dutch submarines with schnorchel were captured in port by the Germans after the invasion of Holland. Schnorchel was further developed by the German Navy late in the war and first appeared in January 1944 fitted to *U-539*. Development was completed and fitting to additional U-boats began in August 1944. Schnorchel was intended to permit a submarine to replenish and exhaust air needed to operate its diesel engines, air for crewmen, and a communication antenna which could be used while the U-boat remained submerged just below the surface. Schnorchel was a mast which ex-

tended the air intake and exhaust and communication antenna slightly above the surface of the water allowing the boat to travel at maximum speed using its diesel engines rather than batteries. Schnorchel also allowed the U-boat to communicate and not expose the full hull or tower to observation or radar. Little more than a stovepipe remained above water. Though schnorchel was detectable by radar, its small size reduced the range by which radar could detect the pipe by about ninety-five percent. German U-boats were not, however, to communicate very effectively using the schnorchel's round dipole antenna.

The British developed a pressure activated mine late in 1944. The decision of whether or not to introduce the mine had to be weighed against the possibility that the Germans may not be aware of the operating principle, capture a mine, and not only reproduce copies for their own use but provide the design to the Japanese as well. Communications intelligence solved the dilemma when in mid-June 1944, a German radio message revealed the shipment of pressure mines to the French coast. The Allies introduced the weapon against German coastal shipping with success. Beesly, p. 240.

SRH-025, pp. 20, 36. Aphrodite was introduced during April 1943 and used throughout that year and 1944. It was a balloon with metal strips suspended beneath. The device was released by a U-boat to confuse British radar. Aphrodite created a radar image similar to that of a U-boat because of the reflective image created by the metal strips. The strips were cut to a length proportional to the length of the hull. Thetis was introduced in January 1944; it was a noise-making device used to confuse hydrophone operators.

60. *SRH-009*, pp. 30-31.

61. *Americana*, Vol. 25, p. 781 and Beesly, p. 202.

62. *SRH-009*, p. 53.

Chapter VIII

1. Dr. Jack Vorona, "The Soviet March Toward Technological Superiority," *Defense 80*, USGPO, monthly periodical, March 1980, p. 11.

2. "U.S. is Losing Science Lead, Technology Expert Warns," *Washington Star*, 4 January 1980, p. A-5.

3. Ibid.

4. VADM W. J. Crowe, Statement before the Seapower Subcommittee of the Armed Services Committee, United States House of Representatives, 13 November 1979, released 13 November 1979 per telecon to Committee Staff on 9 April 1980, pp. 2-9 and Don E. Gordon, "Target-The Spoken Word," *Army*, September 1979, p. 21.

5. Crowe, p. 11.

6. Ibid., p. 13.

7. Ibid., p. 14.

8. Worth H. Bagley, "Sea Power and Western Security: The Next Decade," Adelphi Papers, Number One Hundred and Thirty-Nine, The International Institute for Strategic Studies, London, Winter, 1977, *passim*.

9. Crowe, p. 19.

10. Ibid., p. 22.

11. Channel Command Exercise Winter Wedding, 1979.

12. Admiral Thomas B. Hayward, *United States Marine Strategy for the 1980's*, testimony by Chief of Naval Operations before the Subcommittee on Seapower and Strategic and Critical Materials, Committee on Armed Services, United States House of Representatives, 96th Congress, 1st Session, 20 December 1979, lines 93-114.

13. Ibid., lines 188-96.

14. Ibid., line 268.

15. Ibid., line 29.

16. Ibid., lines 340, 2038.

17. Ibid., line 75.

18. Ibid., lines 84-86.

19. Ibid., lines 206-19.

20. Ibid., lines 275, 277, 301, 329, 768, 1059, 1154, 1170, 1206.

21. Ibid., lines 228, 353.

22. Ibid., lines 228, 224, 210, 542.

23. Ibid., lines 714, 876.

24. Ibid., line 1264.

25. Ibid., line 1474.

26. Ibid., line 280.

27. Ibid., line 1676.

28. Ibid., line 1533.

29. Don E. Gordon, "The Electronic Battle," *Infantry*, May-June 1980, p. 22; David Kahn, *The Code Breakers*, MacMillan Co., 1967, pp. 472-80; Anthony Cave Brown, *Bodyguard of Lies*, Bantam Books, 1976, pp. 97-104; Ronald Lewin, *Ultra Goes to War*, McGraw Hill, 1978, pp. 165-79; F. W. Winterbotham, *The Ultra Secret*, Harper and Row, 1974, pp. 25, 64-72; Ronald Lewin, *Rommel as Military Commander*, D. Van Nostrand Co., Inc., 1968, pp. 407, 122-47; David Irving, *The Trail of the Fox [Rommel]*, Dutton, 1977, pp. 195, 167-203 and see index re: Ultra.

30. Ibid.

31. Ibid.

32. Ibid.

33. Ibid.

34. Ibid.

35. Ibid.

36. Ibid.

37. Ibid.

38. Ibid.

39. Don E. Gordon, "The CEWI Battalion: A Tactical Concept That Works," *Military Review*, January 1980, p. 4.

40. Ibid., p. 5.

41. Ibid.

42. Ibid.

43. Ibid.

44. Ibid.

45. Ibid.

46. Ibid., p. 6.
47. Ibid., pp. 7-12.
48. Ibid., p. 8.
49. Ibid., p. 10.
50. Ibid.
51. Ibid.
52. Ibid.
53. Don E. Gordon, "Army CEWI Battalions," *Journal of Electronic Defense*, Jan-Feb 1980, p. 42.
54. Ibid.
55. Don E. Gordon, "Winning on an EW Battlefield," *Military Intelligence*, Oct-Dec 1977, pp. 39-41.
56. Ibid.

BIBLIOGRAPHY

Books

Arnold, Forster. *The World at War*. Fontana-Collins, London, 1976.
Bagnasco, Erminio. *Submarines of WW II*. Arms and Armor Press, London, 1977.
Baldwin, Hanson W. *Battles Lost and Won*. Harper and Row, 1966.
———. *Great Mistakes of the War*. Harper and Brothers, 1950.
Bauer, Hermann. *Das Unterseeboot*. Mittler and Son, Berlin, 1931, translated by United States Navy, OP-G-20, [V210 B4].
Beesly, Patrick. *Very Special Admiral*. Typescript, to be published by Hammish Hamilton, June 1980.
———. *Very Special Intelligence*. Doubleday, 1978.
Bekker, C. D., alias of Hans Dieter Berenbrock. *Defeat at Sea*. Ballantine, 1955.
———. *Hitler's Naval War*. McDonald, 1975.
Bennett, Ralph. *Ultra in the West*. Hutchinson, 1979.
Blumenson, Martin. *The Patton Papers*. Houghton Mifflin, 1974.
Bradford, Ernle. *The Mighty Hood*. Hodder and Stoughton, London, 1959.
Brown, Anthony Cave. *Bodyguard of Lies*. Bantam, 1976.
Churchill, Winston S. *The Second World War, Vol. I, The Gathering Storm, Vol. II, Their Finest Hour, Vol. III, The Grand Alliance*, Houghton Mifflin Co., 1949.
Clark, Ronald. *The Man Who Broke Purple*. Little Brown and Co., 1977.
Command Decisions. United States Department of the Army, 1960.
Congdon, Don (ed.). *Combat, Vol. I, European Theater, Vol. II, Pacific Theater*, Dell, 1958.
Davis, Burke. *Get Yamamoto*. Random House, 1969.
DeGramont, Sanche. *The Secret War*. Putnam's Sons, 1962.
Doenitz, Karl. *Die Fahrtender "Breslau" Schwazen Meer*. Ullstein, Berlin, 1917, [D582.B5 D6].
———. *Die U-Bootswaffe*. Mittler and Son, Berlin, 1939, [VM365.D56].
Esposito, V. J. (ed.). *The West Point Atlas of American Wars*. 2 Vols., Praeger, 1959.
Farago, Ladislas. *The Broken Seal*. Random House, 1967.
———. *The Game of the Foxes*. McKay, 1971.
———. *Patton: Ordeal and Triumph*. Dell, 1965.
Garlinski, Jozef. *Intercept*. Dent, London, 1979.
Gavin, James M. *On to Berlin*. Viking, 1978.
Gretton, Peter. *Crisis Convoy*. Peter Davis, 1974.
Hackett, John. *The Third World War—August 1985*. Macmillan, 1978.
Haldane, R. A. *The Hidden War*. St. Martin's Press, 1978.
Handbook for U-boat Commanders (translated title). German Supreme Naval Command (translated publishing agency), Berlin, 1942.
Hart, Liddell B. H. *The German Generals Talk*. Berkley, 1948.

Hinsley, F. H., et al. (eds.). *British Intelligence in the Second World War; its Influence on Strategy and Operations*. HMSO, 1979.

Holmes, W. J. *Double-Edged Sword*. Naval Institute Press, 1979.

Irving, David. *The Trail of the Fox*. Thomas Congdon, 1977.

Jones, R. V. *The Wizard War*. Coward, McCann, and Geoghegan, 1978.

Kahn, David. *The Code Breakers*. Macmillan, 1967.

——. *Hitler's Spies*. Macmillan, 1978.

Kerr, Walter. *The Secret of Stalingrad*. Doubleday, 1978.

Leasor, James. *Boarding Party*. Houghton Mifflin Co., 1979.

——. *Green Beach*. Morrow, 1975.

Lewin, Ronald. *Rommel as Military Commander*. D. Van Nostrand Co., 1968.

——. *Ultra Goes to War*. McGraw-Hill, 1978.

Loewenheim, Francis L., et al. (eds.). *Roosevelt and Churchill: Their Secret Wartime Correspondence*. Saturday Review Press, 1975.

Lord, Walter. *Incredible Victory*. Harper and Row, 1967.

Louis, Hagen. *The Secret War for Europe*. Stein and Day, 1969.

Macintyre, D. *U-boat Killer*. Corgi, London, 1976.

"Magic" Background of Pearl Harbor, The. United States Department of Defense, 5 vols w/3 Appendix vols, USGPO, 1977, [E183.8 J3 U55].

Martin, L. F. and Schofield, B. B. *The Rescue Ships*. Blackwood, London, 1968.

Miles, Milton. *A Different Kind of War*. Doubleday, 1967.

Millar, George. *The Bruneval Raid*. Doubleday, 1975.

Montgomery, Bernard Law. *The Memoirs of Field-Marshal Montgomery*. World, 1958.

Morison, Samuel Eliot. *Battle of the Atlantic, September 1939-May 1945*. Atlantic, Little, Brown, 1947.

Pitt, Barrie. *Battle of the Atlantic*. Time-Life Books, 1977.

Price, Alfred. *Instruments of Darkness, the History of Electronic Warfare*. Charles Scribner's Sons, 1978.

Roskill, S. W. *The War at Sea—1939-1945*. 4 vols., HMSO, 1954.

Shirer, William L. *The Rise and Fall of the Third Reich*. Simon and Schuster, 1960.

Speer, Albert. *Inside the Third Reich: Memoirs*. Macmillan, 1970.

Stevenson, William. *A Man Called Intrepid*. Ballantine, 1976.

"Submarine," *Encyclopedia Americana*. 1962, Vol. 25, pp. 763-84.

Taylor, A. J. P. *The Origins of the Second World War*. Fawcett, 1961.

Toland, John. *Battle—The Story of the Bulge*. Signet, 1959.

Tuchman, Barbara. *The Zimmerman Telegram*. Macmillan, 1966.

Wingate, John. *HMS Belfast, 1939-1971*. Profile Publications, London, 1972.

Winterbotham, F. W. *The Ultra Secret*. Harper and Row, 1974.

Wohlstetter, Roberta. *Pearl Harbor: Warning and Decision*. Stanford University Press, 1962.

Young, Desmond. *Rommel—The Desert Fox*. Berkley, 1950.

Zacharias, Ellis M. *Secret Missions*. Paperback Library, 1961.

Periodicals

Berry, Bryan H. "A Secret Revealed—X System," *Popular Science Magazine.* 1979.

"Electromagnetic Spectrum Chart," *Electronics Magazine.* McGraw Hill, 25 September 1972.

Gordon, Don E. "Another View of the Battle of Stalingrad," *Military Intelligence.* United States Army Intelligence Center and School, Fort Huachuca, Az., Jul-Sep 1978.

———. "Army CEWI Battalion—A Tactical Concept That Works," *Military Review.* January 1980.

———. "Army CEWI Battalions," *Journal of Electronic Defense.* Vol. 3, No. 1, Jan-Feb 1980.

———. "The Electronic Battlefield," *Infantry.* May-June 1980.

———. "The Electronic Piranha Can Jam," *The Army Communicator.* Fall, 1978.

———. "Target—The Spoken Word," *Army.* September, 1979.

———. "Winning on an EW Battlefield," *Military Intelligence.* Oct-Dec 1977.

Kahn, David. "Cryptology Goes Public," *Foreign Affairs.* Fall, 1979.

———. "German Military Eavesdroppers," *Cryptologia.* October, 1977.

Pearson, Anthony. "Mayday! Mayday!, The Attack on the U.S.S. [sic] Liberty," *Penthouse.*

Price, Alfred. "That Damned Light," *Journal of Electronic Defense.* Vol. 3, No. 1, Jan-Feb 1980.

Vorona, Jack. "The Soviet March Toward Technological Superiority," *Defense 80.* USGPO, March 1980.

Newspapers

Carney, Robert B. "Letter to the Editor," *Washington Star.* 5 November 1979, p. A-12.

Schumacher, E. G. "Letter to the Editor," *Washington Star.* 17 October 1979.

"The Ultra Secret," *Washington Post.* 24 October 1974.

Miscellaneous

Allied Communication Intelligence and the Battle of the Atlantic. United States Department of the Navy, circa 1945, declassified by United States National Security Agency, 1977, SRH-009.

Allied Strategic Air Force Target Planning. United States Department of the Army, circa 1945, declassified by United States National Security Agency, 1977, SRH-017.

Bagley, Worth H. "Sea Power and Western Security: The Next Decade," Adelphi Papers Number One Hundred and Thirty-Nine, The International Institute for Strategic Studies, London, Winter, 1977.

Battle of the Atlantic, December 1942-March 1944. United States Department of the

Navy, circa 1945, declassified by United States National Security Agency, 1977, SRH-008.

Blockade-Running Between Europe and the Far East by Submarines, 1942-1944. United States Department of the Navy, circa 1945, declassified by United States National Security Agency, 1977, SRH-019.

Controlled Agent Communications Activities, 1944-45. United States Joint Chiefs of Staff, circa 1945, declassified by United States National Security Agency, 1977, SRH-021.

Crowe, W. J. Statement Before the Seapower Subcommittee of the Armed Services Committee, United States House of Representatives, 13 Nov 79, released 13 Nov 79.

Final Report of the Radio Intelligence Section, General Staff: General Headquarters, American Expeditionary Forces, 1918-1919, United States Army Expeditionary Force, circa 1920, declassified by United States National Security Agency, 1977, SRH-014.

Flicke, Wilhelm F. *War Secrets in the Ether.* United States National Security Agency, 1953, declassified 1974, SRH-002.

———. *War Secrets in the Ether.* United States Army Training and Doctrine Command, 1977, unclassified, reprint.

Friedman, William Frederick. *Six Lectures on Cryptology.* United States National Security Agency, 1963, declassified 1977.

German Naval Communication Intelligence. United States Department of the Navy, circa 1944, declassified by National Security Agency, 1977, SRH-024.

Gordon, Don E. Notes of conversation with Patrick Beesly, author of *Very Special Intelligence,* previously cited, on March 18, 1980, at Lymington, England.

———. Notes on Ronald Lewin lecture at Smithsonian Institute, Washington, D.C., on 1 November 1979, Subject: Ultra. Lewin is author of *Ultra Goes to War,* previously cited.

Haines Board Report, Ultra: History of U.S. Strategic Air Force Europe vs. German Air Force, circa 1945, declassified by United States National Security Agency, 1977.

Historical Background of the Signal Security Agency. United States Army Security Agency [deactivated 1977], circa 1946, declassified by United States National Security Agency, 1977, SRH-001.

Narrative of the Combat Intelligence Center, Joint Intelligence Center, Pacific Ocean Areas. United States Department of the Navy, circa 1945, declassified by United States National Security Agency, 1977, SRH-020.

Notes on German Fuel Position by G2 SHAEF, Allied Forces Supreme Headquarters, circa 1945, declassified by United States National Security Agency, 1977, SRH-015.

Raeder, Erich. *Fuehrer Conferences on Matters Dealing with the German Navy.* "Reflections on the Outbreak of War, 3 September 1939," circa 1946.

Reports by U.S. Army Ultra Representatives with Army Field Commands in the European Theater of Operations, circa 1945, declassified by United States National Security Agency, 1977, SRH-023.

"Soviet Missile Coding May Have Prevented Monitoring by U.S.," Associated Press, 15 Feb 80.

Staff Officers' Field Manual, Organization, Technical, and Logistic Data, FM 101-10-1, United States Department of the Army, July 1976.

Synthesis of Experiences in the Use of Ultra Intelligence by U.S. Army Field Commands in the European Theater of Operations, United States Department of the Army, circa 1945, declassified by the United States National Security Agency, 1977, SRH-006.

Technical Intelligence from Allied Communication Intelligence, circa 1945, declassified by United States National Security Agency, 1977, SRH-025.

Trial of German Major War Criminals [*The*]; *Proceedings of the International Military Tribunal Sitting at Nuremberg.* [Title may be transposed] Part 14, HMSO, 1947.

United States Marine Strategy for the 1980's, testimony by Admiral Thomas B. Hayward, Chief of Naval Operations, before the Subcommittee on Seapower and Strategic and Critical Materials, Committee on Armed Services, United States House of Representatives, 96th Congress, 1st Session, 20 December 1979.

United States Strategic Bombing Survey, "German Submarine Industry Report," United States Army Air Force, 1946.

Use of CX/MSS Ultra, United States War Department, circa 1945, declassified by the United States National Security Agency, 1977.

INDEX

Abyssinian Crisis (1936), 32
Admiralty (See Royal Navy)
Aerial Photography, 77, 78-79
Afrika Korps, 2, 146 (see also Rommel)
Allied Control Commission for Versailles Treaty, 14
Altenfjord, Norway, 105-106
Anglo-German Naval Agreement, 14
Anzio, Italy (battle), 9
Aquitania (Royal Navy troop ship), 129
Archangel, USSR, 101
Arctic Ocean, 98-101
Ark Royal (HMS), 81, 126
Asdic (see radar)
Atlantis (German Navy raider), 112
Athenia (HMS), 125
Attaches, 31

Baltic Sea, 77, 82, 116
Barents Sea, 106
Battles
   Anzio, 9
   Atlantic, 10, 12, 129-37
   Bismarck, 80-97
   Britain, 9
   Caucasus, 146
   Coral Sea, 9, 18, 142
   Graf Spee, 73, 74, 75
   Jutland, 28-31, 89, 129
   Kharkov, 146
   Midway, 9, 142
   North Africa, 9
   Pearl Harbor, 9
   Sevastopol, 146
   Stalingrad, 12
   Tobruk (Gazala-Bir Hacheim), 9, 146
Bauer, Hermann (German admiral), 51, 120
Bay of Biscay, 68, 116
B. Dienst (Beobachter Dienst, Funkaufklaerung, naval communications "intelligence" staff), 47-53, 89, 120-21
Befehlshaber der U. Boote (see U.d.B.)
Bekker, C. D., 10, 21
Bhose, Chandra, Subhas, 135
Bismarck, 73, 80-95, 96-101, 109-12, 129
Blockade runners, 113
Blucher, 73

"bombe", 37, 42-43, 105
bombing, by aircraft, 19, 25, 45, 64, 124
Borman (Nazi Party Secretary), 123
British Army, Eighth Army in Africa, 146
British Code and Cipher School, 32, 82, 105, 112, 128
British Foreign Office, 27, 31
British Secret Service, 27

CEOI, 148
Cipher Systems, 6, 7, 9, 34-40, 42-51, 65-71, 111, 112-13, 132-37
   Allied Combined Convoy, 48-49, 121, 132-37
   German Double Cassette, 35
   German Neptun, 85, 94
   German One-Hundred, 112
   German Tibet, 112
   German Triton, 41, 43, 63-70, 112, 132
   Japanese Bertox, 112
   Japanese Purple, 35, 52
Churchill, Winston, 15, 16, 32, 98
Clark, Mark, General, USA, 11
Clausewitz, Von, Carl, 5, 141
Clayton, Jock, Admiral RN, 107, 108
Coastal Command (British), 25
Code and Cipher School (See British Code and Cipher School)
Codes, 6, 7
Combat Electronic Warfare and Intelligence (CEWI) units, U.S. Army, 150-55
Combat Power (as multiplier), 11-15, 22, 34, 45-46, 70, 71-72, 93, 116-18, 121, 149-56
Communication systems, 31, 46
Convoys, 15, 22, 44, 50, 75, 99-110, 114-15, 125, 131
   HX-84, 75
   HX-237, 50
   JW-51, 102
   OB-318, 44
   PQ-12, 102
   PQ-17, 99-110
   PQ-18, 102-110
   QP-13, 104
   SC-129, 50
   sinkings, 21, 50, 109-12, 125, 130

system, 114
  to North Russia, 110
Coral Sea (Battle), 9, 18, 142
Courageous (HMS), 126
Crowe, W. J., Admiral, USN, 140-42
cryptanalysis, 3, 4, 12, 30, 36, 37, 38, 41, 45, 54-55, 105-13, 121, 127-37, 139
  with radar and DF, 58
cryptology, 3, 4, 27, 34-35, 36-39, 102, 105-13, 121-37

deception, communication
  Bismarck, 89-90, 92
  Spikenard, 48, 92
decryption, 6, 41-44
Defense Electronic Warfare Agency, 156
Denmark, 120
Denning, Norman, Sir, Admiral, RN, 78-79
Depth Charges, 131
Deutschland, 73-75
Devonshire (HMS), 112
Direction finding (see radio direction finding)
Doenitz, Karl, Admiral, German Navy, 21, 63, 120-31
Doric Star, 75
Dorsetshire (HMS), 112
Duke of York (HMS), 103

Electromagnetic Spectrum, 2, 3, 148-56
Electronic counter-countermeasures, 6-7, 11, 66
Electronic countermeasures, 6-7, 11-12
  (also see jamming)
Electronic support measures, 6-7, 11-12
  (also see signals intelligence)
Electronic warfare, 1, 5-12, 27, 66, 152-56
  Definition, 6-7
  Korea, 2
  Mideast war, 2
  Modern Battlefield, 151-55
  Policy, 154-56
  Radioelectronic combat, 155-56
  Vietnam, 2
  Weapon, 1
Encryption, 6
English Channel, 116
Enigma, 3, 7, 27, 34-42, 46, 114
  German Air Force, 43, 82
  German Navy, 92, 114-16
  How it worked, 38-42

France, 27, 38, 45, 83, 86, 91, 113, 122
  Allied landings, 122
  Brest, 83, 86, 91
  Cap De La Hague, 113
  Cryptology, 38
  Dunkirk, 113
  Intelligence, 27, 37
  Le Havre, 113
  Resistance, 45
Friedman, William (U.S. Cryptologist), 35

Gazala-Bir Hacheim, Battle of (Tobruk), 146
Geneva Convention of Land Warfare, 5
George, David Lloyd, 16
German Admiralty (Naval High Command, Oberkommando der Marine, OKM), 47
German Air Force (Luftwaffe), 43, 82, 93, 103, 104
  Poor communications security, 43, 93
German Army (Wehrmacht)
  Cipher clerk traitor, 27, 36-37
  Invasion of Norway, 75-80
  OKW (Oberkommando der Wehrmacht) Paratroopers in Norway, 77
German cryptology, 47-52 (see also B. Dienst)
German Navy (surface fleet), 21, 73, 84-94, 98-104, 105
  Headquarters at Wilhelmshaven, 85
  Sinking of *Bismarck*, 84-94
  Submarine fleet, see U.d.B.
  Supreme Command (Oberkommando der Marine—OKM), 21
Germany, 23, 77, 82, 85, 101, 113
  Bremen, 113
  Hamburg, 82
  Kiel, 77, 82, 113
  Rostock, 77
  Stettin, 77
  Swinemunde, 77, 113
  Wilhelmshaven, 85, 102
Giap Nguyen Vo, 141
Gibraltar, 18
Glorious (HMS), 126
Gneisenau, 73, 75, 80
Gotland, 83
Graf Spee, 73-80, 95, 101
Green door, 116 (see also cryptology)

Hardwood, Commodore, R.N., 75
Hayward, Admiral, USN, 143-46
Hipper, 73, 75, 80, 98, 104
Hitler, Adolph, 13, 19, 20, 21, 25, 26, 73, 105, 123
Holland, 14
Hood (HMS), 81, 84, 85

Iceland-Faeroes Passage
  Sinking of *Bismarck*, 88
Ile de France, 129
Indian Ocean, 21
Infrared, 65, 134
Intelligence, 7, 12, 23, 25, 27, 33, 34, 46, 67, 76-81, 84-94, 101-10, 114, 127-33, 147-53
  Cryptologic, 12, 25, 28, 46, 77, 102, 104, 127
  Dissemination, 32-34, 88-89, 110, 127
  Electronic warfare, 6, 150-53
  Failure to use correctly
    Africa, 147
    Bismarck, 86-94
    Invasion of Norway, 77
    Jutland, 26, 28, 32, 96, 129
    PQ-17, 104
  Indicators, 82, 108
  Intelligence Division of British Admiralty, 32, 34, 110
  Success
    Africa, 148
    Bismarck, 80-82
    Invasion of Norway, 80
    PQ-17, 100
Intelligence Organization and Stationing Study, U.S. Army, 150
International Institute for Strategic Studies, 141
Ions, 4
Israeli, 148, 149
  Poor communications security and 1973 Mid-East War, 149
Italy, 112, 119, 147

Jamming, 1, 9, 152-54
Japan, 24, 35, 52, 99, 135
  China, 99
  Communications, 135
  Model 97, Purple, Enciphering Machine, 35, 52
Jellicoe, Admiral, RN, 28-29
Jervis Bay (HMN), 75

Jutland, Battle of, 13, 28, 32, 89, 96, 129

Kemp, Peter, Lieutenant Commander, RN, 88-89
Kerbs, 44
Keylist, 41-44, 111, 121
Kietel, General, German Chief of Staff, 123
King George V, 84, 88
Komet, 112-13
Komoran, 112
Korea, 2, 140

Laconia, 125
Lammers, Hans, German State Secretary, 123
Leigh-light, 68, 131
Liberty Ship, 117, 131
Lucas, John Porter, General, USA, 11
Lutjens, Admiral, German Navy, 86
Lutzow, 98, 104

Magdeburg, 27
Magic, 3, 7
Mahan, Alfred Thayer, Captain, 5
Marshall, George C., General, USA, 13
Mauretania (Royal Navy Troop Ship), 129
Mediterranean Sea, 116, 124
Merchant Marine, 21-22, 51, 99-100, 111-12, 130-33
  Construction, 130
  Shipping, 99, 125
  Sinkings, 21, 50, 111-12, 126-29
  Supplies for 9 divisions for 30 days, 126
  United States, 130-33
Merchant raiders, 110-13
  Atlantis, Python, Komoran, Komet, Togo
Mideast War, 1973, 2, 139, 149
Midway Battle, 9, 142
Mines, Naval, 17
Mistakes by commanders, 81, 85-86, 87-89
Modern battlefield (Third World War), 13, 28, 139-46, 151-53
Montgomery, Bernard Law, Field-Marshal, British Army, 11
Morison, Samuel Eliot, Admiral, USN, 10, 23, 100
Murmansk (USSR), 101

National policy, 10, 14, 155-56

National Security Agency, U.S., 46, 136, 156
NATO, 2, 9, 141-42
Neptun, 94
Netherlands, 120
Nieuw Amsterdam, 129
North Africa, 9, 115, 140
North Sea, 21, 29, 76, 116
Northern Wedding Training Exercise, 1979, 142
Norway, 25, 75-80, 83, 102-13
   Altenfjord, 106
   Bergen, 77
   Blockade runners, 113
   British Defense Plan, R-4, 80
   Christiansand (also Kristiansand), 77, 83
   Egersund, 77
   German invasion, 75-80
   Great Belt, 78
   Leads, 26, 77
   Little Belt, 78
   Narvik, 79
   Oslo, 78
   Ports, 26
   PQ-17, 106-10
   Resistance, 83
   Trondheim, 79, 102

OKM (See German Navy)
OKW (See German Army)
Operation Wilfred (mining of Norwegian leads), 77
Operational Intelligence Centers
   Royal Navy, 12, 31, 33, 68, 82, 88-94, 103-109, 127-30
   U.S. Navy, 24, 130, 136
Orzel, 78

Panther Tank Program, 123
Patton, George, General, USA, 11
Paukenschlag (Operation Drumbeat), 133
Pearl Harbor, Hawaii, 9
Pirate Submarine Case, 33
Poland
   AVA Electric Company, 38
   Cryptologists, 3, 6, 38, 43
   General Staff, 34
   Gdynia, 82
   Intelligence, 36
   Secret Service, 7, 36
Political Objectives, 20, 21, 24, 101

Pound, Dudley, P. R., Sir, 32, 102, 106-109
Prince of Wales, 83, 84, 85-88
Prinz Eugen, 73, 80-85, 95-97, 98, 112
Proforma messages, 45
Purple cipher, 35
Python, 112

Queen Elizabeth (Royal Navy Troop Ship), 129
Queen Mary, 129

Radar, 12, 25, 49, 54-72, 84, 86, 91, 115, 131, 134, 137
   Braun Tube, 60
   British ASV, MK II, 68
   British H2S/U.S. SCR Type, 49, 54, 66
   Captured, H2A, 71
   Centimeter Type (S-Band), 64-67, 131
   Countermeasures, 65
   Detection, 65, 69, 83, 85, 91, 134
      Metox, 66-69; Gema, 69; Hohentweil, 69; Naxos S-Band, 134
   Development, 57-65
   Frequency, 55
   How it Works, 54-55
   Kammhuber Air Defense Radar System, 65
   S-Band, 131
   Schnorchel, 71
   X-Band, 55
Radio Direction Finding, 29-33, 45-48, 55, 66, 74-78, 86-93, 131-32, 148
   Allies, 31-32, 45-48, 55, 67, 74-78, 86-94, 128-32, 148
   Bismarck, 86-91
   German, 47, 86-92
   How it Works, 87, 131-32
   Mideast War, 148
   Success, 131
Radioelectronic Combat, Soviet, 153
Radio Intelligence Bulletin, 48, 51
Raeder, Erich, Admiral, German Navy, 19-26, 73-77, 101
Ramo, Simion, Dr., Chairman, TRW, Inc., 139
Repulse (HMS), 83-84, 85-92
Rio de Janeiro, 78
Rodney (HMS), 91-94
Rommel, Erwin, Field Marshal, German Army, 2, 10, 12, 140, 146, 148
Room 40, 28, 30, 31
Roosevelt, Franklin D., 98

Roskill, S. W., Captain, Royal Navy, 10, 17, 18, 24, 76, 94-95, 110
Royal Air Force, 62, 83, 113, 127
Royal Navy, 15, 17, 26, 31, 32, 73-83, 98, 101, 106-10, 121, 129, 141
  Admiralty, 15, 19, 31, 108
  Staff System, 32
  Home Fleet, 76-79, 88-90, 102, 106
  Intelligence, 74, 76, 83-90, 110
Royal Oak (HMS), 126
Russia (See Soviet)
Russo-Finnish War, 76

Scapa Flow, 28, 79, 82, 126
Scharnhorst, 73-80, 112
Scheer, 73-80, 98-104
Scheer, Admiral, German Navy, 28-29
Schmidt, Hans-Thilo, German Soldier-Traitor, 37, 42
Schnorchel, 71, 117, 122
Sheffield (HMS), 94
Signals Intelligence, 2, 12, 48, 113, 127, 147, 153-56
  Rommel's SIGINT Company, 147
  Two-man U-Boat SIGINT Teams, 48
Signals Security, 46, 134, 136, 148
  CEOI, 148
Skagerrak, 79
Sonar (asdic), 15, 122, 131, 141
Soviet Union, 4, 9, 100, 110, 139, 145
  Archangel, 99
  Caucasus oil fields, 146
  Forces, 99
  Kharkov, 146
  Murmansk, 99
  North Russia, 110
  Radioelectronic Combat, 153
  Sevastopol, 146
  Stalingrad, 12
  Students in U.S., 139
  Typhoon Submarine, 4, 144
  Vaengna Bay, 99
Spanish Civil War, 33
Special Liaison Units (SLU), 34
Speech Security (Cipher System), 5
Speer, Albert, 19
Spikenard (HMCS), 48, 92
Stalin, Joseph, 98, 109
Strait of Denmark, 82, 83
Strategy, 13-15, 22, 26, 46, 63, 76, 94-97, 101, 113, 115-23, 137, 140-45
  Allies, 13, 17, 76, 95-96, 101, 120, 140

Bombing, 25, 45, 62, 124
British Maritime, 22
German, 96-97, 102, 111, 123, 125, 136
Middle East, 96
Modern Battlefield, 146-47
Weapons, 15, 114-16, 125
Suffolk (HMS), 83-85
Sun Tzu Wu, 5, 141
Sweden
  Aid to England, 127
  Aid to Germany, 77, 113
Sydney (HMAS), 112

Technology, 7, 10, 24-31, 35, 56-62, 72, 115, 131-34, 139
  Allied devices, 131-34
  Capability, 9, 23-28, 71, 116, 139
  Policies, 10, 35, 59-62
  Radar, 56-57
Ten Year Rule, 15
Third World War (See Modern Battlefield)
Tirpitz, 73, 95, 98-112
Tizard Committee, 61
Tobruk, 9, 146
Togo, 113
Torch, operation, 96, 115
Tornberg, Major, Chief of Staff, Swedish Secret Service and Norwegian Sympathizer, 83
Torpedoes, 129, 134
Tovey, Admiral, RN, 88-94, 102
Treaty of Versailles, 14
Troop Ships, 129
Troubadour (tanks firing on aircraft from ship deck), 103
Turing, Alan, 42-43
Turing Machine, 42-43
Tuscaloosa, 99
Typhoon submarine, 4

U-Boats, 18, 20-21, 28, 38-46, 50, 54-56, 63-64, 65-67, 111-12, 114-37
  Bombing of, 64, 124-25
  Brake, 135
  Capabilities, 116-25
  Charlotte Schliemann, 135
  Comparison with U.S. Submarines, 117-19
  Construction, 123-26
  Cryptology, 27, 38-51
  Offensive (1943), 129-30

Paukenschlag (Operation Drumbeat), 133
PQ-17, 104-108
Radar, 54-55
Schnorchel, 71, 117, 122
Service, 21, 114-15, 119, 121, 126
U-33, 42
U-110, 27, 42, 111-12
U-111, 27, 38, 42, 44, 111
U-126, 112
U-156, 70, 125
U-333, 69-70
U-456, 129
U-505, 46
U-519, 69
Ultra, 3, 7, 10, 12, 34, 115, 128
U.S. Air Force, 125
U.S. Army
  ASA, 150
  CEWI units, 150-52
  Europe, 141
  Intelligence, 147-53
  Modern Battlefield, 146-55
  Security Agency, 149-50
U.S. Navy, 23, 50, 74, 117, 118-19, 129-30, 134, 140-46
  Intelligence, 23, 51, 74
  Security Group "OPG-20", 50-51, 130, 134

Vaengna Bay (USSR), 99
Victorious (HMS), 83, 84, 92, 102, 103
Vietnam, 2, 45, 139, 140

Warships (defined), 18
Washington, 99, 103
Wichita, 99
Winn, Rodger, Captain, RN, 128-29
WW I, 5, 14-15, 20, 23-24, 27, 116, 119, 121, 125

Z-Plan, 19, 73

ABOUT THE AUTHOR

Colonel Don E. Gordon is a United States Army military intelligence officer presently assigned to the Army's Office of the Assistant Chief of Staff for Operations. He has served as an electronic warfare and cryptologic officer in the 101st Airborne Division, 173rd Airborne Brigade (Separate), the 5th and 10th Special Forces Groups, the United States Embassy, Laos, and recently as the commander of the 313th Combat Electronic Warfare and Intelligence Battalion, 82nd Airborne Division. Col. Gordon is a 1962 graduate of The Citadel and has been awarded a BA, MS, MMAS. He has attended the Army's Command and General Staff College and the National War College; twice awarded the Legion of Merit Medal, and the Training Medal of the Association of Old Crows.

Teresa Smith is Lecturer in Applied Social Studies in the Department of Social and Administrative Studies, University of Oxford, where she teaches community work to social workers. Before joining the Oxford Preschool Research Group, she worked in the Educational Priority Area Project in Denaby Main, South Yorkshire, setting up and evaluating preschool provision, and working with teachers and parents. She latter carried out research on preschool developments in Birmingham and Cheshire. She has been co-Chairman of the Research Committee of the Preschool Playgroups Association. Her interests lie in the combination of community development and preschool provision. She is married and has one son.

The Oxford Preschool Research Project

1. *Under Five in Britain,* Jerome Bruner
2. *Childwatching at Playgroup and Nursery School,* Kathy Sylva, Carolyn Roy and Marjorie Painter
3. *Children and Minders,* Bridget Bryant, Miriam Harris and Dee Newton
4. *Children and Day Nurseries,* Caroline Garland and Stephanie White
5. *Working with Under Fives,* David Wood, Linnet McMahon and Yvonne Cranstoun
6. *Parents and Preschool,* Teresa Smith

Parents and Preschool

Teresa Smith

THE
HIGH/SCOPE
PRESS

First published in England (1980) by
Grant McIntyre Ltd
39 Great Russell Street
London WC1B 3PH

Copyright © Teresa Smith, 1980

**THE
HIGH/SCOPE
    PRESS**
a division of
High/Scope Educational Research Foundation
600 North River Street
Ypsilanti, MI 48197
(313) 485-2000

All rights reserved. No part of this publication may be reproduced in any form or by any means, electronic or mechanical, including photocopy, recording, or any information storage and retrieval system, without permission in writing from the publisher.

Library of Congress Cataloging in Publication Data

Smith, Teresa.
    Parents and preschool.

    (Oxford preschool research project ; 6)
    Bibliography: p.
    Includes index.
    1. Home and school. 2. Preschool education.
    I. Title. II. Series.

LC225.S59   372'.21   80-27701

ISBN 0-931114-14-4

Contents

Foreword by Jack Wrigley — vii
Foreword by Jerome Bruner — ix
Acknowledgements — xi

1 Preschool policy: intervention and participation — 1
2 Parental involvement: research and definitions — 14
3 The Oxfordshire study — 45
4 Fifteen groups observed — 67
5 Fifteen groups and their staff — 96
6 Parents and their involvement in six groups — 110
7 Conclusions: parents and professionals — 150

Short bibliography — 177
Index — 183

To George and Tom

Foreword by Jack Wrigley

In 1971, when a massive expansion of nursery education in Britain was proposed, there was relatively little easily available evidence to suggest how best this should be done. Consequently the Department of Education and Science and the Scottish Education Department initiated a programme of research on nursery education to answer practical questions about provision and to study the effects of expansion. The Educational Research Board of the Social Science Research Council saw the need for a complementary research programme concerned as well with some more fundamental issues which covered the whole range of preschool education.

The work was coordinated in the Department of Education and Science by a management committee on which the Schools Council and SSRC were represented. The original idea, that SSRC should concentrate on fundamental research while DES funded more policy oriented and practical work, proved too simple. What quickly emerged was a view that much of the fundamental work on preschool children had already been carried out. What was lacking was the dissemination of that knowledge and its implementation in the field. Within SSRC a preschool working group was given the task of commissioning projects, and the work of the Oxford Preschool Research Group, under Professor Bruner, reported in this series of publications, was the main element in the first phase of the SSRC programme.

Professor Bruner had already accomplished distinguished fundamental work in this field and was therefore well placed to make the point of the need for dissemination and implementation. Despite the many changes in the economic and political scene in the 1970s the original gap in knowledge remains important and the results of the SSRC research programme will do much to fill the gap. In particular, Professor Bruner's work in Oxfordshire has great value for the rest of the country. The publications of the Oxford Preschool Research Group, together with the results from other participants in the programme, will help give a firmer base on which to build for the future.

Jack Wrigley
Chairman
SSRC Educational Research
Board Panel on
Accountability in
Education

London, 1979

Foreword by Jerome Bruner

This book is one in a series that emerges from the Oxford Preschool Research Group. Like the others in the series, it is concerned with the provision of care in Britain for the preschool child away from home and is the result of several years of research devoted to various aspects of that issue. There are few more controversial and crucial issues facing Britain today. The objective of the series is to shed light on present needs, on the quality of care available and on the extent to which this care meets these needs. The general aim is to provide a basis for discussion of future policy.

The studies have all been financed by the Social Science Research Council of Great Britain. They were commissioned in 1974, a year or two after Mrs Thatcher's White Paper, *Education: a Framework for Expansion,* was published, at a time when it was thought that there would be a publicly financed expansion of preschool care and education in Britain. Since that time events have caught up with the enterprise and Britain finds itself in a period of economic stringency during which many of the hoped-for changes will have to be shelved until better days come again. Nonetheless, the studies are opportune, for careful study and planning will be necessary not only to meet present needs with reduced resources, but to shape policy and practice for an improved future service on behalf of children in Britain and their families.

Developmental studies of the past two decades have pointed increasingly to the importance of the opening years of life for the intellectual, social, and emotional growth of human beings. The books in this series, it is hoped, shed light on the practical steps that must be taken to assure that the early years can contribute to the well-being of a next generation in Britain.

Jerome Bruner

Oxford, 1979

Acknowledgements

I am grateful to all the parents, teachers, and playgroup leaders who gave so generously of their time in allowing us to observe and interview during this study; to Jerry Bruner and my colleagues in the Oxford Preschool Research Group for sharing their work and criticism during the three years of the project; to Sue Draney, who worked with me at the beginning of the study; to Heather Leonard, Henrietta Leyser, and Joy North who carried out observations and interviews in the groups; to Sue North, who carried out the parent interviews, and Rena Shimoni, who worked on the analysis; to all those in the local Pre-school Playgroups Association, and the Oxfordshire Education and Social Services Departments, who contributed to my understanding of preschool provision and the role of parents; to Kathy Sylva and George Smith in particular for commenting on my efforts; to Louise Keegan for typing most of the manuscript, and finally to a forbearing and helpful publisher.

Few books are finished 'works of art', and writing this book raised as many questions for me as it answered. My chief acknowledgement must be to the many friends and colleagues who have shared their ideas with me, since my days in Denaby and before, and have taught me to think about the relationship between education and the community.

1
Preschool policy: intervention and participation

This book is about parents and their role in the education of young children. Parent participation - like community participation - has been a popular phrase over the last decade. Hardly a government report, conference, or publication on preschool provision and the education of the young child has appeared without some prescription for the involvement of parents in the educative process.

Yet we are entitled to ask, like the critics of the notion of 'community participation', whether this is anything more than a passing fashion, based on a short-lived enthusiasm for 'consumer control' and 'self-help'. What, we might ask, are the objectives of and the reasons for involving parents in the educative process, and what is the evidence that their involvement makes any difference to children, parents, or the schools? Although there has been much discussion of how to involve parents, we have remarkably little agreement on what we might mean by parental involvement, or why it might be important. Problems of practice are clearly more vital to workers in the field – the teachers, nursery staff, playgroup supervisors and helpers who organize and run groups of different kinds for young children. Again, problems of policy – how to devise and implement a coherent policy for the under fives and their families, or how to provide a service for, say, working mothers – seem more urgent to most policy makers than do questions of parent involvement. Yet the argument of this book is that parent involvement is a key notion in the development of any preschool policy which attempts to take seriously both the relationship between home and school and the accountability of a service to its consumers.

The first task is to sort out some of the ambiguity. The

question is how to define parent involvement and its objectives. We might argue that objectives and definitions will be demonstrated empirically, in the practice of teachers, playgroup supervisors, helpers and parents in the field: 'Come and see what we do, and that will tell you why we do it and what we mean.' Later chapters in this book report on our study in Oxfordshire, where we attempted to match up observations of practice on the one hand with what professionals and parents had to say about practice on the other. But an understanding of parent involvement and its importance as currently defined depends to a large extent on an understanding of the history of the idea – how, and why, it has reached the agenda, so to speak, in the first place. So the first task must be a historical one: to trace the development of the notion of parental involvement. With this as background, we can then turn to the translation of the idea into practice in the particular example of Oxfordshire.

Parental involvement is a paradoxical and ambiguous notion. For one thing, it is defined, and attempted, in a hundred different ways. For another, it is not a new idea. A hundred years ago, involvement in and responsibility for the child's education and welfare on the part of his family required no justification: indeed, the introduction of compulsory education was seen as 'a revolutionary invasion of parental rights to children' (Musgrove, 1960). The history of education in the last hundred years – and education for the preschool age group is no exception – is the history of the changing relationship between family and non-family institutions over the education and socialization of the young child.

Again, the idea of parent involvement attracts attention from interest groups of very different persuasions. Psychologists, for example, are interested in the influence of parents on cognitive development in early childhood; sociologists in the relationship between parental attitudes, social class, and children's educational achievement; policy makers in the implications of parent involvement for the provision of preschool services. For community development workers and activists, involving parents in their children's education may be a catalyst to further community involvement and organization. Adult educationalists suppose that parents with young children are more likely to be positively interested in education and so potentially open to new forms of learning. Thus parent involvement is for some writers essentially an analytic notion, part of the explanation for, say, the development of intelligence, the process of early learning, or educational achievement. For others, it is essentially practical – carrying potential for certain outcomes. All these groups may use the same phrase; but it will carry different implications and operate within different frameworks. This, perhaps, is its attraction.

In this first chapter, we disentangle some of the threads in the development of preschool policy in relation to parent involvement over the last 20 years. In the second chapter, we look in more detail at some of the research on parent involvement.

Policy and intervention

The history of preschool developments over the last 20 years or so illustrates both the complex interweaving of different interests, and also the difficulties of disentangling the arguments and assumptions that lie behind proposals for preschool expansion from those supporting parental involvement.

There are, however, some common starting points in this history. One such point is obvious in the events and thinking of the early 1960s. These were years of enormous optimism about the possibilities for social change through education and the resulting eradication of poverty and inequality. The key creative idea of educational intervention arose from a coincidence of interests between sociologists and pyschologists, combined with economic expansion – on the one hand, the power of education to affect life chances; on the other, the supposed malleability of the young child's developing intelligence, the interaction between environment and experience, and the link between the parents' and child's 'educational environment' and his intelligence.

First, sociologists continued to accumulate evidence on the relationship between social class and educational achievement – not only in longitudinal studies such as those by Douglas (1964 and 1968) and the National Children's Bureau (1972), but also in official reports such as *Early Leaving* (1954), the Crowther Report *15 to 18* (1959), the Newsom Report (1963) on the 'average child', and the Robbins Report (1963) on higher education. But there was a shift in focus in the discussions about equality of educational opportunity. Throughout the 1950s and the early 1960s, interest had focused mainly on inequalities in access to secondary schooling (e.g. Floud, Halsey and Martin, 1956) and the reorganization of secondary education along comprehensive lines. In the sixties, part of this interest shifted downwards to the preschool years, largely as a result of the longitudinal studies and the work of Bernstein (1971 and following) in demonstrating the differences between social class groups in parents' styles of communication and control that already existed before the child entered school at all.

Secondly, a major revolution occurred in thinking about the psychological nature and development of intelligence and early learning. The work of psychologists such as Hunt (1961) and Bloom (1964) in bringing together studies of the effects of early experience and deprivation was decisive in undermining earlier assumptions of fixed intelligence and predetermined development. Once intelligence could be conceived of as plastic, malleable – to whatever extent – and modifiable, intervention to change children's chances became a reality and a matter for urgency. If intelligence could be seen as 'developmental in nature and modifiable by the environment' (Freeberg and Payne, 1967), then two crucial questions arose: which elements in the environment were the most important, and how did the process work? The investigation of these questions took researchers back into the family and child-parent interaction on the one hand, and on the other hand forward into the school and to questions of organization and the teacher's role.

Economic and academic optimism thus combined powerfully to support the lobby on both sides of the Atlantic for the expansion of educational and welfare strategies of intervention, directed particularly at the lower income groups and the years before compulsory schooling. 'Head Start', 'the War on Poverty', 'compensatory education', and 'positive discrimination' are familiar phrases. These, however, are policies and programmes rather than theories – and the underlying assumptions and objectives were varied. Strictly educational objectives, such as 'increasing children's educational performance', based on assumptions about the links between achievement and factors such as parents' interest and support, overlapped with broader social objectives such as 'breaking the poverty cycle' – based on assumptions about the relationship between educational achievement and occupation which were far from clear (Little and Smith, 1971). Here is how the most recent report on some of the American experimental preschool programmes describes – in most sober language – the euphoric assumptions of those early days (Consortium for Longitudinal Studies, 1979, pp.1 and 13):

> Head Start was built on the assumption that early education, parental involvement, and the provision of medical and social services could enable children of low-income parents to do as well in school as their middle-class peers and thus help them leave the ranks of the poor . . .
> Many preschool intervention programs implicitly contained the following simple model for social change. Preschool programs teach children concrete skills and concepts. But skills and concepts must be built upon over the years, so children must also be motivated to continue to learn and achieve in school. They must believe that school is important and possess enough self-confidence to exert the necessary effort. The

preschool experience should also affect parents so that they may support their children's efforts. With the backing of new abilities, motivations, values and parental support, children should be able to compete better with their middle-class peers.

Some three years after the setting up of the War on Poverty and the Head Start programmes in the States, the Plowden Committee on primary education in Britain was echoing their optimism in its call for positive discrimination in favour of schools and children in poor areas. They asked whether 'such expensive consequences of poor early upbringing (as delinquency, family breakdown and long term dependence on public services) can be diminished if the quality of primary education is improved' and suggested that 'what these deprived areas need most are perfectly normal, good primary schools alive with experience from which children of all kinds can benefit' (Plowden, 1967).

The arguments for preschool expansion in the days of Head Start and the Educational Priority Area programmes sprang essentially, then, from assumptions about the relationship between children's intelligence and development, parents' 'educational environment' and class, and about the impact of intervention on both children and parents and hence on educational achievement throughout school career and so into employment – thus effectively breaking the poverty cycle. One of the keys to 'educational intervention' was to be parental involvement, on the assumption that parents' attitudes and support were crucial for children's development and achievement.

The optimism about education as a force for social change is well illustrated by the figures for public expenditure in Britain on four major social programmes between 1951 and 1981. These show that educational expenditure as a proportion of public expenditure doubled in 20 years, between 1951 and 1971, and in the decade following has risen slightly and then fallen back to the same level. Proportional expenditure on other programmes has risen slightly or remained constant, with the exception of social security, which has more than doubled, largely because of the increase in the dependent groups in the population such as the elderly. These figures on their own tell us nothing about expenditure on preschool education. This did not begin to be

	1951	1961	1971	1972	1974	1976	1978
Education	6·8	9·8	12·4	13·0	11·7	14·5	13·9
Housing	6·9	5·4	5·1	5·3	9·5	8·9	8·1
Health and Personal Social Services	10·1	10·5	11·4	11·8	11·5	12·4	13·6
Social Security	11·8	15·8	17·7	18·7	16·4	20·8	22·6

Source: *Social Trends*

Table 1.1 *UK figures 1951–78: percentage of public expenditure by major social programmes*

	1979	1980	1981
Education	13·2	12·9	12·4
Housing	7·2	7·2	6·8
Health and Personal Social Services	12·5	12·1	12·3
Social Security	25·2	25·4	25·8

Source: *The Government's Expenditure Plans 1980–1981.* Cmnd. 7746. HMSO, 1979

Table 1.2 *Provisional estimates 1979–81: percentage of public expenditure by major social programmes*

significant until the end of the 1960s, with the funding of provision under the Urban Programme. However, during the period 1975/76–1980/81, when overall educational expenditure had ceased to expand, spending on the under fives increased by a dramatic 24 per cent (Barnes, 1978).

But these were enormous expectations. They began to break down with evidence from Head Start programmes that the gains shown at school entry by children who had attended preschool groups apparently 'washed out' after two or three years in primary school. The 'failure of Head Start' became a commonplace, and combined with the attacks of critics such as Jencks (1972) on the notion of equality of educational opportunity to undermine earlier hopes for education as a lever of social change. As Bernstein (1972) summed it up, 'education cannot compensate for society': the school was probably less influential than the family or the neighbourhood for educational achievement; and inequality could more effectively be tackled by a direct attack on employment or housing than indirectly through education. Yet it is ironic that the year Jencks published his book *Inequality* in the States also saw publication in this country of the first of the modestly optimistic reports from the British Educational Priority Area Projects (Halsey, 1972), and the Government's White Paper *Education: a Framework for Expansion* (DES, 1972), which recognized, albeit cautiously, that the preschool child makes not only social but also intellectual advances in his early years, and authorized the first major expansion in preschool education in Britain since the war years of the 1940s.

Policy and participation

If educational intervention, in its varied forms of educational priority, positive discrimination, and compensatory education, was the key creative idea of the 1960s and early 1970s in educational expansion and the pressure for preschool provision, it is less easy to isolate a single influence in the 1970s. The long-awaited expansion failed to materialize: the 1972 White Paper was caustically renamed the 'framework for contraction'. Economic optimism has been overtaken by an overwhelming economic decline: and in the context of cuts practitioners have often feared that academic pessimism over educational intervention would be used by policy makers as licence to reduce rather than expand. Interest has focused on experiments in integrated services and coordinated planning which build on existing provision: family centres or day centres based on existing nursery classes or day nurseries, salaried childminders linked to local day nurseries or drop-in centres, coordinating committees with a brief to review local need and provision. Low cost services and coordination were the key phrases in a joint DES and DHSS conference held in 1976 (DHSS/DES, 1976); a general tightening up of priorities is evident in the DHSS's own priority guidelines published in 1968 and the subsequent guidelines developed by many authorities in the 1970s (e.g. Cheshire Social Services Department, 1976) for provision under social services departments. Yet official definitions of priority categories seem increasingly irrelevant in the face of the discrepancies between supply and demand, the differential rates of take-up of what provision there is between different social class groups, the enormous increase in the numbers of working mothers with under-fives, and the development of voluntary provision in the private sector in the form of playgroups.

There are two main strands here. First, there is the failure of the statutory services to expand to meet demand. A national survey carried out by the Office of Population Censuses and Surveys in 1974 showed that 90 per cent of the parents of three- and four-year-olds and over 70 per cent of the parents of two-year-olds wanted some form of preschool provision – compared with 19 per cent of the two-year-olds, 47 per cent of the three-year-olds and 72 per cent of the four-year-olds actually with a preschool place (Bone, 1977). Thirty-two per cent of the under fives had a preschool place of one kind or another in 1974: the same number again wanted a place. The situation had not changed much by 1977 (Hughes et al., 1980). This had required an expansion of voluntary services to fill the gap. In 1977, voluntary provision catered for 58 per cent of the under fives with a preschool place, compared with 42 per cent provided for in statutory provision (Hughes et al., 1980) – and even this is rather a misleading figure as it includes the rising fives in reception classes in first schools. The Child Health and Education Study national survey carried out in 1975 found that about two in five children in their sample born in 1970 had attended playgroups while only one in five had attended a local authority nursery school or class (Van der Eyken *et al.*, 1979).

Voluntary provision depends for existence on parental involvement, as it is parents who organize, run, and largely finance the preschool groups – whether they employ staff to work alongside the children in the groups or rely on parents to carry out this task on a cooperative basis. Parental involvement here is defined partly in economic terms – in that the service would cease to exist unless parents are involved in its organization and running – and partly in participatory terms, in the notion that parents have both a right and a responsibility for how the service is organized. Thus the failure of the statutory services to expand has resulted in both an enormous expansion of voluntary provision to meet consumer demand and an important shift in the meaning of parental involvement to consumer participation.

Second, there is the tension between what might be called 'professionally defined need', and 'consumer demand'. Priority categories tend to be defined in terms of children at risk because of severe stress or family breakdown, poor housing conditions, or handicap. The DHSS guidelines on provision for 'high risk' and 'medium risk' categories recommend 8 and 40 places per 1000 under fives – that is, places for 0·8 per cent and 4 per cent of the age group. Local authorities' own estimates admit with caution that this may be an underestimate, and the figures appear absurdly low when compared with other indicators of stress. In his study of London mothers, George Brown found that one in three women with preschool children had suffered from depression in the three months before interview, and working class women with children under six were four times more likely than middle class women to develop depression (Brown and Harris, 1978).

But even this view of social need fails to take into account the fact of working mothers. Between 1961 and 1971, the proportion of mothers with preschool children who worked rose from 12 per cent to 19 per cent, and by 1977 to 27 per cent. This means that by 1976 one preschool child in four had a working mother; and of these, just over a quarter of the children under three had mothers who worked for more than 30 hours a week (CPRS, 1978). And we know that substantial numbers of mothers who do not work would like to do so particularly if satisfactory child care were available (Bone, 1977). In the case of the working mother, it is not even clear whether we are talking of 'need' or 'demand': provision for the children of working mothers has not been a priority since the war years, which created their own particular economic pressures – both the Plowden Report and social services departments' guidelines agree on this. Yet if we take female employment as a fact then it could be argued that provision for the preschool children of working mothers follows as a need (Tizard, J., 1975). Factual arguments about working women and moral arguments about a mother's right to choose are inextricably entwined. Patrick Jenkin's exhortation (*Guardian*, 6 November 1979) to mothers to stay at home –

> Quite frankly, I don't think mothers have the same right to work as fathers. If the Good Lord had intended us to have equal rights to go out to work, he wouldn't have created man and woman. These are biological facts; young children do depend upon their mothers.

– stands against the feminists' slogan about 'a woman's right to work'.

The playgroup movement and the feminists represent different attacks on the inadequacy of existing services. Feminist arguments for preschool provision derive largely from assumptions about women's rights, particularly the right to choose whether or not to work – and have merged with shifts in the labour market to press for facilities for working mothers (Fonda and Moss, 1976). The playgroup movement, on the other hand, sees provision for working mothers as only one strand in the network of supporting facilities for parents and their young children. Framework and objectives are thus very different. Yet both movements depend on notions of consumer demand and the right of the parent or consumer to determine how a service should be provided.

The debate about preschool in the 1970s, at a time of economic and political gloom, has been in terms of low cost services, of coordination and integration rather than expansion, of the dilemma over matching provision to precise definitions of 'need' on the one hand or to demand on the other, and of consumer participation. Although some of these developments have been born of economic necessity, they have proved creative in stimulating thinking about new and different forms of service provision, and in highlighting both the dilemma between a universal service based on consumer demand and a selective service based on professionally defined need, and the inadequacies of the present service when judged on any but the most stringent definitions of need. If these were indeed the pressing concerns for expansion in the last ten years, they seem to have bypassed the earlier emphasis on educational intervention and parental involvement. Yet what might be called the post-Plowden orthodoxy of involving parents in the educative process is now well – if quietly – established.

'Participation' here carries notions of a service's responsiveness to its consumers, and consumers' rights to organize the service as they think best or at least to have a say in how it is provided. Involvement in management, as one form of consumer participation, derives less from educationalists' interests – although in the American War on Poverty of the 1960s ideas about educational intervention in the early years ran alongside ideas about parents learning through sharing control of the educational process in the home and in the school – than from the political and sociological notions of participation which developed during the reorganization of health and welfare services and of local government in

Britain in the early 1970s (Hatch, 1973). While involvement in management is taken for granted in the voluntary preschool sector, at least in theory if not in practice, it is slower to develop in statutory preschool provision, although a matter of hot debate at primary and secondary level in the issue of school managers or governors. The Taylor Committee on school managers and governors wrote of the school's duty to be 'sensitive to the needs and wishes of the community it served' and acknowledged the existence of 'interested groups with a keen and legitimate concern' in the school's affairs. Yet they noted that their brief specifically excluded 'the management of nursery schools' (DES, 1977).

Pressure for preschool expansion over the last 20 years has thus built up from two main sources – proposals on the one hand for educational intervention based on sociological and psychological arguments about early learning and the environment, and, on the other hand, a more fragmented discussion about social priority, the labour market, and consumer participation. Broadly speaking, these pressures have been associated with different objectives. In the first, the objective is the child and his social and educational development; if the parent is the focus of intervention, this is in recognition of the primary relationship with the child – 'if you want to work with the child, you have to work with the parent'. In the second, the objective may be the well-being equally of child or parent: but again, if provision for the child is made in response to the parents' need this is in recognition of the probable benefit for the child. In this chapter, we have considered developments in provision and the notions of educational intervention and consumer participation from the point of view of policy. In the next chapter, we focus on the background research on parent involvement.

2
Parental involvement: research and definitions

In the first chapter we sketched an outline of parental involvement in terms of policy. In this chapter, we shall look more closely at the background research. First we summarize the arguments for the importance of parental involvement, secondly consider the evidence for its effectiveness, and third attempt some definitions. What precisely do we know about the relationship between parents' behaviour, attitudes and social class, and children's early learning, development and achievement? What do we know about strategies to change parents' behaviour and attitudes? What evidence is there that changed attitudes and behaviour on the part of parents have any impact on children's development or achievement? Do we have any evidence that some forms of parent involvement are more effective than others?

Definitions of parent involvement depend on an analysis of the relationship between the home and the school, and of the success or breakdown of that relationship. We can already see two different sets of ideas – one broadly educational, to do with assumptions about the relationship between parents' attitudes and children's achievement, and the impact of intervention; the other broadly participatory, to do with assumptions about need and demand, and consumers' rights. What is to be explained is why some children are more successful educationally than others. Can under-achievement be tackled solely by improving school facilities and classroom programmes? Or is change needed in the ways schools relate to other institutions that influence the child's development outside school – the home and the family, the peer group and the community? Different analyses of what has gone wrong in this relationship may lead to different strategies for tackling the problem (Little and Smith, 1971).

One analysis postulates a failure in communication between the school and the home. Parents are poorly educated and apathetic, and understand little of the school's aims or methods; the home fails to support the child in his efforts or learning. The remedy lies in strategies first to improve the links between the home and the school; more information to parents about the school: more open days, better contacts between teachers and parents; and second to improve the educational level of the home, perhaps by special home visiting programmes.

A second analysis is in terms of the power relationship between the school and the home, and is based on arguments that under-achievement depends less on deficits in the learner or the home than failure in the schools. The problem will not be solved simply by providing more information and better contact; the remedy lies rather in strategies to increase community or consumer control of education.

It is important to note that both analyses are in terms of the relationship between home and school environment rather than the failure of either institution on its own, although each analysis is often associated with one or other locus of change. Failure of communication is often linked with assumptions about the home's failure to provide support, encouragement, and an educationally stimulating environment for the child, and the family's ignorance of the school's aims and methods. The second analysis is frequently linked with assumptions about the gap between the values of the home and community and those of the school as demonstrated in school curriculum, organization and class management. The first leads naturally to a focus on change in the home and the family; the second to change in the school, the detail of classroom organization and the teacher's role.

These two analyses and corresponding strategies are not necessarily incompatible – practically speaking, better information often leads to demands for a greater share in how matters are organized. But they may be associated with different theoretical positions. Notions of 'educational intervention' to affect parents' attitudes or behaviour towards their children can easily slide over into something nearer 'interference' – with undertones of 'bad behaviour', 'bad attitudes', or 'poor parenting practice' which has to be changed'. We might call this a 'pathological approach' as it presents attitudes and behaviour as if they stemmed from abnormal views of the world. A more sociological approach would attempt to explain such varied attitudes in terms of differences in social conditions to which families had adapted in different ways. Thus 'child-centred' approaches, favoured by progressive educators as encouraging the child to explore his environment, are appropriate in the small middle-class family, but fit less well the large family in cramped housing. Additionally, different social groups may have different values about child-rearing practices. For these reasons, we should perhaps be less confident about what constitutes 'good parenting' than the proponents of 'parent education' as the chief strategy have appeared to suggest (Fantini and Cárdenas, 1980).

Taking a different tack, we might find it more useful to look at the socialization of the child that occurs in school, and the shift in this process from home to school. The young child who interprets the standard phrase of the nursery class or reception class teacher, 'Would you like to come and have your milk now, dear?' as a question to which one can legitimately answer 'no' rather than a command which has to be obeyed, presents us with a common example of how a different linguistic form gives expression to different behaviour expectations between home and school. Children, and parents, learn rapidly that different kinds of behaviour are appropriate to different situations. And the context may be the best predictor of the behaviour. As in Bruner's delightful paraphrase (1972) of the 'ecological approach', 'The best way to predict the behaviour of a human being is to know where he is: in a post office he behaves post office, at church he behaves church.'

However, this is not simply a matter of 'When in Rome, do as the Romans do.' Analysing appropriate behaviour in terms of settings does not tell us much about the structure.

More fundamentally, we need to understand the relationship between the school or preschool group, parents, and children, as part of the transitional process between the child's home and the wider world (Parsons, 1959). The important idea here is the transfer of power over the child from the home to the school, and the school as a stepping stone in the child's career from family dependence to his independence. In Parsons's analysis, the early stages of schooling closely resemble many aspects of the home to ease the transition. Sarason (1971) also points to the way the nursery of preschool group is frequently isolated as a little community on its own, even when it is set within a bigger school. This analysis provides us with an overall framework to consider the position of parent involvement as part of the transition from home to school.

With this as a framework, we can now turn to consider the importance of parental involvement.

The importance of parental involvement

The evidence on the link between the home's 'educational climate' and the child's development is by now well-rehearsed. Here we pick out some of the main strands.

There is a large body of information on the variation in language use and communication style employed by adults with children – whether parent (e.g. Hess and Shipman, 1965), 'caretaker' (e.g. Tizard, Philps and Plewis, 1976), or both (Tizard, 1979). Bruner (1972) cites studies of mother-child interaction to pick out two factors which he takes to be crucial for early learning and later educational attainment: the 'communication style' – both language use and strategies for problem-solving – between parent and child; and the mother's self-confidence, sense of being in control of what happens in her life. Participation by parents in the process is thus crucial for two reasons: parents' 'style' (particularly the mother's) is the key to the child's 'learning style'; and the mother's aspirations and self-confidence are the key to the child's sense of confidence and competence alike. Involvement here is not a one-way affair, a set of predetermined behaviours – it is an interactive process between parent and child: in Hess's words (1980), 'a pattern of reciprocal responses between parent and child that develop over time'.

There is also continuing evidence for the link between social class and educational attainment (Halsey *et al.*, 1980). Halsey and his colleagues, pursuing the question of educational opportunity and attainment, conclude from their retrospective study of the educational experience in this country since the First World War that social class has continued to exercise a powerful influence on educational achievement and the routes taken through the educational system despite the intentions of the 1944 Education Act. They conclude that 'class differentials in access' to different types of secondary education remain 'depressingly constant'; and that throughout secondary school career 'class differentials widen at each rung up the educational ladder'. A working-class boy, they found, was more likely 'to drop out of school as soon as the minimum leaving age was reached, was less likely to continue his career into the sixth form, and was less likely to enter a university or some other form of education after school' (pp.203–4). At the bottom end of the age range, we know that there are dramatic differences between privileged and underprivileged children showing class differences even by the age of three years (Ainsworth, 1962).

Yet there is unresolved and continuing debate about the intervening variables between social class and educational performance, how social class actually operates; and debate about whether the notion of social class or of parental 'attitudes' is better at explaining differential performance. This is of crucial importance for the question of involving parents in the educative process, at the levels of both analysis and policy – for if we understand more about the family factors that affect children's intelligence and attainment, whether they be the mother's self-confidence, the father's job, the family's communication style, or the level of the educational resources in the home and the community, we should be in a better position to take policy decisions and develop strategies of intervention.

For the psychologists interested in measuring parental influences on children's cognitive performance by observing the fine detail of parent-child interactions, 'social class' has sometimes been too broad a notion because it fails to make sense of the differences observable within social class groups, and too narrow because it is restricted to the father's occupation (Freeberg and Payne, 1967). For sociologists, an exclusive concentration on 'parental attitudes' or 'communication styles' could perhaps be misleading because the concept of class already contains attitudes (Halsey, 1975). Of course there are variations in parents' attitudes, motivations, aspirations, but these are integrally related to class rather than independent individual attributes. What exactly do we find in this ragbag notion of 'parental attitudes'?

Douglas (1964 and 1968), in his longitudinal study for the National Survey of Health and Development, found a close and consistent relationship between social class, children's educational achievement, and parents' attitudes. High interest on the part of the parents in their children's development was linked with high attainment, good examination results, and staying on at school; low interest was linked with poor performance and early leaving. This was found for the population studied as a whole and also within each class group. The assessment of parents' attitudes showed a remarkable consistency: mothers who took little interest in their children's work in their early years at school included a high proportion of those who had been described as 'poor managers' of their homes and their children in the preschool years, and teachers at primary and secondary level tended to assess parents' interest level similarly. Douglas developed a 'parental attitude' scale which included measures of parents' own educational aspirations (whether either parent had wanted to pursue further education after leaving school), their interest in the child's progress (as demonstrated by the father visiting the school to discuss the child's progress on at least two occasions, or as assessed by the teacher), and their aspirations for the child's further education or occupation. He also developed a 'school type' scale which included measures of school amenities, size, staff background, and pupil-teacher ratio. He concluded that home influences are crucial not only throughout school career but also in the preschool years, but that the effects of home and school on achievement are interactive – while 'deficiencies of interest and ambition' may be offset by good teaching, enthusiasm and support on the part of the parents alone may be insufficient to counter school deficiencies.

It is instructive to look in some detail at the discussion of parent attitudes and parental participation in the Plowden Report on British primary education *Children and Their Primary Schools*, published in 1967. The Plowden Committee accepted as orthodoxy the interactive nature of the relationships between early learning and the environment in a single phrase on the demise of the 'old nature-versus-nurture controversy'. Their central research attempt, in a national survey of parents' attitudes, was to analyse the links between occupation, attitudes and achievement – 'how much parents influence children's achievement at school and how their influence operates'. For the last decade the report has been held up as the teacher's and educational administrator's manual for policies of compensatory education, positive discrimination, and parental involvement.

Six associated clusters of parental attitudes and behaviour were distinguished: first, the extent to which parents took responsibility and initiative for their child's education – whether they had talked to the head or class teacher, whether they visited the school and attended school functions, whether they asked for work for the child to do at home, and asked for advice on how they could help their child. Second, the relations between parents and teachers – whether parents thought it was easy to see the teachers whenever they wanted to and did not feel they were interfering if they went to the school uninvited, whether they were happy with the arrangements for seeing the head or class teacher. Third, fathers' interest and support, and fourth, the extent to which mothers devoted time and attention to their children's development – whether parents thought they 'should leave it all to the teacher'. Fifth, there was the parents' interest in and knowledge of the child's work at school – whether the child talked to his parents about his school work and took books home and read, whether parents spent time with their child in the evenings and weekends, whether they were satisfied with the child's progress and the school's teaching methods, and thought they were given enough information and consulted sufficiently by the teachers. And finally, there was the level of literacy in the home – whether the parents belonged to a library, and had books at home, whether the child used a library and did much reading at home.

There is a strong link between attitudes and behaviour and social class in the survey. For instance, middle-class children read more at home than did working-class children, and borrowed books from libraries; while there were no social class differences in parents' wish for children to have work to do at home, fewer working-class children in fact had homework, and middle-class parents were slightly more likely to help their children with it; more middle-class parents visited the schools and talked to the teacher and the head, went uninvited to the school, and expressed worries about teaching methods. And on the six clusters of associated attitudes, class differences showed up consistently, with the slight exception of teacher-parent relations – where middle-class parents were more likely to express dissatisfaction than working-class parents. Yet Peaker, in his analysis of the survey's findings, concludes that only about one quarter of the variation in parental attitudes can be attributed to variation in home circumstances, and that variation in parents' attitudes has a greater effect on children's achievement than does the variation in home circumstances. The committee's conclusion was that 'attitudes could be affected in other ways . . than [by] parents' occupation, material circumstances, and education . . and could be altered by persuasion'.

One might question whether the Plowden Committee's optimistic conclusion was actually supported by their evidence, and therefore whether their policy recommendations for shifts in parental attitudes through 'persuasion' and participation were likely to be successful without other changes, more difficult to achieve, in resources and social and economic factors. Should attitudes be seen as isolated factors, or as an integral part of class and community? And there is also a confusion over what counts as an attitude unless it is translated into a piece of behaviour. Nevertheless, the report usefully points to clusters of behaviours and aspirations which go to make up what we might call the 'educational climate' of the home combining both material resources and support – Bourdieu's 'cultural capital' (Halsey et al., 1980) or 'la famille educogène'. We should note here Wolf and Davé's index of educational environment' (1963 and 1964) which included parents' intellectual expectations for the child, the amount of information the mother had about the child's intellectual development, the opportunities the child had to increase his vocabulary, the extent to which the parents created openings for learning in the home and helped with school and non-school work. The question remains, of course, as to whether 'la famille educogène' or 'cultural capital' are randomly distributed across the population or linked to social class. What is being suggested here is that different patterns of family communication, educational resources, or the 'educational-climate' of the home, are differentially distributed across social class groups. Increasing 'cultural capital', 'educational climate' or 'la famille educogène' is essential, if we are to affect children's chances of educational achievement, and may also be considerably more difficult than the Plowden Committee's view of parental influence and parental participation suggests.

The impact of parental involvement

The background to the interest in parental involvement lies

in the psychologists' and sociologists' evidence on parents' attitudes, aspirations, interest and support. Our second question concerned the effects of parental involvement. What do the studies have to show?

There is a mass of literature following the Plowden Report on what might be called the post-Plowden orthodoxy – that parental involvement in the work of the school, and better communications between parent and teacher, are a good thing. The Plowden Report wrote about the continuous interaction between homes and schools and stressed that 'schools exist to foster virtuous circles'. They were concerned at the discrepancy between headteachers' complacent claims to 'have very good relations with parents', and parents' dissatisfaction with those relationships (one half wanted to be told more about their child's progress in school, and one third thought that teachers should ask the parents more about their children). Their 'minimum programme' for 'participation by parents' was given official endorsement in the DES booklet *Parent/Teacher Relations in Primary Schools* (DES, 1968). Plowden stressed the importance of winning 'cooperation from parents' and encouraging 'support from the home'. Examples of good practices were listed: inviting parents to assembly, holding parents' evenings when parents could experiment with school equipment and learn new methods, mothers helping staff out, fund-raising and making equipment. Practical help and learning often went hand in hand: 'in schools where parents gave practical help of this kind, discussion with teachers about methods used in the school often arises informally over the job and enables parents to understand how the schools work and how to help their children more effectively'.

The 'minimal programme' included a welcome to school for new parents and their children, weekly times for meetings with teachers, class 'at homes' for parents, times when fathers could be available, open days and evenings, booklets of information for parents, a changed format for reports, and tentative proposals for home visiting by class teachers or educational welfare officers. This programme was to be supported by greater parental choice in their child's school, and the development of community schools on the Cambridgeshire village college model, with out-of-school activities for parents and school facilities open to the community.

The post-Plowden literature tends to be description-cum-exhortation of 'good practice' – often written unashamedly by and for practitioners (e.g. Cave (1970); Murton (1971); DES (1968); Parry and Archer (1974); Taylor *et al.* (1972); McGeeney (1969).

> The good school should become an extension of the child's home or family rather than a substitute, and therefore it should co-operate positively with the parents. Lack of understanding and communication between home and school often lies at the root of children's poor school adjustments and performance (Parry and Archer, 1974).

The emphasis is on 'building a relationship' between home and school, 'cooperative parents', communication and information, the importance to teachers of knowing about a child's home background, the teachers' efforts 'to make the transition from home to school a happy one', the importance of parents 'supporting the work of the school'. The menu is a standard one – parents visiting the school, staying to settle their children when they first join the class, teachers welcoming parents and spending time getting to know the children's home backgrounds. The DES booklet on parent/teacher relations lists the standard ways for parents to help the school: practical help like making or mending equipment; fund-raising; helping the teachers with activities or events such as cooking or outings; helping to organize out-of-school activities such as clubs. Almost all these accounts contain 'horror stories' of the 'keep parents out' style and 'no parents beyond this line' – the 'trespassers will be prosecuted' notices, the ban on visits except by appointment, the queues at open evenings – as almost a ritual reminder of the pre-Plowden 'bad old days'. Perhaps the best of this type of 'horror stories' and post-Plowden 'good practice' is McGeeney's survey *Parents Are Welcome* (1969).

Yet while this literature often contains good and vivid descriptions of practice it tells us little about the effects of good practice on children, parents, or schools. The only examples of this are studies by Green (1968) and Young and McGeeney (1968). Both these studies relate their aims closely to the Plowden Committee's thinking. Green describes his as a case study of methods to improve the contact between the home and the school, and sees the problem in terms of communication about the work of the school and its achievements. Green's ideas for his school include a new style of school report, with pages for comment and discussion by the parents; interviews with parents at school and at home; school functions to which parents are invited; a parent-teacher association; and a stream of letters and information. He argues that the result is changes both in parents' attitudes towards the school and in their children's behaviour and work at school. Of the 21 parent groups who said their attitude towards school had changed for the better, 16 attributed this to being visited by teachers at home, four to their easy access to the head teacher and class teacher, and nine to the new style of reports together with home or school interviews. Where parents' attitudes had changed, their children's behaviour in school often improved dramatically, with a rather slower improvement in work performance, as measured by teachers' assessments.

Young and McGeeney describe their work as a small-scale experimental case study to test out some of the ideas 'to promote cooperation with parents' then being discussed by the Plowden Committee, of which Michael Young was a member. Their careful account of teachers' views of parents, and parents' views of teachers and education, before the 'trial' period, gives a picture of separate interests and mutual distance, with few contacts, ignorance on the teachers' part of parents' views or the children's home backgrounds, and ignorance on the parents' part of the school's organization, methods, or objectives. They set up a carefully planned, though brief, programme of open meetings, talks between parents and teachers, discussions on teaching methods, and home visits. Young and McGeeney describe the outcomes as modest. Parents felt that they knew more about their school and the teachers' work, they realized that the teachers were interested, and felt they knew more about helping their child at home. Teachers realized more about home conditions:

> When I look at them now I think of all the things I know about them and realize just what some of them have to put up with (p.54).

Some teachers changed their views quite dramatically:

> It has taken me five years to be convinced that the old methods I used were not the most effective. . . . I'm still changing my ideas as I've changed my ideas about giving talks to parents at meetings like this. A few months ago I resisted the idea strongly and now here I am talking to you about how I teach (p.58).
>
> I suppose when it started I thought of parents coming in and taking over. That's disappeared (p.64).

For the children, there were tests of educational performance before the trial, after six months, and a year later. At six months, the children showed modest gains on verbal and non-verbal, reading and arithmetic tests; and these gains were maintained after a further six months. The authors make no great claims for this. They argue that the improvements were not necessarily the result of parental involvement – they could have resulted from other changes in the school (greater interest from the teachers, for example, as we know from other studies) or they could have been test-taking effects. Comparison with two other local schools, where similar gains were made without parental involvement, complicated the picture, and added to the argument for a possible 'halo' effect. Here the authors discovered that – naturally enough – the head teachers had immediately used the evidence from the low pre-trial scores in their schools to push their case for extra teaching resources, or to introduce a new reading scheme, and so introduce new classroom programmes during the trial period.

The Young and McGeeney study is a perceptive account of strategies for change in parent-teacher relationships. The problems are seen to lie equally in parents' lack of knowledge, and teachers' resistance to change; and the way forward is by way of a combination of small steps designed to reassure both that change is possible and productive.

The pro- and anti-parental-involvement viewpoints are neatly put in the summary of teachers' opinions about home-school relationships in the DES survey of topics for research in the nursery programme (DES, 1975). The objectives of preschool education, to be achieved through parental cooperation, were largely to help parents to learn about children and how they learn, and to help parents understand what the preschool institution was doing so they could give their support. Staff in favour of involving parents stressed the value of a high adult-child ratio so that children could receive a lot of individual attention, and the importance of increased understanding on the part of the parents; but felt that interested parents were frequently unable to help, for instance because of a small baby which could not be left at home. Those against involving parents thought that it was a good thing but impossible in difficult areas because 'the language, habits, and attitudes of the parents conflicted with what the staff were trying to achieve'; that it would take up too much staff time; that parents were not willing to help; that 'it's the teacher's job'; there was a problem of disruptive younger children tagging along; children were more clinging and difficult to settle if their parents stayed to help; and it was bad for the child whose parents did not help. The DES's comment was to urge research on the effectiveness of different forms of involvement, for parents and children.

This collection of studies, then, tells us a good deal about what is seen as 'good practice' in home-school relations, but little about the impact. Its focus is 'communication', 'cooperation' and 'support' for the task of the school – its concern more with 'innovative practice' than research. The key to Plowden's task of 'changing attitudes by persuasion' is more and better communication. Actual involvement is seen mainly in terms of what might be called non-educational tasks – fund-raising, making and mending; or what is rather coyly described as 'giving general help in the school without actually working with children', for instance looking after the library corner or mending equipment – with tentative moves towards classroom activities such as 'knitting, sewing, weaving, [cutting] paper and collage work' or 'reading stories to small groups, supervising cookery or helping with craft materials' (DES, 1968 and 1975).

Yet Barbara Tizard's study of nursery schools and classes trying out new ways of involving parents, suggests that even when teachers make determined efforts to give more information to parents this is not necessarily effective in helping them to understand more about the methods and objectives of the group or their children's learning (Tizard, 1977 and 1978).

There is a second group of studies which suggests that it is active involvement in these educational activities that is most likely to affect parents' attitudes, understanding, and behaviour. What does this second group of studies, of early intervention, tell us? Pessimism about the results of the American Head Start programmes has been widespread (Tizard, B., 1975). Yet the latest results from some of the American intervention programmes give us greater grounds for optimism, and for that reason are worth quoting. Lazar and Darlington conclude from their analysis (Consortium for Longitudinal Studies, 1979) of 12 longitudinal studies in the United States that 'early education programs for low-income children apparently had lasting effects' on children's school performance, with less grade failure and need for remedial education, and also on children's own confidence and self-image of themselves, and their and their parents' aspirations for future education and employment. These were the findings up to 15 years after the original programmes. Their conclusions are relatively modest: that preschool programmes help low-income children to meet the 'minimum requirements' of later schooling – that is, reduce failure in terms of repeated years or special classes. This was not due to higher expectations on the part of the teachers, nor was there any evidence that brighter children or children from one kind of family background benefited more than others.

Which programmes did Lazar and Darlington point to as the most effective? An earlier follow-up study in the same series showed that factors to do with parental involvement, home visits involving both parent and child, and specific goals for working with parents, were strongly related to the effectiveness of the programme. This study concluded that the most effective early intervention programmes were those where the worker worked with the parent and child together in the home. Unfortunately, Lazar and Darlington could not identify from their analysis any one programme of parental involvement as more effective than any other. This was partly because of problems with the data; and partly, they suggest, because their definition of effectiveness – reducing the need for special education – might not have been the most sensitive way of distinguishing between different programmes.

While the evidence is far from unequivocal, this analysis does apparently show considerable long-term effects associated with preschool experience on children's performance and attitudes, and their parents' attitudes. The studies reported here are indeed highly-structured experimental programmes with carefully trained staff, rather than the average Head Start programme or day care regime. Nevertheless, these long-term results should lead us to reconsider the earlier pessimistic conclusions about the 'wash-out' of gains once children join school and look again at the question of whether 'education *can* compensate for society'. This may be over-optimistic, but at least the question is still an open one.

These long-term results are echoed in another longitudinal study from the United States. Weikart and his colleagues

(Weikart *et al.*, 1978; Hohmann, Banet and Weikart, 1979) implemented three different preschool programmes in an attempt to compare the effectiveness of different types of teaching and learning models. They concluded that all the programmes made a long-term impact – gains were maintained by the children in school up to five years after the programme, with less need for special remedial work and less grade failure. This was designed as a comparative study of programme effectiveness, and therefore the conclusions are to do essentially with the components of an effective preschool programme; a well-worked out curriculum, careful staff management and training, and 'quality control procedures'. The study was not designed to test the effectiveness of parental involvement, and all three programmes included home visiting; nevertheless, the data show modest changes in parents' methods of working with their children, related to the programme – for example, the mothers in the programme which emphasized an interactive relationship between adult and child in his exploration were more likely by the end of the programme to ask their children questions and give them information than they were at the beginning. Weikart and his colleagues suggest that the most effective programmes are those which combine school based and home based elements.

Bronfenbrenner, in an earlier review (1974) of intervention programmes, had suggested that family involvement might be the crucial ingredient. Where children and parents worked together on a programme, children's intelligence improved substantially; and the 'wash-out' effect after they entered school was less likely if programmes involving the parents continued. There was some evidence that younger brothers and sisters in the family were also affected by a programme involving the parents, and that effects spread from one family to another in the local community – what might be termed 'vertical' and 'horizontal diffusion' (Gray and Klaus, 1970). Effects were cumulative: children involved in a programme with their parents were also more likely to improve when they joined a group programme later on.

Bronfenbrenner concludes that

> the family is the most effective and economical system for fostering and sustaining the development of the child. . . . The involvement of the child's family as an active participant is critical to the success of any intervention programme. . . . Without such family involvement, any effects of intervention, at least in the cognitive sphere, appear to erode fairly rapidly once the programme ends. . . . The involvement of the parents as partners in the enterprise provides an ongoing system which can reinforce the effects of the programme while it is in operation, and help to sustain them after the programme ends.

The family is thus the means by which intervention is translated into sustained impact. In Bronfenbrenner's words, parental involvement is thus both a 'catalyst' and a 'fixative': and the target of intervention is neither parent nor child on their own but the 'parent-child system'.

These studies do not tell us much about the effectiveness of programmes which do not involve parents in comparison with those that do – as Lazar and Darlington acknowledge in their recommendations for future research. What they do tell us is that programmes may affect both children's and parents' attitudes and behaviour in the long term. If we put together the evidence on the maintenance of children's achievement over time, with the evidence of the impact on parents' and children's attitudes, we may have a clue to the intervening process.

We should be more specific about what these parents did when they were involved in programmes with their children. Some school-based projects brought parents into the classroom as 'teacher assistants' or 'teacher aides' and organized training programmes for them. Others involved the mothers at home with their children, either as a component of a school-based programme or in home-based programmes when mothers were given materials and encouraged to use them with the children between visits. Radin (1972 describes a project in which home visits by a teacher to work with the parent and child ran alongside a school-based programme and a programme of discussion groups. Mothers were shown how to give their children 'positive reinforcement', and how to develop stimulating games during 'routine house-keeping', and were encouraged to develop their children's motivation. Karnes (1973) describes how mothers were given a programme of activities, lent materials, taught positive reinforcement techniques, and encouraged to view themselves as competent.

We can also be more specific about the effects of such programmes on parents. Effects may be small-scale but significant: an increase in mothers' own IQ scores; increased confidence in handling their own and other children; a better understanding of children's development and how to stimulate this, and of the relationship between play and learning; greater confidence in their own abilities and potential. As Radin concluded, involvement can 'enhance mothers' perceptions of themselves as educators of their children and of their children as individuals capable of independent thought'.

One longitudinal study in this country of an early intervention programme illuminates something of this process (Armstrong and Brown, 1979). Five years after the end of a home visiting programme in the West Riding EPA, parents and children were contacted to get a picture of changes that had occurred. The interesting finding of this study is that while after three years of school there were minimal differences in performance between the group of 'home visited' children and a second group who had not been visited, there were substantial differences in attitude between the two groups of parents. The differences lie essentially in the parents' view of education and of their own role in relation to their children's development. Mothers in the 'visited' group were more likely to have helped to prepare the child for school. They felt that talking to the child was preparation in itself. They 'told her what she'd be doing', 'told him he'd be painting like at playgroup'; 'her older sister talked about it'. The few mothers in the comparison group who said they had prepared the child laid more stress on 'teaching him things' – they had 'taught him to write his name', 'told him not much playing, more reading and writing'; and one mother said she had not prepared her child 'because you're told not to teach anything now as all the methods are different'. Again, when the mothers were asked what they thought were the most important activities at school for five-year-olds, those in the visited group talked about 'playing and learning in preparation for work', while those in the comparison group were more concerned with formal educational skills like 'learning to read and write'. Mothers in the visited group were far more likely to say that they had tried to help with their child's education; and they put this in terms of 'answering questions and explaining things' to the child, while the comparison group again stressed formal reading and writing. Although both groups had visited the school with equal frequency, the visited mothers were far more likely to wish for greater involvement in their child's schooling. They wanted to 'go and see more about teaching methods so if I want to help him I could do so', and 'wouldn't like to live there but would like to know more about what the children are doing'. The comparison mothers did not understand 'new methods' and said they were 'quite happy with the present set-up' and 'preferred it as it was'. And finally, more of the visited mothers hoped their child would have further education or training when he left school as it would 'help to get a better job'.

This study apparently confirms the earlier evidence about the 'wash-out' of children's gains after school entry without follow-up programmes. The explanation here may be partly to do with the fact that a new nursery was opened in the control group's village during the study, and many of the children attended this or local playgroups. One might say that parents have done well at least to maintain their children's position against the other group in 'professionally' run provision. But the interesting result is the much wider view of education and early learning, and their role in this, held by the mothers in the home-visiting programme; while the comparison mothers tended to see education as something that only happened in school and involved formal skills above all else. One would like to see a longer follow-up of both children and parents.

Here, then, we have a study of the effects on parents' attitudes of a programme which involved them in working with their children. What about different types of parent involvement? One study worth discussing is that described by Radin (1972). Children were divided into three experimental groups. The first group had a preschool programme, and sessions at home together with their mothers; in addition there were weekly discussion groups for the mothers. The second group did not have the discussion sessions. The third group did not involve the parents at all, as the home visits did not involve the mothers and there were no discussion groups. At the end of the year's programme, all the children had made gains and had improved their classroom behaviour; mothers in the first group provided more stimulating materials for their children to play with and were less authoritarian; mothers in the second group expected higher achievement from their children; while those in the third group showed no change. The surprise came at the follow-up testing of the children after a year in school. The two groups with parent involvement maintained their improvement in achievement scores; while the third group's scores declined. Here is evidence – if on a small scale – that parent involvement can affect both parents' attitudes and children's achievement.

The implications of these early intervention studies are clear – they are that work should be carried out with parents and children together. Two facts about the present preschool scene are therefore rather surprising. The first is that active participation by parents is far from universal. Parents working in the less structured Head Start centres in the States were expected to observe and do routine chores – and the same may be true of traditional nurseries. The second is the emphasis on intervention through the school- or centre-based group rather than the home. Despite the arguments of the critics of the notions of 'compensatory education' and 'equality of educational opportunity' that environmental factors to do with home and community were more powerful than school factors in explaining children's educational performance, efforts have concentrated mainly on parents and children within the school or group setting.

What should we conclude from the early intervention studies? First, parents should be viewed as educators, with a role to play in their children's development. Their participation should be active, working directly with the children, whether at home or in school. Secondly, parents' confidence in their own abilities and their own worth is a crucial component of their competence. Thirdly, we see from both American and British programmes that preschool intervention can make an impact on both children and parents over the long term. And last, we should note the reaction against what has been seen as an over-emphasis on the early years, leading to a re-emphasis of the importance of continuity between what happens before five with the child's experience in school and at home with his parents throughout his school life (Clarke and Clarke, 1976). In short, we should see parental participation as a continuous process – not simply, like a preschool programme, an 'injection before five'.

So far, we have looked at parental involvement within the tradition of educational intervention. Yet, as we have seen, the impetus for expanding preschool provision also derives from consumer pressures, and notions of participation here have had more to do with consumers' rights and the responsiveness of a service to consumer needs and demands than with the education of parent and child. What evidence is there for the effectiveness of this tradition of provision? If educational intervention is not an objective of this form of provision, then it is hardly fair to judge its impact on such grounds. Yet it is relevant. Bruner (1972) quotes Hess's study to suggest that the more the mother feels in control of her life the more likely the child is to do well. We know that many parents lack confidence in themselves as parents, and see the professional as the source of expert advice (Hess, 1980). Mere attendance at a preschool group appears to have little impact by itself on either parents' participation in the centre or further participation out in the community, whether they belonged to community groups or bothered about community problems (Myers, 1972). There is some evidence that playgroups run by parents can be effective in improving children's performance (Turner, 1977). We know that playgroups in priority areas are more likely to keep children as regular attenders if their mothers are involved in helping in the group (Ferri and Niblett, 1977). What happens, then, when parents are responsible for organizing the group, employing the staff, and working alongside the children – what are the effects of this kind of involvement on both parents and children?

We can illustrate some of the effects of this kind of involvement for parents from a scheme in Cheshire, supported jointly by PPA and the local authority, where project leaders worked in priority areas to set up and support playgroups. Mothers described what they felt the playgroups had done for their children in terms of making friends: 'They learn to share and get on,' 'It helped him come out of himself.' Many mothers spoke about 'getting ideas' about what to do with their children at home, and 'learning a lot' about them (Palfreeman and Smith, forthcoming):

> It helps you to understand children. It gave me a variety of things to do with my child – instead of reading silly stories you think of other things to do with them. You understand children more when you see a variety of children together.

Mothers also described the experience for themselves. The enjoyment of a 'feeling of belonging', of doing things in a group, of sharing a common experience, was clearly important:

> It's brought me out of myself. I was very shy and didn't go anywhere – you don't feel so lonely when you have somewhere like here to go to.

> I found they all had some problems – I was not the only one with a wilful child. I enjoyed mixing with the mothers . . . it made me more confident. I was accepted other than in my own home. I was shy before. It made me feel someone.

Alongside this feeling of change in their own lives, mothers spoke about change in their community:

> It's helped people on the estate get involved. . . . . It's helped the community – brought mothers together who wouldn't normally mix . . . brings the children together.

– and about their own growing confidence in getting things done:

> Well, we are thinking of starting a mother and toddler club now, moving on. . . . We are ordinary people, but meeting here together makes you want to do things. . .

For these groups of mothers, the experience of being part of a playgroup which they helped organize and run, clearly helped them to realize their own sense of identity and their collective power and sense of community. There are many similar examples of parents and children finding companionship and self-confidence in playgroups (PPA, 1980). But we do not know what differences in impact on parents or children there would be between playgroups run and organized by parents, and nursery classes or schools run by professionals but involving parents. Studies of this kind need to be done before we can talk with confidence about the effects of parental participation.

The literature on participation illustrates the problems of participation in the sense of parental control. Bacon, in his study of the new-style school boards in Sheffield (1978), suggests that school governors were reluctant to raise issues to do with, for example, curriculum or teaching methods, which might challenge the headteacher's professional judgement or competence, or to become too closely involved in what are traditionally defined as professional matters. As one governor put it, 'I feel convinced that the head teacher is the one person who should judge what is best for our children in terms of curriculum and internal policy.' The new boards were, however, taking more initiative over issues which concerned the relationship between the school and the community – the use of school sports facilities by local groups, for instance. Lynch and Pimlott, in their study of parents and teachers in three secondary schools in Southampton (1976), have additional evidence on this question of professional competence. The majority of the teachers thought that parents had enough say in *what* and *how* their children were taught, and one in four thought that teachers were capable of teaching the child without the parents' help. Roughly a quarter of the teachers thought that too little was provided in the way of opportunities for parents to help at the school, talks on education, and information for parents on what and how their child was being taught and how they could help him. When parents were asked their views, it was clear that although roughly two-thirds thought they did not have enough say in what or how their children were being taught, seven out of ten parents underlined the professional's competence view of education – that the teachers were capable of teaching without help from the parents. In another study parents come at the bottom of the list of groups with power to influence what happens in the school or the classroom (Taylor *et al.*, 1974).

This is a long way from a 'parent power' movement to take control of the schools. The Taylor Committee noted wryly that the structure and composition of school governing bodies might change to include parents without necessarily re-defining their function. Barbara Tizard's research in nurseries suggests that it may be difficult to alter organizational arrangements which reflect assumptions about professional responsibilities unless there is an immediately visible pay-off from the change. In his review of compensatory education programmes, Woodhead (1976) argued that 'since we have greater control over the environment of the school than we have over the home, the emphasis will be on the way the school can be modified'. But perhaps we should be rather more cautious about the possibilities for change in schools and teachers.

The literature on parental involvement gives us grounds for optimism that there are long-term effects for both parents and children. However, as yet we know little about the process by which the effects of involvement are sustained or 'fixed', the relationship between changing parents' attitudes and changing their behaviour, or about the effects of different types of parent involvement. Modest optimism should not allow us to ignore the difficulties in changing people's behaviour, and the organization within which they operate – whether teachers in the schools or parents in the home.

Definitions of parental involvement

Now that we have considered some of the developments in parental involvement and the research evidence, we can at last commit ourselves to a definition. Explicit definitions are hard to find; the discussion so far should at least have demonstrated the variety of implicit definitions to be found in both practice and theory. We have outlined two approaches to parental involvement as preschool provision has developed over the last 15–20 years: the first educational, and the second participatory. In the first, parents are seen as learners and teachers of their own children; in the second, they are organizers, committee members, policy-makers, as well as consumers.

Gordon (1969) outlines a five-point scale which combines the two approaches:

1 *Parents as supporters* – service givers – facilitators – clerical, custodial, maintenance, fund-raising, family nights
2 *Parents as learners* – parent education courses, observation of children with explanation

3 *Parents as teachers of their own children* – taking home toys and books for use with children
4 *Parents as teacher aides and volunteers in the classroom* – prepare materials, read stories, work with children
5 *Parents as policy-makers and partners* – policy-makers, advisory board members

Ferri and Niblett (1977), in their study of playgroups in priority areas, outline four different types or categories of parent involvement: first, involvement in the group's management committee; second, helping in the day to day running of the group, working alongside the children; third, involvement in 'group related activities', whether in the group (making tea or coffee, setting out the equipment), or outside it (parties, fund raising); and a fourth category, more difficult to define or assess, which was to do with the group's 'warmth' – 'the extent to which mothers used the group as a place where they were able and welcome to spend some time and enjoy social contact with staff and other mothers' – 'simply the opportunity to sit down and relax, have a cup of tea and chat'.

These two frameworks do not overlap completely. They both contain what might be called the 'servicing', 'management', and 'volunteering' elements of parent involvement; but Ferri and Niblett do not specifically mention the educational aspects (parents as learners and as teachers), and Gordon is not concerned with group 'accessibility'.

Preliminary analysis of the data from the national CHES (Child Health and Education) survey (Van der Eyken *et al.*, 1979; Van der Eyken *et al.*, forthcoming) suggests three measures of parental involvement – support or practical help, involvement or working in the group, and control or involvement in management. But this classification does not include the notion of a group's accessibility, nor does it permit us to distinguish different types of help when working in the group.

From our review of the literature, we can pick out the

following five categories of parent involvement in preschool groups:

1. Working with the children on 'educational activities' – that is, with little apparent difference in role between the 'professional teacher' and the 'parent as teacher'. This seems to be the crucial factor in the studies of early intervention in the home.
2. Working in the group 'doing the chores' – putting out the equipment, clearing up, making the tea, mixing paints and cutting up paper (what is known in many primary schools as 'tying shoelaces and wiping noses').
3. Servicing the group but not actually working in the group alongside the children – making and mending equipment, fund-raising, helping with outings and the annual Christmas party.
4. A 'miscellaneous category' of factors to do with the 'openness' of the group: parents visiting the group before the child starts, staying to settle the child; visiting to discuss problems with the staff; visiting for special events; parents dropping in casually to see what is going on in the group.
5. Involvement in management.

To what extent does this classification reflect actual practice?

First, how common is it to find parents working in the group? About half the nursery schools and classes in one small survey conducted by the DES (DES, 1975) had parents helping in the classroom, either regularly or occasionally; but the percentage of parents involved in this way was not high, nor are there any details of what the parents actually did. Sixty-two per cent of the primary schools in the Plowden survey reported that parents provided substantial help in money, kind or labour each year; but again there are no details of what proportion of the parents were involved or what they did. A more recent study of 157 groups in Scotland (Watt, 1976) showed that one third of the nursery schools and classes and almost all the playgroups surveyed said parents most often helped with (in order) setting out equipment, giving out milk, and working with a small group of children; and more than three quarters of the parents interviewed said they worked with the children. According to the Pre-School Playgroups Association's figures (PPA, 1979), parents help with the children during playgroup sessions in 81 per cent of all playgroups, and in more than half the groups where parents help there are more than ten involved, but this does not tell us how regularly. Parents helped in half the playgroups in the Ferri and Niblett study of priority areas.

The Scottish study showed that parents thought that 'servicing activities' such as helping on outings and fund-raising were the most appropriate forms of involvement in all types of group. Parents in playgroups were more likely to think 'educational activities' – playing with children – appropriate involvement than were parents in nursery classes or schools. Likewise, staff in nursery schools and classes thought that helping with outings and fund-raising were the chief ways of involving parents, while playgroup staff thought playing with the children was more important. PPA figures (PPA, 1975) suggest that working with the children in the group and raising money rank about equal in practice. Mothers helped with routine jobs in the group, and with group-related activities, in two thirds of the playgroups in the priority area study.

Secondly, what about the openness of the groups? The Scottish survey suggests that playgroup parents had less opportunity than parents in nursery schools or classes to visit the group with the child before he started at the group, or to have a private talk with the staff; more than four fifths of the nursery parents had done so. On the other hand, playgroup parents had more opportunities for social events, general meetings, and outings. In the Plowden survey, 66 per cent of the schools had arranged social functions for the parents, and 63 per cent had arranged meetings on educational matters. Parents tended to go (in order) to open days, social events such as shows or concerts, and fund-raising events; but there were considerable differences between class groups in attendance at these events; and over a third of the parents surveyed had not visited the school to have a talk with the head teacher before the child started school.

Thirdly, how far are parents involved in management? This shows the widest variation between type of group. Playgroups are most often managed by a parent committee – 56 per cent according to PPA figures (PPA, 1979). In the Scottish study, no nursery schools or classes involved parents in any aspect of management; all the playgroups were run by a parent committee, and in three quarters of these parents were in the majority; considerably more playgroup parents and staff thought that parents should take management decisions and appoint staff than did either the parents or staff in nursery classes or schools. Twelve of the 30 playgroups in the Ferri and Niblett study of playgroups in priority areas had some form of management committee, and mothers were represented on five of these. Perhaps the most important fact here is that parents were more likely to be involved in helping with the children in the group when it was run by a parent committee (PPA, 1975).

The Taylor Committee on school governors and managers (DES, 1977) reported that by 1975, 70 out of 82 local authorities had parent representatives on governing bodies. This compares with the Plowden Committee's comment that substantial numbers of primary head teachers and teachers thought that managing bodies were 'unhelpful'. Seventeen per cent of the schools surveyed by the Plowden Committee had parent teacher associations, but fewest of these were to be found in the nursery schools, 'where relations between mothers and teachers are usually very intimate', as the committee commented. The committee did not view PTAs with favour, on the grounds of their middle-class dominance.

Parental involvement is a growing fashion. According to a national survey of primary schools (Cyster, Chift and Battle, 1980), 55 per cent of primary headteachers thought that involvement had increased and that parental attitudes were changing significantly as a result. What can we conclude from the sketch in this chapter? First, that it is extremely difficult to be sure what exactly parents do when they help in a group, whether playgroup or nursery class or school; or to know what proportion of the parents of children in a group are actually involved. Secondly, that parental involvement in management, or in officially-constituted bodies such as PTAs, is far less likely in nursery schools or classes than in playgroups. Third, that there seems to be some evidence for a link between parents being involved in running a group and parents being involved in working with the children in the group – although we do not know exactly what this means. Fourth, there is a wide range of openness in groups, with no clear picture so far of what type of group parents find more welcoming – perhaps we should be more specific about the different kinds of 'welcomingness'.

In this chapter we have attempted to unravel some of the different arguments from different sources about the importance and impact of parent involvement, and how involvement is defined and put into practice. This, then, is the background to our study in Oxfordshire of parental involvement in nursery schools, nursery classes, and playgroups. In the next chapter we outline the study and the questions we proposed to ask.

3
The Oxfordshire study

We began the study of parental involvement in Oxfordshire with a range of questions already suggested in the literature. 'Good practice' in the tradition of the Plowden Report means a 'welcoming' group and a two-way flow of information between home and school covering the child's home background and the school's methods. But it is not clear what 'welcoming' might mean. Involving parents in actually working with their children apparently has an impact on both children's educational performance and also parents' understanding of their part in the educative process – but we know little about how this is related to other forms of involvement. We might expect to find different forms of involvement in voluntary playgroups and statutory nursery groups, but it is difficult to be sure exactly what parents do or how many participate. There is clearly great variety in the definitions and types of parent involvement, yet we do not know how this might be related to differences in educational objectives, say, between different types of group. Which of these questions should we have pursued?*

---

* Let us remind readers of the definitions of the various forms of preschool group referred to in this and following chapters:
   Nursery schools and nursery classes are both statutory forms of preschool provision provided free by the local education authority, and in theory open to all three- to five-year-olds in the catchment area. Nursery schools are separate establishments with their own headteacher; nursery classes are simply classes in a first or primary school.
   Playgroups are voluntary groups, registered with the local social services department and charging a small fee, usually set up by a group of parents who join together to make provision for their children.

The Oxfordshire background

To start with, we had to review what was known about parental involvement in Oxfordshire.

In 1977-8, when we made our study, Oxfordshire had 29 nursery schools and classes, with more than two thirds concentrated in the city and the remainder either located in the larger county towns or serving concentrations of population such as the Brize Norton air base or Harwell. It also had some 290 private groups, 250 of which were members of the Pre-school Playgroups Association. Oxfordshire came fairly low in the league table for statutory provision and slightly higher for voluntary – although obviously some areas were far better served than others. But this is a fairly typical county, with its mixture of relatively prosperous, well-serviced towns and isolated rural villages, no large urban centres except Oxford itself, and no industrial concentrations except Cowley. The one striking fact relevant to preschool provision is that Oxfordshire has the lowest proportion of full-time working mothers with children under five of any county or metropolitan district in the country.

We knew there was considerable interest in parental involvement at what we might call the official level. In the education department, this was not confined to preschool – and, indeed, not necessarily related to preschool provision at all. Questions of school management had been up for discussion since the reorganization of the county boundaries in 1974 – separate managing bodies for nursery schools, with a parent representative, had been recommended by a working party in 1975 – and the publication of the Taylor Report in 1977 provided further stimulus. There was growing interest in involving parents in the work of the schools – indicated by the number of county level discussions and conferences on the topic. And on the other hand, there was an increasingly clear statement from the Pre-school Playgroups Association that parental involvement in playgroups was important.

What was Oxfordshire's policy towards parents? From the

discussions with staff in schools and playgroups, and officers in the Education and Social Services Departments and in PPA, it became clear that parental involvement met with official approval, and was encouraged as 'good practice'. Yet, as the people we spoke to were quick to point out, headteachers and staff in voluntary groups traditionally enjoy considerable autonomy, and 'good practice' could not be legislated into existence.

The most sensitive statement of the relationship between parents and their children's preschool group from the 'official' rather than the 'ground level' point of view is set out in a report produced by a Working Party established to review preschool provision in the county following Mrs Thatcher's White Paper *Education: a Framework for Expansion* (1972) and local government reorganization of 1974, with representatives from the Education and Social Services Departments as well as PPA. This is how the Working Party described the relationship between parents and nursery schools and classes in their report, 'Beginnings':

> It is helpful if parents spend time in the nursery alongside their children, thus linking the small family group with the larger school community. There are also benefits for everyone in the nursery, since parents can offer particular skills and expertise. Most important of all, the involvement of parents promotes a feeling of well-being which is transmitted to the children, and which helps them to learn. It is now well known that parental attitudes and expectations constitute one of the strongest influences upon a child's readiness to gain skill and knowledge. Attitudes and expectations are most easily changed for the better through shared experience within the nursery. It must be said, however, that not all parents are able or willing to play an active part. For a minority of such parents the child's attendance must be seen as largely therapeutic. These parents need a short period away from their child and it

is a great help to them if they are coping with many personal and family problems to be reassured and feel happy about the period of the day that their child spends in a nursery, for they know he is receiving skilled help in an environment especially planned for him.

Here we have a service run by professionals largely for the child, but with a therapeutic objective for those parents who need support. Involvement of parents is an added bonus if they have special skills to offer to benefit the child, or to enable parents to acquire more positive attitudes. Shared experience is the key, to both the child's and the parent's learning.

This is how the working party saw the relationship between parents and playgroups:

> Where there is good communication between groups and opportunities for people to learn from each other and discuss new ideas, playgroups become more community-conscious and less inward-looking. Some results are:
>
> (a) An understanding of the loneliness and desperation of some young mothers, leading to an interest in the development of mother and toddler groups;
> (b) A clearer understanding that parent involvement does not mean just having mothers who are 'good with children', but finding ways of making the not-so-good mothers feel wanted because they badly need the playgroup;
> (c) An attempt to respond to this increased understanding by the provision of informal education programmes for parents.
>
> In playgroups it became obvious in the early years that parents who took on responsibility in the playgroup began to realize their own potential in many

different ways. This involvement of parents in taking the responsibility for their children, both administratively and in the play session, is seen to be the most important contribution that playgroups have made in the field of early childhood education.

Playgroups are concerned with the development and well-being of the whole family as part of the community. They believe that parents and children need to grow together. . . .

Since any effective new learning has to be built on something already properly understood it has been the policy in playgroup courses to work from practical experience: from an acceptance of what the parents were able to provide themselves towards an understanding of theory. Although the standard of provision of play and its management might at first be lower and difficult for the professional to accept, it improves as the parents' understanding grows . . . through group discussion and observations.

The starting point here is that parents and children learn best together, that parents must be accepted 'as they are' before they can learn. Parents carry primary responsibility for the service, which is concerned with the whole family as part of the community. The emphasis is on parents and children together.

'Beginnings' was a careful and sensitive statement of the different sorts of relationship that might be found between parents and statutory and voluntary provision in Oxfordshire. But did it correspond to actual practice? Many people working in the preschool field across the county could point to particular groups as examples of 'good practice' of parental involvement. Yet information on numbers of nursery classes, schools or playgroups involving parents, or parents' activities, and staff's or parents' views, was more difficult to find.

We knew that some 82 per cent of Oxfordshire's 250 PPA registered playgroups were managed by a parents' committee, and 92 per cent had parents helping with children during the group session (PPA, 1978). A small survey of 20 playgroups in Oxfordshire was carried out in 1976 for the Oxford Preschool Research Group (Bradley, 1976). This showed that the most common form of parental involvement was fund-raising; all but one of the playgroups was run by a parents' committee; and all but two had parents helping in the sessions. Twelve had a parents' rota for help with the sessions; eleven had secondary school children or students as additional casual help. Parents were more likely to help with sessions in the larger playgroups and those where fees were low. Only two groups actually discouraged parents from working in the sessions with the children – largely on the grounds that the supervisors wished to create an atmosphere more akin to 'school', but also perhaps because they needed less help in maintaining the premises or clearing away equipment. Bradley concludes that although there were varying levels of parental involvement, 'without parents providing both help in sessions and back-up support, many of the groups would clearly cease to function'. The most important finding of this survey from our point of view was the comment by supervisors that parents were not very clear about their role in the playgroup and needed encouragement to participate.

Preliminary discussions

Thus we did not have much information to hand when deciding what we might attempt in Oxfordshire. It was clear that there were different practices and approaches. The working party's report contained different perspectives on parents and their involvement in statutory and voluntary provision – nursery classes and schools on the one hand, and playgroups on the other. But apart from small-scale surveys and anecdotal examples, we had little to tell us how far these background assumptions and expectations matched actual practice. The literature told us something about types of parental involvement in different types of preschool organization, and something of the strategies for their introduction; yet there was little detail in the studies concerning the different roles taken by parents or 'professionals'. From the preliminary discussions, this was an area of murky confusion between expectation and practice.

We might have set up an action-research study on the Young and McGeeney model (1968), to assess the effects on children and parents of changing patterns of parent involvement and communications between school or playgroup and parents. Our resources, however, were insufficient for both 'action' and 'research'; and we should therefore have had to rely on the chance of finding a group in the process of changing its practice and willing for us to observe that process. But to have concentrated all our energies on this point would have meant neglecting a wider focus. Or we might have documented the 'good practice' already known to be in action in different groups across the county. But to consider only 'good practice' would have meant ignoring the factors that contribute to make some practice 'good' and other practice 'bad' as well as missing an opportunity to probe the definition in the first place.

In a sense, neither of these enterprises was possible until we had more precise information concerning the extent and type of involvement in different types of preschool group, and the attitudes and assumptions held by parents and professionals about parent involvement. But clearly with our resources we could not take a detailed look at all 300 or so preschool groups across Oxfordshire. If we wished to probe differences in practice and assumptions in different types of group with different styles of operating, we had to devise first, some way of observing what happened and of recording people's views; and second, some way of sampling groups to include those with different styles of working with parents. Before we could find an answer to either of these problems, we had to get a clearer idea of the important questions about parental involvement to the staff running the groups, and thus a better 'nose' for differences between groups. So, as a first step, in the Autumn of 1977 and the Spring of 1978 we consulted headteachers and supervisors in about 100 nursery classes, nursery schools, playgroups, private nursery schools and day nurseries and crèches across the county. We viewed this as a 'trawling exercise' – to give us a better sense of probable diversity in practice and background assumptions concerning parents' involvement in their children's preschool groups.

We did not set out on this trawl with a highly-structured theory, but three rather low-level working expectations: first, that there would be considerable differences in practice in how parents were involved; secondly, that there would be considerable differences in attitude as to whether parents should be involved, and if so, how and why; and last, that these differences would be related to organizational differences between groups which would in turn reflect the different objectives which groups were established to meet. Our first two expectations were confirmed without much difficulty; the third was rather more complicated, however, than we had supposed.

We were uncertain when we started in 1977 whether parental involvement would be of any concern at all to people at a time of considerable anxiety in the education service both locally and nationally, with economic cuts, strikes, and threatened closures of provision. Involving parents might simply be the icing on the cake when there was at stake the much more basic bread-and-butter provision of buildings, staff, equipment and materials. Or it might be the issue which set statutory provision against voluntary: 'professionals' threatened by 'do-it-yourself' parents or 'nurseries on the cheap'. However, we found that involving parents, building links between group, home, and community, or learning how to make a reality out of the phrases 'it's your playgroup' or 'it's the parents' school', were taken to be crucially important questions. Occasional sensitivity to the possibility of 'a lot of parents helping providing an excuse to cut staff', as one headteacher put it, arose less as an anti-parent feeling than as a reaction to economic threats to a service. Several headteachers in first schools spoke of the indirect effect that cutbacks in staff might have on parent involvement. 'Volunteer' parents would replace paid helpers in secretarial work or library administration, or even, possibly, in traditional teaching tasks such as hearing reading. 'But why should parents be used as a cheap source of labour?' we were asked. There might also be a more subtle impact on the school's links with the community. One school had formerly had a paid assistant in each classroom – usually a local mother. Now 'Oxfordshire expects volunteers to do the same work' – but local mothers could not afford to volunteer. The relationship between 'involvement' and 'volunteering' was thus a sensitive issue in the current economic climate.

In these preliminary discussions with headteachers of nursery schools and first schools with nursery classes, and with the supervisors or teachers in playgroups and other non-statutory groups – some 100 groups in total across the county – we intended to find out how parents were involved in the groups, why those in charge of the groups thought parents should be involved, and what they meant by parent involvement. We summarize the main threads first, then give some examples. (We should remind readers that the discussion in this chapter is not restricted to the preschool level – some of the examples deal with parents' involvement with older children in the first schools.)

Parents' involvement

First, there was a great variety of help given by parents reported by teachers and playgroup supervisors. They worked with the children in the sessions alongside regular staff; they read stories and cooked with the children, talked to them about what they were doing, tied aprons and shoelaces; they provided cover for staff absences; they made and mended equipment, cut up paper, cleaned the rooms, made coffee, washed paint brushes and towels; they took children on outings, raised money, and served on committees.

Some of our preconceptions took a knock. Following the Bradley survey in Oxfordshire and other literature, we expected, for example, to find more parents involved in management in the non-statutory, self-financing groups than in statutory provision. Overall, this was so; but a surprising number of playgroups were *not* run by a parents' committee – in one area only two thirds had a parents' committee; while it was common practice for statutory nurseries to have parent managers on the management body – although views varied as to their representativeness or their value. Again, we expected that playgroups would involve parents in the sessions to a greater extent than either the statutory nursery classes and schools or the voluntary groups set up by and for working mothers – if only for economic reasons. This was true to some extent. The full-time groups catering for working mothers did not have a parents' rota for help in the sessions, although some had a 'cover rota' for staff illness. But a parents' rota for help in the sessions was by no means universal in playgroups – indeed it was the exception rather than the rule, although the definition of 'rota' varied from a list of fairly regular helpers to the expectation that every mother would help with the sessions; on the other hand there were nurseries with a parents' rota for help with sessions. So, on the two factors of management and organized help with sessions, the picture of practice was by no means as clear-cut as we had expected.

Working mothers were mentioned surprisingly often in view of the fact that among counties Oxfordshire comes bottom of the list for working women – and mentioned not only in those full-time groups which catered for working mothers. This was less common in the country villages (although 'domestic work' was mentioned); but many groups in Oxford itself, in 'suburbs' like Kidlington, and in the army communities round Bicester, had up to 75 per cent of their mothers in work, often part-time jobs on the 'twilight shift' or evening cleaning.

Two points stood out in headteachers' and supervisors' comments. One concerned 'critical activities' or 'critical territory' – whether parents were excluded from certain activities or areas, and to what extent there was a distinction in roles between parents and staff in the group. Hearing reading is one example. Several headteachers of first schools picked this out as an activity unsuitable for parents – or one that was done by parents but with possible conflict with the NUT as a result. Hearing reading thus for some headteachers belonged quite clearly to the professional role rather than the parents' role. Another example was parents' access to the staff room. One headteacher felt that parents came in to the school to help as equals and should be invited into the staff room. Sometimes, however, parents were not welcome in the staff room – where staff wanted privacy to discuss problem children or problem parents. A third, and related, example, concerned the problem of confidentiality – giving parents access to personal details or the background to a particular child's difficulties. Many playgroup supervisors and headteachers thought that they had been given information in confidence by parents which it would be unprofessional to divulge to 'non-staff'. A similar problem arose over discipline – should a parent helper discipline a child or leave this to a regular member of staff? All these difficulties relate to the boundary lines between what can legitimately be done by someone in a 'professional' role and what can or should be done by someone not in that role. We shall return to this later.

The other point concerned parents staying to settle in their child when he first joined the group. This was almost universal practice – expected by most headteachers and playgroup supervisors. However, a few groups did not welcome or expect parents to settle their children. 'It's better to get the crying over – mothers can look through the window if they like,' and 'Children easily become little tyrants,' were the comments made. Reasons given for this exclusion were always to do with the difficulties of the process of separation – if mothers stayed, they would encourage their children to be 'clingy', and it was better for both mother and child 'to get it over quickly'. Parents were discouraged from helping for similar reasons: Their own children are too clinging' – 'the child must learn to be independent'. Here the objective of the group is to wean the child away from family and home, rather than maintain a partnership. Again we shall return to this later.

Definitions of involvement

Second, what did those in charge of the hundred-odd groups mean by the term 'involvement'? Most thought that involving parents was a good practice and to be encouraged. But people attached different meanings to the word. One group leader might say that parents were not involved in her group – but as she meant a parents' rota by 'involvement' fail to include a gradmother who came in to read stories to the children. Another might claim that parents were involved – but there was no parents' rota and only occasional help from parents, although they were welcome to stay informally. And a third might likewise claim that parents were involved – although here she meant that parents stayed to settle in their children and organized a cover rota when staff were absent although they did not normally stay to help with the sessions at all.

The full-time groups catering for working mothers provide an illustration. Although these groups had no parent rota for help with the sessions, supervisors were just as likely as those in other non-statutory groups to say that parents were involved and to think that they should be. But what they meant by involvement was parents 'knowing what's going on', taking turns on a cover rota for staff absences, and, most important of all, staying to settle the child when he first joined the group.

Another illustration is provided by the differences in the meaning of 'involvement' for headteachers of nursery schools and headteachers of first or primary schools with a nursery class. Parents were viewed by both as an extra, practical resource. They undertook tasks which otherwise would have required staff time or school funds. As one headteacher said where parents had painted the school building – he would be considerably worse off but for the labour provided by parents. Nursery school headteachers were more likely, however, to use parents as substitutes or extra pairs of hands when the nursery was short-staffed, and to view this as 'a legitimate reason for asking parents to help'. First-school heads were more likely to bring in trained teachers to cover staff shortages.

Again, nursery heads were more likely to see involvement in terms of parents' own needs, or informal open access, than were first-school headteachers. The latter spoke of involvement in terms of a 'better understanding between home and school' and parents wanting 'to know what is going on', or parents undertaking particular maintenance jobs or activities.

Here we have a clear indication that different types of involvement were thought to be more appropriate in different organizations. Parental involvement was seen as less formal in the nursery. Parents were free to come in and stay with their child, and were welcomed in a very informal way; specific help with outings and parties, repairs or maintenance, or activities in the group such as cooking, were left to the teacher concerned and similarly organized in a fairly informal manner. In the rest of the first school, however, involvement was on a more formally organized basis – often through the parent-teacher association. At the nursery level, involvement was usually judged on the interests of the child, or the parent and child together (even if the actual activity seemed more for the benefit of the nursery) – the first question to be asked when a parent offered to help was whether it would be beneficial or not for the child to have the parent present. In contrast, further up in the school involvement was defined as practical help for the school; the child's or the parent's interests did not come into the matter except for an occasional concern that some parents would prefer not to help in their own child's class.

The differences in viewpoint were neatly summed up by

two headteachers, one from a first school, the other from a nursery school. The first said that 'parents are free to stay in the nursery but they do not participate'. The other set the contrast: involvement in the nurseries was about 'relationships, not only practicalities'.

We should perhaps be wary of making too much of a difference in approach between nursery classes and nursery schools. As several teachers commented, what actually happens in the nursery class may be nearer nursery school practice than headteachers' views suggest. However, we have used these examples to illustrate the diversity of definition.

Reasons for involving parents

Third, we hoped to discover some of the reasons for involving parents. We picked out two recurring emphases. One concerned the question of screening or selecting parents to help in the group. For many nursery staff, there was a dilemma between their wish to involve all parents, and the need to keep the group functioning without being overwhelmed. Some solved the problem by welcoming all comers into the group while remaining highly selective when it came to particular tasks. 'You have to be careful,' – 'Some mothers are not always suitable,' – and 'You can't have inadequate parents with the children,' were not infrequent comments. Other staff rated parents' needs high on their list of priorities and put much time and effort into involving mothers with problems of their own.

Playgroup supervisors seemed less bothered by this dilemma between open access to all parents and selection of the 'suitable'. Most got on well with local mothers, and thought that parents who helped made an important contribution, although sometimes there were problems of the 'regulars' turning into a clique and dominating the group. There were occasional comments about 'immature' mothers and 'going back to work too soon', but on the whole playgroup supervisors welcomed help from any source and were less likely to be selective.

The other emphasis concerned the reasons for encouraging open access or selective approaches. Views in favour of involving parents divided roughly into four. First, social reasons: 'It helps the mothers to feel less isolated.' Second, broadly educational – parents learn through being part of the group: 'It helps parents to gain a sense of perspective on their own children,' 'All mothers should come in if only to watch,' 'It's good for mothers to find out what happens – parents learn to enjoy their children and it gives them ideas.' Parents learning through involvement was a common reason given for involvement in all kinds of group. Third, a sense of parents' rights to participate in the group: 'The parents have a right to be involved – it's a fully democratic group,' and with a shift from rights to corresponding duties – 'It is the parents' playgroup and they should not exploit it as a cheap form of babysitting.' And fourth, a sense of the links between the family, the group, and the community: 'The playgroup should be an extended family,' 'Being involved helps to make a community.' So here involvement is encouraged as therapeutic or educational for the parents, and the group is assumed to be a partnership, or extension, of home and community, with corresponding rights and duties for parents.

In contrast, views in favour of selection or restriction of parental help broke down into three. First, the group should indeed be therapeutic for parents but by giving them a break from their children. Second, the group's focus was the child, and his growing independence. And third, mothers were simply less efficient as helpers than were the regular staff. Here the group is assumed to be primarily for the child's benefit, and is less of a partnership than a stepping stone for the child out of the home and away into the wide world.

So much for a somewhat skeletal summary of the preliminary discussions. To give a stronger flavour of the diversity of practice and definition that we heard, here are a few examples. They are not intended to characterize or define the different organization types of group.

Some examples

For some headteachers in nursery schools, parents' own needs provided a reason for involvement and one criterion for selecting parents to help. One head was anxious to have parents in both to relieve staff and also 'to have mothers in the building so that something can rub off about child handling'. This head was very sensitive to parents' problems and the needs of working mothers. She spoke of a mother who 'used to scream all the time at her child' but who by staying to help in the nursery was 'gradually finding alternative ways of dealing with the child'. She clearly saw the nursery as a means of training parents in child-rearing, and had a deliberate policy of approaching 'those who most need to help' as well as the most able. Another nursery head, who thought that 'parents of priority children often have problems themselves' and needed particular encouragement, persevered with a mother who was gradually learning how to play with and understand her own child – 'but we had to reorganize the entire nursery to cope'. One headteacher was sensitive to the needs of working mothers, and isolated or depressed mothers. She saw the nursery partly as a means of creating social networks – 'mothers have made friendships by meeting here' – and organized *ad hoc* evening meetings which were partly educational but partly 'just plain fun'. She was interested in the question of accountability to the community and thought the managing body should ideally act as the link with the community. Another thought that it was important to work genuinely alongside parents as equals – for example she did not ask about fathers' occupations as she felt this set up a barrier. The opinion of the parent representative on the management committee was important when admissions were discussed or staff appointments made.

Other nursery heads relied on more organized involvement plus more careful selection. Parents helped with specific activities like washing towels, taking children on outings, mending toys, bringing in baby animals, but were not encouraged to stay all day. One head wanted to do without parents if possible – if necessary, she approached 'the better educated', and felt that parents helped out of gratitude for a place for their child. Others were emphatic that 'you can't have inadequate parents with the children'.

Here are some examples from first schools with nursery classes. There was more openly expressed anxiety about the relationship between the school and its community of parents – illustrated in the argument over the advantages or disadvantages of a formal organization to link up the two like a parent-teacher association. One headteacher feared that a PTA would become 'dictatorial' and 'make the rules about what is taught'. 'Some staff want parents, others don't,' was the view. The nursery should not cater for working mothers. Parents tended to be a disruptive influence in the school, 'treating it like a social function' with their cigarettes and toddlers and pushchairs and dogs all over the place. Another stressed that the school was 'open house' to parents, organized social functions, visited the children's homes, and welcomed help with fund-raising and making and mending equipment – particularly from 'fathers out on strike' – while maintaining that it was not school policy for 'parents to help in class': 'You have to be very careful about the type of parent.' There was concern over 'gossippy' parents from local housing estates, and some headteachers preferred to restrict parent involvement to a minimum rather than be seen to be 'selective'. Comments were made about problems of confidentiality, discipline, and favouritism: 'They all gossip over the fence about who's been naughty; if a child's been naughty I'd rather tell the parent myself,' 'You can't let one mother discipline another's child, 'You can't have Mrs X in if you don't have Mrs Y.' Yet good contact at the nursery age was thought to lay the foundations for continuing contact throughout the child's school career.

Another head gave us a different picture. Parents came in to help as equals and were invited into the staffroom – 'We must treat them with respect.' Many parents offered to help because they were lonely and themselves needed help, and they gained both confidence and a better understanding. This head stressed that the school was 'always open', knew exactly how many parents helped and what they did, and was happy for parents to organize activities on their own initiative or on a joint basis.

A different picture again was presented by a headteacher who was acutely aware of the difficulty of separating children's and parents' needs. She was sensitive to the problems of the local community, particularly immigrant families, and spent much of her time doing 'social work'. She was also most thoughtful about the role of the PTA in encouraging parents with difficulties into the school, providing support, and channelling parent involvement. The PTA provided a major link between parent and school, and played a major part in involving parents in the work of the school and encouraging parents to think about how school resources should be used – whether, for example, school funds should be used to subsidize children whose parents could not or would not pay for swimming. This headteacher accepted all offers of help and made many approaches herself to parents who, she felt, needed support. She believed that the school should be accountable to the community and teachers should not be afraid of explaining their work to parents. 'Community accountability' and open access to parents produced two dilemmas in this headteacher's view. The first was the dilemma between teaching responsibilities and support for parents – both properly part of the teaching role. The other was the boundary between community accountability and community politics – should the school, for example, take part in the political argument over the future of nursery provision? Here the answer was no.

Our research design

The preliminary discussions gave us a better understanding of the important questions to do with involving parents in the eyes of staff. They also enabled us to test out the general 'expectations of good practice' contained in the county working party's report 'Beginnings', and take the conclusions of Bradley's survey of actual practice in playgroups rather further. It was now clear to us that statements of 'ideal types' and surveys of actual practice both left large questions unanswered. We began to suspect that if we were to understand the differences both between and within different types of group, organizational labels such as 'playgroup', 'nursery class', or 'nursery school' might conceal as much as reveal the important features.

Returning to our low-level hypotheses at the beginning of the 'trawling exercise', we could see that there were indeed considerable differences in practice, attitudes and assumptions to do with parental involvement. But these differences were apparently more closely linked to the objectives of the group and its staff than to organizational type as such. We were beginning to sketch in two different models of group – one with the focus on the child, and his gradual weaning away and independence from the family, the other more an extension of the family, with parents as partners in the child's learning and experience. Parents were more likely to be involved and welcomed in the second model than the first. Both types could be seen as therapeutic for parents; but this was more likely to be defined in the first type of group as a break for the parents, while the second type was more likely to be therapeutic in its friendly and undemanding welcome and acceptance.

Staff's attitudes towards parents as helpers were a good indication of the differences between the two models. In the first type, parents often were a hindrance, simply less efficient than staff. 'They chatter,' 'The children cling,' 'They're unreliable,' 'They have such different ideas about play,' were frequent comments. In the second type, there was a greater flexibility towards the needs of parents and children together. 'There are extra problems with the children but it's worth it,' 'Their own children may cling but it only worries their mothers, it's not disruptive,' were typical comments. Staff gave examples here of mothers with problems of their own or problems with their children who had gradually sorted themselves out through involvement with a group. A nursery had been reorganized to help one mother. Another mother from an isolated farm, whose first child spent a term under a table, was helped through the playgroup to work with her second child. 'If she's a good mother it helps the group; if she's a poor mother it helps her,' summed up this view of give and take between parent, child, and the group.

On the basis of the preliminary discussions, we argued that an account of parental involvement in Oxfordshire would be incomplete unless it took into account both actual practice – precisely what parents did in relation to the group and how staff in turn approached the parents – and also staff's and parents' views about the parents' role. We decided, therefore, to set up a study using observations in groups of different kinds and interviews with staff and with parents. Our intention was to document the differences in actual practice in greater detail than had been done in previous studies, and to relate this to the assumptions, attitudes and expectations of parents and staff about the objectives of the group, the part played by parents in their child's development, and the relationship between the home and the wider world of school or preschool group. In brief, we hoped to test out the types of parent involvement suggested in Chapter 2, and see how they related to different models of preschool provision.

We carried out the study in three parts. In the first, we conducted observations in 15 groups to give us the detail of what parents did in the group, how much contact there was between parents and staff, whether parents were encouraged to certain activities and discouraged from others. We selected the 15 groups from the Oxfordshire lists to give us a mix of different organizational types (nursery classes, nursery schools, and playgroups)*, of urban and rural groups (some in Oxford and some in the county), and of groups with 'high' and 'low' involvement as indicated by staff in the preliminary discussions. This gave us three nursery schools, four nursery classes, and eight playgroups – ten groups in Oxford and five in the county – eight groups with 'high' and seven with 'low' involvement. We followed the observation sessions with short discussions with helpers and staff from the group to check on the interpretation of particular events, or the typicality of the sessions, which would not be clear from observation alone.

In the second stage of the study, we interviewed staff in the 15 groups to learn their attitudes towards involving parents and their assumptions about the objectives of the group and the parents' part in the child's experience. In the third stage, we interviewed a sample of parents drawn randomly from the registers of six of the 15 groups. These six were selected to give us matched pairs of nursery schools, nursery classes, and playgroups with 'high' and 'low' involvement as shown by the observations and staff interviews – it was not possible at this point to include the city-county dimension.†

The conclusions from each of the stages are open to criticism on the grounds that the data base is small and that situations change rapidly. We have done our best to test the validity of the information by its internal consistency – whether the observations fit with what parents and staff said happened and thought should happen; and to discipline ourselves to limited conclusions and further questions, rather

---

* We excluded the Oxfordshire day nurseries from our study as day nurseries cater for families who are considered high priority cases for one reason or another and almost by definition do not involve parents – although there is an increasing number of day nurseries which take the relationship between the group, the family, and the community seriously and which do attempt to welcome and involve parents (Garland and White, 1980; Hughes et al., 1980).

† The complete material from one nursery class was not available for this analysis. Where comparisons are made between the matched pairs, this group is excluded; otherwise information is drawn from a similar class which had not, however, been matched.

than sweeping generalizations which we cannot substantiate. It remains for other researchers and practitioners to take up our material and use it to test out more detailed hypotheses.

In this chapter, we have attempted first to give some of the flavour of the practice and definitions of parent involvement in Oxfordshire, as this came over in the preliminary discussions, and the questions that arose; and secondly to set out the design of the subsequent study. In the chapters following, we describe our findings. In Chapter 4, we set out the observations in the fifteen groups. In Chapter 5, we describe staff's views, and, in Chapter 6, we look at parents' views in six of the groups.

4
Fifteen groups observed

The preliminary discussions reported in Chapter 3 gave us a sketch of headteachers' and playgroup leaders' views about involving parents. We learnt that most thought this was important, though there was a good deal of ambiguity and ambivalence. Some people thought the important point was that the group should be a welcoming one where parents could simply feel at ease; others that parents were useful extra labour; others, again, that parents learnt by joining in, or that children learnt better with their parents near them. But 'involving parents' is notoriously a dustbin term: it tells us nothing about the actual activities. To learn this, we proposed to look in more detail at a smaller number of groups of different kinds. What do parents contribute, and gain in return? And how does this match up to staff's and parents' views on their contribution?

For this first stage of the study, we selected 15 groups, to provide us with a mix of type of group, area served, and level of parent involvement. We ended up with three nursery schools, four nursery classes and eight playgroups. One nursery school, one nursery class and three playgroups were located in the county, the rest in the city. About two thirds of the groups were known to have parents helping with the sessions.

In each group, we observed throughout two sessions at different times of the week (and of the day, if the group had a morning and an afternoon session). The focus was specifically on adults – first, what parents and other 'non-staff' adults present in the group were doing, and secondly, any interaction between staff and parents. We wanted to know, for example, what happened at the beginning and end of sessions – whether parents usually waited outside for their children or came in to talk to the staff or other parents or to join in the activities; we wanted to know whether parent helpers worked and talked with the children as did the other members of staff, or cut up paper, tied shoe laces, made coffee, washed up; we wanted to know about the conversations between staff and parent helpers – whether staff told them what to do, encouraged them, left them to get on by themselves, or chatted about knitting patterns; we wanted to know about the 'openness' of the groups to other adults – the local builder arriving to mend a window, a grandmother with half an hour free after shopping, or the speech therapist.

Our observations in the 15 groups totalled over 80 hours. Just over half of this total was spent in the eight playgroups, just under a quarter in the four nursery classes, and a fifth in the three nursery schools. We observed throughout two sessions, noting at five-minute intervals and in as much detail as possible what any parents present were doing with the children or with other adults. We tried not to get involved ourselves in these sessions – although children often involved us automatically in their activities and parents were interested to know what we were doing. This we explained; but we kept our own questions for follow-up discussions.

We hoped that the observations would provide us with information about the general organization of the groups, and in particular about what parents did when they stayed to help. But, as one teacher said to us, 'You would have to observe in this class for a year to be sure that you have got the picture right.' Nobody could guarantee that the sessions we observed would be typical. The presence of parents, and the organization of the group, might be affected by seasonal or even weekly changes. For example, there might be more parents staying to settle their children at the beginning of term, or the first half of the school year; a sudden influx of parents and children new to the group, or a number of mothers with young babies, might mean fewer parents willing to help. Again, no-one could predict when a parent might arrive with a problem to discuss, a request for help, or a suggestion. We argued that while such events and their unpredictability were precisely what we were seeking to uncover, it would clearly be wise to cross-check the observations. We therefore decided to follow up the observations in each group by a discussion with the staff, parents, and other adults present during the sessions observed.

Discussions were held in 13 of the 15 groups – that is, in all the groups we observed except for one nursery school and one nursery class which did not involve parents as helpers at the sessions. All the discussion groups had parents present, though not necessarily those parents helping during the sessions we observed; and all but one had staff present. Our questions related to the focus of the observations: how typical were the sessions that we observed, who decided what parents should do, whether staff were selective in what parents took on, how much discussion there was between staff and parents about what parents should be doing or were doing; and whether parents were happy with what they were doing, how they got involved, what problems or advantages there were for both sides.

The discussion groups differed very much in who took part and how issues arose. Some were small and controlled – perhaps a couple of staff and a couple of parents; others large and heated – 15 or 20 parents and staff together. Very little of the discussion dealt with what in the observations we called 'openness' or 'accessibility', with the exception of settling in children, which emerged as obvious and important. Almost all of the discussions focused on parent helpers. Much of what emerged dealt with wider questions of differences between the staff role and parent role and how these were seen in different groups. This will be left until later chapters.

This chapter is based on our observations in the 15 groups and the follow-up discussions with staff and parents. The focus here is parents' activities in the group. We ask two questions in our analysis of the observations in this chapter: first, what do parents do in the group? and second, how open or accessible is the group to parents?

What do parents do in the group?

In the observations and follow-up discussions we looked at the numbers of parents helping in the different groups, how their involvement was organized, what they did when they stayed to help, and what contact they had with staff or with other parents. We consider these in turn.

The number of parents helping in the groups

Parents were present helping in 11 out of the 15 groups we observed, in two nursery schools, three nursery classes, and six playgroups. This fact, by itself, tells us nothing significant about the differences between types of group, as we deliberately chose a mixture of groups to observe. The number of parents helping tells us more. In the two nursery schools, four parents were helping during the sessions observed (an average of two); in the three nursery classes, we observed a total of five (an average of less than two); in the six playgroups, 19 parents were helping in one way or another throughout the sessions with more helping for shorter periods of time, perhaps for half a morning or so (an average of three plus). So the playgroups we observed tended to have more parents helping during the sessions than did either the nursery schools or the nursery classes (although one of the nursery schools at one of the sessions observed had more parents helping than did some of the playgroups when looked at individually). Playgroups also came out well when we look at the consistency of parent help. The six playgroups involving parents had parents helping all the time, while four out of the five other groups had parents helping at only one of the two sessions observed. We should not make too much of this as the number of groups observed is small – but it may indicate a trend.

The discussion groups thought that the sessions we had observed were fairly typical of the numbers of parents who helped and what they contributed. Parents were sometimes said to be involved in parties, outings, jumble sales, fund-raising, or 'cover' when staff were ill: these other events were more likely to be mentioned for the playgroups than other groups. At one of the nursery classes it was pointed out that parents were less involved at the beginning of the year when they were less familiar with the group. As a matter of policy, in several groups parents were not invited to help in their first term, to give the children time to settle down on their own; and in some groups pregnant mothers were not encouraged to help.

Three of the 15 groups had presented us with atypical sessions, according to the discussion groups – all claimed to have more parent help than we had observed. In one of the nursery schools, there was a policy of having two parent helpers each session, and of not using 'new mothers'. In the other nursery school, staff thought that holidays and events at other schools meant that parents were particularly busy at the time of the year when we carried out the observations.

Other factors prevented mothers helping at certain times – getting the housework done, for example, and letting their babies sleep in the mornings.

One group made a distinction between parents coming in as helpers and coming in to settle children when they first started at the group. Settling in a new child was considered by almost all the discussion groups to be essential and typical – whether or not this had been observed by us. With one exception, groups thought there were more parents around at the beginning of term to settle their children. The one exception was a group where this was not encouraged.

	Nursery schools (N=3)	Nursery classes (N=4)	Playgroups (N=8)
Number of groups with parents observed helping during sessions	2	3	6
Total number of parents observed helping during sessions	4	5	19

Table 4.1 *Number of parents observed helping during sessions*

How involvement in the group was organized

Observations could not, of course, tell us how often parents helped, how many helped, or whether they were encouraged to 'drop in' casually or expected to sign up on a rota. This information came out in discussion. A rota was the most usual method of organizing parent help in all types of group. Seven of the 15 groups had 'rota mothers' – two of the nursery schools, one of the four nursery classes, and four of the eight playgroups. But 'rota' was not necessarily a clear term, and there were various other arrangements which either replaced or supplemented a rota system. Three playgroups had 'regular helpers' who came in to help at most or all of the sessions in addition to the paid staff, either instead of or as well as 'rota mothers'. In one playgroup without a rota, a regular helper was about to be replaced by a mother with a child currently in the group who came to help as an 'extra'. In another playgroup, which relied on parents as regular helpers rather than rota helpers, staff talked about the advantages of continuity for the children with regular helpers, compared with 'the constant change of faces' with a rota system. A teacher in one of the nursery classes, where there was a rota list for mothers to sign, nicely illustrates the possible variety:

> With one or two it's a duty – and it's a long morning for some – and unless they're pushed they won't come. About six mothers come regularly, and most occasionally. Only two don't come at all – one's working, and the other – welcomes the break – it's the break really for her isn't it? . . . And Mrs Richards very often comes in and stays half an hour, and she sits in the book corner and then she goes. She doesn't spend the whole morning, but she obviously really enjoys that coming in and sitting for about half an hour and then goes off – and I think if that suits her and suits the children then that's fine . . .

	Nursery schools (N=3)	Nursery classes (N=4)	Playgroups (N=8)
Number of groups with parents observed helping during sessions	2	3	6
Number of groups with 'parent rota'	2	1	4
Number of groups with 'regular parent helpers' observed as well as or instead of 'parent rota'	0	0	3
Number of groups with other help observed (eg. teenagers, parents staying for short time, 'dropping in')	0	1	4

Table 4.2 *Organization of parent help with sessions*

In the observations, it was the playgroups which were noticeable for numbers of other adults helping either throughout or for part of a session. One had two teenagers from the local school helping on a regular basis, in addition to the 'rota mothers' and numbers of other parents who stayed to help for short periods of time. Another playgroup had a former parent helper who, since starting a part-time job, still came regularly to help for half the morning.

We could not tell from the observations whether staff were selective about which parents helped in the group. In one group, a mother helper was a personal friend of the teacher. In other groups, staff made a point of inviting parents to help. Some thought there was no point in pushing mothers who did not want to come; others argued that mothers often enjoyed helping despite initial apprehension and saw this as a justification for a rota system which everyone was expected to join:

> I can name two mothers who said they couldn't cope because that's why they wanted the child to come to playgroup; but you know they *really* enjoyed it – and [said] never mind asking me again if you're short. . .

What parents did in the group

There seemed an endless variety in what parents did in the groups when they stayed to help. They sat with the children by the water tray and in the book corner, helped them dress up, read to them, talked to them about their drawings and their jigsaws, cooked, painted and made collages with them, helped them on the slide and the bicycles. The general picture from observations was of parents getting along on their own, working with the children where they thought best, helping clear up when necessary, with occasional directions of suggestions from the staff.

In the preliminary discussions, we wondered whether parents were guided towards certain activities and excluded from others, and to what extent there was a distinction between the roles of staff and parents in the group. In the analysis of the observations, we made a distinction between two types of activity: 'educational' activities and 'chores'. We classified as 'educational' any activity which involved working with the children, whether or not this included talking with them or being told to do something specific with them: working at jigsaws, taking part in the water play, sitting in the book corner or in the play house, cooking, making paint. By 'chores' we meant general clearing up after the children, or laying out activities for them, setting out the children's milk, making the coffee, washing up, cutting up paper for drawing. There are problems about this distinction. One is that a rigid distinction along these lines breaks down in practice, as we learnt by observation that any activity could be treated as a learning activity for a child. ('Would you mix some more paint?' says a member of staff to a mother; 'Do take Sarah – she'd love to help you.') Thus it is the use made of the activity rather than the activity itself that marks the distinction we intended between education and chores. Another difficulty was that staff sometimes suggested a chore to a parent who was initially too shy to work directly with the children or did not want to, as a way of building up her own confidence in her contribution or as a lead-in to further involvement. Or a mother herself might prefer to work away from the children, so she did not inhibit her own child in the group.

A third difficulty is that the use made of the activity or the intention of the staff or parent was not usually visible to the eye, and emerged only in subsequent discussion. However, with these provisos, we hoped to see whether parents were expected or encouraged to work in the same way as the staff worked with the children.

In all the groups where we observed parent helpers working with the children, they also cleared up generally, as did the staff – wiping tables, picking up bits of jigsaws and crayons, pinning up paper for painting. There were few occasions when parents were expected to do specific chores – the only two examples we observed were making coffee and setting out the children's milk. And there were very few examples of helpers asking to do something specific with the children, rather than 'generally keeping an eye open', as one mother put it.

In striking contrast, we observed a small number of groups where parents did not work with the children at all. In one, mother helpers put out equipment, cleared up the mess, told the children when to wash their hands, put things away, and talked to the staff; but they did not work alongside the children or talk to them about what they were doing. In another, neither staff nor helpers interacted with the children at all except to give them directions for playtime, milk, or story, or to intervene in something 'rather dramatic like the children undressing under the stacked chairs'. In a third, the parent helper sat quietly on her own making up a register for the following year, while the children and staff were outside; occasionally, one of the staff put her head round the door with a friendly comment, and some of the children came in to talk, but this was the only contact. Although in one group the lack of interaction between adults and children was characteristic of the style of the group as a whole rather than just of the parent helpers, these were clear examples from the observations of parents concentrating on chores rather than working with the children.

	Nursery schools (N=3)	Nursery classes (N=4)	Playgroups (N=8)
Number of groups with parents observed helping during sessions	2	3	6
Number of groups where parents engaged mainy in 'educational activities'	0	3	5
Number of groups where parents engaged mainly in 'chores'	2	0	1

Table 4.3 *Type of parent help during sessions*

We also noted whether helpers were directed by staff towards certain activities or away from others. When a story was read as a big group activity – and for many groups this was the main focal activity of the session – parent helpers tended to sit in rather than organize it or read the story; but the only example we observed of parent helpers being excluded from an activity came from one group where staff insisted that a parent should not tell the story as it was to be accompanied with pictures.

For comment, we turned to the subsequent discussions. Two of the groups where we observed parents concentrating on chores were nursery schools; one was a playgroup. Was this a fair judgement?

We asked first whether staff were at all selective in what they encouraged parents to do. Most people in the discussion groups said that parents were 'left to do what they liked' when they came to help – with rare exceptions when parents were 'irresponsible', or 'standing around looking lost' and 'didn't seem to know what to do'. Some people stressed that the choice of activity was the mothers'. As one playgroup supervisor put it:

> Some mothers feel more secure in the kitchen so we leave them to cope there – others hate the kitchen and

then one of us [staff] works there. If they would like to take the story or anything special then we are happy.

– and a member of staff in one of the nursery classes said much the same thing:

> Some mothers are happier with something practical to do – sewing tapes or cutting paper – they feel happier doing something like that than sitting chatting to the children.

At the same time, however, there was a surprising number of comments made by staff in the discussion groups about activities in which parents were definitely *not* expected to take part. There was a 'theme for the week' for the story, which only staff would know about; parents were not expected to take 'group time'; they were asked not to use capital letters for the children's names; reading was a sensitive topic:

> You have to be careful about that – I wouldn't say I mind a parent hearing a child who was quite an adequate reader, but I think when they go slowly and need a lot of – you have to be more careful.

Comments of this kind were made by staff in discussion in five out of the seven nursery classes or schools, and two of the eight playgroups. This did not fit with the general view that parents did what they liked – but perhaps there were other ways of 'inducting' parents into appropriate behaviour than simply directing them, which would be made clear to us later. Here we were left with the impression that staff in the nursery classes and schools were more likely than playgroup staff to be selective about parents' activities in the group and directive about how they went about things, and more likely to be sensitive about what might be called 'professional' areas of work.

Contact between parents, other parents and staff

We wanted to learn how parents knew what to do when they stayed to help in the group. We wanted to know who told them what to do; how much contact there was between parent helpers and staff; whether parents asked staff what to do, or worked by themselves, or were directed by staff; whether parents and staff talked about what was happening in the group, or about other matters. In the observations, we defined as 'contact' all the interactions between adults in the group – conversations, chats, encouragement, requests for help, advice, suggestions, directions, even the quick smile and lifted eyebrow across the room. This, of course, was difficult to observe – many conversations were no more than two or three words exchanged in passing, some will have been missed completely, and it was not possible to grasp even the substance of what passed between two people on the other side of the room. So we clearly cannot place any reliance on fine distinctions between groups.

In the analysis of the observations, we looked at the total amount of contact or exchange between staff and parent helpers in the different groups. We then broke this down into *direction* – staff directing parent helpers or parent helpers asking staff what to do; *discussion* – discussion or comment about what the parent helper was doing, the group, or the parent's own child; and *social conversation*, about matters not connected with the group. We also looked at the amount of contact between the parent helper and other 'non-staff' adults present in the group.

The first surprise is the small amount of contact of any kind observed between adults in any of the groups. The second is that direction – parents being told or asking what to do – came bottom. Discussion and social chat came out roughly the same. Most exchanges between parent helpers and other parents took place in the playgroup, and none at all in the nursery schools. More discussion was about what the helper was doing or what was happening in the group than about the helper's own child; but most of both kinds occurred in nursery classes, and very little in the nursery schools or playgroups. Most direction occurred in playgroups: this tended to be staff directing parent helpers – helpers asked for directions more frequently in the nursery schools. Most social conversation, when averaged out, occurred in nursery schools.

The picture may be clearer if we look at the different types of group. There were most exchanges in total in the playgroups. Staff directed parents more often, and parent helpers talked more to parents. There was a good deal of social conversation, but not much discussion. There were fewest exchanges all together in the nursery schools, although there was on average most social chat, and a certain amount of discussion about the helper's own child. Parent helpers did not talk to other parents, staff did not direct helpers at all, and there was hardly any discussion about what the helper was doing, although helpers asked for directions more often than in any other type of group. Nursery classes came out highest on discussion, lowest on direction. There was a certain amount of conversation between parent helpers and staff.

If we look at individual groups as well as averaging out the number of contacts by type of group, it becomes clearer that

	Nursery schools (N=3)	Nursery classes (N=4)	Playgroups (N=8)	Totals
Base: number of groups with parents observed helping during sessions	2	3	6*	11
Total number of contacts observed between parent helpers, staff, and other parents	14 (7)	37 (12·3)	92 (18·4)	143
Total number of contacts observed between parent helpers and staff	14 (7)	36 (12)	53 (10·6)	103
Total number of contacts observed between parent helpers and other parents	0	1 (0·3)	39 (7·8)	40

* Information was available from only five playgroups. Figures in brackets are average numbers of contacts per session.

Table 4.4 *Numbers of contacts observed between parent helpers, staff, and other parents during sessions*

	Nursery schools (N=3)	Nursery classes (N=4)	Playgroups (N=8)	Totals
Base: number of groups with parents observed helping during sessions	2	3	6*	11
Type of contact observed between parent helpers and staff:				
Direction:	2 (1)	1 (0·3)	11 (2·2)	14
Staff directs	0	1	10	11
Parent helper asks staff	2	0	1	3
Discussion:	3·5 (1·75)	21 (7)	8 (1·6)	32·5
Comment on parent's activity or group in general	0·5	14·5	7	22
Comment on parent's own child	3	6·5	1	10·5
Social conversation:	8·5 (4·25)	10 (3·33)	15 (3·0)	33·5
Total number of contacts observed between parent helpers and staff	14	36	53	103
Unattributed contacts (observed but too far away or brief to analyse)		4	19	23

* Information was available from only five playgroups. Figures in brackets are average numbers of contacts per session.

Table 4.5 *Type of contact observed between parent-helpers and staff*

there was a contrast between the nursery classes and schools on the one hand and the playgroups on the other in the type of contact. In the nursery classes involving parent helpers there was discussion between staff and parents about what they were doing, about their own child, and about other matters; but in only one of these groups did parents talk to other parents. In contrast, in playgroups involving parent helpers, parents talked to other parents and to staff about non-group matters, but were far less likely to discuss what they were doing in the group, or their own child.

Various points stand out concerning who directed and initiated activities. What we had learnt about the selection of activities and guidance of parents led us to expect staff to be more directive in nursery schools and classes than in playgroups, when we looked at the contact between parents and staff. The observations gave us a surprisingly different picture. First, there was very little exchange of any kind with parent helpers in the nursery school. What there was tended to be social conversation. Occasionally helpers asked for direction. Staff did not apparently take the initiative in directing parent helpers or discuss what they were doing, and parents were left very much on their own to get on. Secondly, although in the nursery classes there was very little direction of parent helpers, there was a good deal of discussion, comment and explanation about what they were doing and what was happening in the group. Third, parent helpers in the playgroup were more directed by staff although they did not talk much about what they were doing or what was happening in the group; conversation tended to be either social chat with staff or with other parents. All this was rather surprising.

We tried to fill out this picture from the follow-up discussions. We asked staff whether they thought parents wanted to be directed or not, and parents for their views. In some groups, both parents and staff thought parents preferred not to be directed, except when they needed to know where things were kept or how to do something, or were new to the group. In others, staff thought that 'it depends on the parent' – some parents might be shyer than others and need more help and direction. The first view was more typical of playgroups, the second of nursery classes and schools. We also asked who was responsible for planning activities in the session and for deciding what parent helpers should do. While there was general agreement that parents were left to get on by themselves, in all except one of the groups responsibility for planning activities was said to rest with the supervisor, sometimes together with the staff. The one exception was a playgroup where responsibility for planning and for directing activities was said to be shared equally between staff and parents.

We then asked whether staff and parents ever discussed what parents should do or were doing in the group. Few of the groups mentioned discussion of any kind. We distinguished here between, first, some sort of 'formal' introduction (this might be a formal meeting of parents or parent helpers and staff, at the beginning of term or of the year – a visit before the child started in the group to explain what was expected – or a formal briefing from the supervisor when parent and child first arrived); second, a more informal 'learning by watching the others' (usually when staying to settle in a child); and third, 'discussion on the job'. Formal induction was mentioned in four groups. One of the nursery schools and classes had a formal meeting for staff and parents at the beginning of the year or the term; in one of the playgroups, the supervisor visited families before the child started in the group, and in another there was a briefing on the parent helper's arrival. 'Watching others' was mentioned in one of the nursery schools and two of the classes, and one of the playgroups ('parents guide each other').

'Discussion on the job' was said to be comparatively infrequent – it was mentioned in only one of the nursery classes, two of the playgroups, and not at all in the nursery schools. At two of the playgroup discussions, people talked of committee meetings as a forum for discussing policy and the contribution of parent helpers.

From the observations and discussions, there appeared to be surprisingly little discussion or explanation for parents, whether formal or informal. Both parents and staff thought that parents often knew the routine from staying to settle their child. As one mother put it,

> I went with my daughter for six weeks, settling her in – so I knew what was going on more or less.

Or it was assumed that helpers would 'pick it up' without much difficulty:

> You usually take your cue from the parents in the room at the time – and watch the children playing and the staff. If I'm not sure I will ask, because they will

come up and say will you fetch me this, or if I am not sure where something is I will ask . . . . You take your general cue from the other adults in the room. The children teach you anyway. . . . The first time is the most difficult – you feel useless – you don't know where anything is . . .

Occasionally staff and parents were explicit about there being no need for discussion:

It's not necessary as parents mainly do domestic chores.

Here are the mothers in one nursery class describing the mixture of explanation and observation of the routine:

Well you just sort of take it naturally – you do what you think will help, really. . . . The first time when I came, [the teacher] said sit at the table and the children will come to you – that's all, really, isn't it? – there might be the odd occasion when [the teacher] would say, 'Oh would you go and do . . .?', but it's not very often.

The teacher then continued the discussion with the mothers:

I think the mothers who come in have obviously all got children here, so they know there's lots of things to talk to them about. And [mothers] do use words like big and little and how many colours. I mean if there were any others who didn't – I'd perhaps sit down and say 'It's quite a good idea to talk about what we're doing'; but you just instinctively knew. We always suggest that they sit at a table and move from table to table and that the children'll come – and I think you saw that yourselves and just took it from there . . .

Learning by observation is neatly summed up by the following comments by a mother:

The first day I came I just watched what [the staff] did – and the next week I just knew where to go from there.

– and by a teacher in another nursery class:

> They see how we talk to the children and how we cope with situations and it'll just come – they do recognize the way it's done and follow suit – but I always try to talk to the mothers and say the sort of things we are trying to do . . .
>
> I think a good way of learning is by observing . . . I would say the same to all the mothers: observe, watch. If you tell people what to do, nine times out of ten if you leave them they see things for themselves – what they enjoy doing – and they see different things from you.

But some mothers would clearly have liked more explanation at the beginning:

> MOTHER: When I first came I didn't know what to do – well I mean I sat at the table with the children, but I didn't really know if I was doing the right thing or not – if I was helping or hindering – they were making a clock one day and I thought well should I do it – but I thought if they didn't like it they would come and tell me – about numbers. . . . But now, well I just do what I think and no one seems to complain.
> STAFF: You would have liked some pattern to be laid down?
> MOTHER: Yes, really: I didn't know if I was helping you or hindering.

What parents do in the group and how they know what is expected of them is tricky territory. Most staff seemed to assume that parents would 'pick it up as you go along', perhaps with a minimum of guidance and explanation. Guidance tended to be informal and implicit rather than formal and explicit. 'Instructing mothers' was seen by some staff as patronizing and insulting: 'It's not my place,' as one teacher put it. On the other hand, some parents felt that they were not given enough guidance: 'I was just left standing around.' So informal and implicit procedures were inadequate at times. One solution would be for staff to assume total control over what was done in the group and to instruct parents accordingly: some groups approached this style. The opposite possibility would be for parents to have complete freedom over what to do in the group: the only example of this style we found was in one playgroup where parents and staff agreed that mothers, like the supervisor, brought in their own ideas for what to do and mothers said they liked the freedom of choice rather than direction. But this was unusual.

The sort of difficulties and uncertainties that could arise over what parents were expected to do in the group were forcibly illustrated for us in the discussion group at one of the nurseries. The diversity of parents' expectations, and of staff's expectations, came out most strongly in this discussion, possibly because it was a bigger discussion group than elsewhere. Some parents said they felt free to make suggestions, and were given simple and helpful directions about what to do. Others felt they were treated like children and not expected to behave responsibly. Some mothers thought they had a right to some say in what went on in the group, as their child was their responsibility. Others argued in turn that teaching was the teacher's job: 'If I came into a school and found the staff doing the chores and the parents doing the teaching I would take my child away.' Others said they were grateful to the staff and should do what they could to help. Parents asked for more explanation of the reasons for inviting in some parents rather than others, and for encouraging certain activities and excluding others: for example, reading stories, or being left in charge of a group. Staff pointed out that they also had a responsibility for training students and that sometimes there were not enough activities to go round. There was also some feeling amongst the nursery assistants that the chores were left to them rather than being shared with parents. A number of suggestions were made for putting communication between staff and parents on a more formal footing as the best way to clarify these uncertainties about the parents' role: formal meetings, a 'parent representative' who would discuss with staff what parents were expected to do, and a mothers' room where they could meet. This nursery decided subsequently to solve the problem of who did what with a policy of parents' helping under the direction of the staff rather than working with the children on their own.

How 'open' are groups to parents?

We turn now to what we have called the 'openness' or 'accessibility' of groups to parents. What we have in mind is the extent to which a group is defined as 'professional' or 'shared' territory, with the presence of parents or other 'non-staff' adults limited to certain times or particular tasks.

We wanted to see, for example, what happened at the beginning and end of sessions. Do parents shove their children in through the door without a word and run, or do they come inside, wander around, talk to staff, and to other parents? This may be a crude caricature, but the 'openness' or 'accessibility' of a group may be indicated by the accumulation of such tiny pointers. We wanted to see whether the door was kept closed until the end of the session, with parents waiting outside, or whether parents might wander in at any time to join in with their children; whether 'delivery' and 'collection' were rapid exchanges completed on both sides as fast as possible, or relaxed periods which merged into the normal activities; whether parents visited the group before their child started, or stayed to settle him in; whether they brought staff their problems.

We could see that most groups had a generally welcoming and friendly air, with apparently no fixed time of arrival – parents arriving early, coming inside with their children, being greeted by staff, and talking both to staff and to other parents. A certain amount of administration was completed first thing in the morning – paying fees in the playgroups, paying for trips or collecting jumble. Occasionally parents helped to put out equipment: in one group, a mother went straight to the book corner on arrival with her child to find a book about an anticipated visit to the dentist. But this was fairly unusual, and only happened in the groups which were notable for involving parents in other ways.

Similarly most groups had a friendly and relaxed end to the session – parents arrived early, came inside, talked to staff and other parents. In some groups parents joined in whatever their child was doing.

Four groups stood out as exceptions to this welcoming and relaxed atmosphere – two nursery classes and two playgroups. Parents waited outside until the end of the session, when the door was opened and the children sent out rapidly to the waiting parents, who only came into the room if they wanted to catch one of the staff or collect a child's coat or painting. Parents did not get equipment out with their children, or join in activities with them. Similarly, at the beginning of the session, parents tended not to arrive early, or come in with their children or talk to the staff or other parents. In these four groups the 'exchanges' at the beginning and end of the session were very rapid in comparison with the lengthy and informal arrivals and departures of parents and children in other groups.

In the analysis of the observations, the nursery schools stood out as the most welcoming of the groups at the beginning and end of sessions, and parents tended to join in whatever their child was doing more.

We did not see many parents staying to settle their children in, or visiting the group before their child started. In two of the three nursery schools, a handful of parents stayed for half an hour or so to settle their children and one or two parents were visiting the group to see the head teacher or to sit in the group with the child. In one of the playgroups five mothers stayed for the whole session to settle their children – in another some stayed short periods of time and came back before the end of the morning. Parents stayed to settle children in two of the three nursery schools, and five of the eight playgroups. Parents were visiting in two of the nursery schools and two of the classes, but only in two of the playgroups. We have too little information to say to what extent new parents talked to staff or headteachers or other parents, or were left to wander round with their children on their own. In some of the groups there was clearly a lot of conversation between parent helpers and parents visiting or staying with their children. In others, nobody at all in the group spoke to a visiting parent.

Very few parents were observed bringing problems to staff. One parent talked to a teacher about bringing her handicapped child. Another brought a child with her leg in plaster. Another talked about her sleepless nights. An Asian mother left a younger child with the group while she visited the doctor. One Pakistani father brought his daughter's new earrings for a teacher to deal with, the rest of the class looking on with interest. Examples, although few, were found in all types of group, but most in the nursery schools.

	Nursery schools	Nursery classes	Playgroups
Base	3	4	8
Number of groups observed to have:			
Relaxed beginnings to sessions	3	2	7
Relaxed endings to sessions	3	2	6
Parents pre-visiting or settling children	2	1	5
Parents bringing problems to staff	3	1	2
'Non-staff' other adults present:	1	3	6
High (5 or more other adults present and/or adults not connected with the group)	0	1	5
Low (fewer than 5 other adults present and/or adults connected with the group)	1	2	1

Table 4.6 *Groups' 'accessibility'*

We also wanted to know how open the groups were to other, 'non-staff' adults during the sessions – how many other people came in and for what reasons, and what contact they had with the staff. Here it is the playgroups which stand out in striking contrast to the rest. Three quarters of the playgroups had numbers of people coming in and out – ranging from parents who came to help for a short time although they were not on the rota, the supervisor's daughter who was a registered childminder and brought the minded child with her, ten mothers with their toddlers, committee members setting up a shop, to a builder to mend the windows, the community centre warden who put his head round the door, and a steady stream of people waiting in the clinic room where the playgroup was held. This contrasted with the nursery schools and classes, where only one group had any number of other adults present during the session – a nursery class where parents passed through the room and greeted staff and children on their way to another class. Except for this group, other adults were observed in two of the three nursery schools and only one other nursery class, and very few of them – the school secretary, the speech therapist, two parents bringing problems. The playgroups on the whole tended to have more adults present for one reason or another during the session, and more adults who were not connected with the institution. The nursery schools and classes, by contrast, had very few non-staff adults present during the session and these tended to be connected with the group in some way.

It is worth noting that the four groups we picked out earlier as less welcoming to parents at the beginning and end of sessions, also tended to have fewer non-staff adults present. Only one person was visiting in any of these groups, nobody brought a problem, and only two of the four had a parent settling a child in for a short period of time.

When we consider the openness or accessibility of the different types of group, then, the nursery schools tended to come out as more open than the rest. They were more welcoming to parents at the beginning and end of the sessions, parents tended to come in more with their children and talk more to staff and other parents, to stay more to settle their children, to visit more and bring their problems. The exception to this was the presence of non-staff adults in the groups. Here the playgroups came out in striking contrast to the rest. And there was a small number of playgroups and nursery classes which were significantly less open or accessible both to parents and to other adults.

Conclusions

The tables offer a concise summary of the observations we carried out in the 15 groups. Groups differ in their organization of parental involvement, the activities parents undertake, parents' 'induction' or 'introduction' into the group, the contact parents have with staff, and groups' openness or accessibility.

Through the observations, we have clarified a number of useful categories for analysing parents' activities as parent helpers and the relationship between parents and the group; in short, the differences between groups in their approach to parents. First, when we consider groups' accessibility to parents, we can distinguish factors such as rapidity of 'transfer' between parents and staff at the beginnings and endings of sessions, the openness of staff to parents with problems, parents visiting and settling in their children when they first join the group, the presence of 'non-staff' adults. Second, we can distinguish between 'educational activities' or 'chores' when we consider parents' activities during the session – roughly speaking, that is, whether parents work with the children or spend their time clearing up. Third, we can distinguish between direction, discussion, and general conversation as types of contact between parents and staff during the session – that is, parents asking or being told what to do by staff, discussing parents' activities or events in the group, and general chat about matters unrelated to the group. These categories are derived from observation. From the follow-up discussions, we can add two more useful variables. One is to do with methods of introducing parents to the organization of the group and the part they play – here we can separate formal induction, informal 'pick it up as you go along', and 'learning through discussion on the job'. The other is the extent to which a group is hierarchical or democratic in its decision-making – whether staff are selective and directive or not about parents and the activities they undertake in the group.

So far, in analysing the observations and the follow-up discussions we have taken organizational differences between groups as the basic factor. Thus, for example, we have argued that when we 'cluster' nursery schools on the one hand and playgroups on the other, the nursery schools were more likely than the playgroups to have relaxed beginnings and endings to sessions and to welcome parents with problems, whereas the playgroups were more likely than the nursery schools to treat the group as 'shared territory' with large numbers of 'non-staff' adults present unconnected with the group, and more freedom for parent helpers to talk to other parents. To take another example, we suggested that both staff and parents were more likely to be sensitive to 'professional boundaries' in the nursery schools, where we observed parents clearing up rather than working alongside the children, than in either nursery classes or playgroups. But, as we suggested in the previous chapter on the preliminary discussions, if we concentrate on this organizationally-based 'clustering' of nursery schools, nursery classes, and playgroups we may miss other important differences. What other patterns are revealed if we 'cluster' the groups in a different way?

We have noted earlier a puzzling discrepancy between the observations and the follow-up discussions over the question of the direction of parents and selection of activities. In discussion, nursery schools appeared as the most directive of parent helpers and selective of the activities permitted them – while in the playgroups both staff and parents thought that helpers preferred to be left to get on by themselves and that staff tended not to direct or select. However, in the observations of the eleven groups where parents helped with the sessions, playgroup staff were more likely and nursery school staff least likely to direct parent helpers. One explanation of the discrepancy is to shrug our shoulders and accept that we picked atypical days for the observations. Another would be to argue that people simply fail to notice the complexity or amount of verbal exchange when they themselves are involved. A third explanation is that the contact observed between parents and staff in the group makes sense only if it is interpreted within the context of the parents' 'introduction' into the group, and the group's decision-making – that is, the contact we observed may make most sense if we know about other contact between parents and staff. Obviously we cannot tell from simple observation whether the fact that parents are left by themselves when they stay to help indicates a firm structure previously laid down by staff which parents follow without further discussion or direction, or, on the other hand, a democratic group where parents exercise equal responsibility with staff for making decisions about activities during the sessions. Nor can we always tell from observation whether parents are confidently following a routine or desperately anxious for further explanation by staff. We found examples of all four situations.

If we 'cluster' the groups where parents were observed to be helping apparently without any direction from staff, we may perhaps find a solution to the puzzle.* There were four such groups. In two, we observed a considerable amount of discussion between parents and staff during the sessions – in one of these 'discussion on the job' was particularly mentioned in the follow-up discussions as a way of parents learning the ropes when they stayed to help. In three of the groups it was staff who were responsible overall for making the decisions and directing the activities, and if parents were thought to prefer to get on by themselves this was 'within a framework' of direction by staff.

Similarly if we 'cluster' the six groups where parents were observed being directed by staff or asking for direction, we find more clues. In this cluster there was noticeably more attention paid to the parents' introduction into the group and

---

* Information on contact between parents and staff was not available from one of the eleven groups where we observed parents helping.

the part they can play; a formal meeting, visit or briefing was mentioned in three of the follow-up discussions, 'discussion on the job' in two, and 'watching others' or while settling in their own children in four. In addition, two groups mentioned discussions in committee meetings. Most of this increase is accounted for by two groups. These two groups were the only ones where staff were said not to be selective of either parents or activities, and parents took their own decisions. They were also the groups with the largest numbers of helpers and non-staff adults observed during the sessions.

Here, then, we begin to make sense of the discrepancy. The contact between parents and staff observed during the sessions is easier to interpret when put alongside what else we know about groups' methods of inducting new members and making decisions. On the one hand, parents can work on their own within a framework of discussion 'on the job' or a staff-based routine. On the other, it is not suprising to see staff directing parents or parents asking for direction in groups which have large numbers of helpers and other adults around, or where parents can take their own decisions, or where the routine is determined by staff.

Three patterns stand out from the observations and discussion material.

First, there is a strong clustering to do with groups' openness or accessibility – whether groups had relaxed beginnings and endings to the sessions, whether parents were visiting or settling in their children and bringing their problems to staff. On these four factors, we found five groups with a 'high' score (four 'pluses'), four with a medium score (three 'pluses'), and six with a low score (under three 'pluses'). If we add in the further factor of the group's openness to 'non-staff adults', we find ten groups – four with high scores and six with low (five had none). Only two groups overlap, with high scores on the first four factors as well as 'non-staff adults'; and these were both playgroups. If we exclude 'non-staff adults', nursery schools came out top – with two out of three scoring highly compared with only one in four of either nursery classes or playgroups. None of the nursery schools scored low on the first four factors, compared with one in two of the nursery classes and playgroups alike.

Second, there is the distinction we drew between 'educational activities' and 'chores' when we observed parents in the groups. This factor does not by itself produce any distinctive pattern. But if we relate it to the 'openness' pattern, we can see that those groups with a high score for 'non-staff adults' encouraged parents to work alongside the children – three of these groups were playgroups and one a nursery class. We can also see that groups which scored low on the other openness factors were less likely to involve parents at all in the sessions – here we found one in two of both the nursery classes and the playgroups we observed.

Third, we can discern the outline of a pattern which we shall call 'democratic/hierarchical'. By 'democratic', we mean groups where staff were apparently neither selective about parents staying to help nor directive about the activities they undertook. By 'hierarchical', we mean groups where staff appeared to be both selective and directive. Three groups stood out as most democratic, and four most hierarchical – for these seven groups the pattern was fairly clear. Again, we can relate this to our other patterns. The three most 'democratic' groups all had high 'openness' scores, including openness to non-staff adults in two of the three; and parents in all of them worked alongside the children rather than clearing up. Two of these were playgroups and one was a nursery class. Three of the four most 'hierarchical' groups scored low on all the 'openness' factors – only one came out with a high score, excluding non-staff adults; parents were less likely to work alongside the children, if they helped at all. Two of these were playgroups, one a nursery class, and one a nursery school.

In plain language, what we are suggesting is this. On the basis of the observations there appears to be a cluster of groups which strive to be open and accessible to parents. Those which make themselves 'open territory' to other adults as well as parents as part of their general accessibility are more likely to involve parents in the work of the sessions, and to encourage them to work with the children rather than limit them to clearing up. And there appears to be a relationship between the openness of a group and its staff's policy of selection or direction towards parents and their activities in the group. In the next two chapters, we shall see what the views of staff and parents add to this picture.

5
Fifteen groups and their staff

We turn now to the interviews we conducted with staff in the 15 groups. Staff had varied views on parents and their contribution, the reasons for parents' involvement, the objectives and style of the groups in which they worked. In the preliminary discussions with staff reported in Chapter 3, we began to sketch in two different models of a preschool group and its relation to the parents of the children it served – one a partnership model where parents and children and staff worked together and the group functioned as an extension outwards from the child's home into the wider community, and the other where the group functioned more as a stepping stone for the child in his search for independence from his family, where the focus was on the child and the parents were largely excluded. In this chapter, we look now at staff's views in greater detail. We must ask ourselves whether the outlines of the earlier sketch can stand – or whether the picture should be redrawn. At the same time, we consider whether staff's views add to the patterns we began to outline from the observations reported in the last chapter.

Let us start with some examples of staff's views about parents, their relationship with the group, and the group's objectives. Here is the first group:

> It's nice for us to know the parents – we're always around, a few minutes to spare if anything's bothering them.

> It's nice when parents stay a little with their children, not just rush in and rush out again. When they come up and say thank you for looking after their children, you feel they're really appreciative of what you do. It's really nice when they're interested in what the children

do; it's a shame when some of them whisk the child off, and don't even look at what the child's made. I like to talk to them – when you've noticed how he's developed, and the parent says 'Oh yes, I've noticed that too'.

You have to get to know the parents; obviously you have to know if it affects the child – if the father's gone off, for instance. Most of my parents just come up to tell me things; it's nice to know what's going on at home for the child's sake – you get told sometimes without realizing it.

Staff in this group impressed as warm, welcoming, and friendly, anxious to talk to parents and to make time for parents to bring their problems; and information about the home was important for staff in their work with the children. But there is nothing about parents helping in the group, or playing much part in the child's life in the group. Here, for contrast, is a different group:

It's nice for the parents to be involved with us. More important that they help with the children than anything else: the more adults there are the more the children can learn from them . . . . Since I have been here, there have been many changes. Talking to parents at the beginning of term, asking them to come in – telling them they are as important as the teachers in educating their child.

Education must be a partnership. Parents are most important. . . . Parents always talk about the nursery – they understand it is not just play. A lot of learning going on . . . talking about this seems helpful for parents then they feel so left out. . . . Parents begin to feel they have something to offer.

Here parents are seen as partners in the educational process: they play an equal role, and through involvement they learn that they have something to offer in that process. In the third example, parents are members of the group almost by definition since it is an extension of the home:

> I used to see the group more as an opportunity for the children to develop and play. Now I see it more and more as important for the parents. I started as 'a teacher' – I used to think about the parents, 'When on earth are they going to leave?' Now I like the contact; it is very good for the children – it's much more natural than cutting them off from the adult world, which creates an artificial situation. I'm still just as strong about children's development, but I think it helps the parent to see her child in relation to others. . . . Younger children add to the enrichment and enjoyment of the group. . . . I used to find it very disturbing at first, but now I think there are many advantages particularly for children without younger children at home. I've changed my mind about several things. . . . Parents should be involved because it is an extension of the natural relationship.

In the fourth group, by contrast with the first, there is little feeling of a boundary between staff and parent – the relationship is that between equals:

> This is a very open group – parents or staff discuss problems as and when they arise . . . there is no hierarchy here so parents quickly get on and do things as they think best . . .

Parents learning through involvement in the group – learning about child development, about education, learning new confidence in their own abilities to cope or work with children, or simply learning to relax – are common themes. It is already apparent in the second and third examples. Here are some more examples of how staff saw parents learning in the groups:

> Parents are always talking about the nursery. They understand that it is not just play – a lot of learning going on – and children learn to share things. . . .

Children become more independent – talking about this seems helpful for parents . . .

Parents learn very quickly – one mother started to cut out certain shapes for the children to copy – by the second time she had done this, she said perhaps I should cut out more abstract shapes for them. That's an example of parents learning.

Parents are always saying 'Where can I buy this?' – they see puzzles that the child likes using and they want them for home. . . . And we hope that involvement and interest in the child's development and education will continue after the group . . .

I think that what you must find interesting is seeing other children and the way they react to each other. And you can see your own children in a different light. I think it's really reassuring to see that other people have children who can throw tantrums and be really horrible and naughty – I think that in itself is a relief for mothers, that your child is quite normal in the way he behaves and the things that he does.

In the sixth group, involvement is seen as therapeutic for the parent:

One mother – I like *her* to stay – she needs us. She likes to stay for five or ten minutes. Her English is quite bad. Staying is for *her* sake – it's a break from the house. . . . We're the only English people she talks to . . .

Here the group plays a therapeutic and social function for parents who may be shy and lonely or isolated.

We have here then six different examples of the relationship between staff, parents, and the groups their children attend. The first example came from a nursery school with an extremely welcoming and friendly approach to parents, but no parents helping in the classroom. The second was a nursery class which put a lot of effort into visiting parents and encouraging them to get involved; parents helped freely in the group with a wide range of activities. The third and fourth examples both came from playgroups, both with rotas of parents helping with all the activities. The fifth examples came from two nursery classes; and the last from a nursery school. We cannot claim that these examples are necessarily typical – we have selected them to illustrate the range of views across different types of group.

Staff's comments show different ways of encouraging parents to help in a group or making a group accessible to parents. If we use the same methods to analyse the interviews with staff as we used on the observations, we can begin to see two distinct patterns of attitudes and assumptions about parents and their contact with the group. We shall then ask if there is any relationship between these patterns of attitudes and assumptions and the patterns in the observations.

'The group is here for the child'

In the first approach, the focus of the group is primarily the child, and the beginning of the process of his weaning away from the world of home to the world of school. We found examples of this in playgroups:

> The group is here for the children – that's the only reason I come – not for the parents.

> The group functions primarily for the child, to educate them generally, to help them learn to socialize.

> To mix and learn to play with other children . . . the group is really for children to come and play. It does the parents good to have a break from them for a couple of hours. . . . It gives the parents a break, and the child a break, and it's good for both.

> The group it here mainly to help the children – to get them ready for school – they learn to mix.

It gives them independence and the parents get a break.

in nursery classes:

It's primarily for the children – if the children are happy here they will be happy at school. . . . It's a lead-up to school.

and nursery schools:

The group is there to begin the child's education.

It functions primarily for the children.

The nursery is there to prepare the child for the world of school – to help them learn to explore themselves, and their capabilities with the minimum of direction.

The group is here for the child to get used to being away from parents and to learn things that they would not necessarily do at home.

For these the touchstone of any arrangement was whether it was to the benefit of the child: a decision to have parents in the group, or a matter of altering arrangements to bring or collect their children was always met with 'it all depends on the child'.

Parent involvement is basically to help the child . . . .
The reason for involving parents is to help the child.

If the children seemed unsettled then staff discouraged parents from staying to help. 'Parents stay too long,' and 'It makes the children clingy,' were frequent comments.

Involving parents was often seen in terms of parents providing information about children's home background and behaviour. Some members of staff described in detail how their understanding of children's difficult home backgrounds helped their work.

Getting to know the parents helps us to know why the child behaves as it does.

> I wish they'd tell you when something happens at home – we need to know for the child's sake.

> It's so enjoyable to have contact with the parents of the children that we are responsible for – it means that we can do more for the child if we know about the family.

Some staff stressed the therapeutic value of contact for parents – particularly for parents with problems; although if staff saw possible conflicts of interest between parents and children they usually gave children the priority:

> There's the view that you have to help the parent, understand the parent, before you can help the child; but you can get too involved, and then the rest of the children suffer.

> We bring parents in to help *them* – they know nothing about children – nothing about nurseries . . .

> We try to fulfil a need for parents – lonely parents, for instance; we put them in contact with each other.

But most often, contact was described in terms of pleasant, shared experience for staff, child and parent, as in the example quoted at the beginning of this chapter:

> The aim of the group is to make their preschool days happy for the children. It's helpful having contact with the parents – they become our friends – they enjoy coming and can share in the learning of their children.

> Parents enjoy being here – seeing their children growing and developing.

> If parents can see that their child is happy then we shall have a happier child.

> The emphasis is on the child. . . . But it makes things more relaxed if parents are free to come in if they want to. It is nice for the children and parents to see each other in other surroundings – it relaxes the child to

have the mother here and makes the mother feel at ease.

> They like to know what's going on – they're interested.

As more than one member of staff summed it up:

> It's nice to have contact – you become more human to each other. You become a human face.

It almost comes as a surprise to think of parents as helpers after this picture of friendly contact. The most common comment about parents as helpers in the group was that they would be useful 'for the general clearing up' – 'as an extra pair of hands', or to free staff 'for more time with the children'. However, many staff admitted to being selective about inviting parents in to help in the group and about activities that parents 'would and would not be asked to do'. Comments that 'parents were not reliable, they did not know what to do, and the children played up' were not uncommon as explanations for a reluctance to involve parents with the children.

The strongest thread common to these approaches was the free and easy contact between parents and staff and the sense of open access to the group. This was stressed time and time again.

> We've no special open times – we're open all the time – parents can feel free to come. We have very flexible times for them to collect the children. . . . We're open all the time for parents to talk about problems . . .

> Problems? We're flexible – if they've just moved house and someone else has to pick up the children late, why not? The facilities are here.

> I think the thing that parents find most helpful is that they can come and talk to us whenever they feel like it.

> We're very flexible if there are difficulties – if the

mother works, then we don't mind if she brings the child a bit early.

Here we have a picture of groups which are very open and welcoming to parents, where staff are keen for friendly and relaxed contact, and the focus is strongly on the welfare of the children. The group may serve a social or therapeutic function for parents, particularly parents with problems, but parents do not play an active part. The key here in the notion of parental involvement is contact and information – information for staff about the child's family, and information for parents about the child's development in the group. Thus the parent is a passive recipient of information rather than an active participant in the group. We can see this first approach neatly summarised in the following comment from a teacher:

> The most helpful thing about contact with the parents is that we learn about the child and that there is a continuity between school and home. This way both groups learn to know what is best for each of them [to do] with the child.

'The group is here for the parents *and* the child'

This is the second approach, and the focus of the group is on both parents and children together:

> You can't separate the home and the group . . .

> The group is here for the parents and the child – it is impossible to separate the two. If the parents are not involved the educational part won't necessarily get back to the home, and it's much better if it does.

We immediately have a sense of partnership and mutual learning between home and school. There are scattered references to parents acquiring a different perspective, but the strongest emphasis is on notions of partnership or equality, economic sharing, and the group as a natural extension of the home.

For some staff, the parents were seen as the teachers' equals in the relationship with the child, and the professional boundaries between parent and staff had to be broken down:

> The group is primarily for the child's sake; but that means working with the parents as well, as they are as important as the teachers.

And as in the example quoted at the beginning of the chapter:

> Parents are as important as the teachers in educating their child – education must be a partnership.

For others, the question of the parent's relationship to the professional did not arise – involvement of parents in the work of the group seemed much more matter-of-fact and taken for granted. Sometimes activities such as the parents' rota, coffee mornings, and the introduction of new parents to the group, were organized through a parents' committee; and questions such as who did what in the group, and whether to select or guide parents, could be discussed in this context. Sometimes staff's comments showed that parents were active and equal participants in the group with an equal share of the responsibility, and this was seen to need no further discussion.

Economic necessity was mentioned by several playgroups: as one supervisor said, 'The group couldn't function without parents being involved.' Another supervisor commented on the difficulty of running a parents' rota with more mothers going out to work; she proposed to take the problem to the parents' committee with the suggestion that children would get more care and individual attention if the number of sessions was reduced.

The notion of the group as a natural extension of the home, with parents as equal partners, is well summarized in these quotations:

> It's an extension of the natural relationship . . . .
> Involving the parents is good for the children – it's

much more natural than cutting them off from the adult world.

> The reason for the contact [with parents] is the tie . . . it's part of the child growing away from the family, forming relations with other adults. . . . We can't say we know your child – we probably know more about child development – but we can't say you must leave your child in our care. . . . The ties with mother and ties with the home are much stronger than later on: they'll always want mummy if something is really wrong. We act as intermediaries . . ..

Here then we have a picture of groups based on assumptions that parents play an equal role in the child's educative process and can take equal responsibility for running the group. Questions of selection of parents and of the educational or social function of the group for parents arise less often. The presence and participation of parents is assumed as a fact – rather than a proposition for which the argument has to be made.

More patterns?

The examples so far have given us a flavour of staff's views on parent involvement and groups' objectives, but no sense of how these different attitudes are distributed across different groups. Let us look at the interviews in more detail.

Six of the 15 groups were child-centred – that is, staff said the primary focus of the group was the child. Parents helped during sessions in three of these six groups: in two of these groups staff thought it was important to select parents and activities with care, and the third had a regular parent helper rather than 'rota mothers'. Where parents did help, staff tended to think of reasons for their involvement in terms of benefit to the group and the staff: parents were 'extra pairs of hands', or they could provide staff with information about the child's home background or his problems. Staff in two groups thought that involvement was for the child's benefit, and would help the parent gain a better understanding of the child and a 'different perspective'.

Nine groups were more of a partnership – that is, staff said that the group was for the benefit of parent and child together and that work with the child of necessity involved the parent. Parents helped with sessions in all but two of of these groups – one was a group catering for working mothers. In four of the groups involving parents, staff thought it important not to be selective of parents or their activities – all parents and all offers of help were welcomed. Again, reasons for involvement were different. Staff tended to talk in terms of a 'partnership' with parents, a feeling of 'equality' in the group rather than a hierarchy, the group acting as a natural extension of the home, and parents learning a new role for themselves in the educational process.

So far the data appears to confirm two distinct patterns. How do these map on to the patterns in the observations reported in the last chapter?

Three points stand out at once. First, the partnership groups were more likely to involve parents in the sessions working alongside the children rather than clearing up. In only two of the child-centred groups did parents work in this way – both groups with a regular helper.

Second, the partnership groups were more likely to pay attention to the parent's 'induction' into the group. In six out of the nine groups at least one method of introduction was mentioned by staff and parents in the discussion groups following the observations, and most mentioned a variety – discussion on the job, watching others, learning the routine while settling in the child – whereas only one of the child-centred groups mentioned any form of induction, and this was a formal meeting between staff and parents.

Third, the partnership groups were slightly more consistent in their openness and accessibility to parents when we looked at the beginnings and endings of sessions, parents visiting and settling in their children, and parents bringing their problems to staff. This was more marked, however, if

'Child-centred' groups:
- were less likely to have parents helping with the sessions
- staff were more likely to take the decisions, and direct and select parents when they did help with the sessions
- were less likely to 'induct' parents into the group, unless formally
- were less likely to have 'non-staff adults' present in the group, or helpers 'dropping-in'

'Parent-and-child' groups:
- were more likely to have parents helping in the sessions
- staff were less likely to be selective or directive of parents and their activities
- were more likely to think about methods of 'introducing' the parent into the group
- were more likely to have 'non-staff adults' in the group, and helpers 'dropping in'

Table 5.1 *Staff's views of 'child-centred' groups and 'parent-child' partnership groups*

we look at the aspect of 'shared territory' – the extent to which groups welcomed other adults. More of the partnership groups had other adults present, and in greater numbers, as well as casual helpers dropping in for, say, half a morning. When we observed adults other than staff or parent helpers in the child-centred groups, they tended to be people connected with the group.

We may ask how the distinction we are suggesting between the partnership and child-centred types of group relates to the organizational caregories of nursery school, nursery class, and playgroup. So far all we can say with confidence is that each type contains all three – there is no monopoly.

So when we match up the observations with the staff interviews – that is, match observed behaviour of staff and parents in the groups with staff's views about the parents' role and the groups' objectives – the data does apparently indicate two broadly differing styles of preschool group. One is focused fairly precisely on the child, and the environment and teaching strategies best fitted to his development and growing independence. The boundaries of the group, both its physical territory and the activities permitted within it, are fairly tightly defined and there is a clear distinction between the role of the parent and the role of the teacher or supervisor. The other is more likely to operate with parents and children together and to consider parents in their own right. The boundaries of the group are far less defined, and the distinction between parent and staff usually less obvious. In the next chapter, we must add parents' views into the picture.

6
Parents and their involvement in six groups

What parents thought and felt is the final piece of our jigsaw. Following the observations and discussions with staff in the 15 groups reported in the previous chapter, we interviewed a total of just under 60 parents from six of the groups to collect their views. We wanted to know what parents had to say about their involvement in different types of group, what role they thought they played or should play and whether this differed from the role that staff expected them to play. If they were involved with the group, we hoped to find out how this came about, and what they had gained from their experience. For those who were not involved, we wanted to know if this was because they did not wish to be, or because for some reason the group had failed to make contact with them.

These are the questions asked in this chapter. In the next chapter, we put together all the information from the observations and interviews with staff and parents, so that we can begin to see whether the evidence is cumulative or contradictory – whether we have a jigsaw or merely different pictures. Here, however, we confine ourselves to parents. The information is slanted to the extent that although we picked parents at random from the registers of the six groups – ten parents from each – we matched the six groups to give us a 'high' and 'low involvement' playgroup, nursery school, and nursery class. As with the rest of our information, we thus cannot lay claim to general truths – what we have is case studies which illuminate parts of the field more clearly. Nor can we claim to have anything but a 'snapshot' in time for any one group: as parents repeatedly reminded us, groups change their character as their membership and staff change, and what may be characteristic at one time may not be so at another time with a new year's intake of children and parents, or a new teacher or supervisor. But the general picture may still hold good: what is surprising is the clarity which marks different styles of involvement, and different types of group.

Let us start with what parents said about their involvement. There are three broad headings: parents' activities, their role, and groups' accessibility. So first, how did parents actually help in the group or in other ways? How much explanation or induction was there concerning what they should do, and how much did they want? Second, what did parents think about their role in relation to the group, and what did they think was expected by the staff? And third, how open or accessible were the groups? Did staff welcome parents to visit the group, settle in the children, bring their problems, and play a part in the group – or did they keep parents at arm's length?

Activities

First, then, parents' activities with the groups. Bearing in mind that the groups were deliberately selected to give us matched 'high' and 'low involvement', what can we say about the extent and nature of parents' activities?

To start with a catalogue is simplest. Parents helped in all of the six groups in one way or another – working with the children, making or maintaining equipment, fund-raising, and so on – although the numbers varied. For instance, all the parents we spoke to in one of the playgroups helped with fund-raising, and all the parents in one of the nursery schools helped with maintaining equipment. The commonest ways of offering help were fund-raising, general maintenance (this included looking after the rabbits or cleaning the rooms as well as mending toys and books), and parties or outings. If we distinguish between three different kinds of help or involvement – working in the group alongside the children, servicing or offering practical help outside the day-to-day sessions, and management – we can see that servicing is the most common.

Servicing the group
Here are some examples:

> I wash the towels – one of the fathers made the climbing frame – jumble sales – Christmas cards: one of the children drew them and I'm having them printed . . .
> I took the clock home, made it work and painted it . . .
> We've looked after the rabbits and we've had toys to mend; I've done sewing for them; I've collected bits and pieces for their pictures and cooking.
> I run a puzzle library; that entails making wooden frames and net bags, mending and making new pieces of jigsaw, and keeping track of who's got them . . . We went in the summer and concreted round the swings.
> We make cakes and biscuits and organize the sale: you do a poster and publicity, and we ask everybody to make a cake, and we have half an hour at the end of the afternoon. We have quarter of an hour to set it out and price it, and we do cups of tea and sell the cakes; and we ask half a dozen mums to help us and we sit and talk. We do at least one a term; we made £27 in half an hour last time.
> Children's parties – basically providing food; we go and clean every so often, we have a rota for cleaning; fund-raising – bingo sessions – we get a good response if we plan on a night when nobody else has one, about once a month. Bazaar – making pies etc. to sell – getting people to help on stalls.
> I provide food for outings and parties – *endless* jumble sales.
> Clean up after each session – sweep the floor, wash cups. Make decisions about toys to buy and that sort of

thing. ... All the parents contribute fantastic food for the evening parties ...

Parents who had very little other contact with a group would often mention the inevitable jumble or donation box:

They have notices up asking us to donate money or anything for the children to play with – they have a little box for you to donate the money.

They write to us – many call for jumble – jumble sales (a Pakistani father).

Management

While more parents were involved in servicing the groups than in any other form of support, fewest were involved in management. We spoke to two mothers in nursery schools who were involved – one as a parent manager, the other as secretary to the nursery. Apart from this, in one of the playgroups almost half the parents said they were involved in the parents' committee which ran the group. Even with the low level of involvement in management, more parents were involved in help of a supportive nature outside the group than were involved in actually working in the group alongside the children. This is a salutary reminder that in practice not all involvement means working with children – whatever the argument at a theoretical level, or the expectation of practice.

Working in the group

Three of the six groups had no parents at all helping at the sessions – not surprisingly, as this was the main criterion for involvement when we selected the groups for the parent interviews. But in the three groups where parents did help with the sessions, the number of parents involved and the work they did showed considerable variation. In the nursery school, a couple of parents out of the ten we interviewed said they helped; in the nursery class, just under half; and in the playgroup, two thirds. In two of the groups, parents said they did the same work as the paid staff; in the third, they usually cleared up. Here are some examples of what parents did in the groups.

> I'd go in some mornings and see if they wanted paper cut and they'd say no but can you do this – you see what interests you and join in . . .

> Helping with their puzzles and drawings . . . just generally playing and helping with the children outside – I like to be with young children.

> Occasionally cooking and making ginger beer, and occasionally making pictures – pasting collages . . . ginger beer with one lot of children took nearly all the morning . . .

> We do everything – we read to the children in the book corner, mend toys, sew things – anything the teachers ask us to do, we do.

> This morning I finished painting a cupboard. I made coffee and washed up, mended the Wendy house, got cups ready for lunch time, kept an eye on my daughter. . . . I've been asked to re-cover the settee there. If there's books to be mended, I mend them. I make play dough – general clearing up – jigsaws – tying children's aprons . . .

> I took over the washing as a lady was doing it who wasn't keen on it.

> Well this term I think I'll be washing up most of the time but in between I sit with the children.

> You help them, read to them. You're virtually like the teachers. It's up to you what you do.

There is already a distinction here between joining in with the children, or keeping an eye open for what needs to be done – 'anything', 'everything', 'it's up to you what you do' – and a rather more restricted concentration on mending, washing or generally clearing up; although there is considerable overlap. Parents in the nursery school tended to talk more about mending and clearing up, while parents in the nursery class and the playgroup tended to refer to clearing up and supervising and working with the children and talking with them all in one breath – 'you do as the teachers do and it's up to you'.

Expectations and explanations

What do parents expect when they offer or are asked to help? Some clearly thought that the basic help required was financial – like the parents who offered money or help with fund-raising events, and those who regularly mentioned the donations box. There was a general view that parents played a part when there was an obvious need for funds – as with the playgroups – or for staff – obvious again with the playgroups but also with other groups during staff absences. But where groups were well-staffed, parents were less likely to see an obvious opportunity for their help.

How did parents know what to do when they stayed to help? Did they think they had been given enough explanation? What was the process of induction? Again let us look at some examples of what parents said.

> The staff tell you at the beginning of term what they'd like you to do. . . . Sometimes I ask staff as I like to be busy.

> After four years I think I can see what needs doing.

> It's up to you – if you go in and see a child trying to do something, you'd sit down and see if they wanted help – like getting a pinafore on, or stringing beads. I picked it up as I went along. But if something needed to be done they'd say 'Would you like to help over there . . .'

> Common sense – whatever you feel like doing. At first the staff would say that whatever you can do the

> children will be interested: if you sit and knit all morning they'll be interested.

> It's fairly free – but staff would explain if a mother did not know what to do.

Parents spoke of more direction by staff in the nursery school than in the other two groups: staff told them what to do, and there were formal meetings where staff explained the policy on parents helping with the sessions. In the other two groups, although staff would occasionally direct or explain, parents were left more to decide themselves what they wanted to do or what they thought needed to be done. Some parents would have liked more explanation, especially at the beginning:

> I was never sure whether I was helpful . . . I was never sure where things went so I didn't put things away.

But on the whole, where parents were left to decide for themselves what to do, their views were well expressed by this mother:

> I think it's about the right mixture – you're given a lot of freedom – maybe some mothers, if they've never had any contact, they'd tell them what to do – but it's just obvious if the children are sitting there glueing things to sit down and glue too.

A good illustration of the process of induction concerned what *not* to do. In the nursery school, parents spoke approvingly of a recent meeting at which staff had explained what they liked parents to do and not to do. This had clearly been helpful, and more than one parent wished it had been held earlier during their time with the group.

> Not anything really involved with the children as we're not trained.

> They prefer us not to chat to each other but to talk to the children.

With the children – not to tell them off or tell them what to do – if they're fighting let them get on with it . . . just helping out generally.

Not to show the children what to make or do – it has to come from them. It was a great success, this meeting, and they're doing it every term now. There's a theme every week which I hadn't realized – this week it's wheat and flour.

In this group parents had a good deal of direction from staff about what to do in the group when they stayed to help, but they would have liked more explanation at the beginning. This apparently is what the formal meeting provided: some explanation of the organization of the group, and of the staff's objectives with the children and their assumptions about child development. At the same time, there were clearer boundaries in this group between what parents might and might not do, and between what parents did and what staff did, than in any other group. Perhaps it is to be expected that where there are sharper demarcations parents need more formal explanation and more formal direction.

How was helping organized? A mixture of parents volunteering help and staff asking for particular jobs was the general pattern for both helping with the sessions and other types of support. In the nursery classes and schools, involvement was usually organized by the staff, who took the initiative about what needed to be done, when, and how; in one of the playgroups, this was the responsibility of the parents' committee. One group had a policy of not encouraging mothers to stay to help in the group until the term after their child had started. Parents spoke of the rota as the most usual system for organizing involvement: this usually meant a list on a notice board of jobs to be done or sessions when help was required, and parents signed up if they were available. It was not clear how regularly parents offered help – except for those helping 'on the rota' with sessions in the playgroup and the nursery school, where they came regularly once a week or once a fortnight at the same time.

Parents who were not involved

There were clear contrasts, then, in the amount and type of involvement across the six groups. What of those parents who did not help? Many said they had helped some time in the past but were no longer involved. Why was this? Some were no longer involved because of changes in their own circumstances: in four of the six groups mothers said they would not help at the moment because they were pregnant or had young children who could not be left at home but were too troublesome to bring to the group, but looked forward to the time when they could offer help once again.

> I used to help out one afternoon a week; but I get too tired now, having my fourth baby.

> I had the baby and I've just started work full time, so I can't help now. But I stopped when the baby was born as it interfered with his feeds. . . . I'd still like to go over and help. . . . I like to be with young children.

Some mothers felt too shy and did not think they could cope:

> I don't go there to help – it's just that I feel inadequate – I don't have any self-confidence. The teacher asked me once to bake some cakes and I said I can't – I'm no good at cooking.

A few of the mothers we spoke to did not want to help because they wanted the time for themselves or because they thought the group should be run 'professionally' by trained people. One had been coping for a year with an ill and difficult baby:

> It's the only time of day when I have two hours without them both – and it's marvellous to have those two hours without her, and to be able to change the nappies all the time without 'Isn't that woman doing anything else?'. Then I can survive the day. I couldn't help there – I must have that time.

One mother helped in another group taking handicapped

children swimming, but was very much against mothers helping with the sessions:

> I don't agree with it at all: the staff are trained. They have a rota and there's a couple of mothers every morning and every afternoon – it's expected by the teacher. But I think it's quite wrong.

But this was the only example we met of parents using the argument of 'professionally trained' staff to justify a wish not to get involved. More often it was the other way round. A large number of parents said they would like to help but had not been asked or their offers had not been taken up:

> I did ask her if there was any help she wanted, but she said no. . . . They've got the time to do it themselves. . . . There are three of them and they seem to be so happy; and I've noticed that the children start playing up when they see the mums.

> I often get down there early and help clear up. I would love to help if I was asked – but it's all so well organized.

> They used to do everything themselves: they never asked parents to help, only to donate things.

One mother was afraid that her child was penalized in the group because she had never helped:

> No, I've never helped – no, nothing – not even empty washing up bottles and things – they never asked for them so I didn't take them. So I wondered if this was why he never had things he'd made. . . .

Overall, about one quarter of the parents we spoke to said they were not involved at the moment and would like to help in some way, but had not been asked. At the very least, this suggests an untapped interest in the work of the group with their children which surely might have been exploited or used or explored in some way.

Table 6.1 presents one way of summarizing parental

Parents helped with:	Nursery Schools (N = 2)	Nursery classes (N = 2)	Playgroups (N = 2)
'servicing' activities outside the group (maintenance, fundraising, etc.)	A lot in one group, some in the other.	A lot in one group, some in the other.	A lot in both groups.
involvement in the day to day sessions	A few parents involved, mainly clearing up, in one group; parents not involved in the other.	A lot involved in one group, working with the children; parents not involved in the other.	A lot involved in one group, working with the children; parents not involved in the other.
management	One parent involved in each group.	No parents involved.	A lot of parents in one group; none in the other.

Table 6.1 *Parents' activities in six groups*

involvement in the six groups. We note that about one quarter of the parents interviewed would have liked to help and had not been asked.

Role

Secondly, we come to parents' views of their role. How does what parents think about their involvement compare with what actually happens?

We expected that parents might talk about their involvement in terms of learning about their children and about child development, or in terms of therapeutic experience for themselves. This had been our general impression from the discussions we had held when we observed parents and staff in the groups, and when we interviewed staff. However, we got a rather different picture from the parents. Closer contact between staff and parents, cooperation with the staff, taking an interest in the children, general help and support, shared information about family background, shared experience – these were the comments that parents made.

We can pick out five different strands in what parents had to say.

Practical support

The first is a very practical view of parents' role. The parents' part is to support the staff in their job by doing the practical jobs that have to be done and providing essential practical support:

> Anything that needs doing . . . anything the staff want done . . . it's a help to do the jobs that they haven't got time to do – repairing things, running jumble sales. . . . I'm a general dogsbody.

> We mainly help by sending things – things for the children to play with – we just help when we're asked to by sending jumble, fruit and veg, sending flour for dough, food for Christmas parties. . .

It is interesting that in one group with a heavy emphasis on practical help from parents this approach was criticized as a form of exploitation by one mother who said she would be more than willing to help in a crisis like staff illness, but thought that it was 'wrong to ask so much from the parents':

> I think there are some who are willing and some who aren't, and I think the willing ones are taken advantage of.

The view that the group depended for its existence on practical help from the parents was put in a very matter of fact way for one of the playgroups:

> They need parents because they don't have any money . . . staff think they need more funds, and so more parents should be involved. . . . They really need the parents and they really help a lot – everything there has been done by the parents.

So when the emphasis was on practical help, parents responded when they saw there was a need.

Shared experience and open access

The second strand is a mixture of contact and cooperation, shared experience and shared territory, information and open access, and feelings of encouragement and welcome. Parents thought they should know what was going on, and felt generally welcomed by staff:

> You get every encouragement to join in, in any way you want – they like the parents to be involved.

> Parents should know what's going on.

More information was important – for staff, a better understanding of the child's home background, and for parents, shared experience with the child in the group. There was an assumption here about continuity between the home and the group. The group was seen as an extension of the home.

> It's so natural there – you can stay for the afternoon and they give you a cup of tea – the staff and parents chat . . .

> I think the staff think that it's important that the mothers show an interest for their children's sake as they are so young – it helps the child that you help.

> I think you should take an interest in it, because they are looking after *our* children.

> I like the feeling I know the staff as people and they know my home background – for instance, they know what's going on at home . . . staff want the parents to communicate their ideas about their child. The emphasis is on a smooth transition from home to nursery and back.

The feeling is very much one of a warm welcome and free access for parents. Yet it is not clear whether parents can be said to play any role here at all, except in this sense of shared experience. Several parents said 'I don't really think they do play much part.' One mother expressed this well:

> I don't see parents as playing a part. I see that they

should be totally relaxed about coming and going with their children, and a mother's views should be respected. . . . A child should be seen as a unit of the child and its parent – they're a unit – parent and small child – you can't separate them.

But when parents do play a part, it is very much a supportive back-up for the teacher – practical help with jobs for which teachers do not have time. So here the emphasis is on parents being welcomed into the group as a natural extension to the home, sharing their knowledge with the staff, and sharing the child's new experiences in the group, but not necessarily taking a more active part.

Boundaries and appropriate tasks

The third strand is to do with the boundaries between the staff role and the parents' role. Parents in some of the groups gave vivid descriptions of their exclusion from certain activities. They did not necessarily resent the fact that there were boundaries. On the whole, parents accepted without much question the style of involvement and the roles and tasks presented as appropriate by the group their children attended, with only occasional dissent or dissatisfaction from a parent who hoped for a different style of involvement or role. Two examples will illustrate this.

In one group, where parents were closely involved with the work of the group and were warmly welcomed, but discouraged from undertaking more than practical taskes, this was seen as appropriate.

> Staff don't like parents to . . . come in and tell stories as they have set routines – they do very much have a routine there.
>
> They don't want the mums to take over . . . or bring their ideas into it.
>
> I'm just a helper really. I'd like to think that the people looking after my children are qualified, and

parents there to do the menial tasks to leave the staff free to attend to the children.

Parents acknowledged that there had been friction between parents and staff over what parents should do in the group:

> We had a meeting – a debate – and people said they were being asked to do a lot of things they didn't want to do – like gardening and cleaning out the animals – they didn't think this had anything to do with children and I think it has. And nobody knew what they were supposed to do when they came in fresh – and now it's all made clear. They particularly want parents to be there to talk to children . . .

Two points are important to note here. First, that the friction was not only to do with the boundaries between staff's and parents' roles, but also to do with the explanation and direction given to parents. What was in question was not only what parents were permitted to do – although this was certainly important – but also whether they understood what the staff were trying to achieve and how they worked with the children. This takes us back to the question of shared experience. While parents wanted more information about what was appropriate, very few of them questioned those boundaries. The second point is that this debate over boundaries and information occurred in a group which made most strenuous attempts to involve and welcome parents in its work, while maintaining a very professional stance to the parents' contribution.

In the other example, the boundary was drawn in a different place – in three groups where parents were not encouraged to help with the sessions in any way at all. Here the most usual comment was that the groups were so well run and well organized that no further help was needed: again, parents thought this was perfectly appropriate.

> I think it's up to the teachers: it's their job and should be left to them. . . . They're trained.

> The teachers just have everything organized and they seem to want it like that . . .

I think it was efficiently run – I don't really know if you could improve on it. . . . They had everything very well organized and the children loved it.

There was a feeling that parents played no part beyond taking and fetching the children on time:

You leave the children at the door and the teachers take over from there . . .

They just take the kids and leave them – I suppose if you're anxious about your child you can have a word.

Again, most mothers seemed to be happy with this arrangement:

I'd doubtless have far more ideas if I didn't think it was such a well run nursery.

And parents were happy to leave the staff to get on with the job:

Otherwise there's too many parents dabbling. . . . I'm sure she finds it much easier without a lot of parents around as the children behave much better when their parents aren't there.

But some mothers clearly felt excluded, because no help of any kind was needed:

They're very well organized. If they needed help and they'd asked for it I would have given it to them – but they are very professional.

– but more often because they felt they did not have sufficient information about what was going on in the group:

It would be nice if you could go every three months and discuss the child . . .

Parents felt excluded most often in the one group where they were not made to feel welcome but kept on the other side of the threshold. And it is striking that in this group eight out of the ten parents we spoke to had no idea what part staff expected parents to play – although most were happy with the way the group was run. Dissatisfaction stemmed partly from a sense of inadequate information about the group and what was going on with their child, and partly from a sense of help rejected.

Staff are trained for the job – the group is efficiently run – these were the comments made by parents who thought that some sort of boundary between roles for parents and roles for staff was reasonable and appropriate. But the most interesting comment on professional boundaries was made by this mother:

> It's a socially very mixed group – so the staff prefer to do it all themselves.

The suggestion is that involving parents will naturally produce cliques or favouritism, as one group of mothers will dominate the rest. The solution is for the staff of the group to remain in control, to maintain some sort of professional boundary, and either reject involvement and help, as in the second illustration, or, as in the first, control and limit it. Yet there were groups with very similar social composition which had adopted quite different approaches to parental involvement.

Boundaries and shared tasks

Our fourth strand is also to do with boundaries between parents' and staff's roles – but from the opposite starting point. This time the assumption is that everyone is equal – staff and parents – and that everyone has a part to play in helping to run the group and making decisions. The only example of this view of the roles comes from one of the playgroups.

> Everyone's equal – the staff and the mothers are not divided. The playgroup supervisors and the mums run the thing between them.
>
> We should have the choice of an active role. . . . I like to think if we're unhappy we could suggest changes.

The feeling about involvement is immediately very different. Far from involvement being determined by the staff, with occasional problems about what parents should be encouraged or allowed to do, here problems only arise in terms of turnover of parents willing or able to help:

> About half [the parents help]: half of them are very active in helping and doing things for the group, and others work or don't want to be involved. . . . There's quite a turnover of children – that's what you notice – and you have to involve more parents and that becomes hard at times. It's better this term – we've got a lot more interested.

Again, changes in the parents' role were seen as problems of turnover rather than of boundaries:

> There have been changes because we have had different committee members – the parents are changing constantly.

But not all the parents in this group held the same assumptions of automatic equality. As some parents noted, there was a strong network heavily involved in all aspects of running and working with the group; those outside the network were not so familiar with this style of involvement, and clearly felt that they did not have sufficient information about how the group was run or what they were expected to do.

Parents as learners and teachers

Our fifth strand is to do with parents' learning. How many parents thought that their role should be an educational one, for themselves or their children? The answer is surprisingly few. Here are two examples. The first is a mother talking about staff's views of the parent's role:

> They expect them to be responsible informed helpers – but mothers with little or no experience of theory of child rearing and the experience and importance of play

need an opportunity to say how they could best be helped.

The second is a comment on the part parents should play:

> Speaking for myself as only I can – I like to stand back and observe Kelly and sometimes she'll say 'I didn't paint today' and I know that she wants to. I'll give her all the help I can give her and encourage her to do what she wants.

Quite a number, however, thought they had learnt more about children, and enjoyed seeing how the children learnt; and it gave them ideas for working with the children at home:

> I get a greater knowledge of children – the scope of ideas to do at home with him – much more things to do at home with them. I would never have thought of giving a two-year-old a jigsaw. . . . It's widened my ideas about young children.

> We're learning things – how children react and behave . . .

> I enjoy helping the children with puzzles – they're quicker than I am and it's nice to get them to think a little bit.

> . . when I'm able to help a child do something new for themselves – for instance, an Asian girl learning some new words.

> I'd get ideas on how to teach him to read and write.

> It teaches you what teaching children at this age means – I wouldn't have their job for £100.

To sum up our discussion of parents' roles – our first strand was strictly practical involvement; our second open access, warm welcome and shared experience; our third and fourth to do with professional boundaries and assumptions of equality; and our last to do with parents' learning. To what extent do these overlap, or stand independently on their

	Nursery schools (N = 2)	Nursery classes (N = 2)	Playgroups (N = 2)
Practical help for groups and general support for staff	Both groups yes	One yes; the other very little	One yes; the other very little
Shared experience for parents and children, and open access to groups	Both groups yes	One yes; the other no	Both groups yes
Boundaries between staff and parent roles	Both groups yes	One very little; the other yes	One group no; the other very little
Parents spoke of 'learning' or 'teaching' in the group	One a little; the other no	One yes; the other no	One yes; the other a little

Table 6.2 *Summary of parents' comments on their roles*

own? Are they characteristic of particular types of group? Which of these strands is the most common?

Shared experience, a strong sense of professional boundaries, and practical help were the three most common descriptions of their role put forward by parents. 'We're all equals,' applied to only one group; and hardly any parents thought of their role in an educational sense – either learning or teaching.

Very roughly speaking, parents in the nursery schools thought of their role in a context of professional boundaries, sometimes with open access and shared experience, and sometimes close involvement in practical help. Parents in one of the nursery classes had no sense of professional boundaries, and in the other the strongest feeling of boundaries and the weakest feeling of contact or access of any of the groups. Parents in one playgroup usually talked of it as a democratic organisation with no boundaries and with everyone involved in everything; in the other playgroup there was more feeling of a boundary between parents and staff. We should note that more examples of parents using 'educational language' come from the two groups without a strong sense of professional boundaries between staff and parents – one of the nursery classes and one of the playgroups. We can hardly claim, however, to make general statements about typical roles in nursery school, nursery class, or playgroup on the basis of this evidence. We might do better to characterize the different styles of involvement and parents' roles and set them out as case studies. This we shall do at the end of the chapter.

Access

Our third broad category concerned the accessibility or openness of groups to parents. But is this a type of parental involvement, or is it rather a characteristic of the groups? A group's openness to parents – whether they can come in and out freely, talk to staff about problems, stay to settle in their children, for example – certainly tells us something about that group; but it is also indicative of the contact between staff and parents and therefore, possibly, of the relationship between them and the expectations of both sides. So here our question is the contact parents thought they had with staff and the groups, and what they gained from it.

We first asked parents whether they had visited the group before their child started, and whether they had then stayed to settle him in. A visit was expected in all the groups – as parents said in one group, 'It helps to show that you're interested.' Most had visited once or a few times, usually with the child: in one group, parents made weekly visits for a term or sometimes a year or over before the child actually started in the group. Many children became familiar with the group through collecting an older brother or sister. Again, most parents in most of the groups had stayed to settle in the child when he first started, and had found this helpful.

> It was helpful for me to stay because he was rather clinging and he got used to the children while I was

there. He'd go and play and come back and see me. For me it was helpful in the way that I knew he was all right. I'd have hated to leave him crying.

Hardly any parents actually wanted to leave their children without settling them (one mother who disapproved of parents being present in the group at all was an unusual exception); although there were some who felt that it was unnecessary from the child's point of view – they were perfectly happy and joined in the activities without a backward glance. But, as one mother said, 'Perhaps she wouldn't have been so happy if I hadn't stayed.'

Two groups stood out as exceptions here. In one, although parents stayed on the whole, staff preferred them to leave their child to settle on his own if he started clinging or crying. In the other, parents were not encouraged to stay, and none of the ten we spoke to had done so for more than a few minutes.

> I think I just stayed to see he was settled – we had crying every morning for a week and they preferred me not to stay – said he'd be better if I went . . . after the first week he'd walk in without saying goodbye . . .

Most parents were happy with the arrangements; but at the same time more than half the parents in this group said they would have liked more opportunity when their child started to stay longer and talk to the staff about the organization of the group and about what their child was like:

> I would have welcomed a chance to talk to the staff about his interests and development. You weren't encouraged in . . . you left them in a little room where they hang their coats.

> We didn't know what they did in the day – I would have liked to know that. . . . I would definitely have liked to know more about their teaching methods.

Parents in all the other groups with this one exception were happy with the amount of time they had had to settle the child, and the contact with staff; these parents were upset by the lack of both access and information.

Our second question was to do with contact with staff once the child was in the group. Did parents have opportunity to talk to staff about their child's progress or problems? And were staff helpful? Most parents felt they had plenty of opportunity to talk to staff, when they took or collected children:

> They'll always tell me what he's been doing . . .
>
> She'll always look up and say something. . . . She'll tell me if he's said or done anything funny, or he's had a good day . . .

were fairly typical comments. One group in particular stood out for the sensitivity staff showed to both parents' and children's needs. Parents described how staff had helped with their problems:

> I had a lot of sleep problems with her and I was whacked – they'd take her and send me home to sleep. You come to regard them as friends; you could talk to them about anything. . . . I've had a lot of problems in the past year and I found them very sympathetic and they'd really try and solve the problems and suggest something.
>
> When I was concerned about the children – one stutters and the other was very backward talking – they arranged for them to see a speech therapist – she made that decision and it's really helped. . . . The girl who runs it helped me and got them meals at the nursery. They never seem too busy to help.

But this group was unusual for the amount of help of a social work nature offered by the staff as a normal part of their work.

By way of contrast, one group discouraged contact with staff once the children were in the group. More than half the parents interviewed said they would have liked more chance to talk to the staff about the child's progress or problems:

> Every mother is anxious to know what her child is interested in. I felt nobody seemed to want to know how he was coming on. You had to use your own knowledge of what was going on.

> I'd like to have known more about what was going on – in what he was doing and how he was coping with things – like controlling a pen. . . . They never told you how they were progressing.

One mother was clearly anxious that the staff had failed to notice her child's problems:

> They didn't realize that he was having problems – he forgets to go to the toilet in time . . .

Parents needed confirmation of their own views of what their child was like and capable of. As one mother said:

> I'd like to have known how he was getting on in his behaviour, and whether they considered he was quick or slow to learn – what they thought of him.

They needed to test out with staff their ideas for helping the child at home and best continuing the work of the group:

> They didn't seem to want to discuss her or what she could do. I wanted to talk about whether to teach her to read. They should tell you what they're doing and capable of. . . . It would have been nice to join in and get an idea what they're doing and what you can do with them at home – because with her I've had a lot more time and I'd have liked to know what to do to help her and I could have got to know that from the nursery. . . . You should be told how you can help your child and what they're doing and what you can do to help at home . . .

> I didn't really know what they taught, what their teaching method was. If you knew, when you were at

home you could sort of carry on what they were doing, and it would make their job easier.

Our third question concerned the events laid on for parents by the group. Were there any such events, and did parents know about them? Did they go, and what did they get out of them?

In parents' eyes, there were two types of events. One included social events such as coffee mornings, social evenings, barn-dances, suppers: parents enjoyed these for their social value, the chance to meet other parents and to relax with staff, and for new parents to get to know the group. Most events parents mentioned were of this kind. The other included open evenings or similar occasions where parents had an opportunity to see their children's work or a performance by the children, or, less often, an educational event such as films about child development or nursery education.

Groups differed in the amount of energy they put into events. In one group nearly half the parents said there were none – 'no money', commented one mother – or they did not know of any. Another group laid on something once a month. In four out of the six groups, parents said they would like more events. There are two important points here. In one group, more than half the mothers said they could not go because of young children and husbands on shift work. In another, the only social event of any kind was an open evening shared with the first school – the one occasion parents had to discuss children's progress or to see their work. Whether events are social or educational occasions, there are clear implications from parents' desire for more in these two examples. On the other hand, events may be 'superfluous', as one mother felt about her social contact with her daughter's group – 'every day is an open day'.

Finally, we asked parents whether there was a parents' committee or association or representative of any kind, and if they were involved. This question overlaps our earlier discussion of involvement and the present one of access or openness. A parents' committee may have either a management function or an information function, or a mixture of both. The presence of such a body may tell us something about parents' involvement in making decisions, or something about the openness of the group – or both. In two of the groups, parents said there was no such body. In the other four, a few parents mentioned some kind of committee, or a parent manager; but even in those groups which apparently had flourishing committees or associations, there was considerable confusion as to the nature of the body and its membership. We can illustrate this with the example of a group run by a parents' committee to which every member of the group in theory belonged. Six of the parents we interviewed knew about the committee, and that they were members and could attend meetings, even if they were not all certain how members were allocated jobs on the committee. The other four parents either did not know of the existence of the committee, or were unsure whether they were members or not. It so happens that these four were the parents

Parents:	Nursery schools (N = 2)	Nursery classes (N = 2)	Playgroups (N = 2)
made a pre-visit	All Most	Most Some	Most Some
settled child in	Most Most	Most None	Most Some
wanted more contact and time with staff	No No	No Most	No No
went to social events and thought there were enough	Yes Most	Most Some	Most Most
did not go or wanted more	No Some	Some Some	No Some
members of a parents' organization or managing body		Parents in four groups were members. Parents in five groups said they did not know of any such body.

Table 6.3 *Parents' views on groups' 'accessibility'*

whom we noted earlier as uninvolved and 'outside the network'.

Let us summarize this discussion on contact and accessibility. We have considered four different types of contact which we called visiting and settling in, access to staff, social events, and parents' committees. Clearly these differ in the importance attached to them as signified by their visibility in parents' comments. The most important is the process of starting a child in the group – visiting beforehand and settling him in – and maintaining contact with the staff once he is there. Social events, whether of an educational/information or a social kind, figure rather less prominently, and parents' bodies of one kind or another least of all.

Another way of looking at this is to ask whether there are different styles of contact across different groups. The answer to this is no, with one exception: our study showed less variation between the groups in their style of contact between parents and staff, than in their style of involvement or the roles parents take on. The one exception is one group which consistently showed less contact of any kind than any other group – whether visiting, settling the child, talking to staff, or social events. More than half the parents interviewed from this group would have liked more chance to talk to staff, and to spend time with their children in the group – two thirds said their only chance of contact was the one open evening; and nearly half wanted more social events for parents and staff to meet.

The important question is how these three pieces of information which we have considered so far separately – involvement, roles, and access – can now be put together. What picture do we get of parents and their children's groups?

Shared experience, or an educational role?

Parents' comments certainly indicated what they thought they had got out of involvement in their child's preschool group. At its simplest, there was a feeling of enjoyment, and of belonging:

> Pleasure – I do enjoy it. I feel useful – doing something worth while . . .

> Comfortable – feeling of pride . . . good to feel part of the group.

To counterbalance this, one mother said she only came out of duty – but only one. Several mothers spoke about sharing their child's experience:

> The best thing is my daughter really likes me to be there – she really gets excited – 'This is my mum . . .'

> I like helping there – it helps Paul as he'll be going there soon and Suzanne likes me to be there so I can see what she's doing.

And the fascination of working with children, and learning how they learn, comes over at times as strongly as the sense of shared experience with one's own child.

Yet we can see from Tables 6.1, 6.2, and 6.3 that parents in different groups are involved in different ways and have different views about their involvement.

Is there a common pattern? The most striking impression from the interviews is parents' sense of shared experience with their children. Almost without exception, they talked of their children's attendance at a group as something that was important to both parent and child and that should be shared. This was so in spite of the diffidence many expressed about their role – teachers and supervisors were 'trained' and 'knew their job' – and the shyness and lack of confidence, or the exhaustion with younger children, which prevented others from giving much time or help. The importance of knowing what happened in the group was stressed again and again: 'You've got to know what is going on.' The sharing of the child's new experience in the group was seen as an extension of the previous shared experience between parent and child in the family – an extension that was, perhaps, all too brief, as the child moved out into the wider world:

> I think parents should play as large a part as they want to. I think it's nice for them to be involved because when the children start school they don't have much involvement – they're so soon grown up . . .

As one mother said, 'You *should* take an interest – the staff are looking after *our* children.' The welcome offered by some groups to parents emphasized this natural extension:

> Staff think parents play an important part and like to involve them. . . . It's so natural there – you can stay for the afternoon and they give you a cup of tea – the staff and parents chat . . .

Similarly shared experience was recognized as important from the child's point of view – as with the mother who said that the best thing about helping was that her daughter really liked her to be present. Staff were quoted as wanting parents to be involved because 'they think that if parents take more interest in school and are involved in it this should help the children':

> They think it's important that the mothers show an interest for their children's sake as they are so young – it helps the child that you help. . . . I feel the same. . . . I can't imagine not taking an interest . . .

The sense of shared experience was most clearly expressed by these two mothers:

> They're a unit – parent and small child – you can't separate them. . . . Parents should feel totally relaxed about coming and going with their children; and a mother's views should be respected on a child's tiredness . . .

> It's not like years ago when you took the child, handed him over, and that was it. . . . She gets a better understanding of me – it brings us closer together – it's not a world I can't step into.

The sense of 'belonging', or 'shared experience' and a 'shared world' came over powerfully when parents were talking about what they had gained from being involved in their child's group and what they thought their role should be. It came over equally powerfully when they talked about their first visits to the group, their first conversations with staff, the period of settling in the child, their contact with staff once the child was in the group, and the educational and social events provided by the group. Parents clearly wanted to know how the child had passed his day and whether there had been any problems, just as they thought staff should know if there were any difficulties at home:

> I wasn't sure how she'd settle in as she was one of the youngest and she got tired, so they watched her carefully – and they always told me about her – they were very willing to give me all the information I wanted.

Parents' sense of frustration and anxiety if this experience was not shared was demonstrated in their comments when staff apparently missed a child's problems, or failed to inform parents of an accident; and equally when parents had to rely on the child to tell them what he had been doing: 'I find out by asking her what sort of a day she's had,' was one sad comment. The clearest illustration comes from the group quoted earlier where parents were not encouraged to stay with their children or to help, and where the only occasion when they could talk to staff or see children's work was an open evening shared with the 'big school'. Two parents from this group felt strongly about the benefits of shared experience for themselves and their children. One mother with more determination than most had in fact stayed with her child for short periods, and had developed her own ideas for helping him, despite lack of contact with the staff:

> I've stayed up there about ten minutes some mornings and watched what he's doing . . . sometimes he's asked me to see what he's doing and I've just sat and

> got him started. . . . I suppose staff think parents should encourage the children at home with drawing and sort of back up what they're doing at the nursery – but this is what I've seen that he likes there, not what they've told me about what he does.

The other mother thought that shared experience would benefit her child:

> I think it does good to go round and give a hand with the children once or twice a week – just general helping – read stories, do what's needed doing. I think it's better for the children if the parents help – it builds a better relationship between parents and teachers and then you find out what's going on. Because now I have to ask her all the time. I think it would be a good idea for parents to take it in turns to help out. There must be things that parents can do to help. . . . It seems to help the children . . .

and herself:

> The staff are nice – she likes to go – she looks forward to it – the teacher is very nice – it's just that we'd like to go in there more and have more to do with it . . .

while in the same breath praising the staff for running a pleasant group.

So we can see that the common phrase 'It's nice to see what they are doing' hides something very complex to do with shared experience between parent and child and the extension of that natural relationship from the family into the child's group. Parents want to know what their child does day by day; they want to know how the group is organized, and what methods the staff use. There is an assumption that the child's experience at home and in the group forms, or should form, a continuity. Parents seek confirmation from those they consider more skilled or experienced that their view of their child is basically sensible and correct; and they need information and confirmation about what to do with the child at home to strengthen that continuity: 'how to back up the work the staff are doing' or 'how to make sure that I am doing the right thing at home', as many parents express it. The notion of shared experience is thus a very basic one. It includes questions about the relationship between staff and parent, about the openness or accessibility of the group and staff to the parent. Parents were clearly upset, dismayed, disappointed, or plain angry if the relationship with their child's group denied this shared relationship – if they felt excluded, for whatever reason. They might nevertheless believe that the group was a good one and the staff praiseworthy, and recognize that the child was happy – yet there would still be something missing.

We have seen that shared experience between group and home was defined as part of the natural relationship between parent and child. To what extent was it defined as an educational relationship? We saw in the last chapter that very few staff in any of the groups thought of parents as 'teachers' of their children, or as sharing a 'teaching relationship' with the 'professionals'; we should now compare the parents' view. To what extent did the *parents* see themselves as teaching their children, and did involvement in their child's group affect their views?

It is difficult to get a clear picture. A handful of parents who were discouraged from contact with their child's group felt this hindered them in their attempts to help the child at home or to maintain continuity from home to group and back again. Whether or not they actually spoke of 'teaching' or 'learning' (one mother indeed spoke of teaching her child to read), they thought of what happened at home as continuing or reinforcing the learning the child did in the group, and saw that they had a role in this process. One or two parents talked to staff about the child's difficulties in 'learning his colours':

> I was told by one of the helpers that she was very good at painting, so I bought paints – I talked to them once about not knowing her colours but she soon learnt.

Some parents clearly learnt something about child development – not through a textbook but from direct observation of children playing and learning – and put it to good use at home:

> Once I did stay. . . . I was sat at the lego table, and it fascinated me watching them, what they were doing.

> I get a greater knowledge of children – the scope of ideas to do at home with them. . . . I would never have thought of giving a two-year-old a jigsaw. . . . It's widened my ideas about young children . . .

But for some parents to learn, there might have to be more direct explanation and positive demonstration, as this mother pointed out:

> Put it this way: it should be explained to parents that the stuff at the group is good for children. You get children who won't play with water because they're not allowed to at home; boys tend not to play with girls' things . . . because they don't at home. It does them good to get wet and dirty and enjoy themselves . . .

This mother may not have used the languge of adult education or child development, and the process may have to be less directive than she suggests, but she was at least clear that learning for parents is not necessarily an automatic process but one that may have to be planned for deliberately and with care.

Yet such examples, although striking when they do appear, are few. It seems that parents do not commonly see their shared relationship with their children in terms of a teaching or learning relationship. Why should this be so? We may hazard a guess. There is considerable muddle and confusion surrounding the notion of 'teaching' children of this age. Parents described how staff had carefully explained the policy of the group that they 'did not teach children at this age, merely channelled them' or 'would not teach them things unless they actually came and asked'; yet, as one mother retorted, 'I wouldn't agree with that, as my child would never leave the sandpit to go and ask if he could learn to write.' If teachers are reluctant to use the language of teaching or learning for what they do with preschool children, while maintaining a strictly professional stance about their training and competence for this work, it is surely hardly surprising to find that parents believe they do not or should not teach their children. And perhaps parents with the strongest ideas about 'teaching' receive least encouragement from the staff.

Does involvement in a preschool group affect the parents' view of their own role as educational? Earlier in this chapter we looked at the extent to which parents saw learning or teaching as part of their own role or as one of the benefits of involvement (we use 'learning and 'teaching' here to mean the awareness of role in relation to the child's activity and learning). Although very few people actually *described* learning or teaching as part of their role in the group – few parents said they were in the group to teach the children – some parents did say they helped in the group with the same activities as the staff, and others mentioned increased understanding of how children play and learn as a spin-off from their involvement. We cannot say that people's views changed as a result of their involvement unless this was actually claimed.

But was there any evidence that parents were more likely to think of their role in educational terms if they were involved in a group where, for example, their involvement was itself of a more educational kind, working with the children in the same way as staff rather than offering practical support, or where staff made particular attempts to involve parents in the 'educational partnership'? There was indeed some evidence for this. When we interviewed parents, it was striking that one group of parents in particular gave examples of what they had learnt about how their children learnt, ideas for what to do at home, and specific activities for the group. This was a group where parents worked with the children rather than giving practical help to the staff, where they had very open access to the staff, and where staff gave a lot of support to parents with their own problems and a lot of encouragement to parents lacking in self-confidence. It was also a group where staff talked specifically about parents as 'educators' of their children and about an 'educational partnership'. On the other hand, one of the clearest statements of a parent's growing understanding of how children learn came from a group where parents were involved in offering help of a practical kind, and made extremely welcome in the group, but not encouraged to work with the children on the grounds that they were not trained.

What are we to conclude from this pattern? We cannot argue that there is only one way to learn an educational role – that is, to be aware of the interactive relationship between parent and child and the parent's role in the child's development. Clearly some parents spoke of 'learning' and 'teaching', and of 'getting ideas to do at home' when they were involved in educational activities working alongside the children; but other parents who were only doing the chores also used these terms. It may be the case that involvement 'by doing' is a more efficient way for some to learn than involvement 'by observation'; but parents, like children, learn in different ways. However, both the groups we have taken as examples were groups where staff put much time and energy into involving parents – although with different styles. We may at least suggest that it requires strenuous efforts on the part of both staff and parents to help parents recognize that, in their shared experience with their children, not only can they take on an educational role, but they also learn themselves.

A major question to tackle in seeking to explain these differences in parental involvement is whether social class makes any difference to the role played by parents in their children's group or to the expectations of parents or staff. What is the key factor in explaining differences in parental involvement between groups – group style, social class, or the formal organization of the group, whether it is a nursery school, nursery class, or playgroup? What is it that makes one group apparently readier or more willing to involve parents, or to involve them in different ways? The data that we have relates to groups rather than to individual parents because the questions that we have been asking relate to groups. Of the six groups where we collected information on the 'consumer population' through the parent interviews, two served very mixed populations of manual workers on the one hand and highly-educated professionals on the other, and the remaining four served populations predominantly of manual workers with little education beyond compulsory levels. Yet the first two groups, although they served very similar populations in terms of parents' occupations and education, and numbers of working mothers, approached the parents very differently. One was a nursery school with a very welcoming and friendly attitude, but no involvement of parents in the classroom; the other was a playgroup, with parents heavily involved in the work of the group, its management, and other activities, as well as an 'open door' to other adults. We see a similar variety with the other four groups, although again they were broadly similar in terms of parents' occupations and education. One was a nursery school with a very friendly and open approach to parents, who were closely involved but in carefully defined and supervised tasks; one was a playgroup, friendly and welcoming to parents but with no parental involvement in the sessions. The two remaining groups were nursery classes; one kept parents at arm's length and discouraged them from helping or even coming into the room; the other made strenuous efforts to bring parents in (with staff visiting families on the waiting list) and spoke of parents as 'partners' in the educational process. So we can see that groups apparently serving very similar catchment areas have very different styles of approach towards parents.

We have argued that formal organizational differences – whether nursery school, nursery class, or playgroup – are less powerful in explaining differences in approach towards parents than are factors to do with group style – whether staff and parents define the group and its involvement of parents in 'partnership' or 'professional' terms, whether this is the result of explicit decisions or implicit in the way the group operates and parents respond. We can see that group style cannot be explained solely by social class factors – as groups similar in terms of social class demonstrate considerable variations in group style. Although we should expect there to be a link between social background and parents' willingness to be involved, and the role they expect to play in the group and with their own child, the evidence suggests this is not a sufficient explanation for the variations in involvement to be found between different groups in this study. However, this was a limited investigation. The picture may be a complicated one of interaction between parents, social background, and staff style – and we need further work on the detail.

Six snapshots

We asked earlier whether some forms of involvement or access were more typical of some groups than others. Do playgroups involve parents more in working with the children than do nursery schools? Are nursery schools more welcoming towards parents than nursery classes? Our discussion so far has told us little about the interrelationship between different types of involvement and different types of group.

General statements about playgroups, nursery classes, and nursery schools may be too simplistic – and not just because we only looked at six groups. What we have in mind instead is different styles of involvement, role and access, which do not correspond neatly to organizational type. To conclude this chapter, therefore, we present six snapshots to show up the detail of these different styles.

The first two are of nursery schools. Both are very accessible, relaxed, and welcoming to parents – parents clearly feel they can spend a lot of time in the groups with their children and talking to staff. One groups organizes a highly successful mothers' club for social events. Parents are encouraged to help in one of the groups, and a few do, although there is more involvement with practical services outside the day-to-day sessions. In the other, there is no involvement with the sessions, but occasional help outside the group. Both have strong professional boundaries and a strong emphasis on trained staff. Staff organize the help; there are 'set routines'; parents' task is to 'help the staff to do their job better'. Parents are enthusiastic about the welcoming style; and although a few are critical, most are in favour of a well-run, well-organized and professional group with a strong emphasis on the child.

The third and fourth snapshots are of a nursery class and playgroup. Both make parents very welcome; both have more parents than any other group working with the children in the day-to-day sessions; neither group has much sense of boundaries between parents and staff. Two points stand out about 'community': in one group the community it serves, in the other, the community within it. The nursery class serves a largely working class community of an isolated housing estate, where parents know most of the staff socially. The teacher in charge of the class visits each family before the child starts in the class, to establish a link. This group has built up a strikingly close relationship with parents, many of whom spoke about their personal difficulties and the help staff had given them, and what they and their children had gained through the group and the staff's efforts. The playgroup likewise operated on a partnership rather than professional lines and – unlike any other group – attempted to run as a democracy: for example, staff were reluctant to direct what parents should do when they stayed to help in the group, and decisions about management, activities, staffing, fees and so on were taken at parents' meetings. However, like all democracies, some seemed more equal than others. From what parents said, it was clear that some people felt more comfortable than others, more part of 'the network', more involved and 'in control', more familiar with the organization. This was often a very subtle process. One mother commented on the way the friendship network made it more difficult for new mothers to integrate or to understand what was expected. And it was noticeable in this group how social class, education, and ethnic group separated those 'in' the network from those 'outside'. So our fourth snapshot is of a group which runs along the most democratic lines of all, with more parents involved in management than anywhere else, but paradoxically split within itself.

The fifth snapshot is of another playgroup. Here we have a group that is very welcoming and relaxed towards parents, but has no parental involvement at all in the sessions with the children. Some parents welcome this as a relief; others would like to take a 'more active interest' and share their children's experience. But one comment made was that in a very 'socially mixed' group professional boundaries may be one way of solving the problem faced by the previous playgroup, without open selection or discrimination.

Our final snapshot is of another nursery class. This group stands out for its lack of contact with parents on every front – whether access or involvement. Parents left and collected their children at the door; they sent things rather than offered any other more active support; they had little idea of what staff expected of them or what staff did with the children. The most usual view was that this group was well-run and the children were happy – but it was expressed with the occasional sad rider, 'We should like to know more about what goes on'. We were left in no doubt that parents regretted their exclusion.

The picture is a complicated one. The style and the objectives of the groups are reflected in the parents' comments: one group attempts a democracy, but fails to make equal contact with all its constituents; another attempts to give parents a break, but risks ignoring their desire for a more active part; another attempts partnership by reaching out to parents; one runs the group apparently entirely for the benefit of the children; and others involve parents strenuously but within tightly defined boundaries. Parents' styles of involvement and roles largely match their views of the group.

In the next chapter, we must finally ask whether parents' views match staff's views and what we observed in the groups.

7
Conclusions: parents and professionals

In the first two chapters we set out the background research behind the present interest in parental involvement and attempted a definition. In the rest of this book we have presented material from our study of parents in playgroups, nursery classes, and nursery schools in Oxfordshire. Our final task is to draw conclusions from the study, and to look again at the questions raised in the first two chapters in the light of the evidence we now have from the observations in groups and interviews with staff and parents, and in particular the two models of involvement we have distinguished, 'professional' and 'partnership'.*

Process or impact? the experience of involvement

Most research studies in the preschool field deal with the *effects* of preschool intervention or comparisons of different programmes, not with the actual process or experience of intervention. The question that is usually asked about parental involvement is thus 'Is it effective? Does it work?' This study, however, does not tell us much about the long-term effectiveness or impact of involving parents in their children's preschool experience, for either parent or child; except in the very short-term sense of changing people's definitions of the activity in which they are engaged and their part in that activity. (This, of course, may be a requirement

---

* We use the terms 'professional' and 'partnership' as a way of analysing group style rather than describing staff characteristics. Thus we do not mean to imply that a group with a 'partnership' approach necessarily has staff who are any less trained or exacting in their standards of work than a group we term 'professional'.

for long-term effectiveness – but we have not tested that here.) A study of the long-term effectiveness of parental involvement, using the material we have gathered, could ask the following questions: Which type of involvement is more effective in affecting what children 'extract' from education (in Weikart's phrase) – involving parents in their children's activities in the group, involving them in their child's experience but without actively taking part, or involving them in the management of the group? Which type of involvement has more effect in changing parents' attitudes about the educational process, and the part they play in their child's development? Recent studies (Consortium of Longitudinal Studies, 1979; Weikart *et al.*, 1978; Armstrong and Brown, 1979) suggest that involving parents in their children's preschool education can change parents' attitudes towards education, and their aspirations and expectations for their children, as well as changing children's performance, over the long term. We also know that parents are involved in very different ways – but we know little about the long-term impact of different kinds of involvement.

This study is about the process rather than the impact of involvement. What actually happens when parents are involved in their children's preschool groups? What do they do? Why and how do they get involved? What role do they see themselves as playing? What is the structure or style of the different groups we have been studying? These are the questions we have been asking.

The Oxfordshire study – types of involvement and group style

In the second chapter, we quoted Gordon's (1969) five-point scale for parent involvement: parents as supporters, learners, teachers of their own children, teacher aides or volunteers in the classroom, and policy makers. How does this compare with the evidence from Oxfordshire?

Gordon's first category is our *servicing* category – parents giving help outside the sessions, making and mending equipment, fund-raising, looking after the animals. His last is our involvement in *management*. The others are more problematic. tic. His fourth category, teacher aides and volunteers in the classroom, corresponds closest to our category of *involvement with the day-to-day sessions* of the group – but we have made a further distinction here between working alongside the children in the group and clearing up after them. This is a fundamental distinction if we are concerned with the roles played by parent and professional. Similarly, Gordon's second and third categories of parents as learners and teachers of their own children restrict what we have called the parent's 'educational' role to work with his own child – we are interested in the parent's role in the group as such. So we do not have information in the Oxfordshire study on the parent's role specifically with his *own* child, except incidentally from comments about the carry-over of learning from the group to the home. Instead, we have information about the parent's 'educational' or 'servicing' role in the classroom or playgroups as it compares with the role of the teacher or the playgroup supervisor.

There is a sixth category which Gordon does not include but to which we have given considerable space in this study – parents as sharers or partners in their children's experience. This is not necessarily the same as being a teacher or a learner – both of which require active participation – although they may overlap. This is the category which elsewhere we have considered under the heading of the openness or accessibility of a group – to what extent parents are welcomed into the group and encouraged to see it as a natural extension of the home experience, with shared information between staff and parent and shared experience between parent and child.

Which of these types of involvement ranks highest in frequency in the study of Oxfordshire nursery schools, classes, and playgroups?

More than half the parents we inteviewed were involved in servicing or support roles – they made cakes for fund-raising events, painted furniture, concreted the playground, collected jumble, mended books. Almost one quarter were involved with the day-to-day sessions – whether working with the children or clearing up after them. Only one parent in nine was involved with management. According to this study, then, servicing activities are the most usual form of involving parents in the work of the group, followed by helping with the day-to-day sessions, with involvement in management a very long way behind. This formulation, however, obscures a further distinction which we found to be important – whether helping with the sessions meant working with the children or clearing up after them. Only one in five parents said they worked with the children. If we take clearing up as another kind of servicing, although in the sessions, then this category becomes even more dominant. Another way of putting this is the fact that in all the groups more parents were involved with servicing than any other form of help.

What can we add to this picture if we look at the information from the point of view of the *groups* rather than the *parents* involved? We can see that more groups involved parents in servicing than any other form of help. (We cannot say anything about the number of groups involving parents in the sessions, as this was our main criterion for selection in the first place; so numbers of parents are a more important guide here.) Three out of the six groups from which we interviewed parents involved them in some form of management or administration of the group. *Type* of group tells us rather more, although we should remind ourselves that the number of groups is too small to give us very reliable information. Of the three types of group, playgroups came out highest on all forms of involvement – servicing (fund-raising rather than maintenance), management, and help with the sessions; playgroups also came out with the most parents involved in working with children during the sessions as distinct from clearing up, and they were least likely to be selective about the activities parents undertook in the sessions.

When we turn to the groups' openness or accessibility to

parents, we can see that the nursery schools were more welcoming and open than any other kind of group to parents at the beginnings and ends of sessions; parents came in more with their children and talked more to staff and other parents, stayed more to settle their children, visited more and brought their problems. The only exception to this picture of general welcomingness was the presence of 'non-staff' adults in the group – here playgroups came out significantly higher. From the staff interviews, we have seen that the nursery school staff tended to place most emphasis on parents visiting before the child started at the group, and staying to settle him. In the interviews with parents, we asked about four types of contact, all of which could be said to be ways for parents to share in their children's experience – visiting and settling in, access to staff, social events, and parents' committees. Of these, the most important was the process of starting a child in the group and maintaining contact with the staff while he was there; social events were less important, and parents' bodies least important of all. There was not much difference here between different types of group. The one striking exception was a nursery class which consistently had the least contact of any group with parents – whether as sharers in their children's experience, settling them and talking to staff, or as helpers in the group or outside.

More parents, in all kinds of group, had this contact – the process of starting the child in the group and maintaining contact with the staff while he was there – than were involved in either servicing, management, or help with the sessions. If we include in the list of parental involvement this basic contact, where the parent shares in the child's experience but is not necessarily an active participant in the group, we can see this will head the list.

If we summarize the information from the Oxfordshire study on the roles played by parents in their children's preschool groups, we can see that they are, first of all, sharers in their children's experience, with open access to the group, whether playgroups, nursery school or class; second, servicers or supporters – providers of practical help outside the group; third, helpers or 'aides' in the day-to-day sessions of the group; and fourth, 'teachers' in the group working alongside the children in the same way as regular members of staff. This is in rank order, but does not tell us the relative frequency; for example, we know that numerically speaking the third category – helpers in the group – is far more frequent than the fourth. This is a similar picture of parents' roles for Oxfordshire as we sketched in the second chapter for elsewhere in the country (Watt, 1976; Van der Eyken *et al.*, 1979; Ferri and Niblett, 1977).

Can we relate this summary of parents' roles to group style? We agreed earlier that a classification of groups on the basis of their organizational type – playgroup, nursery class, nursery school – might tell us something about their style but might also obscure important similarities and differences on other dimensions. We suggested the following categories as a useful way to begin analysing the differences between groups in their approach to parent involvement.

Open or closed groups

Do groups have relaxed beginnings and endings of sessions, or are these points rapid 'transfers' of the child between parent and staff? Do parents visit and stay to settle their child? Can they stay and watch? Is there sufficient opportunity for parents to discuss their children's problems and progress, and their own problems? Are there social or educational events, and plenty of information for parents? Is the group open territory to other 'non-staff adults' or restricted fairly closely to staff and parents, and do parents feel it is sufficiently their territory for them to talk freely to other parents? We have seen that the nursery schools in our study came out highest on the whole for this friendly and welcoming accessibility to parents – with the exception of open territory to other adults, where playgroups came out top. It was unusual to find groups which were not open and accessible to parents, but we have examples of this in both nursery classes and playgroups.

Helping in the sessions or servicing

Do parents help with the day-to-day sessions of the group? Or are they encouraged to offer practical help, but kept at arm's length from the actual sessions? Practical necessity was recognized by both staff and parents as a legitimate reason to ask for help – either for help with the children, when staff were ill or when a group had insufficient funds to employ helpers; or with practical maintenance and fund-raising. We have seen that overall the playgroups in our study were more likely than any other kind of group to involve parents in servicing, management, and working with the children – and since they are self-help groups this is perhaps not surprising. However, what perhaps is *more* surprising is the number of playgroups which do *not* involve parents either working with the children or in management, and the number of other groups such as nursery classes and nursery schools, which do not have to be self-sufficient yet do involve parents in the sessions, with servicing, and less frequently in management. Economics and self-help cannot provide a complete explanation of parental involvement.

Working with the children or clearing up

If parents help with the sessions, do they 'do as the staff do', as one parent put it, or are they restricted to certain activities? We have noted that playgroup staff were the least likely in our study to be selective about the activities that parents might undertake; but we also have examples from all three types of group – nursery classes, nursery schools, and playgroups – of parents being asked not to undertake certain activities because they were not trained or would not understand the rationale behind them.

Direction or autonomy

When parents stay to help, do they 'keep their eyes open and do what needs to be done', as one parent described it, or are they told what to do by staff? We observed very few instances either of staff directing parents or of parents asking for directions. Somewhat paradoxically, it might seem, most instances of staff instructing parents occurred in the playgroups, while most instances of helpers asking staff what to do occurred in the nursery schools. Yet parents 'using their common sense' or 'getting on by themselves' might either indicate genuine autonomy, or mask a situation where parents did not really know what to do but were too shy to ask. There were examples in the interviews of parents from all types of group saying they would have liked more explanation and instruction at first: 'I felt like a spare part,' 'I didn't know if I was doing it right.' Direction and explanation go together – we found that we could not ask questions about the extent to which parents were instructed or left to get on with the job, or understand their own comments, unless we also knew the context of explanation and induction, formal or informal.

Formal induction or informal learning on the job

Are parents given a formal 'introduction' to the group, with an explanation of its objectives and organization and their own contribution? Or are they expected, as some parents said, to 'pick it up as you go along'? Very few groups had a formal 'introduction' or 'induction' for parents. But neither was there much 'explanation on the job'. We noted in the observations that what little discussion there was between parents and staff about activities or objectives tended to happen in the nursery classes rather than the nursery schools or the playgroups. Apart from these few examples there was little, either formal or informal. Why is this? One explanation might be that what staff do in the way of introduction or explanation is presented so informally that parents do not recognize it as such. ('When he starts, this is what he'll be doing – ' or 'Did you notice how he's matching colours?' is to the parent a comment about her individual child, rather than generalizable into a statement about how the group is organized or how children learn.) Another might be that staff are reluctant to organize formal sessions for parents, as they do not wish to impose their structure but would rather allow parents to develop their own ideas together with the children. This confuses instruction with explanation. A third reason might be that staff expect parents to learn, and understand, from simple observation or involvement without any further help from them.

Explanation and instruction may indeed overlap, as in the example given in an earlier chapter of a meeting between staff and parents when there was confusion over what parents might and might not do in the group. What parents found useful about this meeting was not only that it clarified what they were expected to do, but that the staff had explained their objectives and methods in working with the children. As one mother said, 'I now understand the theme they have for the week and why the staff read the stories – this week it's wheat and flour.' This is a good example of a parent's failure to understand what lay behind a particular activity until something of the staff's methods of working was explained directly to her.

Democratic or hierarchical decision-making

How are decisions made in the group? Is this entirely the responsibility of the person in charge – the teacher, head-teacher, or supervisor? Do parents have any formal part in policy-making? Are they consulted? We have seen that playgroups were more likely to involve parents in the management of the group, if they were run by a parents' committee. (Other groups had parents' committees too, which were discussion-cum-social bodies rather than management bodies.) The nursery schools had parent managers, and so did the nursery classes though not necessarily from amongst the class's parents; but we did not ask specifically about parent managers and have little information.

One example to note is the playgroup run by a parents' committee, of which every parent in the group was theoretically a member, although there were elected officers. This was the only example of parents' taking control, and making decisions about the running of the group and about staff appointments. The feeling of involvement – the flavour of it – was quite different in this group from any other. There was an automatic assumption of membership, with a right to have some say about the group, how it was run, what activities it offered – and a corresponding duty to contribute time and effort. At the same time, there was a strong feeling of membership of a friendship network, which overlapped the group membership – but had the effect of subtly excluding those not 'on the network', who tended not to be so closely involved, as some of the parents pointed out. We may ask whether a group seriously attempting to run itself in a democratic fashion faces an even greater risk of excluding those for some reason or other not 'on the network' than an autocratic or hierarchical group.

And this is the one example where social factors apparently did come into play, as the friendship network was clearly made up of the better educated and professional members of the group. However, this is the only group where social background appeared to be so important on a group level.

Following the interviews with staff and with parents, we added two more categories:

'Child-centred' or 'parent-and-child-together'

In the interviews with staff, we used these categories to distinguish two different ways of thinking about the relationship between parents, their children, and the group, and about the role that parents played in the group. In the first approach, the group was seen as primarily for the child's benefit; the emphasis was on a relaxed and friendly atmosphere; parents were to be involved, to know about their child's experience, to provide staff with information about the child's home background, or to provide practical help as 'extra pairs of hands'; and where parents were involved there was a careful selection both of the parents and the activities they undertook. In the second, there was more of a joint focus on both parent and child in the group; and an assumption that parents played an equal role in the child's education and development, and often in the management of the group as well; neither parents nor their activities were subject to selection. From the evidence on staff's attitudes in the 15 groups, both 'child-centred' and 'parent-and-child-together' approaches were to be found in all three types of group.

'Professional' or 'partnership'

In the interviews with parents, we used these categories to refer to parents' senses of the boundaries round their children's preschool group. These might be boundaries between parent and 'professional' – that is, boundaries to do with the roles played by parent and 'professional' (for example, whether groups had 'set routines' and staff organized and selected the help offered by parents) or they might be boundaries to do with objectives of the group (for instance whether parents felt the group was focused wholly on the child or also recognized their needs and contribution as parents). Questions arose here of who made decisions, what part parents thought they played in helping their child, and also sometimes questions of physical territory – whether or not parents felt welcome in the group.

When we put together the data from the categories in the observations and the staff and parent interviews, what do we find?

First, we can see there was a 'cluster' of groups which stood out conspicuously as open and accessible to parents, with a friendly and welcoming approach to parents whether they were visiting or staying to settle in their child, bringing problems to discuss, or fetching and delivering children at the beginnings and endings of sessions. Nursery schools came out particularly well for this friendly approach. If, however, we look for openness to adults staying around in the group or 'dropping in' to help for a brief period, whether or not they were expected to visit or help that day, it is the playgroups which stand out. Only two out of the 15 groups combined both types of openness – and they were both playgroups.

Second, we can combine the measures of parents helping in the sessions alongside the children or clearing up, staff's selection of parents when they stayed to help, and their direction of the activities parents undertook, and groups' opennesss or accessibility. We can then see one 'cluster' of groups where parents worked alongside the children with minimal selection of either parents or activities, groups which tended to be welcoming and accessible to parents and other adults; and another 'cluster' which tended to be staff-controlled and directed, and less welcoming to parents or other adults. We called these two clusters 'democratic' and 'hierarchical' in the observations.

Third, if we combine these measures with the distinction we drew from the staff interviews between 'child-centred' groups and those where the focus was on parent and child together, we can see that the 'child-centred' groups were more likely to be staff-directed and controlled, less likely to encourage parents to help with the sessions or to let them work alongside the children if they did stay to help, and less likely to offer a welcome to other adults unless they had a particular reason for being in the group. The groups where the focus was on parent and child together were more likely to be open to other adults, and non-selective about parents or their activities when they stayed to help.

Fourth, we can now bring in parents' views about their involvement and the welcome they received in the groups.

The groups where parents were most likely to express feelings about 'set routines' or 'professionally-run' groups where staff 'did not seem to need any help', and on occasions felt excluded from the group and its activities, tended to be those groups where parents were not expected to help with the sessions, where staff were strongly in control, where the focus was on the child rather than parent and child together, and where the group was least open to other adults. Those groups where parents were less likely to express feelings about exclusion or 'professional boundaries' tended to be the groups which were least selective, which involved parents most in the work of the sessions with the children, and which were most open to both parents and other adults. These are the two approaches we have called 'professional' and 'partnership'.

Our measures add up to a general question about 'boundaries' – the extent to which a group operates, and is seen to operate, as a self-sufficient or 'bounded' entity with restricted contact with those defined outside its boundaries. We have distinguished two aspects here. One is to do with 'shared' or 'closed' territory – the extent to which parents and other adults have access to the group and are seen to have legitimate concerns there on an equal footing with staff. The other is to do with the roles played by parents and staff in the group, and the extent to which there is a sharp distinction between staff's and parents' roles. Here we have to consider perceived and expected roles as well as actual ones – what parents and staff think they should be doing and expect of each other as well as their actual tasks in the group. This is closely linked to staff's and parents' views of the group's objectives and focus.

Throughout the analysis of the data from the observations and the interviews, we have been uncertain as to the relationship between these two aspects. At times, the data has indicated a link between 'partnership' roles for parents and staff, and a sense of 'shared territory' in the group; at other times, these factors apparently operated independently. One way of combining them is to think of the groups as distributed along two dimensions – the first the 'openness' or 'closedness' of the group, the second whether it operates on a 'professional' or a 'partnership' approach towards parents and their role.

We find that most of the groups in the study fell into either the 'open/partnership' or the 'open/professional' categories. That is, they were all friendly and welcoming places, with parents visiting and settling in their children, talking to staff about problems and progress, and encouraged to see what their children were doing. Some, however, welcomed parents as partners in the process of educating their child, and encouraged them to work freely in the group with the children. Here the focus was on parent and child together, and there was a feeling of shared territory with staff, parents, and other adults. These were the 'open/partnership' groups. Others thought of the group as primarily for the child's benefit, with parents involved to provide continuity and information about home experience, but not encouraged to participate except to give practical support outside the sessions or to clear up after the children. These groups tended to be staff-controlled and directed, and were not so open to other adults. These were the 'open/professional' groups. We found nursery classes in the first category, nursery schools and playgroups in both.

Fewer groups in our study came into the 'closed/professional' category. None of the nursery schools were of this type. Their professional approach was strongly bound up with a view of parents as sharers in their children's experience and therefore a determination to be as open and accessible as possible to parents. But we find some of the nursery classes; and also some of the playgroups, and other forms of private groups – particularly those with regular helpers rather than parents on rota, and without a parents' committee.

But two of the groups in the study did fall into the 'closed/partnership' category. This is perhaps surprising – that a group where parents were seen as partners or where the focus was on parent and child together rather than the child on his own should discourage parents from settling in the child, say, or from free access to the staff. Both these groups restricted parents' access, although they intended to operate as partnerships rather than focus on the child alone, and one had parents helping in the group with clearing up after the children. One of these groups was a crèche set up for working mothers, the other a playgroup. But we do not have sufficient information from the study to see whether these groups were atypical in other ways or to explain why they fell into this category.

Parents who were not involved

This study has little to say about working mothers or ethnic minority groups – two groups picked out in the literature on preschool policy as in need of special attention (CPRS, 1978; CRC, 1975). Yet this in itself is important. Half the mothers we interviewed were working, most part-time – yet there were no apparent attempts on the part of staff to think through the question of how to involve working parents. We heard a number of comments about mothers working with young children, or going back to work 'too soon', or groups not being in business to cater for mothers to 'dump' their children. Working parents often regretted the difficulty of being involved, or felt guilty about not putting in their fair share of effort. Several spoke of the negative attitudes of staff – one had felt harassed to pick up her child on time. With groups dependent on parent help to keep open, like playgroups, some parents felt increasingly guilty about 'not pulling their weight', and staff acknowledged the increasing difficulty of maintaining a parent rota.

Immigrants or overseas visitors formed a small proportion of our sample of parents. Nevertheless, it is important to note that they consistently came out lower on any dimension of involvement. At times it was clear that parents did not understand what staff required or expected, far less the educational objectives of the group. One Pakistani father explained that his wife had attended an open day but had understood nothing. Staff felt that immigrant families were less willing to be involved; on the other hand, there were clear indications that the parents were willing but did not understand that they had ever been asked.

What of the parents who were not involved and wished to be? In the groups that did not involve parents except for servicing, two in three parents would have liked to be involved in some way or other, and half of these had not been approached. In the groups that did involve parents with the sessions, 12 out of 30 would have liked to be more involved than they were; some were obviously withdrawing for the moment because they were pregnant or had young children to cope with, but others had developed new ideas through being involved. That is, more than half the parents in this study would have liked to play a larger part in their child's group and share his experience more closely. This is the strongest possible indication of the waste of interest on the part of parents – interest in their children's experience and development that could have been built on for both parent and child.

Shared experience or an educational role?

Recent research on preschool programmes suggests that involvement of parents with their children as active teachers and learners may be one of the key ingredients of success in affecting children's achievement and intelligence over the long term (Fantini and Cárdenas, 1980) or changing parents' attitudes about education and their own role with their children in the short term (Armstrong and Brown, 1979). Critics of the 'parent education' approach argue that the flavour is far too didactic – learning, whether for children or adults, should be gently assimilated through active experience, rather than *taught*. However, our evidence suggests that it may not happen like this – at any rate, not all the time or not for the parents we interviewed. We found remarkably few examples of parents being aware of preschool as a specifically educational experience for themselves – a place where they could learn about child development, how children learnt – or of a specifically educational role for themselves with their children. We did find examples of parents gaining ideas for activities to carry out with the child at home, watching children with fascination, extending their understanding of children's needs and capacities. But we should have expected far more examples of this kind, if indeed parents were learning through simple exposure. It is also true that we have no evidence about parents' actual practice with their children, as distinct from what they said about it; and we do not know whether parents would talk about an educational role which they then failed to put into practice, or change their approach to the child and be unable to express this in words.

The emphasis in involving parents, as we have seen from both the parents' and the staff's interviews, was overwhelmingly on sharing the child's experience as a natural extension and continuity of the home experience and as a vital support for the child. Learning for parents was part of shared experience with the child, rather than a separate activity.

The notions of 'parents as learners' or as 'teachers of their own children', in Gordon's phraseology, look somewhat uneasy in the British context. None of the groups we studied contained a home-teaching component, as do many American programmes; nor did they explicitly instruct parents to work with their children – far from it, indeed, as many staff expected parents to work with other children rather than their own if they stayed to help in the group. Yet there were staff who spoke of parents learning in the group about child development, and parents who talked of learning how to carry on the work of the group with their child at home. The emphasis, though, was informal rather than formal, and not always couched in educational terms. Asked about their role in the group, parents tended to talk about 'general support', 'taking an interest', or 'shared experience' with their child. When they did talk about 'learning' or 'teaching', it was to give specific examples of something that had struck them – the fascination of watching children working with lego or finding new words, of learning to stand back and observe their own child, or of 'getting ideas for what to do at home'. Only occasionally were there comments of a more general kind – 'learning about children's reactions or behaviour', or 'explaining' the importance of different kinds of play to parents.

So it was unusual to find parents acknowledging an explicit learning or teaching slant to their role, and even more unusual to find this put in educational language. But if we turn to what staff had to say about the parents' role, we find a more explicit statement of educational aims. When asked about the value to parents of involvement, staff were more likely to say that it gave them a better understanding of or a different perspective on their child. Perhaps staff and parents have similar things in mind, although the language they used was different.

Did the explicitness of parents' educational understanding vary with the type of group? Were parents more likely to think of their role in educational terms in groups where they were involved more closely with the work of the group, where they helped in sessions alongside the children rather than in servicing or chores, where staff were more explicit in their attempt to involve parents in educational partnership? Certainly there seems to be a link. Parents were more likely to give examples of situations that had struck them in those groups which put most effort into involving parents with the day-to-day sessions, and particularly where parents worked alonside the children. In the case of the playgroup with a strong democratic orientation, it is strikingly those parents who were 'in on the network', rather than those for some reason outside it, who spoke of their role and involvement in this way.

Two points stand out here. The first is that parents – and staff – were most likely to see the role of the parents in educational terms in groups where parents were most closely and actively involved and where there was least barrier between staff and parent. This cuts across all types of group. The second point is that this understanding of the role of parents was not at all formally expressed. Nowhere did we find a formal 'programme' for parents. They were not instructed in child development, or in activities to use at home. The nearest approach to anything formal was a meeting, sometimes held at the beginning of term, when the organization of the group was explained to parents and they were encouraged to become involved. But this was the exception rather than the rule. Not that an informal approach by staff was any more usual. Although staff might hold the view that involvement was a means of learning for parents, there was very little discussion between staff and parents about the group's activities or objectives. We noted in the observations that discussion was comparatively infrequent, and what little there was of it tended to happen more in nursery classes than either nursery schools or playgroups.

So we might say that in the Oxfordshire groups we studied, parents operated as teachers or learners more by accident – a happy, spontaneous flash of insight, as it sometimes appeared from parents' accounts in the interviews – than by deliberate, carefully planned design.

We have here two different views of learning and how to foster it. One is the view associated with traditional English nursery education, with its emphasis on free play, enriched environment, and learning through exploration. On this view, parents will learn simply through exposure – through sharing their children's experience in the group. The other is a structured programmed teaching approach, where teachers teach and parents or children learn. On this view, parents need a structured 'parent programme'. But there is a third way, which combines both structure and learning at the learner's own pace, when opportunities for learning are created or picked up and then developed. On this view, staff should take the parents' experience in the group and make the learning explicit.

We do not know which of these views of parents learning is the most effective. It may be that exposure and shared experience is simply too low-key, and not sufficiently explicit, for parents to learn as much as they could about how to foster their child's development. Our evidence certainly suggests that opportunities were missed to build on parents' excitement or flashes of understanding and insight, or their desire for more information. We should note Barbara Tizard's comment (Tizard, 1978) that parents' greater knowledge of what went on in the group did not necessarily bring with it any greater understanding of these activities. But is this so because parents fail to understand, or because staff do not build on the opportunity to help parents learn?

We should now ask what we are to consider the objectives of involving parents in their children's preschool groups. If the goal is the educational orientation of the parents – helping them to grasp the educational process and their role in it – then no group in our study achieved this totally, even those that tried. It is interesting that the groups which had little sense of a professional boundary between parents and staff were those where staff talked most clearly in terms of an educational partnership; but their energies went more in attempts to make the group more open and welcoming than in developing a more deliberate programme for parents. If the goal is shared experience for parent and child, and enjoyment of that experience, then some of the groups in our study did achieve this, but only those most open and welcoming to parents. Only one of the six groups where we spoke to parents failed in this conspicuously. And the effort involved by staff for either achievement is considerable.

What might be – and indeed was – considered good practice in the groups in our study reminds us of the Plowden Committee's exhortations on parental involvement and good home–school relations – open access for parents, free exchange of information between parents and school on the child's home background and between the school and parents on educational objectives and methods, and much practical involvement (Plowden, 1967). The similarity is striking – there is the same emphasis on shared experience and exchange of information. The assumptions are also similar – that exposure and information is sufficient to bring about changed attitudes and behaviour. If we are to conclude that good practice for the groups in our study was parental involvement on the Plowden model, then we need evidence over the long term to compare this with other forms of involvement for long-term effects. What, for example, does involvement in management as in committee-run playgroups add to the open access and shared experience kind of involvement? Bruner has argued that the mother's sense of control or power over her own life is a crucial factor in her effectively taking an educational role with her child (Bruner, 1972). We have seen that for parents involved in playgroups the sense of control over the organization and objectives of the group is a powerful one, but we do not know if this is related to a keener sense of educational involvement with the child.

Two questions remain unanswered. The first we considered briefly in the chapter on parents – the relationship between social class and the differences in parental involvement between groups. Our conclusion is that what we have called group style is more important than the background of parents in explaining at a group level why one group involves parents and another does not or adopts a different approach. And the differences between groups has been the focus of the present study. The reason why one parent rather than another becomes involved when their children attend the same or a similar group, may well be strongly influenced by social class factors. However, we cannot say conclusively from the Oxfordshire study whether middle-class parents were more likely than working-class parents to be involved in their children's groups, to take on an educational role in the group, or to speak of their experience in educational terms – as other studies might lead us to expect. There is some evidence for this. However, it is also clear from the study that parents from very different social backgrounds were involved in their children's groups, and were equally likely to talk of what they did and learnt in educational terms. But the questions we asked and the information we collected related to groups rather than individual parents, and we cannot compare parents across the six groups. What we were interested in were differences between groups in their approach to parents, and explanation in terms of group characteristics, rather than questions as to the motivation of individual parents, as Shinman considers in her study of the take-up of preschool provision (1975).

The second question relates to the distinction we have drawn between 'professional' and 'partnership' styles in approaching the involvement of parents. Our conclusion in this discussion of shared experience or an educational role for parents is that learning by parents was informal and unplanned in the groups we studied – a spontaneous flash of insight, as we have described it, without follow-up or development. Critics may argue that if we plan for and programme this spontaneity so that parents can develop and build on it more effectively, this may simply reinforce existing pressures towards a 'professional' approach with strict boundaries between parent and professional roles. Although 'parent programmes' smack of the didactic approach, this does not have to be so. We do know that programmes to work with parent and child together can operate by building on the parent's existing competence and confidence (Armstrong and Brown, 1979), rather than laying down a pre-planned programme that must be followed. As with parent involvement in groups, there are many different approaches. There can be 'professional' or 'partnership' approaches to parent education as to parent involvement.

Professional or partnership?

We come finally to the relationship between group styles and parent involvement. We suggested that we could summarize group style into two categories, 'open' and 'closed', and 'partnership' or 'professional', and then cluster the 15 groups we studied in Oxfordshire along these dimensions. How does this relate to the literature we considered in the first two chapters?

If we remind ourselves of Parsons's (1959) analysis of the structure of school as a transitional stage between home and the wider world, and Sarason's (1971) notions of boundaries and context, what we have is two different definitions or descriptions of this transition via the means of the preschool group. In one, the process of transition for the child is accomplished through a partnership between his parents and the staff in charge of the group. His parents have a part to play in education and socialization outside the family as well as inside, and so do other members of the community. The professionals do not have exclusive control of the process or the wider contexts in which that process occurs for the child. Here the boundaries between group and community, between parent and professional, are less defined and more permeable. In the other description, the process of transition for the child from the family into the wider world is accomplished as rapidly as possible, under the control of the professional, and with the minimum of interaction with the parents, except perhaps that they should be aware of the child's growing independence. Here the boundaries between group and community, parent and professional, are more rigidly defined and strictly applied. The first approach we can label 'partnership' and 'open', the second 'professional' and 'closed'.

The difference is essentially to do with 'boundaries' – boundaries between the preschool group and the community of which it is part, and boundaries between professional and parent in respect of the roles they play in the group. The notion of boundaries came up throughout the Oxfordshire study – when we considered staff's views about welcoming parents into the staff room or which activities it was appropriate for parents to undertake; the distinction between 'educational activities' and 'chores'; the restriction of some groups to parents who might be said to have legitimate business there and the exclusion of other adults; the sense of exclusion for parents in some groups from the activities of the group and their children's experience; and the roles that staff thought appropriate for parents.

Conclusions

The stance throughout this book has been a pluralist one – parental involvement comes in many shapes and sizes, and the primary task of a research study is to disentangle them and determine the constraints and contexts, before deciding that one is better than another. Yet there is more to say than this. Preschool experience is an educational experience – for parent and child. The research literature shows that what happens between parent and child at the preschool age matters vitally in an educational sense, as well as any other. So, at the very least, we can argue that preschool provision that neglects either the participatory tradition or the educational tradition as we set them out in the first two chapters, is missing a vital opportunity.

This study is about the organization and experience of involvement rather than its long term impact on either parent or child. We can therefore make no claims for the effectiveness of one or other approach. However, we can argue that the literature on preschool provision, the effectiveness of certain types of programme, and the link between parents' attitudes and behaviour and their children's performance, should be subjected to far more careful scrutiny. Research is called for on the long-term impact of different forms of provision on children's performance and competencies. Yet studies of outcome may be premature until we know more about the process. The categories we have outlined in this study for analysing patterns of involvement in preschool provision provide a means to greater precision about this process. This is our first recommendation.

Most parents interviewed in this study wanted to be involved in their children's preschool experience. More than half wished to play a larger part in their children's preschool group. More than two in three parents who were not involved would have liked to be, but they had not been asked or their offers of help had not been taken up by the staff running the groups. We have not concentrated on individual parents' motivations, as for example Shinman does in her study of the take-up of preschool provision (1975). What we have focused on is the mismatch between parents' expectations of the situation and staff's objectives and interpretations, and the characteristics of groups which may help to explain different types of involvement. This is the strongest possible indication of the waste of interest on the part of parents – interest in their children's experience and development that could have been built on to the advantage of both parent and child. In the groups in this study which involved parents only in practical support outside the sessions, two in three parents would have liked to be involved in some way or other, and half of these had not been approached. In those groups which did involve parents in the day-to-day sessions, nearly half the parents interviewed would have liked to be more involved than they were – although here the reasons for a lower level of involvement may have been more to do with personal commitments such as young children to cope with, than a lack of interest on the part of staff. This, then, is our second conclusion. We have evidence that parents show considerably greater interest in their children's preschool experience than the staff in charge of their children's groups appear to take into account. This is a striking waste of potential. Our recommendation is that staff should be willing to recognize parents' interest and exploit and develop it.

The overwhelming evidence from both observations and interviews is that involvement was defined in terms of shared experience and shared information. We have called this the Plowden model of 'good practice', as it is in line with the report's recommendations for open access and the assumption that good communication would be sufficient to change parents' attitudes and behaviour. Yet even in those groups which tried hard to involve parents and make them welcome, there was evidence that parents did not have enough information about the organization or objectives of the group. Most groups neglected opportunities to explain to parents the aims and methods of the group. In particular, there was little consideration given to making involvement relevant for working mothers or parents with poor command of English. Although some staff saw the parents' role and their involvement in educational terms, this was by no means universal – and even less common for parents.

This is our third conclusion and recommendation. We should recognize that open access and shared experience, even when they are achieved, do not necessarily on their own bring about better understanding or greater knowledge about an educational role in the interaction between parent and child. Parents may need far more explanation and discussion than they are given at present at every level about the group, their children, and their role. We may have to exploit opportunities for learning, and for creating or maintaining the continuity between home and the group, far more deliberately and throughly than we do at present. At the same time, we have to recognize that as yet we do not know whether this will be more effectively done within what we have called the 'professional' or the 'partnership' approach to parental involvement. But we can see that just as there is a waste of parents' interest in their children's development, so there is waste of learning opportunities for parents.

Our fourth and final conclusion is that neither organizational differences between nursery schools, nursery classes, and playgroups, nor the social class mixture of the populations served by the different groups, are sufficient to explain the striking differences in approach to parents and their involvement. The major point to emerge from the study is the distinction between two models of operation which we have labelled 'partnership' and 'professional'. We might say that these are manifestations of two different views of the transition for the child from his home into the wider world. In the first, the process is a partnership between parent, child and professional, and the parent plays a role that is educational in its widest sense in the child's education and ment. In the second, the process is under the control of the professional, and the transition is as rapid as possible, with the parent sharing in the process only to the extent of seeing or being kept informed about his child's progress.

Yet we know that the parent's role in his child's development, and his encouragement of the child's learning, is crucial from the point of view of the child's long-term life chances. Most groups in our study in Oxfordshire were concerned to welcome parents as sharers in their children's experience in the sense of observing what they did rather than participating more actively. If parental involvement is to mean more than communication or sharing information on the Plowden model, then we must work hard for a more participative approach. We must recognize the boundaries and barriers that exist between the roles of parents and professionals in many groups, whether subtly or openly, and experiment far more boldly with different ways of putting the partnership between parent, child, and professional into practice.

Short Bibliography

AINSWORTH, M. D. (1962) The effects of maternal deprivation: a review of findings and controversy in the context of research strategy. In *Deprivation of Maternal care: a Reassessment of its effects: Public Health Papers*. New York and Geneva: World Health Organization.

ARMSTRONG, G. and BROWN, F. (1979) *Five Years On: A Follow-Up Study of the Long-Term Effects on Parents and Children of an Early Learning Programme in the Home*. Oxford: Social Evaluation Unit, Department of Social and Administrative Studies.

BACON, W. (1978), *Public Accountability and the Schooling System: A Sociology of School Board Democracy*. London: Harper & Row.

BARNES, J. (1978) Resources for schools. In Educational Studies E361: *Education and the Urban Environment: Block 111: Policy and Priority*. Milton Keynes: Open University Press.

BERNSTEIN, B. (1971) *Class, Codes and Control: Vol. 1: Theoretical Studies Towards a Sociology of Language*. London and Boston: Routledge, Kegan & Paul.

BERNSTEIN, (1972) Education cannot compensate for society. In RUBINSTEIN, D. and STONEMAN, C. (eds) *Education for Democracy*. Harmondsworth and Baltimore: Penguin).

BLOOM, B. S. (1964) *Stability and Change in Human Characteristics*. New York: Wiley.

BONE, M. (1977) *Preschool Children and the Need for Day Care*. London: Office of Population Censuses and Surveys.

BRADLEY, J. (1976) Playgroup Survey (Oxfordshire). Oxford Preschool Research Group. Mimeo.

BRONFENBRENNER, U. (1974) Is early intervention effective? Facts and principles of early intervention: a summary. Reprinted in CLARKE and CLARKE, *op. cit.*

BROWN, G. W. and HARRIS, T. O. (1978) *Social Origins of Depression*. London: Tavistock; New York: Free Press.

BRUNER, J. S. (1972) Poverty and childhood. In *The Relevance of Education*. London: Allen & Unwin; New York: Norton.

CAVE, R. G. (1970) *Partnership for Change – Parents and Schools*. London: Ward Lock Educational.

CENTRAL ADVISORY COUNCIL FOR EDUCATION (ENGLAND) (1954) *Early Leaving*. London: HMSO.

CENTRAL ADVISORY COUNCIL FOR EDUCATION (ENGLAND) (1959) *15 to 18*. London: HMSO (The Crowther Report).

CENTRAL ADVISORY COUNCIL FOR EDUCATION (ENGLAND) (1963) *Half our Future*. London: HMSO. (The Newsom Report).

CENTRAL ADVISORY COUNCIL FOR EDUCATION (ENGLAND) (1967)

Children and their Primary Schools. London: HMSO. (The Plowden Report).
CENTRAL POLICY REVIEW STAFF (1978) *Services for Young Children with Working Mothers.* London: HMSO.
CHESHIRE SOCIAL SERVICES DEPARTMENT (1976) *Report of the Working Party on Day Care of Children.* Mimeo.
CLARKE, A. M. and CLARKE, A. D. B. (1976) *Early Experience: Myth and Evidence.* London: Open Books; New York: Free Press.
COMMITTEE ON HIGHER EDUCATION (1963) *Higher Education.* London: HMSO. (The Robbins Report).
COMMUNITY RELATIONS Commission (1975) *Who Minds?* London: CRC.
CONSORTIUM FOR LONGITUDINAL STUDIES (1979) *Lasting Effects after preschool: Summary Report.* U. S. Department of Health, Education and Welfare.
CYSTER, R., CLIFT, P. S. and BATTLE, S. (1980) *Parental Involvement in Primary Schools.* Slough: National Foundation for Educational Research.
DAVÉ, R. H. (1963) The identification and measurement of educational process variables that are related to educational achievement. Chicago, Ill.: University of Chicago. Unpublished doctoral dissertation.
DAVIE, R., BUTLER, N. and GOLDSTEIN, H. (1972) *From Birth to Seven.* London: Longman.
DEPARTMENT OF EDUCATION AND SCIENCE (1968) *Parent/Teacher Relations in Primary Schools.* London: HMSO.
DEPARTMENT OF EDUCATION AND SCIENCE (1972) *Education: A Framework for Expansion.* Cmnd. 5174. London: HMSO.
DEPARTMENT OF EDUCATION AND SCIENCE (1975) *Preschool education and care: Some topics requiring research or development projects.* Mimeo.
DEPARTMENT OF EDUCATION AND SCIENCE and WELSH OFFICE (1977) *A New Partnership for our Schools.* London: HMSO. (The Taylor Report).
DEPARTMENT OF HEALTH AND SOCIAL SECURITY and DEPARTMENT OF EDUCATION AND SCIENCE (1976) *Low Cost Day Provision for the Under-Fives.* Papers from a conference held at the Civil Service College, Sunningdale.
DOUGLAS, J. W. B. (1964) *The Home and the School.* London: McGibbon and Kee.
DOUGLAS, J. W. B., ROSS, J. M. and SIMPSON, H. R. (1968) *All Our Future.* London: Peter Davies.
EYKEN, W. van der, MICHELL, L. and GRUBB, J. (1979) *Preschooling in England, Scotland, and Wales.* Report from the Child Health and Education Study (CHES).
EYKEN, W. van der, OSBORN, A. and BUTLER, N. (forthcoming) *Preschooling in Britain.*
FANTINI, M. D. and CÁRDENAS, R. (1980) *Parenting in a multicultural society.* New York and London: Longman.
FERRI, E. with NIBLETT, R. (1977) *Disadvantaged Families and Playgroups.* National Children's Bureau/NFER.
FLOUD, J. E., HALSEY, A. H. and MARTIN, J. M. (1956) *Social Class and Educational Opportunity.* London: Heinemann.
FONDA, N. and Moss, P. (1976) *Mothers in Employment.* Brunel University Management Programme and Thomas Coram Research Unit.

FREEBERG, N. E. and PAYNE, D. T. (1967). Parental influence on cognitive development in early childhood: a review. *Child Development*, **38**(1).

GARLAND, C. and WHITE, S. (1980) *Children and Day Nurseries*. London: Grant McIntyre; Ypsilanti, Michigan: High/Scope.

GORDON, I. J. (n.d.) *Parent Involvement in Compensatory Education*. ERIC Clearinghouse on Early Childhood Education: University of Illinois Press.

GORDON, I. J. (1969) Developing parent power. In GROTBERG, E. (ed.) *Critical Issues in Research Related to Disadvantaged Children*. Princeton, New Jersey: Educational Testing Service.

GRAY, S. W. and KLAUS, R. A. (1970) The early training project: a seventh year report. *Child Development*, **41**. Reprinted in CLARKE and CLARKE, *op. cit.*

GREEN, L. (1968) *Parents and Teachers – Partners or Rivals?* London: Allen & Unwin.

HALSEY, A. H. (ed.) (1972) *Educational Priority: EPA Problems and Policies*, Vol. 1. London: HMSO.

HALSEY, A. H. (1975) Sociology and the education debate. *Oxford Review of Education*, **1**(1).

HALSEY, A. H., HEATH, A. F. and RIDGE, J. M. (1979) *Origins and Destinations: Family, Class, and Education in Modern Britain*. Oxford: Clarendon Press; New York: Oxford University Press.

HATCH, S. (ed.) (1973) *Towards Participation in Local Services*. Fabian Tract 419.

HESS, R. D. (1980) Experts and amateurs: some unintended consequences of parent education. In FANTINI and CÁRDENAS, *op. cit.*

HESS, R. D. and SHIPMAN, V. C. (1965) Early experience and the socialisation of cognitive modes in children. *Child Development*, **36**(4).

HOHMANN, M., BANET, B., and WEIKART, D. P. (1979) *Young children in action*. Ypsilanti, Michigan: High/Scope.

HUGHES, M., MAYALL, B., MOSS, P., PERRY, J., PETRIE, P. and PINKERTON, G. (1980) *Nurseries Now: A Fair Deal for Parents and Children*. Harmondsworth and New York: Penguin Books.

HUNT, J. McV. (1961) *Intelligence and Experience*. New York: Ronald Press.

JENCKS, C., SMITH, M., ALLAND, H., BANE, M. J., COHEN, O., GINTIS, H., HEYNS, B., and MICHELSON, S. (1972) *Inequality: A Reassessment of the Effect of Family and Schooling in America*. New York: Basic Books; London: Allen Lane.

KARNES, M. B. (1973) Evaluation and implications of research with young handicapped and low-income children. In STANLEY, J. C. (ed.) *Compensatory Education for Children Ages 2 to 8: Recent Studies of Educational Intervention*. Baltimore and London: Johns Hopkins University Press.

LITTLE, A. and SMITH, G. (1971) *Strategies of Compensation: A Review of Educational Projects for the Disadvantaged in the United States*. Paris: Centre for Educational Research and Innovation/Organization for Economic Cooperation and Development.

LYNCH, J. and PIMLOTT, J. (1976) *Parents and Teachers*. London: Macmillan.

MURTON, A. (1971) *From Home to School*. London: Macmillan.

MUSGROVE, F. (1960) *Family, Education, and Society.* London: and Boston Routledge & Kegan Paul.
MYERS, L. F. (ed.) (1972) *The Family and Community Impact of Day Care: Preliminary Findings.* Pennsylvania: College of Human Development, Pennsylvania State University.
MCGEENEY, P. (1969) *Parents are Welcome.* London: Longman.
PALFREEMAN, S. and SMITH, T. (forthcoming) *The Cheshire Project: Co-operation and Preschool Provision in Cheshire.* Cheshire County Council.
PARRY, M. and ARCHER, H. (1974) *Preschool Education.* London: Macmillan.
PARSONS, T. (1959) The school class as a social system: some of its functions in American society. *Harvard Educational Review* **29**.
PRESCHOOL PLAYGROUPS ASSOCIATION (1975) (1978) (1979) *Facts and Figures 1974, 1977, 1978.* London: PPA.
PRESCHOOL PLAYGROUPS ASSOCIATION (1980) *Report on Parental Involvement in Playgroups.* London: PPA.
RADIN, N. (1972) Three Degrees of Maternal Involvement in a Preschool Program: Impact on mothers and children. *Child Development,* **43**.
SARASON, S. B. (1971) *The Culture of the School and the Problem of Change.* Boston: Allyn and Bacon.
SHINMAN, S. (1975) Parental response to preschool provision. Brunel University mimeo.
TAYLOR, P. H., EXON, G. and HOLLEY, B. (1972) *A Study of Nursery Education.* Schools Council Working Paper 41. London: Evans/Methuen.
TAYLOR, P. H., REID, W. A., HOLLEY, B. J., and EXON, G. (1974) *Purpose, Power and Constraint in the Primary School Curriculum.* Schools Council Research Studies. London: Macmillan.
TIZARD, B. (1975) *Early Childhood Education: A Review and Discussion of Research in Britain.* Slough: Social Science Research Council/National Foundation for Educational Research.
TIZARD, B. (1977) No common ground. *Times Educational Supplement* 27 May 1977.
TIZARD, B. (1978) Carry on communicating. *Times Educational Supplement* 3 February 1978.
TIZARD, B. (1979) Language at home and at school. In CAZDEN, C. B. (ed.) *Language and Early Childhood Education.* Washington, D. C.: National Association for the Education of Young Children.
TIZARD, B., PHILPS, J. and PLEWIS, I. (1976) Staff Behaviour in Preschool Centres. *Journal of Child Psychology and Psychiatry,* **17**.
TIZARD, J. (1975) The objectives and organization of educational and day care services for young children. *Oxford Review of Education,* **1**(3).
TURNER, I. F. (1977) *Preschool Playgroups: Research and Evaluation Project* Belfast: Queen's University mimeo.
WATT, J. S. (1976) *Preschool Education and the Family.* Report to the Social Science Research Council. Aberdeen: Department of Education, University of Aberdeen.
WEIKART, D. P., EPSTEIN, A. S., SCHWEINHART, L. and BOND, J. T. (1978) *The Ypsilanti Preschool Curriculum Demonstration Project: Preschool Years and Longitudinal Results.* Ypsilanti, Michigan: High/Scope.
WOLF, R. M. (1964) The identification and measurement of environmental

process variables related to intelligence. Chicago, Ill: University of Chicago. Unpublished doctoral dissertation.

WOODHEAD, M. (1976) *Intervening in Disadvantage: A Challenge to Nursery Education*. Slough: National Foundation for Educational Research.

YOUNG, M. and MCGEENEY, P. (1968) *Learning Begins at Home: A Study of a Junior School and its Parents*. London and Boston: Routledge & Kegan Paul.

Index

achievement
  and social class, 4, 18–22
  and underachievement, 14–16
Armstrong G. & Brown F., 32. 151, 165, 171

Bacon W., 37–8
Barnes J., 7
Beginnings (Oxfordshire's preschool proposals), 47–9, 62
Bernstein B., 4
Bloom B.S., 4
Bone M., 9, 11
Bradley J., 50, 54, 62
Bronfenbrenner U., 30–1
Brown G.W. & Harris T.O., 10
Bruner J., 16, 17, 35, 170

Cave R.G., 24
Central Policy Review Staff (CPRS), 11, 164
Child Health & Education Study, 10, 40, 155
Cheshire
  local authority, 36–7
  Social Services Department, 9
Clarke A.M. & Clarke A.D.B., 35
Community Relations Commission (CRC), 164
Consortium for Longitudinal Studies, 5, 28–9, 31, 151
Crowther Report (*15 to 18*), 4

Davé R.H., 22
Department of Education & Science (DES), 9, 23, 24, 27, 28, 41
Department of Health & Social Security (DHSS), 9, 10
Douglas J.W.B., 4, 19–20

Education: a Framework for Expansion, 8, 47
educational intervention, 3–4, 8, 13, 15, 30, 34
Educational Priority Area programme (UK), 6, 8
  West Riding EPA, 32–4

Fantini M.D. & Càrdenas R., 16, 165
Ferri E. & Niblett R., 36, 40, 43, 155
Floud J.E., Halsey A.H. & Martin J.M., 4
Freeberg N.E. & Payne D.T., 4, 19

Garland C. & White S., 64
Gordon I.J., 39–40, 151–2, 166
Gray S.W. & Klaus R.A., 30
Green L., 25

Halsey A.M., 18, 19, 29
Hatch S., 12
Head Start programme (USA), 5, 6, 7, 8, 28, 34
Hess R.D., 18, 35, 36
  & Shipman V.C., 17
Hohmann M., Banet B. & Weikart D.P., 30
Hughes M., 9, 64
Hunt J., 4

Jencks C., 8
Jenkin P., 11

Karnes M.B., 32

Lazar & Darlington, 5, 28–9, 31, 151
Little A. & Smith G., 5, 14
Lynch J. & Pimlott J., 38

INDEX

McGeeney P., 24, 25
Murton A., 24
Musgrove F., 2
Myers L.F., 36

National Children's Bureau, 4
National Union of Teachers (NUT), 55
Newsom Report, 4

Office of Population Censuses & Surveys, 9, 11
Oxford Preschool Research Group, 50

parental involvement
　definitions of, 56
　rotas for, 72–3
　selection for, 73, 76–7, 94–5
parental involvement in,
　'critical activities', 54–5, 123–7
　management, 41–4, 46, 53, 60, 113, 151, 153, 170
　'openness' of group, 41, 53, 86–90, 93, 95, 122–3, 130–6, 146, 153–4
　servicing group, 41–4, 53, 57–8, 74–7, 94, 115, 151
　settling in, 55–6, 82, 136
　working in group, 41–4, 53, 74–7, 94–113, 151–2, 155–6
　working with children, 41–4, 53, 57–8, 74–7, 94, 113–15, 121, 151–2, 155–6
parent participation, 1–3, 10, 12–13, 14–44, 45, 53–6, 59–62, 90–5, 128–30
　arguments against, 27–8
　definitions of, 14, 20–1, 31–2, 34, 39–44, 56–8
　effectiveness of, 14, 23–39, 136–47
　importance of, 14, 17–22, 58–9
　in Oxfordshire, 46–50, 64–5, 151–5, 168
　models ('professional' and 'partnership') for, 150–1, 155, 160–1, 162–4, 171–6
　parents' views of, 110–49, 162
　recommendations for, 173–6

research methods into, 51–3, 62, 70
social class and, 144–6, 170–1
staff views of, 96–100, 115
parent-staff contacts, 78–86, 92–3, 115–20, 123–7, 136, 156–9
parent-teacher associations (PTAs), 61, 62
Parrry M. & Archer H., 24
Parsons T., 17, 172
Plowden Report (*Children and their Primary Schools*), 6, 11, 20–5, 28, 41, 42, 45, 169–70, 174
preschool
　child centred, 100–4, 106–9, 159–60
　child-and-parent centred, 104–9, 159–60
　comparison of types of, 45, 46, 54, 58, 70, 76, 79, 89–90, 113–14, 129, 146, 147–9
　consumer demand for, 10, 12
　ethnic minority groups and, 164–5
　expansion, 6, 8
　feminist arguments for, 11–12
　parents as learners in, 127–8, 152, 166–9
　professionally defined need for, 10–11
　voluntary provision of, 10
　'wash-out' effect, 8, 30, 33
　working mothers and, 10–11, 54, 56, 164
Preschool Playgroups Association (PPA), 36–7, 42, 43, 46–7, 49
public expenditure, 6–7

Radin N., 31–2, 34
Robbins Report, 4

Sarason S.B., 172
Shinman S., 171, 174

Taylor P.H., 24, 38
Taylor Report, 13, 38, 43, 46
Tizard B. & J., 11, 17, 28, 38, 169
Turner I.F., 36

Van der Eyken W., 10, 40, 155

War on Poverty programme (USA),

5, 6, 12
Watt J.S., 41–2, 155
Weikart D.P., 29–30, 151
Wolf R.M., 22

Woodhead M., 38–9

Young M. & McGeeney P., 25–7, 51